Fodor's

THE AMALFI COAST, CAPRI & NAPLES

WELCOME TO THE AMALFI COAST, CAPRI & NAPLES

Few regions of Italy claim as many iconic images as the corner of Campania that holds the Amalfi Coast, Naples, and the sun-splashed islands of Capri, Ischia, and Procida. If the colorful cliffside houses don't win your heart, the azure sea will. Driving the curving coastal road is exhilarating, so unwind with memorable Neapolitan fare, or go island hopping and explore grottoes and beaches. Cultural highlights are always nearby too, from the ruins of Pompeii and Herculaneum to the echoes of classical history in the vibrant streets of Naples and Sorrento.

TOP REASONS TO GO

★ **Food:** The home of great pizza, mozzarella, limoncello, and *spaghetti con le vongole.*

★ **Views:** The bluest bay in the world dazzles from Ravello's Belvedere of Infinity.

★ **Beaches:** Scenic, hidden coves line the Bay of Naples and make boat trips rewarding.

★ **Archaeology:** Pompeii and other evocative ruins transport you back to Roman times.

★ **Baroque Art:** Museums and churches shelter masterworks including three Caravaggios.

★ **Walking:** Slow exploration beckons—hiking Anacapri or strolling Naples' Spaccanapoli.

Fodor's THE AMALFI COAST, CAPRI & NAPLES

Publisher: Amanda D'Acierno, *Senior Vice President*

Editorial: Arabella Bowen, *Editor in Chief*; Linda Cabasin, *Editorial Director*

Design: Fabrizio La Rocca, *Vice President, Creative Director*; Tina Malaney, *Associate Art Director*; Chie Ushio, *Senior Designer*; Ann McBride, *Production Designer*

Photography: Melanie Marin, *Associate Director of Photography*; Jessica Parkhill and Jennifer Romains, *Researchers*

Maps: Rebecca Baer, *Senior Map Editor*; Mark Stroud (Moon Street Cartography) and David Lindroth, *Cartographers*

Production: Linda Schmidt, *Managing Editor*; Evangelos Vasilakis, *Associate Managing Editor*; Angela L. McLean, *Senior Production Manager*

Sales: Jacqueline Lebow, *Sales Director*

Marketing & Publicity: Heather Dalton, *Marketing Director*; Katherine Punia, *Senior Publicist*

Business & Operations: Susan Livingston, *Vice President, Strategic Business Planning*; Sue Daulton, *Vice President, Operations*

Fodors.com: Megan Bell, *Executive Director, Revenue & Business Development*; Yasmin Marinaro, *Senior Director, Marketing & Partnerships*

Writers: Martin Bennett, Fergal Kavanagh, Fiorella Squillante

Editors: Róisín Cameron, lead project editor; Danny Mangin

Production Editor: Carolyn Roth

7th Edition

ISBN 978-0-8041-4213-7

ISSN 1542–0728

SPECIAL SALES

This book is available at special discounts for bulk purchases for sales promotions or premiums. For more information, e-mail specialmarkets@randomhouse.com

PRINTED IN THE U.S.A.

10 9 8 7 6 5 4 3 2

CONTENTS

Fodor's Features

CONTENTS

MAPS

ABOUT THIS GUIDE

Fodor's Recommendations
Everything in this guide is worth doing—we don't cover what isn't—but exceptional sights, hotels, and restaurants are recognized with additional accolades. Fodor's Choice★ indicates our top recommendations. Care to nominate a new place? Visit Fodors.com/contact-us.

Trip Costs
We list prices wherever possible to help you budget well. Hotel and restaurant price categories from **$** to **$$$$** are noted alongside each recommendation. For hotels, we include the lowest cost of a standard double room in high season. For restaurants, we cite the average price of a main course at dinner or, if dinner isn't served, at lunch. For attractions, we always list adult admission fees; discounts are usually available for children, students, and senior citizens.

Hotels
Our local writers vet every hotel to recommend the best overnights in each price category, from budget to expensive. Unless otherwise specified, you can expect private bath, phone, and TV in your room. For expanded hotel reviews, facilities, and deals visit Fodors.com.

Restaurants
Unless we state otherwise, restaurants are open for lunch and dinner daily. We mention dress code only when there's a specific requirement and reservations only when they're essential or not accepted. To make restaurant reservations, visit Fodors.com.

Credit Cards
The hotels and restaurants in this guide typically accept credit cards. If not, we'll say so.

Top Picks
★ Fodor's Choice

Listings
- ✉ Address
- Branch address
- ☎ Telephone
- Fax
- Website
- E-mail
- Admission fee
- Open/closed times
- M Subway
- Directions or Map coordinates

Hotels & Restaurants
- Hotel
- Number of rooms
- Meal plans
- ✕ Restaurant
- Reservations
- Dress code
- No credit cards
- $ Price

Other
- ⇨ See also
- ☞ Take note
- Golf facilities

EXPERIENCE THE AMALFI COAST, CAPRI & NAPLES

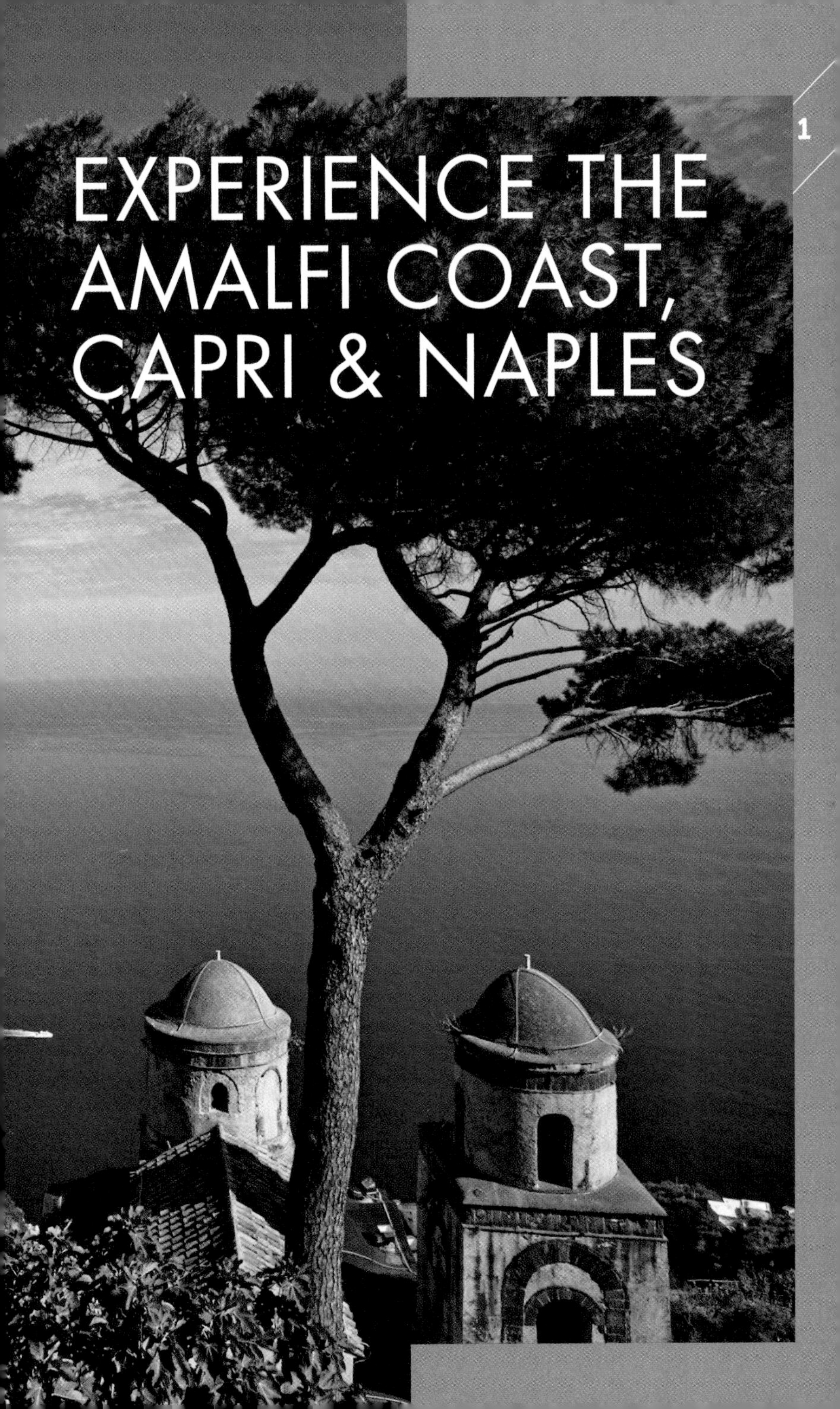

WHAT'S WHERE

1 The Amalfi Coast. One of the most achingly beautiful places on Earth, this corner of Campania tantalizes, almost beyond bearing, the visitor who can stay but a day or three. South of Sorrento you espy the spectacularly scenic Amalfi Coast, traversed by a road that must have a thousand turns, each with a view more stunning than the last. Here, sunbaked towns compete to win nature's beauty contest. They include **Positano,** the world's most photographed fishing village; **Amalfi,** adorned with the coast's grandest cathedral; and sky-high **Ravello,** perched 1,500 feet over the famously blue Bay of Salerno.

2 Capri, Ischia, and Procida. History's hedonists have long luxuriated on Campania's islands. The most famous, rocky **Capri,** mixes natural beauty and *dolce vita* glamour. In summer, the day-trippers are legion, but even crowds don't spoil the charm. Twice the size of Capri, **Ischia** has Campania's most beautiful white-sand beaches and great spas and springs. Nearby **Procida** is a rugged island with houses so multihued that you'll be reaching for your paintbrush.

3 Sorrento and the Sorrentine Peninsula. A Belle Epoque treasure, with picturesque alleyways, palm-shaded cafés, and "queen-for-a-day" grand hotels, **Sorrento** has one of the world's most charming old towns, and a peninsula perfect for escaping the madding crowds.

4 The Bay of Naples. East of Naples lie **Pompeii** and **Herculaneum,** the most completely preserved cities of classical antiquity, along with **Vesuvius,** which buried them in ash and mud in AD 79. West of Naples is a fabled region, one where Nero and Hadrian had summer villas, Virgil composed his poetry, and the Apostle Paul landed to spread the gospel. Track their footsteps in ancient Baia and Cumae.

5 Naples. Perhaps the most operatic city in the world, Napoli can seduce you one moment and exasperate you the next: it's lush, chaotic, friendly, scary, amusing, confounding, and very beautiful. Unfolding like a pop-up book of history, the city's canyon-like streets are packed with people, cafés, pizzerias, great museums, and an amazing number of Norman and baroque churches.

Parco Regionale del Partenio
A1
A16
A30
Nola
Avellino
Monteforte
Casavatore
Pomigliano
Casoria
Marano di Napoli
S Anastasia
Somma
Capodimonte
Ottaviano
Campi Flegrei
5
Parco del Vesuvio
Cercola
S Giuseppe
Naples
A1
18
Vesuvius
Terzigno
Portici
A30
Sarno
Mergellina
Herculaneum
Poggiomarino
Mercato
Golfo di Pozzuoli
Marechiaro
Boscotrecase
Boscoreale
Isola di Nisida
Torre del Greco
4
Pompeii
Nocera
Torre Annunziata
A3
A3
Circumvesuviana Rail Line
Bay of Naples
S António
Castellammare di Stabia
Gragnana
145
Vietri
Salerno
Piano di Sorrento
Marina di Equa
Ravello
Meta
Cetara
Sorrento
SORRENTINE PENINSULA
1
Amalfi
Marina di Puolo
3
145
Positano
Praiano
Metrano
Sant' Agata sui Due Golfi
THE AMALFI COAST
Termini
Isola di Capri
Marina Grande
Grotta Azzurra
Bocca Piccola
Bay of Salerno
Anacapri
Capri
2
Marina Piccola
0
10 mi
0
10 km

THE AMALFI COAST, CAPRI, AND NAPLES PLANNER

When to Go

In April, May, and early June, southern Italy is at its best—the weather is generally pleasant and flowers are in bloom. Easter is a busy time for most tourist destinations; if you're traveling then, have lodging reserved in advance. In May the ocean water is warm enough for swimming and beaches are uncrowded.

Temperatures can be torrid in summer. The archaeological sites swarm with visitors, and the islands and Amalfi Coast resorts are crowded. If you seek a beach, keep in mind that during August all of Italy flocks to the shores.

From late September through early November you'll find gentle, warm weather, and acres of beach space; swimming temperatures last through October. Watch the clock, however, as the days get shorter. At most archaeological sites you're rounded up two hours before sunset—but by then most crowds have departed, so afternoon is still a good time to see Pompeii and Herculaneum.

Early winter is relatively mild, but later in the season cold fronts can arrive and stay for days. In resort destinations, many hotels, restaurants, and other facilities close from November until around Easter.

Getting Here

Major gateways to Italy are Rome's Aeroporto Leonardo da Vinci, better known as **Fiumicino** (FCO), and Milan's **Aeroporto Malpensa** (MXP). To fly into most other Italian cities you need to make connections at Fiumicino and Malpensa or another European airport.

Located just 8 km (5 miles) outside Naples, **Aeroporto Capodichino** (NAP) serves the Campania region. It handles domestic and international flights, including several flights daily between Naples and Rome (flight time 45 minutes). In Rome you can also take the airport train to Termini station and catch a train to Naples. It typically takes about an hour to get from the airport to the station, and the fastest train from Rome to Naples takes around 70 minutes.

Italy's airports are not known for being new, fun, or efficient. Security measures, including random baggage inspection and bomb-sniffing dogs, may seem daunting, but they don't pose any problems for the average traveler. *For further information about getting into the region, see the Travel Smart chapter at the end of this book.*

What to Pack

In summer stick with light clothing, but toss in a sweater in case of cool evenings, especially if you're headed for the islands. Sunglasses, a hat, and sunblock are essential. In winter, bring a coat, gloves, hat, and scarf. Winter weather is milder than in the northern and central United States, but central heating isn't always reliable. Bring comfortable walking shoes in any season.

As a rule, Italians dress well. Men aren't required to wear ties or jackets anywhere except in the most formal restaurants, but are expected to look reasonably sharp—and they do. A certain modesty (no bare shoulders or knees) is expected in churches, and strictly enforced in many.

Restaurant Basics

The standard procedures of a restaurant meal throughout Italy are different from those in the United States (and most other places). When you sit down in a *ristorante*, you're expected to order two courses at a minimum, such as a *primo* (first course) and a *secondo* (second course), or an antipasto (starter) followed by a primo or secondo, or a secondo with dessert. Traditionally, a secondo is not a "main course" that would serve as a full meal. The crucial rule of restaurant dining is that you should order at least two courses. It's a common mistake for tourists to order only a secondo, thinking they're getting a "main course" complete with side dishes. What they wind up with is one lonely piece of meat. Eateries are quite used to diners who order courses to split; but, if you're not so hungry, you might head for a pizzeria or *bacaro* to sample some quick bites.

All prices include tax. Prices include service (*servizio*) unless indicated otherwise on the menu. It's customary to leave a small tip in cash (from a euro to 10% of the bill) in appreciation of good service. Do not leave a tip on your credit card. Most restaurants have a "cover" charge, usually listed on the menu as *pane e coperto*. It should be modest (€1–€2.50 per person) except at the most expensive restaurants. Some instead charge for bread, which should be brought to you (and paid for) only if you order it. When in doubt, ask about the policy upon ordering.

Hotel Basics

Hotels in Italy are usually well maintained (especially if they've earned our recommendation in this book), but in some respects they won't match what you find at comparably priced U.S. lodgings. Keep the following points in mind as you set your expectations, and you're likely to have a good experience:

Rooms are usually smaller, particularly in cities. If you're truly cramped, ask for another room, but don't expect things to be spacious. A "double bed" is commonly two singles pushed together. In the bathroom, tubs are not a given—request one if it's essential. In budget places, showers sometimes use a drain in the middle of the bathroom floor. Washcloths are a rarity. Most hotels have satellite TV, but there are fewer channels than in the United States, and only one or two will be in English. Don't expect wall-to-wall carpeting; tile floors are the norm.

Speaking the Language

Because Naples and the surrounding resort areas see many English-speaking tourists, in restaurants and hotels you're bound to find someone with a rudimentary understanding of English. On the other hand, if you're fluent in Italian you still may not be able to follow conversations heard on the street; locals often use dialect that even fellow Italians have a hard time deciphering. But locals speak standard Italian as well, so you can still benefit from knowledge of the language.

Italy from Behind the Wheel

Having a car in Italian cities is almost always a liability—nowhere more so than in Naples. In the towns of the Amalfi Coast, parking is hard to come by and up to 35 euros for 24 hours, and on the islands of the bay, car access is very limited. If you do rent a car, be aware that Italians tend to be aggressive drivers—expect tailgating and high-risk passing. Your best response is to stick to a safety-first approach; the *autostrada* is one place where you don't want to "go native." On the upside, Italy's roads are well maintained. Note that wearing a seat belt and having your lights on at all times are required by law.

THE AMALFI COAST, CAPRI, AND NAPLES TODAY

. . . is losing its distinctive character.

Put on the map by 19th-century Grand Tour travelers, the Amalfi Coast has recently come under assault by international hotel chains. One by one, its richly atmospheric hotels, veritable time machines that offer sepia-toned dreams of the past have given way to grotesque face-lifts, all in the name of progress. This is especially tragic in that last outpost of old-world refinement, Ravello.

First, the Palazzo Avino was Las Vegasized by Richard Branson with the addition of hot tubs on the roof, glass elevators, and roaring fountains with Playboy Mansion statuary. Then the Orient-Express luxury chain eviscerated the magical Hotel Caruso-Belvedere, trading its antiques and lace-trimmed ambience for dreary rattan sofas seen from Kansas to Katmandu, beige-on-beige cocktail lounges, and, almost prosecutable, destroying the fabled medieval Belvedere Window, seen on a 1,001 travel posters, by encasing it alive within a plastic Lucite wall.

Next up was the Hotel Cappuccini Convento in Amalfi, which once delighted Longfellow and Wagner, dukes and duchesses. Now, contemporary furniture and art, supermodern facilities, and other high-rolling luxuries have displaced the royal sense of civility this hotel used to have.

Happily, there are still some hotels left on the *Costiera Divina* that retain the patina of the past—but hurry!

. . . remains different from the north.

Southern Italy is slap bang in the middle of the Mediterranean, so it's no wonder that it has experienced invasions and migrations for millennia, many of which have left their mark culturally, linguistically, and architecturally.

The southerners, despite the homogenizing influences of television and education, really *are* different from Italians farther north. Under an ostensibly sociable and more expressive exterior, they are more guarded when dealing with strangers, less at home with foreign languages, and more oriented toward the family than the community. The trappings of affluence, like cars and scooters, become essential status symbols here, which in part explains why Naples is congested and noisy.

. . . has issues when it comes to local politics.

Politics tends to be clientalistic in large swaths of the south. In this climate of mutual back scratching and with unemployment rates twice the national average of 12%, the main preoccupation for many voters is *il posto fisso* (a steady job).

Votes are all too often cast for the politician who promises opportunities for career advancement—or lucrative contracts—preferably in the public sector. Over the years, this approach has insured inefficiencies, if not outright corruption.

. . . endures national political upheaval.

The political landscape in Italy as a whole is less stable than in any other industrialized nation. The country has had a new government an average of about once a year since the end of World War II, and hopes are slim that the situation will change much in the near future.

This virtual turnstile outside the prime minister's office takes a toll on Italy in any number of ways: economic growth is slow in part because businesses are continually adapting to new sets of government policies, and polls show that rank-and-file Italians are increasingly

cynical about their political institutions. As a result, they're much less likely to trust in or depend on the government than neighbors elsewhere in Europe do.

. . . has its economic ups and downs.

While the north has developed relatively rapidly in the past 50 years, the Italian entrepreneurial spirit in the south struggles to make good. Despite a pool of relatively cheap, willing labor, foreign investment across the entire south is merely one-tenth of that going to the northern region of Lombardy alone.

The discrepancy can be attributed in large part to the stifling presence of organized crime. Each major region has its own criminal association: in Naples, it's the *Camorra*. The system creates add-on costs at many levels, especially in retail.

It is not all bad news though. Southern Italy has woken up to its major asset, its remarkable cultural and natural heritage. UNESCO lists 14 World Heritage sites in southern Italy alone, while the last decade has seen the creation of several national parks, marine parks, and regional nature preserves. Environmental and cultural associations have mushroomed as locals increasingly perceive the importance of preserving across the generations.

In general, the small average farm size in the south (5.8 hectares, under 15 acres) has helped preserve a pleasing mosaic of habitats in the interior. Landscape and product diversity have been aided by the promotion of traditionally grown products by the European Union and its PDO (Protected Designation of Origin) project.

. . . lives with the black market.

Nobody knows how big Italy's black-market economy is, though experts all agree it's massive. Estimates place it at anywhere from a fourth to a half of the official, legal economy. Put another way, if the highest estimates are correct, Italy's black-market economy is about as large as the entire economy of Mexico or India. If the black-market figures were added to Italy's official GDP, the country would leapfrog France, the United Kingdom, and China to become the world's fourth-largest economy.

The presence of the black market isn't obvious to the casual observer, but whenever a customer is not given a printed receipt in a store or restaurant, tobacco without a tax seal is bought from a street seller, or a product or service is exchanged for another product or service, that means the transaction goes unrecorded, unreported, and untaxed.

. . . is eating well?

The old joke says that three-quarters of the food and wine served in Italy is good . . . and the rest is amazing. In some sense, that's still true, and the "good" 75% has gotten even better.

Ingredients that in the past were available only to the wealthy can now be found even in the remotest parts of the country at reasonable prices. Dishes originally conceived to make the most of inferior cuts of meat or the least flavorful part of vegetables are now made with the best.

Italian restaurateurs seem determined to make the most of the country's reputation for good food. The same is true of Italian wine. Through investment and experimentation, Italy's winemakers are figuring out how to get the most from their gorgeous vineyards. It's fair to say that Italy now produces more types of high-quality wine from more different grape varieties than any other country in the world.

THE AMALFI COAST, CAPRI & NAPLES TOP ATTRACTIONS

Spaccanapoli, Naples

(A) To learn why people fall in love with Naples, stroll down this arrow-straight road through the heart of the city. It's all here: gorgeous churches, café-lined piazzas, colorful shops, and, most of all, the exuberant Neapolitans, engaged in the drama of their daily lives. *(⇨ Chapter 6)*

Museo Archeologico Nazionale, Naples

The National Archaeological Museum has arguably the world's finest collection of classical artifacts. The most impressive finds from Pompeii and Herculaneum—everything from sculpture to carbonized fruit—are on display; a visit before heading to the ruins makes the experience significantly richer. *(⇨ Chapter 6)*

Pio Monte Misercordia, Naples

(B) Among the many impressive landmarks in Naples, this one bears special mention for its altar painting, Caravaggio's *Seven Acts of Mercy,* the city's most heralded artwork. *(⇨ Chapter 6)*

Sorrento

(C) Sorrento's old town quarter is one of the most romantic places in Italy—be sure to dine in front of the Sedile Dominova, a 16th-century frescoed loggia that is a colorful backdrop for a café and serenading waiters warbling "Come Back to Sorrento." *(⇨ Chapter 4)*

The Ruins around Vesuvius

(D) This may be the closest you'll ever get to time travel. Thanks to Vesuvius blowing its top in AD 79, the towns at its base were carpeted in fallout and preserved for posterity. Allow a good half day to look round bustling Pompeii or the more compact, less busy Herculaneum. For the best Roman frescoes, head to the Villa of Oplontis between the two ancient cities and once home to Nero's wife Poppea. *(⇨ Chapter 5)*

La Piazzetta, Capri

(E) Sitting in one of the cafés on this main square, watching the world go by, is a classic Capri experience. It's at its best in the evening, when day-trippers have departed and locals make an appearance. *(⇨ Chapter 3)*

Belvedere of Infinity, Villa Cimbrone, Ravello

(F) This sky-kissing terrace, set amid gorgeous gardens and overlooking the bluest bay in the world, is the high point, in more ways than one, of any trip to the Amalfi Coast. *(⇨ Chapter 2)*

Villa San Michele, Capri

(G) Emperor Tiberius himself would have been impressed by this antique-rich 19th-century villa. Make a wish while standing on the Sphinx Parapet; here, high atop Anacapri, it feels as if anything is possible. *(⇨ Chapter 3)*

The Amalfi Drive

The road along the Amalfi Coast combines the thrills of a roller-coaster ride with spectacular views. If you're taking a car, you'll need a confident driver who can keep his eyes on the road. Go by bus if you want a seasoned pro behind the wheel. *(⇨ Chapter 2)*

Positano

(H) Whitewashed houses cascade down to the azure sea in this remarkable village, described by the artist Paul Klee as "The only place in the world conceived on a vertical rather than a horizontal axis." *(⇨ Chapter 2)*

The Temples of Paestum

(I) Some of the best-preserved ancient Greek monuments found anywhere (including Greece) are here. Paestum's remoteness means it's seldom overrun by crowds. The best times to absorb the grandeur are daybreak and dusk. *(⇨ Chapter 2)*

IF YOU LIKE

Archaeological Sites

When the rich of ancient Rome—emperors included—had time off, they would head south to Campania and many of the surviving ruins qualify the region as an archaeologist's treasure garden. In Naples, below medieval, Byzantine, then Roman remains often lies another layer going back to the Greeks.

Anfiteatro Flavio, Pozzuoli. Rome's Colosseum's only slightly smaller twin is better conserved than that of its travertine big brother.

Cumae. Stand where the Greeks first landed and then proceed to the cave of the Sybil, where ancient prophecies were handed out.

Herculaneum. Smaller than Pompeii, but due to the pyroclastic flow of the 79 AD eruption of Vesuvius—which preserved organic materials such as wood—this site is even more evocative and in places breathtakingly well-preserved. Thanks to virtual technology, watch before your very eyes crusty ruins take on new life and color.

Museo e Scavi Santa Restituta, Lacco Ameno, Ischia. Accidentally unearthed in 1950, this site under the church of Santa Restituta is evidence of the earliest Greek settlement in the area.

Pompeii. More a city than a site, a visit gives you the chance to stroll ancient streets; observing along the way ancient houses, shops, temples, frescoes, graffiti, and plaster casts of people killed by the eruption.

Villa Jovis, Capri. On Capri's second-highest peak, it is easy to understand why the emperor Tiberius shunned Rome and chose to reign from here until his death in 37 AD.

Art

Italy has the largest collection of art works in the world, and a large portion of these are in the Naples area. A stroll though the city center is like a walk through an open-air gallery, and it is, in fact, on the UNESCO World Heritage List.

Caravaggio, Naples. Naples is home to three masterpieces by Michelangelo Mersi da Caravaggio, produced in his final years here.

Certosa di San Martino, Naples. Perched on the hilltop just below Castel Sant'Elmo, this former monastery houses one of Europe's finest collections of baroque art, for which the city is famous.

Madre, Naples. Contemporary exhibitions of established international artists as well as temporary shows, along with the occasional evening time *aperitivi,* make this one of Naples's most exciting spaces.

Museo Archeologico di Pithecusae, Lacco Ameno, Ischia. Nestor's Cup, the oldest known kotyle vase in existence, is the highlight at the site of one of Italy's earliest Greek settlements—the inscribed poetic verse is the earliest example of ancient Greek writing known to scholars.

Museo di Capodimonte, Naples. Built in the 18th century to house the magnificent Farnese collection, this is the best place to see examples of paintings of the Neapolitan School from the 13th to the 18th centuries.

PAN, Naples. The Palazzo delle Arti di Napoli is an 18th-century palazzo with more than 6,000 square meters of exhibition space for contemporary works, including photography, film, and sculpture.

Walking

Lace up your hiking boots, pack your sunblock, grab a few *panini,* and enjoy some of the most unspoiled scenery in Europe far from the madding crowds. The added advantage is that these peaks lead down to the beach, so don't forget your towel.

Capri. Quite simply, Capri is a walker's paradise. Walk along the west coast past the four Saracen fortresses? Climb Mont Solaro (or cheat and take the chairlift)? Take the Scala Fenicia from Marina Grande to Anacapri just like the ancient Greeks? Take a walk to help you decide!

Lungomare, Naples. The city's mayor closed the 2-mile (3-km) seafront to traffic in 2012 and a *passeggiata* here past the Castel dell'Ovo, with a stop at one of the many pizzerias or for an ice cream at Mergellina, is de rigueur.

Monte Epomeo, Ischia. At 2,582 feet this is a challenging climb, but it is worth scaling the now-dormant volcano (don't worry, the last eruption was in 1301) for the 60-degree view of the gulf.

Mount Vesuvius. Mainland Europe's only active volcano is also a national park, with paths winding along the lava flows. Visitors to the crater negotiate a steep, winding gravel path with the Bay of Naples far below.

Sentiero degli Dei, the Amalfi Coast. Beginning at Agerola and snaking high above the coastline for 5 miles (8 km) the Pathway of the Gods is as close to paradise as hikers can get.

Valle del Dragone, Ravello. Take the path from Ravello down to Atrani and follow in the footsteps of locals before motorized transport hit the coast.

Beaches

The region is famed for its dramatically scenic beaches—stretches of sand, rocky plateaus above the big blue, crowd-pleasers and isolated coves all compete for your beach towel. Unsurprisingly, the islands offer the best fare, although the Amalfi Coast's secluded bays are also a firm favorite.

Bagno della Regina Giovanna, Sorrento. Take the bus to Capo and it is a short walk to this rocky beach where it is said Queen Joan of Anjou bathed in the 14th century. It is indeed worthy of a monarch, with crystal clear water in a stunning setting.

Cetara. The clean, shallow water, adjacent park, and boats for hire make this one of the best spots on the Amalfi Coast for kids.

Citara, Ischia. This stretch of sandy beach is one of the island's best, with the thermal waters of the Giardini di Poseidon occupying the final section.

Conca dei Marini, Amalfi Coast. Take the steps down to this drop-dead gorgeous cove below a 16th-century Saracen tower—crowded, but worth it.

Lido del Faro, Anacapri. Not technically a beach, but these natural seawater pools make a refreshing change, as do the rocky plateaus under Capri's Fariglioni, frequented by those with deep wallets.

Spiaggia del Fornillo, Positano. With excellent standards of water quality, safety, and services, the Spiaggia has the glorious, rainbow-hued backdrop of Positano, but for a more informal atmosphere and lush vegetation, follow the Via Positanesi d'America to the Fornillo beach.

TOP EXPERIENCES

I Dolce Far Niente

"The sweetness of doing nothing" has long been an art form in Italy—particularly in southern Italy. This is a place where life's pleasures are warmly celebrated, not guiltily indulged.

Of course, doing "nothing" doesn't really mean nothing.

It means doing things differently: lingering over a glass of wine for the better part of an evening as you watch the sun slowly set; savoring a slow and flirtatious evening *passeggiata* along the main street of a little town; and making a commitment—however temporary—to thinking that there is nowhere that you have to be next, and no other time than the magical present.

Along the Amalfi Coast, it's easy to achieve such a state of mind. No matter where you choose to situate yourself, you can hardly go wrong: there's quiet little Ravello, stunningly positioned on a hilltop lookout; the vertical fishing village of Positano, where a tranquil sunset is a balm to the soul; and Amalfi with its Moorish passageways and other hints of a long, multicultural history.

On Capri the pace picks up a little, and in Naples a lot, but there's still a sense of taking life's pleasures where you find them. The sense of enjoyment is, fortunately, infectious.

Simply Fabulous Food

It's no wonder *la cucina Napolitano* has won the hearts (and stomachs) of millions: the rich volcanic soil and fertile waters surrounding the city provide abundant and varied seafood, Vesuvian wines, vine-ripe tomatoes, and luscious fruits. This food is simple and earthy, at once wholesome and sensual, as sophisticated in its purity as the most complex cuisine, as inspired as the great art and architecture born out of the same culture.

Like Michelangelo freeing the prisoners that dwelt within the stone, chefs in Campania seem intuitively to seek out the essence of what they are preparing—Exhibit 1 being that Neapolitan delight, pizza.

It's worth noting that in Campania, as in much of Italy, the most revered (and most expensive) restaurants are often found in the countryside or in small, remote towns. These are places for food pilgrimages, where you can escape the city and indulge in a long, opulent meal free from distractions.

A notable example is Don Alfonso 1890, the region's most famous temple of fine dining, located in the mountainside village of Sant'Agata on the Sorrentine Peninsula.

Neapolitan Baroque

Of the numerous artistic styles on display in Naples, none suits the city's temperament better than the baroque—the style that came to the fore in the 17th century and continued in the 18th century under the Bourbon kings.

In a city of volcanic passions, the flagrantly emotional, floridly luxurious baroque—a style that seems perpetually on the point of bursting its bonds—found immediate favor.

With untrammeled individualism given full play, the results, visible throughout the city center today, are dramatic, dynamic, and sometimes wonderfully showy.

Like the city itself, the decorative scheme is diffuse and disjunctive, with little effort to organize everything into an easily understood scheme.

Taking to the Water

Despite its miles of beautiful coast, Campania's beaches can be disappointing—most are small stretches of coarse sand. That doesn't mean you shouldn't pack your swimsuit, but leave any Caribbean-inspired expectations behind.

The area around Positano has good beach-going options: Spiaggia Grande (the main beach) is pleasant; a little farther west, Spiaggia di Fornillo gets better; and you can go by boat to the remote Spiaggia di Laurito for a leisurely day of swimming and lunching on seafood.

On Ischia, the best sandy beach is at Citara, south of Forio, and on Capri you can take a dip in the waters around the famous Faraglioni rock formation.

You may not be won over by the sand, but the water itself is spectacular, with infinite varieties of blue shimmering in the sun, turning transparent in the coves. And you may have as much fun on the water as in it. In particular, boating around Capri is a classic experience, allowing you to see sights that are either remote or entirely inaccessible by land.

Edenic Gardens

"What nature gives you makes you rich," they say in Campania. One look at Capri's perfectly tonsured palm trees, Sorrento's frangipani, and Amalfi's lemon trees laden with golden fruit, and you know what they mean.

So it's not surprising to learn that one of the major joys of this region is the abundance of spectacular gardens. Many of the most celebrated gardens were created by English green thumbs, such as the 19th-century medieval-style garden designed by Sir Francis Reid at Ravello's Villa Rufolo, and Lord Grimthorpe's relentlessly picturesque paradise created in the early 20th century at Ravello's Villa Cimbrone. When it comes to gardens, Campania is incomparabile.

The Glories of Spring

In April and May, all of Campania seems like a garden. Wherever you look—roadsides, archaeological sites, public gardens, even along railroad tracks—you're likely to see a dazzling array of natural colors.

From seemingly untended fields of scarlet poppies, to overflowing flower boxes on the streets of Naples, to the yellow umbels of giant fennel on Capri, this is the Mediterranean at its most explosive. Come back in June and much of the tapestry will have faded, with plants dispersing their seeds for next year's show.

Stepping Back in Time

The regions to the west and east of Naples are two of the world's greatest treasure troves of Greek and Roman antiquity.

Quick to appreciate the sybaritic possibilities of Campania Felix—"happy land"—the ancient Romans built palatial country residences and luxurious resorts.

Although the finest art relics have been moved to the Museo Archeologico in Naples, there's still plenty to see at the original ancient sites.

The most famous, rightly, is Pompeii, but it's well worthwhile to check out some of the many other notable locations, including Baia, pleasure spot of the Roman emperors; Lake Averno, legendary entrance to Hades; Oplontis, perhaps once home to Mr. and Mrs. Nero; and Cumae, where from her cave the famous Sibyl announced to kings and emperors her portents of the future.

QUINTESSENTIAL AMALFI COAST, CAPRI & NAPLES

Il Caffè (Coffee)

The Italian day begins with coffee, and more cups of coffee punctuate the afternoon. To live as the Italians do, drink as they drink, standing at the counter or sitting at an outdoor table of the corner bar. (In Italy, a "bar" is a coffee bar.)

A primer: *caffè* means coffee, and Italian standard issue is what Americans call espresso—short, strong, and usually taken very sweet. *Cappuccino* is a foamy half-and-half of espresso and steamed milk; cocoa powder (*cacao*) on top is acceptable, cinnamon is not.

If you're thinking of having a cappuccino for dessert, think again—Italians drink only caffè or caffè *macchiato* (with a spot of steamed milk) after lunchtime. Confused? Homesick? Order caffè *americano* for a reasonable facsimile of good old filtered joe.

Il Calcio (Soccer)

Imagine the most rabid American football fans—the ones who paint their faces on game day and sleep in pajamas emblazoned with the logo of their favorite team. Throw in a dose of melodrama along the lines of a tear-jerking soap opera. Ratchet up the intensity by a factor of 10, and you'll start to get a sense of how Italians feel about their national game, soccer—known in the mother tongue as *calcio*. On Sunday afternoons throughout the long September-to-May season, stadiums are packed throughout Italy, and one of the biggest teams, Napoli, is based in the city of Naples.

Those who don't get to games in person tend to congregate around television sets in restaurants and bars, rooting for the home team with a passion that feels like a last vestige of the days when the country was a series of warring medieval city-states. How calcio mania affects your stay in

If you want to get a sense of contemporary Italian culture and indulge in some of its pleasures, start by familiarizing yourself with the rituals of daily life. These are a few highlights—things you can take part in with relative ease.

Italy depends on how eager you are to get involved. At the very least, you may notice an eerie Sunday-afternoon quiet on the city streets, or erratic restaurant service around the same time, accompanied by cheers and groans from a neighboring room.

If you want a memorable, truly Italian experience, attend a game yourself. Availability of tickets may depend on the current fortunes of the local team, but they often can be acquired with help from your hotel concierge.

Il Gelato (Ice Cream)

During warmer months, *gelato*—the Italian equivalent of ice cream—is a national obsession. It's considered a snack rather than a dessert, bought at stands and shops in piazzas and on street corners, and consumed on foot, usually at a leisurely stroll (⇨ *see La Passeggiata, below*).

Gelato is softer, less creamy, and more intensely flavored than its American counterpart. It comes in simple flavors that capture the essence of the main ingredient. Standard choices include pistachio, *nocciola* (hazelnut), caffè, and numerous fresh-fruit varieties. Quality varies; the surest sign that you've hit on a good spot is a line at the counter.

La Passeggiata (Strolling)

A favorite Italian pastime is the *passeggiata* (literally, the promenade). In the late afternoon and early evening, especially on weekends, couples, families, and packs of teenagers stroll the main streets and piazzas of Italy's towns.

It's a ritual of exchanged news and gossip, window-shopping, flirting, and gelato eating that adds up to a uniquely Italian experience. To join in, simply hit the streets for a bit of wandering. You may feel more like an observer than a participant, until you realize that observing is what la passeggiata is all about.

MAKING THE MOST OF YOUR EUROS

Eating

Pizza rules the roost here, not just culturally, but also price-wise. The classic Margherita is likely to be the cheapest option on the menu, and even in costlier establishments will not break the bank (beware of the cover charge in some restaurants, however). Many pizzerias also have an outside counter selling inexpensive fried delicacies, ideal for a quick snack. Keep an eye out for *tavole calde* (warm tables), which sell portions of pasta and *secondi* from behind a large counter—these are often take-away, and seating areas are generally very basic, but the food is good. Rustic trattorias are generally a better value than the classier joints, and the menu offers the same local ingredients, often prepared by the owner's *mamma*. Opt for the house wine—not only is it less expensive, it may well come from the family's own vineyard. You will probably be offered a complementary *limoncello* to round off your meal.

Lodging

While five-star hotels will hit your wallet hard, there are many good value alternatives in the area. Bed-and-breakfasts and family-run hotels are a good bet, and the owners' warmth and hospitality is a golden opportunity to integrate with the local culture—some services may be basic, but there is every chance they offer the same stunning views as the more upmarket establishments. Many hotels have half-board options, particularly in high season, and promote special offers on their websites. If you can avoid the peak summer season you will find that rates often drop by up to 30%. Consider also choosing a smaller town as a base, rather than the main urban areas.

Shopping

The open-air markets are the place to head for money-conscious shoppers. There are a number of these in Naples, selling discount clothing, household items, and food. Bargains are harder to come by in the resort areas, but stores drop prices by up to 70% in the summer sales—this is generally for three weeks in July. Outside that period you may have to dig deep for those one-of-a-kind pieces (e.g., Capri sandals, Positano beachwear), but think of the saving on the high street prices back home. Make sure to ask about tax-free shopping for foreign visitors.

Travel

As European standards go, it is not expensive to travel around the region. The very best bet is the 3T Tourist Travel Ticket, which costs just €20 and allows three days unlimited use of all trains and most buses in the area—including the airport Alibus and the Pompeii-Vesuvius line. Museum buffs will want to invest in the three-day Campania Arte Card (🌐 *www.campaniartecard.it*), which includes transport, as well as free entry to two sites and discounts to others, for €32. If the Amalfi Coast is your destination, invest in the UnicoCostiera ticket; a day pass for all SITA buses costs €7.60 and gives you a 25% discount on Sorrento's City Sightseeing bus. On the islands, however, it is wiser to avoid the 24-hour ticket—you will probably not make enough trips to justify the cost. Full details of all these fares can be found on 🌐 *www.unicocampania.it*. Bear in mind, too, that walking is often an option for shorter distances, and that those hundreds of steps on the Amalfi Coast are indeed easier to tackle going down rather than up!

THE AMALFI COAST

WELCOME TO THE AMALFI COAST

TOP REASONS TO GO

★ **A world made of stairs:** Built like a steep amphitheater, Positano may well be the best triathlon training ground imaginable. The town's only job is to look enchanting—and it does that very well.

★ **Amalfi, city of the sea doges:** Offering a dazzling layer cake of civilizations—Norman, Saracen, and Arab-Sicilian—this medieval city is so picturesque it will practically click your camera for you.

★ **Furore, art in the hills:** This "town that doesn't exist," with no discernible center, is perched between the sea and sky and decorated with murals by local and international artists.

★ **Villa Cimbrone, Ravello:** No one should miss the spellbinding gardens of this villa and its Belvedere of Infinity, set like an eagle's nest 1,500 feet over the sea.

★ **Grecian glory:** Paestum has three sublime temples sitting side by side—some of the best preserved of ancient architectural monuments anywhere (including Greece).

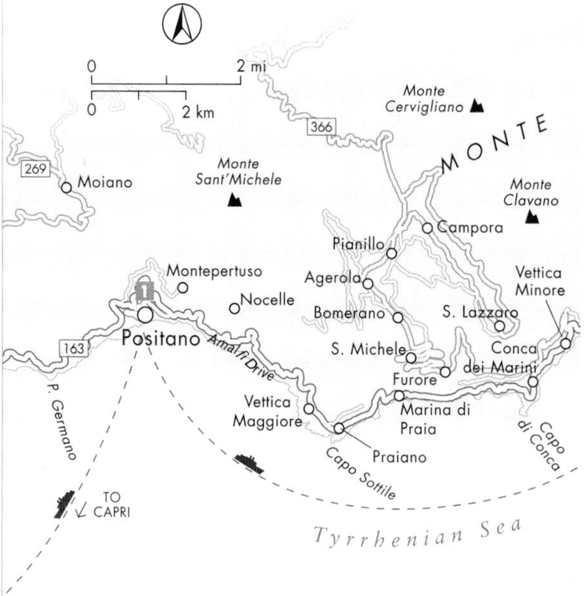

1 Positano, Conca dei Marini, and Nearby. Emerging from Sorrento's peninsula, the Amalfi Drive wriggles its way 5 miles south to Positano, the seaside village that, brilliantly two-faced, moves between luxe-sophisticated and beachcomber-casual. Sheltered by Monte Comune (which keeps the town warm in the winter and cool in the summer), Positano's three districts—the Sponda Lower Town, the central Mulini area, and the Chiesa Nuovo Upper Town—are all connected by endless staircases offering views well worth the blistered feet. Farther south along the Amalfi Drive is picturesque Praiano; the adorable anchorage-lido of Marina di Praia; a tchotchke hamlet called Furore; and Conca dei Marini, noted for its Emerald Grotto and gorgeous Santa Maria della Neve harbor.

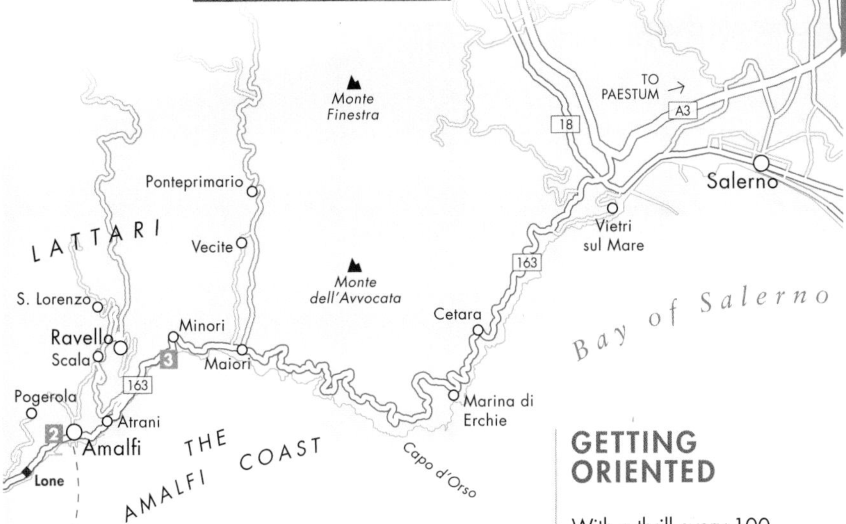

GETTING ORIENTED

With a thrill every 100 yards and a photo op at nearly every bend, the Costiera Amalfitana is about the most satisfying 30 miles of coastline to be found in tourist Europe. Rugged and craggy, the Amalfi Coast extends around the Bay of Salerno from Positano on the west to Vietri sul Mare on the east. When driving round-trip, many choose to go only in one direction on the coastal roads, going the other way via the highway or by train from Salerno, or by boat from Amalfi or Positano. Most travelers opt to wind their way south of Sorrento along the spectacular Amalfi Drive—the "road of a 1,001 turns"—which threads through a famous string of towns.

2 Amalfi. Nestled between the green Valle dei Mulini and the blue Gulf of Salerno, Amalfi is threaded with rambling, Moorish passages, testimony to the city's Norman and Arab-Sicilian past. The glory of the city's days as a medieval maritime republic is most evident in its fantastic cathedral. The transportation hub of the coast, Amalfi's waterfront Piazza Flavio Gioia serves as the terminus for SITA's major bus routes.

3 Ravello, Paestum, and nearby. Just beyond the Valley of the Dragon lies Ravello, perched "closer to the sky than the sea" atop Monte Cereto and set over the breathtaking Bay of Salerno. Famed for its medieval gardens (one of which inspired Wagner) and its bluer-than-blue vistas, this mountain aerie is one of Italy's most beautiful towns. Return to earth along the Amalfi Drive past modern Maiori and Cetara's quaint fishermen's beach. Leapfrog over chaotic Salerno to the Cilento Coast where Paestum's legendary Greek temples make a rousing finale to any trip.

Updated by Fergal Kavanagh

One of the most gorgeous places on Earth, this corner of the Campania region tantalizes, almost beyond bearing, the visitor who can stay but a day or two. Poets and millionaires have long journeyed here to see and sense its legendary sights: perfect, precariously perched Positano; Amalfi, a shimmering medieval city; romantic mountain-high Ravello; and ancient Paestum, with its three legendary Greek temples. Today, the coast's scenic sorcery makes this a top destination, drawing visitors from all over the world, who agree with UNESCO's 1997 decision to make this a World Heritage Center. This entire area is also a honeymoon Shangri-la—it is arguably the most divinely sensual stretch of water, land, and habitation on Earth.

Legends abound, but the Greeks were early colonizers at Paestum to the south, and Romans fled their own sacked empire in the 4th century to settle the steep coastal ridge now called the Lattari Mountains because of the milk, or *latte*, produced there. Despite frequent incursions by covetous Lombards, Saracens, and other hopefuls, the medieval Maritime Republic of Amalfi maintained its domination of the seas and coast until the Normans began their conquest of southern Italy in the 11th century. By 1300, Naples, the capital of the Angevin Kingdom, had become the dominant ruler of the region and remained so until Italy unified in the mid-19th century.

By the late 19th century tourism had blossomed, giving rise to the creation of the two-lane Amalfi Drive, what has come to be called the "Divina Costiera." A thousand or so gorgeous vistas appear along these almost 40 km (25 miles), stretching from just outside Sorrento to Vietri, coursing over deep ravines and bays of turquoise-to-sapphire water, spreading past tunnels and timeless villages.

The justly famed jewels along this coastal necklace are Positano, Amalfi, and Ravello, but today's traveler will find the satellite baguettes—including Conca dei Marini, Furore, Atrani, Scala, and Cetara—just as sparkling. The top towns along the Amalfi Drive may fill up in high season with tour buses, but in the countryside not much seems to have changed since the Middle Ages: mountains are still terraced and farmed for citrus, olives, wine, and dairy; and the sea is dotted with the gentle reds, whites, and blues of fishermen's boats. Vertiginously high villages, dominated by the spires of *chiese* (churches), are crammed with houses on, into, above, and below hillsides to the bay; crossed by mule paths; and navigated by flights of steps called *scalinatelle* often leading to outlooks and belvederes that take your breath away—in more ways than one. Songs have been composed about these serpentine stone steps, and they may come to haunt your dreams as well; some *costieri* (natives of the coast) count them one by one to get to sleep.

Considering the natural splendor of this region, it's no surprise that it flaunts some of the most beautiful beaches in the world. Crystal lagoons lapped by emerald green water; cliffs hallowed out with fairy grottoes; white, sunbaked villages dripping with flowers. The larger masterpieces, like Positano, are easily accessible, but the magic often lies in finding treasures hidden among the cliffs, such as Vallone di Furore, a tiny beach below an equally tiny village. Sun beds and umbrellas cost plenty—up to €10. Operators in Positano and Amalfi can ferry you to smaller beaches—prices depend on whether it's a drop-off (and pick up) or a full-day excursion with a light lunch.

Semitough realities lurk behind the scenic splendor of the Divina Costiera, most notably the extremes of driving (potentially dangerous, although accidents are reassuringly rare), the endless steps, and virtually nonexistent parking. Furthermore, it often rains in spring, parts of the hills burn dry in summer, museums are few, and until you adjust, people seem to talk at maximum decibels. So what? For a precious little time, you are in a land of unmarred beauty.

THE AMALFI COAST PLANNER

WHEN TO GO

The coast is at its best in April, May, and early June. The weather is generally pleasant, and hotels and restaurants have just reopened for the season. By May the seawater is warm enough, by American standards, for swimming, but you can often have the beach to yourself, as Italians shy away at least until June. Temperatures can be torrid in summer, and the coast is swarming with visitors—during August all of Italy flocks to the shores. The early fall months are more relaxing, with gentle, warm weather; swimming temperatures often last through October. Many restaurants and hotels close down for the winter.

PLANNING YOUR TIME

The Amalfi Coast is laid out in the easiest possible way for touring—beginning to the west in Positano, proceeding east along the coastline for 19 km (12 miles) to Amalfi. From here it's less than 7 km (4½ miles) farther east to Ravello, the coast's other absolute must. If an overview of these three fabled spots is all you seek, three days will suffice. To experience a few more of the area's splendors, you'll need a minimum of five days. If staying in one place is a priority, and you will not be exploring much, pick a base—the obvious candidates are Positano, Amalfi, and Ravello—but it's best to arrange to stay overnight in at least two of these destinations.

FESTIVALS

Yearlong, the Positano calendar is filled with festivities and religious *feste.* At Christmas, wreaths are fashioned from bougainvillea, and orchestra and choir concerts pop up all over town. The *Nuovo Anno* (New Year) is greeted with a big town dance and fireworks on the main beach, as well as other events. In neighboring Montepertuso, a living crèche is enacted. Amalfitans also love to celebrate holidays. The Good Friday candlelight procession, Easter Sunday, and Christmas pageants with crèche competitions (with cribs mounted in the city fountains) are all excuses for lavish family occasions, with special foods and church ceremonies.

Fodor's Choice ★ **Festa dell'Assunta** (*Feast of the Assumption*). Positano's star event of the year—and its main religious feast—is held on August 15, with the painting of the Madonna with Child carried from the church to the sea, commemorated by evening fireworks and music on the main beach. ✉ *Positano.*

Corso Internazionale di Musica da Camera (*International Chamber Music Camp & Festival*). As part of this July festival devoted to chamber music, free summer concerts are staged in atmospheric settings throughout Positano and Sorrento. Lessons and master classes also take place. ✉ *Positano* 🌐 *www.icmcfestival.com.*

Mare, Sole e Cultura (*Sea, Sun, and Culture*). In early July Positano hosts national and international authors, who read from their books in the shady gardens of Palazzo Murat. Concerts take place on the Spiaggia Grande. ✉ *Positano* 🌐 *www.deliacultura.it.*

Positano Premia La Danza Léonide Massine (*Positano Prize for the Art of Dancing*). The first week in September sees this celebration of dance that includes music concerts, dance performances, gallery exhibitions, panels, and an awards ceremony. ✉ *Positano* 🌐 *www.positanopremialadanza.it.*

Ravello Music Festival. Starting in the 1950s, Ravello became famed as the "City of Music," when concerts began to be performed in the spectacular gardens of the Villa Rufolo. The celebrated Ravello Music Festival runs from June to October, with full orchestras performing Wagner, Bach, Mozart, Beethoven, Brahms, Chopin, and slightly less well-known Italian composers such as Scarlatti and Cimarosa. The most popular event is the *Concerto all'Alba* (dawn concert), when the entire town wakes up at 4:30 to watch the sunrise over the bay to the accompaniment of music from a full symphony orchestra; this event takes place on August 10 to coincide with the shooting stars on the night of San Lorenzo. ✉ *Viale Wagner 5, Ravello* ☎ *089/858360* 📠 *089/8586278* 🌐 *www.ravellofestival.com.*

Regata Storica delle Antiche Repubbliche Marinare (*Historical Regatta of the Ancient Maritime Republics*). In this pageant staged every four years in Amalfi, mock battles take place in which four boats, each with eight oarsmen, represent the medieval maritime republics of Amalfi, Pisa, Genoa, and Venice. The prize, held by the winner for a year, is a scale-model gold-and-silver replica of an antique sailing ship. Each of the former republics is represented by 80 participants; Amalfi's musical contingent is adorned in jewel-encrusted costumes on loan from the town museum—doges, dogaressas, merchants, and commoners from the prosperous past come colorfully to life, with the day's festivities culminating in a show of fireworks. Held yearly on the first Sunday in June, with the four cities alternating as the urban stage sets, the pageant is scheduled to be in Amalfi in 2016.

Sagra del Pesce (*Fish Festival*). The last Saturday in September brings this fabulous fish festival on Fornillo beach, with live music and plenty of fish and seafood dishes to taste. ✉ *Positano* 🌐 *www.festadelpesce.net.*

St. Andrew Race. Dedicated to Amalfi's protector of seamen, this race, which takes place on June 27 and November 30, is a religious celebration commemorating the defeat of Barbarossa and the Moslem fleet in 1544. A procession of white-robed men carry a silver-gilt replica of the saint to the harbor, and fishermen at the beach run it back to the cathedral and—in one dramatic dash—straight up its 62 steps. Later, the statue gleams silver in the sunshine of the piazza, as fishermen hang tiny wooden and gilt fish amulets from the saint's left wrist as tokens of gratitude. In the evening, guitar music drifts from many boats, and candlelight flickers. ✉ *Amalfi.*

Fodor's Choice ★ **Torello.** At the foot of Ravello's mountain sits the satellite seaside *borgo* of Torello. On the second Sunday of September, this medieval hamlet reenacts its Saracen invasion with an unforgettable fireworks display. Replete with exploding stars that whiz through the streets on cables, this has to be seen to be believed. In addition, the town is illuminated for the preceding week, a magical sight even when viewed from Ravello, set 1,000 lofty feet up the hill. ✉ *Ravello.*

GETTING HERE AND AROUND

BOAT TRAVEL

To get to smaller towns, make arrangements with private boat companies or independent fishermen recommended by the tourist office or your hotel. Ferries operated by Linee Marittime Partenopee and Travelmar serve Positano, Amalfi, Salerno, and other locations within the region. Tickets can be purchased at booths on piers and docks.

Contacts Linee Marittime Partenopee ☎ *089/227979* 🌐 *www.consorziolmp.it.* **Travelmar** ☎ *089/872950* 🌐 *www.travelmar.it.*

BUS TRAVEL

Most travelers tour the Amalfi Drive by bus. SITA Sud (Sicurezza Trasporti Autolinee South) buses make the trip many times daily between 6 am and 10 pm (less often on Sunday, bank holidays, and major festival days). The bus from Sorrento to Amalfi stops at Positano (at Chiesa Nuova and Sponda), Praiano, and Conca dei Marini along the way. SITA bus drivers will stop anywhere on the main route as long as you state your destination when boarding. Tickets are called Unico Costiera, and cost from €2.50 for 45 minutes to €18 for three days. They must be purchased in advance and inserted in the time-stamp machine when you enter the bus. Ticket vendors can be found in cafés, bars, and newsstands. *For more about bus travel along the coast, see the feature "Buckle Up for the Amalfi Drive" in this chapter.*

Contact SITA Sud ☎ *080/5790211* 🌐 *www.sitasudtrasporti.it.*

CAR TRAVEL

Running between the Sorrentine peninsula and Salerno, Strada Statale 163 (State Highway 163), the Amalfi Drive, can be reached from Naples via the A3 Autostrada to Castellammare di Stabia, then linked to Sorrento via Statale 145. When driving round-trip, many choose to go only in one direction on the seaside road, going the other way via the inland highway threading the mountains. If you drive, be prepared to pay exorbitant parking fees, and consider yourself lucky when you find a parking space.

TRAIN TRAVEL

The towns of the Amalfi Coast aren't directly accessible by train, but you can take one to Sorrento or Salerno and then board a SITA Sud bus. The Circumvesuviana railway, which runs along the curve of the Bay of Naples from Naples to Sorrento, runs approximately every half hour. The Milan–Reggio Calabria state-railway train stops in Salerno, whose station here is a good place to pick up buses serving the Amalfi Coast.

Contact Circumvesuviana ☎ *800/211388* 🌐 *www.eavcampania.it.*

RESTAURANTS

No surprise here: dining on the Amalfi Coast revolves largely around seafood. Dishes are prepared using the short, rolled handmade *scialatelli* or large *paccheri* pasta and adorned with local *vongole* (clams) or *cozze* (mussels) and other shellfish (*al coccio*). Octopus, squid, and the fresh fish of the season are always on the menu for the second course. Cetara has been famous for its *alici* (anchovies) since Roman times, and even produces *alici* bread. Eateries range from beachside trattorias to beacons of fine dining with stupendous views. *Prices in the reviews are the average cost of a main course at dinner or, if dinner is not served, at lunch.*

HOTELS

Most lodgings in this part of Campania have been owned by the same families for generations, and whether the owner is plain mamma-and-papà or an heir to a ducal line, personality is evident. Along with local management may come quirks, even in the fanciest establishments, but the 21st century has wrought change, and with it, numerous 19th-century cliff-side villas and palazzi, with their big gardens and grand staircases, huge baths and tile floors, have been transformed into luxury hotels. Happily, you don't need to be a millionaire to enjoy comfy lodgings along the Costa Divina: there are many "cheaper" options; the quote marks are used because many of these places cost more than €100 a night, due to their prime real estate overlooking the sea, but there are also plenty of bargains to be had.

When booking, note that a few hotels *require* half or even full board, usually with a minimum stay of two or three nights. Some hotels have minimum stays for the peak periods of July and August and around holidays. If you're traveling by car and reserving rooms in advance, ask about parking fees. Many guests staying in Positano and Amalfi suffer a nasty shock when they find they have to pay up to €20 per day. *Prices in the reviews are the lowest cost of a standard double room in high season.*

TOURS

City Sightseeing Sorrento offers multiple trips daily from Amalfi to Maiori and to Ravello in open-top minibuses. The fare is €3 per ride (€10 for a daily four-ride ticket). The Naples-based company Vesuvius vs. Pompeii also conducts tours (prices vary) of the Amalfi Coast.

Tour Operators City Sightseeing ✉ *Sorrento* ☎ *081/8774707* 🌐 *www.sorrento.city-sightseeing.it.* **Vesuvius vs. Pompeii** ✉ *Sorrento* ☎ *333/6409000* 🌐 *www.vesuviusvspompeii.com.*

VISITOR INFORMATION

The online resource Amalfi's Coast provides detailed information about all the major towns on the coast, as well as maps, weather updates, and a handy booking service. A related site, at 🌐 *www.theamalficoast.net,* has similar information, along with links to bus and ferry timetables.

Amalfi's Coast 🌐 *www.amalfiscoast.com.*

POSITANO, CONCA DEI MARINI, AND NEARBY

As you head past the Sorrentine Peninsula and onto the coastal Amalfi Drive, we trust you are not driving your own car. If you are, you will have to make the trip later, with someone else driving, in order to properly enjoy one of the world's most beautiful scenic roads, because it is likewise a tortuous road, writhing its way along a coast that wriggles past caverns, little inlets, cliffs, and gardens, curving sharply every 20 feet. So save your nerves and tempers by leaving your car behind and get ready to savor this stretch of the Amalfi Drive, between Positano and the city of Amalfi. Indecently beautiful, the Costiera Amalfitana remains the scenic showstopper of the entire Campania.

POSITANO

56 km (35 miles) southeast of Naples, 16 km (10 miles) east of Sorrento.

When John Steinbeck visited Positano in 1953, he wrote that it was difficult to consider tourism an industry because "there are not enough [tourists]." Alas, there are more than enough now. What Steinbeck wrote, however, still applies: "Positano bites deep. It is a dream place that isn't quite real when you are there and becomes beckoningly real after you have gone."

The most photographed fishing village in the world, this fabled locale is home to some 4,000 *Positanesi,* who are joined daily by hordes arriving from Capri, Sorrento, and Amalfi, eager to celebrate the fact that Positano is, impossibly, there. The town clings to the Monti Lattari and has been called by artist Paul Klee "the only place in the world conceived on a vertical rather than a horizontal axis." Its arcaded, cubist buildings, set in tiers up the mountainside, reflect the sky in dawn-color walls: rose, peach, purple, some tinted the ivory of sunrise's drifting clouds. In fact, the colors on these Saracen-inspired dwellings may have originally served to help returning fishermen spot their own digs in an instant.

It may have started with bread. Roman Emperor Tiberius, son of poison-happy Livia, sent his three-oar boat to a mill in Positano, understandably afraid that his neighbors on Capri would poison him. The mill, now modernized, still grinds healthful flour, but Positano has evolved into well more than just a grocery stop. Its name could be a corruption of the Greek "Poseidon," or derived from a man named Posides, who owned villas here during the time of Claudius; or even from Roman freedmen, called the Posdii. The most popular theory is that the name "Positano" comes from Pestano (or Pesitano), a 9th-century town by a Benedictine abbey near Montepertuso, built by refugees of Paestum to the south, whose homes had been ransacked by the Saracens.

Pisa sacked the area in 1268, but after an elaborate defensive system of watchtowers was put in place, Positano once again prospered, briefly rivaling Amalfi. As a fiefdom of Neapolitan families until the end of the 17th century, Positano produced silk and, later, canvas goods, but decline began again in the late 18th century. With the coming of the steamship in the mid-19th century, some three-fourths of the town's 8,000 citizens emigrated to America—mostly to New York—and it eventually regressed into a backwater fishing village. That is, until artists and intellectuals, and then travelers, rediscovered its prodigious charms in the 20th century, especially after World War II; Picasso, Stravinsky, Diaghilev, Olivier, Steinbeck, Klee—even Lenin—were just a few of this town's talented fans. Lemons, grapes, olives, fish, resort gear, and, of course, tourism keep it going, but despite its shimmery sophistication and overwrought popularity, Positano's chief export remains its most precious commodity: beauty.

GETTING HERE AND AROUND

SITA buses serve Amalfi from Sorrento. Purchase tickets prior to boarding at a *tabaccheria* (newsstand). The buses pass through town every 40 minutes or so in both directions, departing from Amalfi or Sorrento from 6:30 am until 10 pm. The bus has two main stops in Positano: Transita, or Upper Town—near the large church of Santa Maria delle Grazie, or Chiesa Nuova—and Sponda, closer to the Lower Town, to the east of the main beach. Summer ferries serve Positano from Sorrento, Capri, and Salerno. The ferry and hydrofoil ticket office in Positano is beside the Spiaggia Grande; ferries to Amalfi, Sorrento, and Capri are available at the dock under Via Positanesi d'America, near the public beach in the center of town. By car, take the Statale 163 (Amalfitana) from outside Sorrento or Salerno.

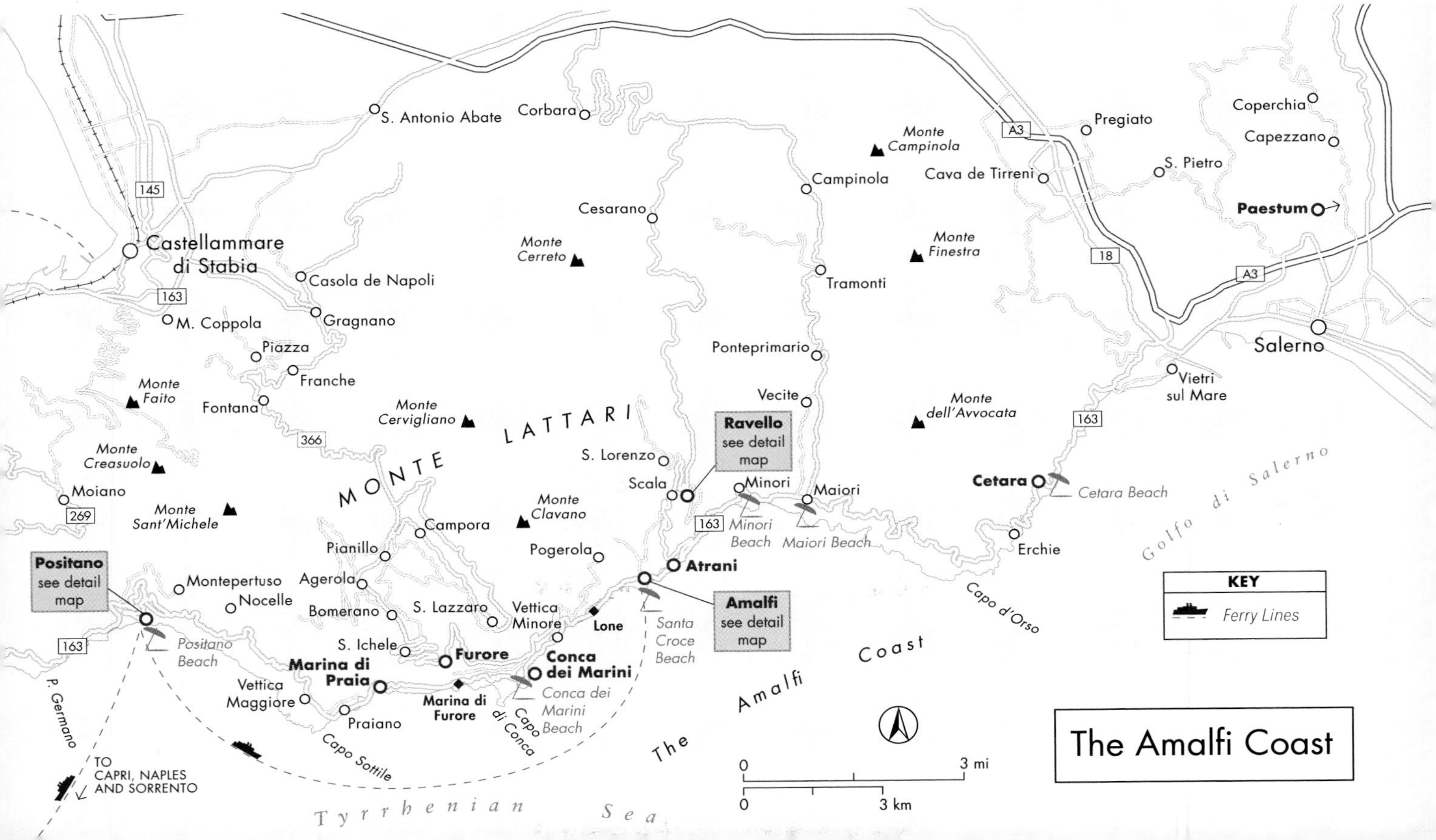
The Amalfi Coast
KEY
Ferry Lines
S. Antonio Abate
Corbara
Coperchia
Pregiato
Capezzano
Monte Campinola
S. Pietro
Campinola
Cava de Tirreni
A3
145
Paestum
Cesarano
Castellammare di Stabia
Monte Cerreto
Monte Finestra
18
Casola de Napoli
Tramonti
163
M. Coppola
Gragnano
Salerno
Piazza
Ponteprimario
Franche
Monte Faito
Fontana
Vecite
Vietri sul Mare
Monte Cervigliano
Monte dell'Avvocata
Ravello see detail map
MONTE LATTARI
366
Monte Creasuolo
S. Lorenzo
Cetara
Cetara Beach
Moiano
Scala
Minori
Maiori
Golfo di Salerno
269
Monte Sant'Michele
Monte Clavano
Campora
Minori Beach
Maiori Beach
Erchie
Pianillo
Pogerola
Positano see detail map
Atrani
Montepertuso
Agerola
Nocelle
Amalfi see detail map
Capo d'Orso
Bomerano
S. Lazzaro
Vettica Minore
Lone
Santa Croce Beach
Positano Beach
S. Ichele
Furore
Conca dei Marini
The Amalfi Coast
Marina di Praia
Vettica Maggiore
Marina di Furore
Conca dei Marini Beach
Praiano
Capo di Conca
P. Germano
Capo Sottile
TO CAPRI, NAPLES AND SORRENTO
0
3 mi
3 km
Tyrrhenian Sea

Local Flavio Gioia orange buses regularly ply even the smallest roads and make more stops than the SITA buses. Look for the ceramic sign and wait there. The local orange bus frequently plies the one-and-only one-way Via Pasitea, hairpinning from Transita to Piazza dei Mulini then up to the mountains and back, making a loop through the town every half hour. The taxi rank is at the top of Via dei Mulini. Service on most Flavio Gioia routes begins at 7:30 am and ends at midnight; departures are usually every half hour on the main lines.

SAVE THE BEST FOR FIRST

The first town on the Amalfi Drive is, to many travelers, the best: Positano. People head for this most popular of Amalfi Coast destinations, which is set in a natural amphitheater, as though to a hit play. The show does not disappoint.

If their hotels don't provide parking, most car travelers leave their wheels either in one of the few free parking spaces on the upper Sorrento–Amalfi main road or in one of the scarce and pricey garages a few minutes' walk from the beach. The best bet for day-trippers is to get to Positano early enough so that space is still available. (Even those arriving by SITA bus should get a morning start, as traffic on the Amalfi Drive becomes heavy by noon.)

A word of advice: Wear comfortable walking shoes and be sure your back and legs are strong enough to negotiate those picturesque, but daunting and ladderlike *scalinatelle*. In the center of town, where no buses can go, you're on your own from Piazza dei Mulini: To begin your explorations, make a left turn onto the boutique-flanked Via dei Mulini and head down to the Palazzo Murat, Santa Maria Assunta, and the beach—one of the most charming walks of the coast.

VISITOR INFORMATION

Contact Azienda Autonoma Soggiorno e Turismo ✉ *Via del Saracino 4* ☎ *089/875067* 🌐 *www.aziendaturismopositano.it* ⏲ *Mon.–Sat. 8:30–4:30 (June–Sept., until 7, plus Sun. morning).*

NEED A BREAK?

Bar Internazionale. More than just a place to wait for the bus—it's at the main SITA Chiesa Nouva bus stop—Bar Internazionale is a meeting place for locals and visitors alike, a happy spot where you can read newspapers from several countries while nursing a creamy cappuccino. ✉ ***Via G. Marconi 306*** ☎ ***089/875434.***

EXPLORING

Palazzo Murat. Past a bevy of resort boutiques, head to Via dei Mulini to view the prettiest garden in Positano—the 18th-century courtyard of the Palazzo Murat, named for Joachim Murat, who sensibly chose the palazzo as his summer residence. This was where Murat, designated by his brother-in-law Napoléon as King of Naples in 1808, came to forget the demands of power and lead the simple life. Since Murat was a Continental style setter, it couldn't be *too* simple; he built this grand abode (now a hotel ⇨ *; see Where to Stay, below*) near the church of Santa Maria Assunta, just steps from the main beach. ✉ *Via dei Mulini 23* ☎ *089/875177* 🌐 *www.palazzomurat.it.*

Found just down the street from the Lower Town bus stop, this copy of Pompeii's famed bronze faun welcomes visitors to someone's house, and to all Positano.

Santa Maria Assunta. The Chiesa Madre, or parish church of Santa Maria Assunta, lies just south of the Palazzo Murat, its green-and-yellow majolica dome topped by a perky cupola visible from just about anywhere in town. Built on the site of the former Benedictine abbey of Saint Vito, the 13th-century Romanesque structure was almost completely rebuilt in 1700. The last piece of the ancient mosaic floor can be seen under glass behind the altar. Note the carved wooden Christ, a masterpiece of devotional religious art, with its bathetic face and bloodied knees, on view before the altar. At the altar is a Byzantine 13th-century painting on wood of Madonna with Child, known popularly as the Black Virgin, carried to the beach every August 15 to celebrate the Feast of the Assumption. Legend claims that the painting was once stolen by Saracen pirates, who, fleeing in a raging storm, heard from a voice on high saying, "*Posa, posa*"—"Put it down, put it down." When they placed the image on the beach near the church, the storm calmed, as did the Saracens. Embedded over the doorway of the church's bell tower, set across the tiny piazza, is a medieval bas-relief of fishes, a fox, and a pistrice (the mythical half-dragon, half-dog sea monster). This is one of the few relics of the medieval abbey of Saint Vito. The Oratorio houses historic statues from the Sacristy; renovations to the Crypt have unearthed 1st-century Roman columns. ✉ *Piazza Flavio Gioia* ☎ *089/875480* 🌐 *www.chiesapositano.com* ⏲ *Church daily 8–noon, in summer also 4–9.*

NEED A BREAK?

Bar Mulino Verde. Come here for an espresso, a slice of *Positanese* (a chocolate cake as delectable as its namesake), or a fresh-fruit iced granita. Deservedly famous for its lemon profiteroles as much as for its tree-lined terrace, suspended on a wooden platform above the Lower Town, Bar Mulino Verde is also ideal for morning coffee, a predinner *aperitivo*, or postdinner *digestivo*. ✉ *Via Cristoforo Colombo 1* ☎ *089/811701*.

Fodor's Choice ★ **Via Positanesi d'America.** Just before the ferry ticket booths to the right of Spiaggia Grande, a tiny road that is the loveliest seaside walkway on the entire coast, rises up and borders the cliffs leading to the Fornillo beach. The road is named for the town's large number of 19th-century emigrants to the United States—Positano virtually survived during World War II thanks to the money and packages their descendants sent back home. Halfway up the path lies the Torre Trasìta (Trasìta Tower), the most distinctive of Positano's three coastline defense towers. Now a residence occasionally available for summer rental, the tower was used to spot pirate raids. As you continue along the Via Positanesi d'America, you'll pass a tiny inlet and an emerald cove before Fornillo beach comes into view.

BEACHES

The Marina is the main boating area, with taupe, semi-sandy Spiaggia Grande the largest and widest beach of the six or so in the area. Fishermen—once the dominant workforce—now function as a cooperative group, supplying local kitchens; they can be seen cleaning their colorful, flipped-over boats and mending their torn nets throughout the day, seemingly oblivious to the surrounding throngs. To the west of town is the less-crowded Spiaggia del Fornillo, which you can get to by walking the gorgeous Via Positanesi d'America (leading from Spiaggia Grande). Fornillo is worth the walk, as it is vast and hemmed in by impressive cliffs. To the east of Positano is a string of small, pretty beaches, separated by coves—La Porta, Arienzo, San Pietro, and Laurito—most of which are accessible only by boat.

Spiaggia del Fornillo. Positano received a Bandiera Blu (Blue Flag) in 2010—the only beach on the coast to do so—in recognition of its water quality, safety, and services offered. The Spiaggia Grande (large beach) has the glorious, rainbow-hued backdrop of the town, but for a more informal atmosphere and lush vegetation, follow the Via Positanesi d'America to the Fornillo beach. Almost 300 meters long, the beach was a favorite of Pablo Picasso because of its position between the medieval Trasita and Clavel Towers. **Amenities:** food and drink; lifeguards; showers; toilets; water sports. **Best for:** snorkeling, swimming.

Spiaggia Grande. The walkway from the Piazza Flavio Gioia leads down to the Spiaggia Grande, or main beach, bordered by an esplanade and some of Positano's best restaurants. Surrounded by the spectacular amphitheater of houses and villas that leapfrog up the hillsides of Monte Commune and Monte Sant'Angelo, this remains one of the most picturesque beaches in the world. Although it faces stiff competition from Spiaggia di Fornillo beach, which is a far bigger and whiter strand of sand, the Spiaggia Grande wins the beauty contest hands down. **Amenities:** food and drink; lifeguards; showers; toilets; water sports. **Best for:** snorkeling, swimming. ✉ *Spiaggia Grande*.

Palazzo Murat 1
Santa Maria Assunta 2
Via Positanesi d'America 3

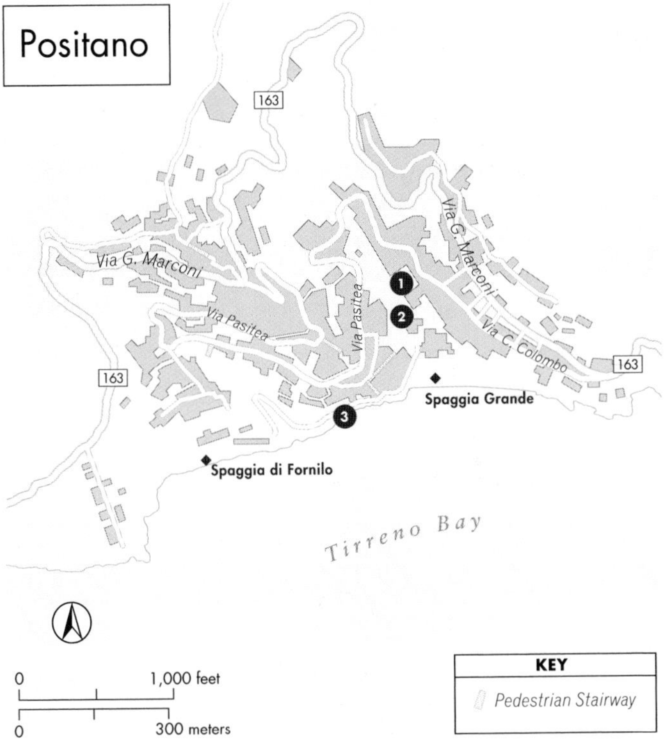

WHERE TO EAT

$$ SOUTHERN ITALIAN **Chez Black.** A local institution, allegedly nicknamed after owner Salvatore Russo's eternal tan, this nautically themed place (the waiters even wear sailor uniforms) cannot be beaten for its location (right on the Spiaggia Grande) or as a great spot for people-watching. Regular visitors include Denzel Washington, who was best man at Salvatore's son's wedding. Despite catering to the day-tripping coachloads, the friendly staff will guide you through the restaurant's specialties, including *zuppa di pesce* (fish soup) and *spaghetti con ricci di mare* (spaghetti with sea urchins). Start with the house *aperativo*, the *grotta dello smeraldo*—gin, lemon, and crème de menthe. *Average main: €20 Via del Brigantino 19 089/875036 www.chezblack.it Closed Nov.–Feb.*

$$ SOUTHERN ITALIAN **Da Adolfo.** On a little beach where pirates used to build and launch boats, this laid-back trattoria has long been a favorite Positano landmark. The pirates are long gone, but their descendants now operate the free ferry to and from Positano (every half-hour in the morning)—look for the boat with the red fish on the mast named for the restaurant—or make the steep descent from the main coastal road at Laurito. Sit under a straw canopy on the wooden terrace to enjoy *totani con patate* (squid and potatoes with garlic and oil); then sip white wine with peaches until sundown. Some diners even swim over, so bathing suits are fine. **TIP→ Da Adolfo gets busy, so ask your hotel to book a table for you:**

personal reservations are often not honored. $ *Average main: €15* ✉ *Spiaggia di Laurito, Via Laurito 40* ☎ *089/875022* 🌐 *www.daadolfo.com* ⊙ *Closed Oct.–Apr.*

> **WORD OF MOUTH**
>
> "Positano is the most spectacular town on the Amalfi Coast. Amalfi may feel/be less touristy, more authentic, but it can't compare in terms of raw beauty and incredible views."
>
> —WWK

$$$ SOUTHERN ITALIAN ✕ **Donna Rosa.** Locals in Montepertuso prefer to dine in this family-run establishment on the main square, slightly more upmarket than neighboring Il Ritrovo. Watch your meal being prepared in the main room with its open kitchen, find a seat on the terraces, or join the smokers on the main square. The menu includes fresh homemade pasta, or a selection of fresh meat and fish, depending on the day's catch. Digest in style with a glass of homemade limoncello. $ *Average main: €25* ✉ *Via Montepertuso 97/99, Montepertuso* ☎ *089/811806* ⊙ *Closed Tues. and mid-Nov.–mid-Mar.*

$$$ SOUTHERN ITALIAN ✕ **La Cambusa.** The two bronze lions guarding the steps leading up to this "pantry" off the Spiaggia Grande aren't actually part of the restaurant, but they aptly guide you to this longtime haven for tasty local cuisine. Linguine with mussels and fresh fish with potatoes and tomato sauce are among the favorite dishes here. Owners Baldo and Danielle are well known for maintaining high standards even during the hectic summer season. The outdoor dining terrace holds pride of place directly above the beach. $ *Average main: €25* ✉ *Piazza Amerigo Vespucci 4* ☎ *089/875432* 🌐 *www.lacambusapositano.com* ⊙ *Closed Nov. and Dec.*

$$ SOUTHERN ITALIAN ✕ **La Pergola.** Occupying a prime location near dead center on Spiaggia Grande, this arbor-covered seating area offers a fabulous (and festive, due to the happy crowds) beachside setting. Often confused with the equally good Buca di Bacco upstairs, it was a dance club until the 1970s. Seafood, unsurprisingly, is the main fare—be sure to try the *scialatielli ai frutti di mare* (fresh pasta with shell fish) or sea bass in *acqua pazza* (poached in a herb broth). Pizza and chicken breast with fries are also on the menu and there's self-service counter, helpful for those on a budget or heading out to the beach. ■ **TIP→ La Pergola stays open until 1 am, giving you time to digest before trying the homemade dolci (desserts) and ice cream, prepared around the corner at Via della Taranta 6.** $ *Average main: €22* ✉ *Via del Brigantino 35* ☎ *089/811461* 🌐 *www.bucapositano.it* ⊙ *Closed Nov. and Dec.*

$$ SOUTHERN ITALIAN Fodor's Choice ★ ✕ **Lo Guarracino.** In a supremely romantic setting, this partly arbor-covered, poised-on-a-cleft aerie is about the most idyllic place to enjoy lemon pasta and a glass of vino as you watch the yachts come and go. Set a few steps above Positano's prettiest seaside path, the terrace vista takes in the cliffs, the sea, Li Galli islands, Spiaggia del Fornillo, and Torre Clavel. The charming backroom arbor, beneath thick, twining vines, where tables are covered in cloths that match the tint of the bay, is *the* place to sit. Fine fish specialties are top delights on the menu. The day's catch is often cooked, with potatoes, in the wood-fired pizza oven, which gives it a distinct flavor. $ *Average main: €20* ✉ *Via Positanesi d'America 12* ☎ *089/875794* 🌐 *www.loguarracino.net* ⊙ *Closed Jan.–Mar.*

Continued on page 46

BUCKLE UP FOR THE AMALFI DRIVE

The vertical village of Positano

If travelers do nothing else along this coast, they have to experience the Amalfi Drive, a cliff-hugging stretch of road that tests their faith in civil engineering. One of the most beautiful coastal drives in the world, this roller-coastal "route of 1,001 bends" offers views that are drop-dead breathtaking—literally, it sometimes seems.

When visitors to the Amalfi Coast take the spectacular 50-minute bus ride along the sea and begin to note the bus soaring and banking along the cliff-side concrete ribbon, they may well wonder if the driver has a hankering to mature his insurance policy. As the road wiggles in and out hundreds of feet above the water (while it's still there—landslides, you know), the Mario Andretti at the wheel seems to shift into juggernaut speed. Bottles begin to roll around on the floor and a lady takes out her rosary. With car-chase determination, the driver negotiates a whiplash twist in the road. Terrifying though some switchbacks are, what meets travelers' eyes (when they can bear to open them) is breath-stopping beautiful: bays of turquoise-to-sapphire water, timeless cliff-top villages, vertiginous pinnacles of rock. As the bus finally pulls into Amalfi, passengers congratulate themselves on surviving the ride of their life.

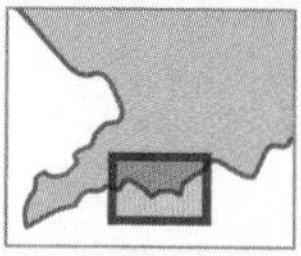

POSITANO TO CONCA DEI MARINI

Positano

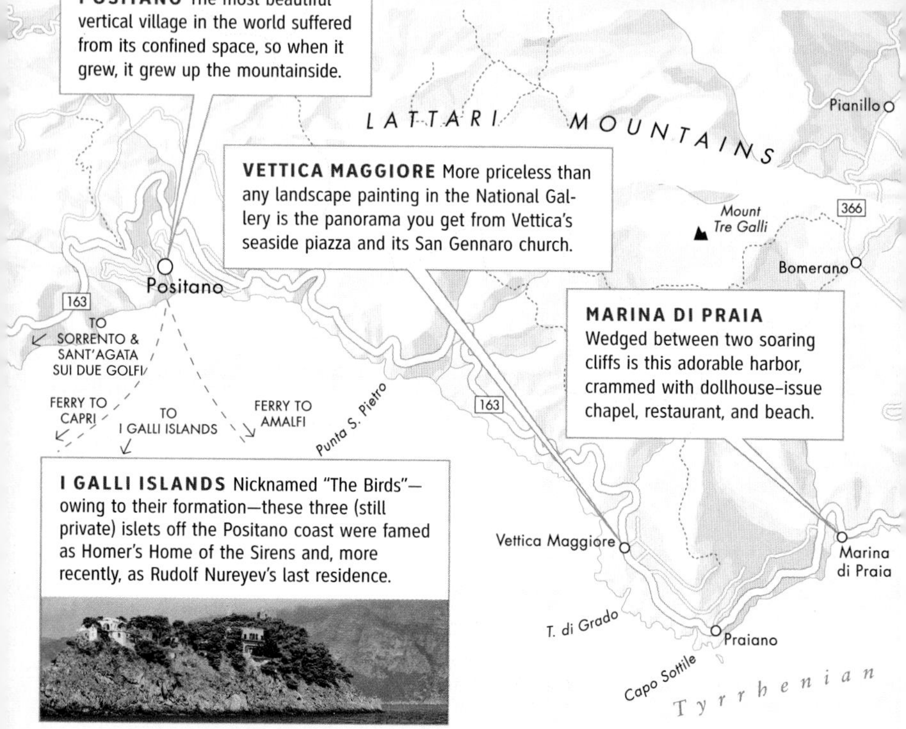

POSITANO The most beautiful vertical village in the world suffered from its confined space, so when it grew, it grew up the mountainside.

VETTICA MAGGIORE More priceless than any landscape painting in the National Gallery is the panorama you get from Vettica's seaside piazza and its San Gennaro church.

MARINA DI PRAIA Wedged between two soaring cliffs is this adorable harbor, crammed with dollhouse-issue chapel, restaurant, and beach.

I GALLI ISLANDS Nicknamed "The Birds"—owing to their formation—these three (still private) islets off the Positano coast were famed as Homer's Home of the Sirens and, more recently, as Rudolf Nureyev's last residence.

A GUIDE TO THE DRIVE

Statale (Highway) 163—the Amalfi Drive, as we call it—was hewn from the lip of the Lattari Mountains and completed in 1852, varying from 50 feet to 400 feet above the bay. You can thank Ferdinand, the Bourbon king of the Two Sicilies, for commissioning it, and Luigi Giordano for designing this seemingly improbable engineering feat. A thousand or so gorgeous vistas appear along these almost 40 km (25 miles), stretching from just outside Sorrento to Vietri. John Steinbeck once joked that the Amalfi Drive "is carefully designed to be a little narrower than two cars side by side" so the going can be a little tense: the slender two lanes hovering over the sheer drops sometimes seem impossible to maneuver by auto, let alone by buses and trucks.

Many travelers arrive from Sorrento, just to the north, connecting to the coast through Sant'Agata sui Due Golfi on

San Gennaro church, Maggiore

Il San Pietro di Positano

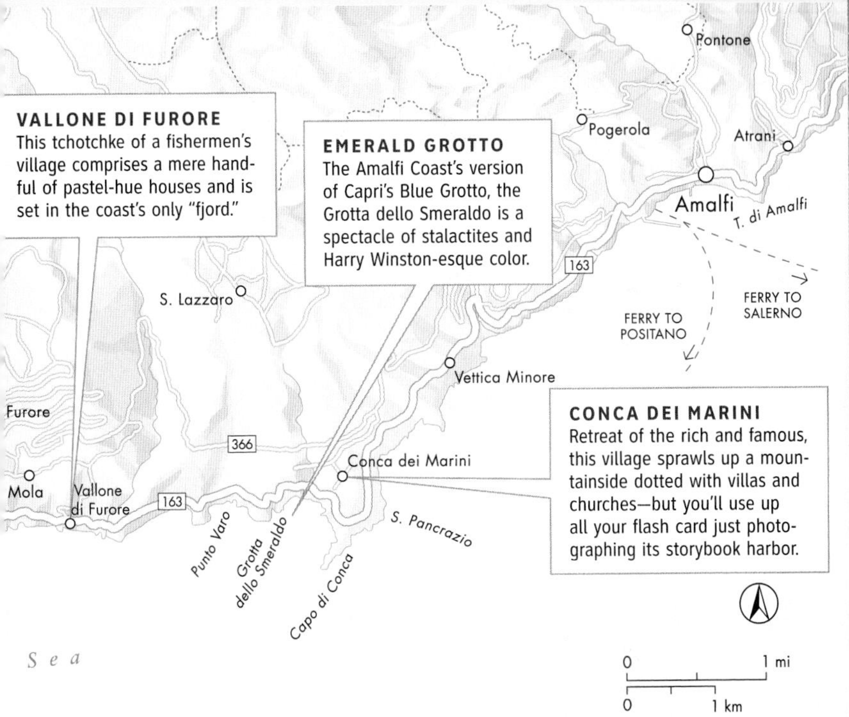
VALLONE DI FURORE
This tchotchke of a fishermen's village comprises a mere handful of pastel-hue houses and is set in the coast's only "fjord."
EMERALD GROTTO
The Amalfi Coast's version of Capri's Blue Grotto, the Grotta dello Smeraldo is a spectacle of stalactites and Harry Winston-esque color.
CONCA DEI MARINI
Retreat of the rich and famous, this village sprawls up a mountainside dotted with villas and churches—but you'll use up all your flash card just photographing its storybook harbor.
Pontone
Pogerola
Atrani
Amalfi
T. di Amalfi
163
FERRY TO SALERNO
FERRY TO POSITANO
S. Lazzaro
Vettica Minore
Furore
366
Conca dei Marini
Mola
Vallone di Furore
163
Punto Varo
Grotta dello Smeraldo
S. Pancrazio
Capo di Conca
Sea
0
1 mi
0
1 km

the Statale 145—the Strada del Nastro Azzurro (Blue Ribbon Road), whose nickname aptly describes its width, and the color at your alternating right and left. The white-knuckle part, or, as some call it, the Via Smeraldo (Emerald Road), begins as the road connects back to Statale 163, threading through coastal ridges at Colli di S. Pietro, and continuing to wend its way around the Vallone di Positano. From ravine to ravine, Positano then begins to beckon out your window, appearing and disappearing like a flirtatious coquette. Just east of Positano, at Punta San Pietro, Statale 163 again winds sharply around valleys, deep ravines, and precipices, affording more stunning ridge views. Past Praiano, the Furore gorge is crossed by viaduct. From here on to Amalfi, the ridges soften just a bit.

CHICKEN?

If you think a road is just for getting from here to there, the Amalfi Drive is not for you. So if you want to leapfrog over all the thrills, opt for the high mountain pass called the Valico di Chiunzi, easily reached via the A3 Naples–Salerno Autostrada from the exit at Angri.

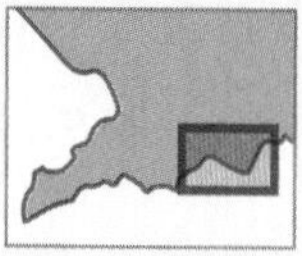

AMALFI TO CETARA

Villa Rufolo, Ravell

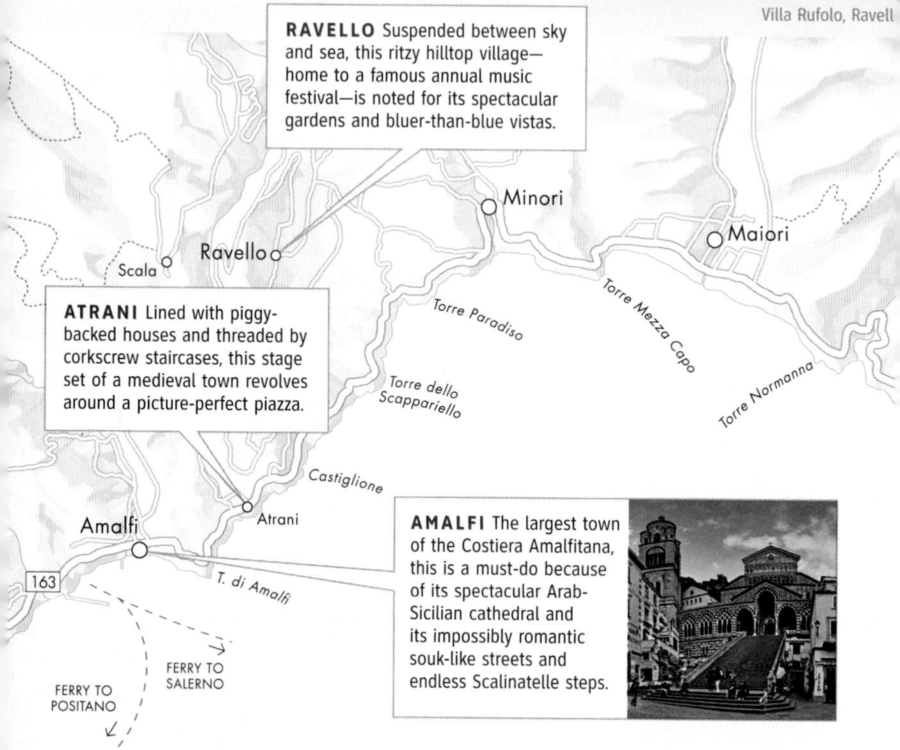
RAVELLO Suspended between sky and sea, this ritzy hilltop village—home to a famous annual music festival—is noted for its spectacular gardens and bluer-than-blue vistas.
Minori
Maiori
Scala
Ravello
Torre Paradiso
Torre Mezza Capo
Torre Normanna
Torre dello Scappariello
ATRANI Lined with piggy-backed houses and threaded by corkscrew staircases, this stage set of a medieval town revolves around a picture-perfect piazza.
Castiglione
Atrani
Amalfi
163
T. di Amalfi
FERRY TO SALERNO
FERRY TO POSITANO
AMALFI The largest town of the Costiera Amalfitana, this is a must-do because of its spectacular Arab-Sicilian cathedral and its impossibly romantic souk-like streets and endless Scalinatelle steps.

DOING THE DRIVE BY CAR

With countless twists and turns, the Amalfi Drive succeeds in making every driver into a Gran Turismo pro. In fact, at times you may feel you've entered the Amalfi Indy: The natives joke that the English complete the "course" in two hours, the Italians in a half hour. The drive is studded with stops built off the roadside for you to pull into safely and experience what your passengers are oohing and ahhing about. The round reflecting mirrors set along major curves in the road intend to show if others are coming around a bend, but honk before narrow curves to let oncoming traffic know about you, and listen for honks from oncoming curves. Buses and trucks will sometimes require you to back up; if there's a standoff, take it in stride, as it goes on all the time. At various points on the drive, stewards will stop larger vehicles so that cars can pass. Note that the road inevitably is closed some days due to landslides.

Villa Cimbrone, Ravello

Atrani

Cetara

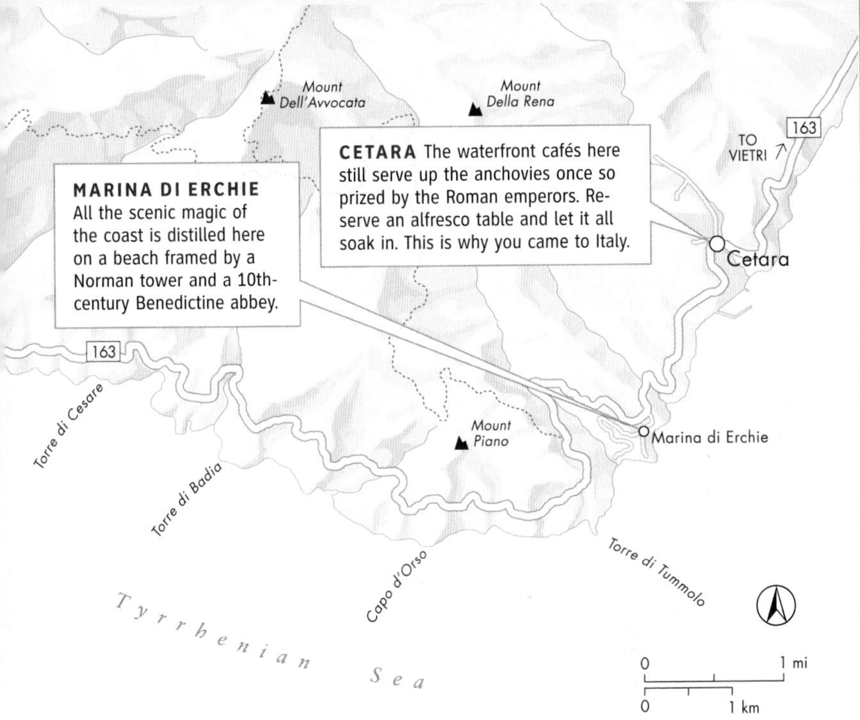
Mount Dell'Avvocata
Mount Della Rena
CETARA The waterfront cafés here still serve up the anchovies once so prized by the Roman emperors. Reserve an alfresco table and let it all soak in. This is why you came to Italy.
MARINA DI ERCHIE All the scenic magic of the coast is distilled here on a beach framed by a Norman tower and a 10th-century Benedictine abbey.
TO VIETRI
163
Cetara
163
Torre di Cesare
Mount Piano
Marina di Erchie
Torre di Badia
Capo d'Orso
Torre di Tummolo
Tyrrhenian Sea
0
1 mi
0
1 km

DOING THE DRIVE BY BUS

There's one main reason why you should forget the car and opt for taking one of the convenient and inexpensive SITA buses that travel the route (usually once an hour: *see* www.sitasudtrasporti.it): The view is much better, thanks to the mighty elevation of bus seats, which allows you to drink in mountain-meets-sea vistas, often missed in a car because of the highway's low stone barrier. The best views can be yours if you sit on the sea side of the bus (on your right as you board the bus if you're starting in Sorrento, on your left if you begin in Amalfi). The trip between Sorrento and Amalfi generally takes between 90 and 120 minutes. Buses make regular stops at all the main destinations: happily, the driver will stop anywhere on the main route as long as you inform him of your destination, be it hotel or fork in the road, when boarding. Note that buses fill up in the summer months, and the locals aren't usually orderly when it comes to making a line.

$$ SOUTHERN ITALIAN **Next2.** Wrought-iron gates open from the main thoroughfare of Via Pasitea into Next2's outdoor dining area, which has a stunning view over Positano. The decor is invitingly simple yet sophisticated, with white tablecloths and comfortable lounge chairs. The two owners are passionate about fine cuisine, particularly seafood—try the pan-seared *bonito* (local tuna) with spinach and sweet-and-sour onions—and they'll walk you through the menu and wine list. *Average main: €22 Via Pasitea 242 089/8123516 www.next2.it Reservations essential.*

$ SOUTHERN ITALIAN **Pupetto.** A long terrace overlooking the sea is the main feature of this simple spot along Fornillo beach that's set under heavily perfumed lemon trees. Opt for the excellent grilled fish, best followed by the homemade limoncello. The restaurant is part of the Hotel Pupetto, most of whose spacious guest rooms also have lovely sea views. **TIP→ To get here from the Upper Town, take the elevator from the parking lot.** *Average main: €12 Hotel Pupetto, Via Fornillo 37 089/875087 www.hotelpupetto.it Closed Nov.–Mar. All meals.*

$$ SOUTHERN ITALIAN Fodor's Choice ★ **Ristorante il Ritrovo.** Sitting in the tiny town square of Montepertuso, 1,500 feet up the mountainside from Positano, the Ritrovo has been noted for its cucina for more than 20 years. Call for the free shuttle service to and from Positano, and take a seat on the terrace's frescoed wood-paneled dining area. The menu showcases food from both the sea and the hills—try the *scialatielli ai frutti di mare* (seafood pasta) accompanied by well-grilled vegetables, or the house specialty, *zuppa saracena,* a paella-like affair brimming with assorted seafood. Leave space for the lemon tiramisu, owner Salvatore's own recipe, paired with one of 80 different kinds of a homemade liqueur (try the carob or even chamomile). Salvatore also runs a cooking school, at which you can learn to whip up his creations at home. *Average main: €20 Via Montepertuso 77, Montepertuso 089/812005 www.ilritrovo.com Closed mid-Jan.–mid-Feb.*

$ SOUTHERN ITALIAN **Santa Croce.** About 1,400 feet above sea level on the Path of the Gods, this is the only restaurant in the dreamy little hamlet of Nocelle where the dress code is decidedly hiking gear. Try to get a window seat with its view fit for the gods. Gazing over Positano, Li Galli islands, and the Fariglioni of Capri, you can sample fresh pastas or grilled meats. On Saturday evenings, the olive wood–fired pizza oven produces godly delights. *Average main: €12 Via Nocelle 19, Nocelle 089/811260 Closed weekdays mid-Nov.–mid-Mar.*

$$ SOUTHERN ITALIAN **Saraceno D'Oro.** Although open also at lunchtime, this restaurant, one of the few patronized by the *Positanesi,* is most definitely an evening venue. Living up to the name, the ambience is distinctly Moorish without being kitschy. *Antipasti misti* is a favorite starter, and the bass with leeks, the veal with provolone, and the local wines are all delicious. Pizza is also served. **TIP→ The outside tables are on the opposite side of Via Pasitea, great for experiencing the bustle that is Positano, but if you're sensitive to the smell of car exhaust, sit inside or away from the street.** *Average main: €15 Via Pasitea 254 089/812050 Closed Nov.–Dec. 26 and Jan. 8–Feb.*

CLOSE UP

Rules for the Amalfi Drive

As submitted by Az to the Forums at *www.fodors.com*:

1. Don't look down.

2. Don't look up.

3. Don't look—it's easier that way.

4. Forget about camels not passing through the eye of a needle.

5. Timidity will get you nowhere—literally.

6. The solid center line in the middle of the road is merely a suggestion.

7. Whoever gets to a lane first has the right of way—it doesn't matter whose side the lane is on.

8. Traffic mirrors are put there so that you can see what you are about to hit head on.

9. Tour buses *will* back up. (This one is true; they don't want a fender bender that will upset the itinerary of all their passengers.)

10. Garbage trucks *won't* back up.

11. Motorcyclists are fearless.

12. Pedestrians are fearlesser.

13. Five headlights coming toward you equal two cars plus one motorcycle, or one car plus three motorcycles, or five motorcycles, all equally probable.

14. The probability of an accident is very low; at 40 mph around a hairpin curve 1,000 feet above the sea *everyone* pays attention. (Same is true for the Autostrada: at 130 mph, nobody's attention wanders.)

15. Have plenty of *limoncello* on hand at the end of a day spent driving the coast.

Rosenatti, another Forums user, added the following coda:

"If the large, orderly group of people approaching your car from the opposite direction looks like a marching band, this is because it is a marching band. No, it will not turn around."

WHERE TO STAY

$$ HOTEL **Casa Albertina.** Clinging to the cliff, this little house is well loved for its Italianate charm, its homey restaurant, and its owners, the Cinque family. **Pros:** a home away from home; open all year. **Cons:** slightly removed from the action; 300 steps down to (and back up from) the main beach. *Rooms from: €170 Via della Tavolozza 3 089/875143 www.casalbertina.it 20 rooms Some meals.*

$$$$ HOTEL **Covo dei Saraceni.** Sea and town interact in Positano, and you see this best from the Covo dei Saraceni, perched on the main beach at the foot of Monte Comune, just steps from the pier. **Pros:** top location; rooftop pool. **Cons:** a hike to get here unless arriving by boat; the entrance can be difficult to negotiate as the hordes of travelers arrive by boat. *Rooms from: €320 Via Regina Giovanna 5 089/875400 www.covodeisaraceni.it 1 suite, 65 rooms Closed Nov.–Mar. All meals.*

$$$$ HOTEL **Hotel Buca di Bacco.** A fisherman's tavern later converted into a guesthouse, this hotel has long held center stage on Spiaggia Grande beach. **Pros:** right on the beach; uninterrupted sea views from many rooms; a Jacuzzi with a view. **Cons:** tricky to get to if not arriving by boat; uneven

service; noisy "Times Square" location. *Rooms from: €305 Via Rampa Teglia 4 089/857699 www.bucadibacco.it 47 rooms Nov.–Mar. Breakfast.*

$$$$ HOTEL Fodor's Choice ★ **Hotel Eden Roc.** The closest hotel to the Sponda bus stop, this family-run luxury property provides spectacular views and service. **Pros:** huge rooms; magical views. **Cons:** on the main road (take care as you exit the hotel); a bit of a climb from the town center. *Rooms from: €345 Via G.Marconi 110 089/875844 www.edenroc.it 25 suites Closed Dec.–Feb. Some meals.*

$$$ HOTEL **Hotel Poseidon.** More than yet another place with an amazing view and a terrace restaurant, the Poseidon aims at those who wish to holiday and keep themselves trim at the same time. **Pros:** a perfect base to organize your holiday; a holiday within a holiday. **Cons:** a steep climb from the town center. *Rooms from: €300 Viale Pasitea 148 089/811111 www.hotelposeidonpositano.it 48 rooms Closed Nov.–mid-Apr. Some meals.*

$$$ HOTEL **Hotel Villa Franca.** Bay blue, lemon yellow, and cool white are the palette here, making for a stress-dissolving retreat, set halfway up the town from the beach. **Pros:** the only pool in Positano with 360-degree gulf views; all rooms with terraces. **Cons:** a steep climb from the town center; small pool. *Rooms from: €220 Viale Pasitea 318 089/875655 www.villafrancahotel.it 37 rooms Closed Nov.–Mar. Breakfast.*

$$$$ HOTEL Fodor's Choice ★ **Il San Pietro di Positano.** Extraordinary is the word for this luxurious oasis set on a cliff high over the sea. **Pros:** picture-perfect views from the terrace; mixing with the Modigliani-sleek jet-setters; superambitious and stylish restaurant menu. **Cons:** too far away from Positano to take a stroll; not all rooms served by the elevator. *Rooms from: €570 Via Laurito 2 089/875455 www.ilsanpietro.it 60 rooms Closed Nov.–Mar. Breakfast.*

$$ HOTEL Fodor's Choice ★ **La Fenice.** This tiny unpretentious hotel on the outskirts of Positano beckons with bougainvillea-laden views, castaway cottages, and a turquoise seawater pool—all perched over a private beach. **Pros:** paradise; 250 steps to private beach. **Cons:** a 10-minute walk to town. *Rooms from: €155 Via G. Marconi 4 089/875513 www.lafenicepositano.com 14 rooms No credit cards Breakfast.*

$$$$ HOTEL Fodor's Choice ★ **Le Sirenuse.** As legendary as its namesake sirens, this 18th-century palazzo has long set the standard for luxury in Italian hotels. **Pros:** unrivalled views; many rooms have whirlpool tubs; close to the bus stop. **Cons:** a bit of a climb from the town center; lower-priced rooms are small. *Rooms from: €460 Via Cristoforo Colombo 30 089/875066 www.sirenuse.it 59 rooms Breakfast.*

$$$ HOTEL Fodor's Choice ★ **Palazzo Murat.** A perfectly central location above the beachside church of Santa Maria Assunta—and an even more perfect entrance through a bougainvillea-draped patio and garden—help make the Murat a top lodging contender. **Pros:** once a regal residence; stunning surroundings. **Cons:** only five rooms have seaside views; constant stream of curious day-trippers. *Rooms from: €270 Via dei Mulini 23 089/875177 www.palazzomurat.it 31 rooms Closed Nov.–Mar. Breakfast.*

2

EATING WELL ON THE AMALFI COAST

Locals say they have "one foot in the fishing boat, one in the vineyard"—and a fortunate stance it is, as you can count on eating simple, fresh, seasonal food, and lots of it, with *tutti i sapori della campagna verace* (all the true flavors of the countryside). From the gulfs come *pesce alla griglia* (grilled fish), *calamari* (squid), *aragosta* (lobster), and *gamberone* (shrimp). Wood oven–baked thin-crust pizzas start with the classic *Margherita*—tomato sauce, basil, and cheese—and marinara—"marinated" with tomato, garlic, and oregano—and go from there to infinity.

La Cucina Costiera seems more sensuous amid all this beauty. Sun-dried tomatoes and chili peppers hang in bright red cascades on balconies and shopfronts. (*"Viagra naturale"* boasts a hand-lettered sign in Amalfi.) Ingredients grown in terraced plots include plump olives pressed into oil or eaten whole, tiny spring *carciofi* (artichokes), and sweet figs. *Sponzini,* or *pomodori del pendolo,* the tomatoes carried from Egypt long ago by fishermen, grow in the mountains and muddy fields of Furore and Conca dei Marini. Eggplant, asparagus, and mushrooms thrive in the Tramonte uplands, while tomatoes come from Campora. Soft *fior di latte* (cow's-milk cheeses) are from the high hill pastures of Agerola, while the world's best buffalo mozzarella comes from Paestum.

Pasta is often served with seafood, but regional dishes include *crespelle al formaggio*—layers of crepes with béchamel sauce—and fettuccine-like *scialatielli,* often a house specialty, served with varied sauces. Clams and pasta baked in a paper bag—*al cartoccio*—is popular in Amalfi. In Positano, try traditional squid with potatoes, stuffed peppers, and slow-simmering ragù (tomato sauce with meat, garlic, and parsley). Around Cetara, salted anchovies, eggplant, and peppers in oil are the base of the famed sauce called *garum,* handed down from the Romans. A lighter version is *colatura di alici,* an anchovy sauce developed by Cistercian monks near Amalfi, served on spaghetti as a traditional Christmas Eve treat. South of Salerno, you can visit working farms, and make friends with the buffalo, before sampling the best mozzarella known to mankind. Artichokes are also a specialty of the Paestum area. For the sweet tooth, don't miss Maiori's chocolate-covered eggplant.

Wine here is light, drinkable, and inexpensive, and often consumed mere months after crushing; don't be surprised if it's the color of beer, and served from a jug (*sfuso*—loose wine). Practically all of it comes from Campania, often from the town or village in which it's poured, perhaps even from the restaurant's own centuries-old vines. Little of it transports well. Furore, Gragnano, and Ravello produce good bottled wines, both *rosso* (red) and *bianco* (white) with Furore's Cuomo perhaps the finest white wine.

Although a few restaurants are world renowned, most are family affairs, with *papà* out front, the kids serving, and mamma, aunts, and even old *nonna* in the kitchen. Smile a bit, compliment the cuisine, and you're apt to meet them all.

DID YOU KNOW?

The hotel Sirenuse is where John Steinbeck stayed while writing his famous essay "Positano" for *Harper's Bazaar* in 1953. He called the town "a dream place that isn't quite real when you are there and becomes beckoningly real after you have gone."

$ B&B/INN **Pensione Maria Luisa.** With two resident cats and many other felines who are "regular visitors," this place should be avoided by those suffering from allergies, but it's a real find for cat lovers. **Pros:** ideal for cat lovers; almost like staying in a real Positano home. **Cons:** not for cat haters; a bit far from the main town action. *Rooms from: €70 Via Fornillo 42 089/875023 www.pensionemarialuisa.com 10 rooms No credit cards Breakfast.*

WORD OF MOUTH

"If you are fit and healthy, go to Positano.... I suggest one of the hotels at least halfway down the hillside or lower to avoid the crowds. There are no roads to the bottom, only footpaths and steps."
—JanieMac

$$ RENTAL **Villa Flavio Gioia.** If you are eager to settle in for a while, this villa has bright mini-apartments, each with its own terrace or large balcony, and a cooking area. **Pros:** convenient location; ideal for longer stays. **Cons:** one-week minimum stay in high season; no pool. *Rooms from: €190 Piazza Flavio Gioia 2 089/875222 www.villaflaviogioia.it 15 rooms Closed Feb. No meals.*

NIGHTLIFE

Despite its past as a bohemian haven, nowadays Positano is remarkably quiet in the evenings. For entertainment, head down to the waterfront, where the restaurants lined up along the border of the Spiaggia Grande turn into an open-air party on summer nights.

La Brezza. A few steps up from, and overlooking, the Spiaggia Grande, popular La Brezza is a fine spot to enjoy a cocktail or one of the bar's signature smoothies. *Via del Brigantino 1 089/875811 www.labrezzapositano.com Closed Nov.–Mar.*

La Zagara. Come evening, things heat up at this bar and pasticceria where a local pianist tickles the ivories on the leafy terrace. *Via dei Mulini 8, Positano www.lazagara.com Closed Nov.–Mar.*

Music on the Rocks. The owners of the restaurants Chez Black and Le Terrazze run this popular bar that occasionally hosts live music. Set in a seaside cave off Spiaggia Grande, it is favored by the likes of Lenny Kravitz, Kate Moss, and Denzel Washington. Special events excepted, entrance is free as long as you buy a drink for about €10. *Via Grotte dell'Incanto 56 089/875874 www.musicontherocks.it Closed Nov.–Mar.*

Paradise. By day this place provides the least expensive view in town, with an outdoor terrace overlooking the Spiaggia Grande. It's an ideal stop for a coffee, a sandwich, or an ice cream. By night, music pumps from the stereo and sports from the four large-screen TVs, as movers and groovers sip cocktails after a hard day on the beach. *Via del Saracino 32, Positano 089/811915 Closed Nov. and Dec.*

SPORTS AND THE OUTDOORS

BOAT EXCURSIONS

From Spiaggia Grande you can board a scheduled day boat or hire a private one for as long as you'd like, to visit Capri, the Emerald Grotto in Conca dei Marini, or coves and inlets with small beaches. Close by, in the large caves of La Porta (650 feet east of the town center), Mezzogiorno and Erica, tools, utensils, and hunting weapons from the Paleolithic and Mesolithic ages have been discovered, the oldest known remains on the coast. The favorite boating destinations, however, are the rocky Li Galli islets (6 km [4 miles] southwest), seen from any point in Positano (as they are from the beaches of the peninsula), whose name derives from their importance in Greek mythology—resembling pecking birds, the islands were said to be the home of the sirens, part human, part feathered. Originally the site of an ancient Roman anchorage, the islands then became medieval fiefdoms of Emperor Frederick II and King Robert of Anjou. The isles remain tempting enough to lure purchasers in search of an exclusive paradise: Russian choreographer Leonide Massine in 1925, and, in 1988, dancer Rudolf Nureyev, who discovered the islands in 1984 when he came to accept the Positano Prize for the Art of Dancing, given each year in honor of Massine. The islands now belong to a Sorrento hotelier, who also purchased the renowned Villa Treville (🌐 *www.villatreville.it*), formerly owned by the famed film and opera director Franco Zeffirelli. This is a pricey destination, though. The suite named for Zeffirelli runs €5,500 per night in high season, and even a "budget" room costs €1,250.

Cassiopea. Boating excursions can also be organized through Cassiopea, which also rents motorboats and Zodiacs by the hour. ✉ *Spiaggia Grande* ☎ *089/8123484 home, 339/1115538 mobile* 🌐 *www.cassiopea-positano.com.*

L'Uomo e il Mare. Brothers Gennaro (whose wife is English) and Salvatore Capraro conduct boating excursions along the Amalfi Coast. Rides cost from €90 per person, including lunch onboard, less if you skip the meal. ✉ *Spiaggia Grande pier* ☎ *089/811613* ☎📠 *089/875475* ☎ *368/455818* 🌐 *www.gennaroesalvatore.it.*

HIKING

Hikers often pass through Positano on their way to the region's most famed mountainside trail, the **Sentiero degli Dei** (Pathway of the Gods), which can be picked up outside nearby Nocelle. For less professional hikers, Ponte dei Libri (a bridge several miles west) spans a pretty valley with soaring rock pinnacles and is a moderate walk. More serious climbers can hike up to Santa Maria del Castello (just more than 2,000 feet) from where paths radiate out eastward and westward along the Lattari Mountains. Plant lovers will find hillside walks particularly rewarding in May, when the mountains turn into a flowering rock garden with fine displays of orchids. As a general rule, allow plenty of time for what look like short distances on paper, take lots of water, and stick to the paths mapped out in red-and-white stripes by the CAI (Italian Alpine Club). Julian Tippet's hiking guide, *Landscapes of Sorrento and the Amalfi Coast,* available at stores here, is worth investing in. You can also purchase the CAI's official map detailing all paths in the area.

Set on its own clifftop promontory, the Grand Terrace of the San Pietro hotel is lined with beautiful majolica-tiled benches (inspired by those of the cloisters of Naples's Santa Chiara church).

SHOPPING

Although the traditional gaudily colored and lace-trimmed Positano-style clothes have started to look frou-frou and dated, some contemporary designers are putting a 21st-century spin on the fashion. Goods still range from haute to kitsch, often-tight tops and casual skirts in vibrant hues, with prices generally higher than in other coast towns. The fabric industry here began long ago with silk, canvas, and hand embroidery, then made headlines in 1959 when Positano introduced Italy to the bikini. The most concentrated shopping area, and the least difficult to maneuver, is the souklike area near the cathedral by the beach, where the crowded pedestrian pathway literally runs through boutiques. Lining steep alleyways covered with bougainvillea, small shops display items such as local foodstuffs, wood, lace, pottery, wines and limoncello, and ceramics; you'll even find artisans who can hand-stitch a pair of stylish sandals while you wait.

ART GALLERIES

Franco Senesi Fine Art. This gallery and its branches in Capri and Ravello exhibit contemporary art by Italian and international artists. ✉ *Via dei Mulini 16* ☎ *089/875257* 🌐 *www.francosenesifineart.com.*

CERAMICS

Ceramica Casola. The tempting ceramics at this gorgeous factory showroom include vases, plates, decorative tiles, and wall hangings, and outdoor sculptures. ✉ *Via Laurito 49* ☎ *089/811382* 🌐 *www.ceramicacasola.com.*

CLOTHING

Antica Sartoria. Come here for colorful local fashions at reasonable prices; there's also a location closer to the beach, on Via del Brigantino. ✉ *Piazza dei Mulini 1/3* ☎ *089/875089* 🌐 *www.anticasartoriapositano.it.*

Marilù. It's worth splurging at Marilù if you want to take home something unique in Positano wear. ✉ *Via del Saracino 20* ☎ *089/875631.*

FOOD AND CANDY

Delikatessen Positano. You can pick up your limoncello or biscuits here, and also candles and soaps made from lemons. ✉ *Via dei Mulini 5, 13, 15* ☎ *089/875489.*

I Sapori di Positano. Here you can find anything it's conceivably possible to make from citrus fruits. ✉ *Via dei Mulini 6* ☎ *089/812055.*

MARINA DI PRAIA

3½ km (2 miles) southeast of Positano, 2 km (1 mile) west of Vallone di Furore.

"Whoever wants to live a healthy life spends the morning in Vettica and the evening in Praiano," according to a local adage. The larger township of Praiano may not fulfill that advice, but its scenic satellite, Marina di Praia, indeed does; it's home to a landmark eatery and famous disco. Nestled by the sea at the bottom of a dramatic chasm, this is the only anchorage along this rocky stretch where you can hire a boat and dock it and where ferries depart for points and islands along the coast.

GETTING HERE AND AROUND

By car, take the Statale 163 (Amalfitana) from outside Sorrento or Salerno. SITA bus from Sorrento–Positano–Amalfi, local bus from Praiano. The town itself is easily walkable.

EXPLORING

The picturesque hamlet, with its year-round nativity scene perched on the cliff above, has a few parking spaces, a small sand beach tucked within cliffs, some excellent seafood restaurants, a hotel, and a tiny church. The legendary L'Africana disco is tucked away on a pretty, winding path along the sea. All in all, Marina di Praia is like a little miniature and magical world nestled between two ageless cliffs.

WHERE TO EAT AND STAY

$$ SOUTHERN ITALIAN

✕ **Alfonso a Mare.** A landmark restaurant and hotel nestled in the Marina di Praia cove, Alfonso a Mare occupies a rustic flagstone structure that once was a dry haul for boats. Among the noteworthy offerings at the restaurant are the antipasti, the fresh locally caught fish, and the seafood pastas. Dining is on a deck partly open to the sea breezes on one side with an open kitchen on the other, and there's an indoor area with country-style wooden tables, netting, and ceiling baskets. Outside, colorful boats, peasant dwellings, and the chasm's sheer rock walls catch the eye. The hotel's small rooms have ceramic-tile floors and a few antique touches. Some rooms have windows that open out to terraces overlooking the gulf. Service can be patchy, but the restaurant is as romantic as it gets. [$] *Average main: €22* ✉ *Via*

Marina di Praia 6 ☎ 089/874091 🌐 www.alfonsoamare.it ⇨ 16 rooms ⊙ Closed mid-Nov.–Feb. 🍴 Some meals.

$$ HOTEL **Hotel Onda Verde.** On a rock jutting dramatically over the tiny cove of Marina dei Praia, this popular, picturesque hotel overlooks a Saracen tower and coastal ridges. **Pros:** with the hotel's fine services, there's no need to go into town at all; great views. **Cons:** a bit of a walk to get here; not great for mingling as you may never leave the hotel. [$] *Rooms from: €190 ✉ Via Terramare 3 ☎ 089/874143 🌐 www.ondaverde.it ⇨ 24 rooms ⊙ Closed Nov.–mid-Mar. 🍴 Some meals.*

NIGHTLIFE

L'Africana. Off a mile-long footpath from the Marina del Praia—or accessed via an elevator from Statale 163— L'Africana is a golden-oldie classic from the 1960s. With an open-to-the-sea atmosphere, a cave for a dance floor, and wildish shows with partial nudity, you can party the night away here, as Jackie Kennedy once did. **■ TIP→ The nightclub runs boats from Positano on Saturday—transfer is also arranged from other points along the coast.** *✉ Via Terramare 2, Praiano ☎ 089/874858, 331/5330612 mobile 🌐 www.africanafamousclub.com.*

FURORE

18 km (12 miles) northeast of Positano, 14 km (9 miles) northeast of Praiano.

Furore, the *paese che non c'è*, the "town that doesn't exist," stretches for 8 km (5 miles) along the panoramic winding road climbing the Monti Latteri hills toward Agerola. Its nickname comes from the absence of any real focal point, or piazza, in the town, but, endearingly, it has billed itself as the *paese dipinto*, the "painted town," as the walls of the homes of local fishermen and wine cultivators are the "canvas" for an array of murals by local and international artists, who have mostly represented the traditions and culture of their town. This open-air "gallery" was first initiated in 1980 with just three murals, and is regularly added to, with a different scene appearing around every bend. Other than artists, the most important residents of Furore are the local vintners. Townsfolk are said to live with one foot in a boat and one in a vineyard, and terraced vineyards cling to Furore's hillsides. Many vines uniquely grow horizontally from the stone walls, maximizing the use of the land here.

GETTING HERE AND AROUND

By car, take the Castellammare exit from the A3 motorway and follow the signs to Gragnano and Agerola, or take the Statale 163 (Amalfi Drive), and climb the hill 2 km (1 mile) west of Amalfi. There's a SITA bus service from Sorrento, and Positano. As for the Vallone di Furore, by car, take the Statale 163 (Amalfitana) from outside Sorrento or Salerno. There's SITA bus service from Positano and Amalfi. Walking around the town is not the ideal option, as it stretches 8 km (5 miles). The murals are on the sides of walls and houses along the winding main road.

EXPLORING

Cantine di Marisa Cuomo (*Marisa Cuomo Cellars*). The most famous of Furore's vineyards is the Gran Furor Divina Costiera estate, where top-quality "extreme" wines (so-called because of the grape-growing conditions) have been produced since 1942. Now named for owner Andrea Ferraioli's wife, the winery has won countless awards all over the world. Among the most lauded vintages is the Bianco Fiorduva, a white wine made from grapes that are allowed to over-ripen a bit. Daughter Dorotea organizes tastings for a minimum of six people, and the cellar, hewn from the hillside Dolomitic limestone rock, can be visited from January into August (call for details). Andrea is also a talented photographer so don't miss the opportunity to see his stunning shots of the surrounding region. **■ TIP→ If you visit, ask to view the part of the stone wall (not far from the cellar) where you can see a magnificent 100-year-old horizontal vine.** ✉ *Via G.B.Lama 16/18* ☎ *338/9213237* 🌐 *www.marisacuomo.com.*

Fodor's Choice ★ **Marina di Furore.** From the lofty township of Furore, 944 steps (count 'em!) lead down to Marina di Furore, Italy's only fjord. Set on the coast, this enchanting hamlet—perhaps 10 houses?—beckons to most travelers as their SITA buses pass over it on a towering viaduct that in July is the site of the Mediterranean Cup High-Diving Championship. The locale's name derives from the "furor" of stormy water that once rushed down the Torrente Schiato here, now a mere trickle. Adorning the gorge is a tchotchke of a fishermen's village (once a favored hideout of bandits and smugglers, with some houses renovated by Ingrid Bergman and Anna Magnani during the filming of Roberto Rossellini's *L'Amore* in 1948); these monazzeni ("places to live in solitude") and the adjoining paper mill were abandoned when the tiny harbor closed. Today, the hamlet has been restored and the paper mill transformed into an "ecomuseum," with short botanical trails on which it's possible to see rare peregrine falcons as well as ancient species of plants found nowhere else in the region. From the beach, the sentiero della Volpe Pescatrice ("the fox-fish's path") and the sentiero dei Pipistrelli Impazziti ("the mad bats' path") climb up some 3,000 steps and were built to portage goods from the harbor to the town of Furore. The hard walk up takes a couple of hours, as you climb from sea to sky. To see any of this by car, you have to pay to park in the lay-by some 450 yards away on the Amalfi side of the gorge, just before the gas station. Unless you're in pretty good shape, it's better to boat to the beach and just rubberneck.

WHERE TO EAT

$$ SOUTHERN ITALIAN ✕ **Bacco.** The Cuomo wine family runs this restaurant, a longtime area favorite named for the Greek god of wine. The terrace is one of the best vantage points on the coast, with a cockerel weather vane lording over the view. The simple but delicious fare includes *ferrazzuoli alla Nannarella* (named after actress Anna Magnani, a past patron)—fresh pasta with tomatoes, tuna, swordfish, and pine nuts—and *vermicelli cu o' pesce fujuto*, a dish with no *pesce* (fish) despite its moniker: the sea flavor of the local tomatoes provides the *piscine parfumo*. The local dish *totani alla volpe pescatrice* (flying squid with potatoes) is another good option. [$] *Average main: €15* ✉ *Via G.B.Lama 9* ☎ *089/830360* 🌐 *www.baccofurore.it* ⏲ *Closed Feb.*

DID YOU KNOW?

The tiny Marina di Furore sits some 3,000 steps below its town. The harbor was once the site of a paper mill, which has been transformed into a museum of paper.

CONCA DEI MARINI

2 km (1 mile) east of Vallone di Furore, 4 km (2½ miles) southwest of Amalfi.

Fodor'sChoice ★ Long a favorite of the off-duty famous and rich, Conca dei Marini (the name means "seafarers' basin") hides many of its charms, as any sublime forgetaway should. On the most dramatic promontory of the coast, the town was originally a province of ancient Rome called Cossa and later became an important naval base of the Amalfi Republic. Much later, it became a retreat for high-profile types, including the writer John Steinbeck, automaker Gianni Agnelli of Fiat, and film producer Carlo Ponti, who erected a white villa here by the sea (for his first wife, not Sophia Loren). You can see why: the green of terraced gardens competes with (and loses to) the blue sea, while the town's distinctive houses flanking the ridges have thick, white walls, with cupolas, balconies, and external staircases, testimony to former Arabic, Moorish, and Greek settlements. Below, on Capo di Conca, a promontory once used as a cemetery, a 16th-century coastal tower dramatically overlooks the sea. On a curve in the road sits the village's most noteworthy attraction, the Emerald Grotto. Coral is still harvested in the waters off the coast here, and boats fish for sardines and squid through the night, their prow lanterns twinkling as if stars had slipped into the sea.

GETTING HERE AND AROUND

By car, take the Statale 163 (Amalfitana) from outside Sorrento or Salerno. There's SITA bus service from Positano and Amalfi. The town is easily walkable, but be prepared to climb!

EXPLORING

TOP ATTRACTIONS

FAMILY **Grotta dello Smeraldo** (*Emerald Grotto*). The tacky road sign and squadron of tour buses may put you off, but this cavern is worth a stop. The karstic cave was originally part of the shore, but the lowest end sank into the sea. Intense greenish light filters into the water from an arch below sea level and is reflected off the cavern walls. You visit the Grotta dello Smeraldo, which is filled with huge stalactites and stalagmites, on a large rowboat. Don't let the boatman's constant spiel detract from the 20-minute experience—just tune out and enjoy the sparkles, shapes, and Harry Winston–esque color. You can take an elevator from the coast road down to the grotto, or you can drive to Amalfi and arrive by boat (€10, excluding the grotto's admission fee). Companies in Positano, Amalfi, and elsewhere along the coast provide service. ■ **TIP→ The light at the grotto is best from noon to 3 pm.** ✉ *Beyond Punta Acquafetente by boat, or off Amalfi Dr.* ☎ *089/871107 Amalfi tourist board* 🎟 *€5* ⏲ *Apr.–mid-Oct. daily 9–4; mid-Oct.–Mar. daily 9–3. Closed in adverse weather conditions.*

Santa Maria della Neve. A must-do in Conca dei Marini is the jaunt down the staircase to the left of the Hotel Belvedere that delivers you to the town's dollhouse-size harbor, Santa Maria della Neve, and darling little chapel of the same name. You'll pass by some gorgeous houses on your way to one of the most idyllic sights along the entire coast. ■ **TIP→ The view of the harbor from the Amalfi Drive high atop the hill is a prime photo op.** ✉ *Santa Maria della Neve.*

WORTH NOTING

San Pancrazio. For Conca *in excelsis*, head up the hill on Via Don Amodio, opposite the Hotel Belvedere, to Conca dei Marini's northern reaches. Your reward after a short climb up the hillside roads and steep *scalinatelle* is the stunningly sited neo-Byzantine church of San Pancrazio, set in a palm-tree garden. Opposite this church, in the direction of Positano, is a road leading to Punta Vreca, a sky-high lookout over the coast. Climbing farther up the Scalinatella San Pancrazio will take you to the tiny town piazza. ✉ *Via Don Gaetano Amodio.*

Sant' Antonio di Padova. Spectacularly cantilevered hundreds of feet over the coastline on a stone parapet, this elegant Neoclassical white church is also known as Chiesa Principale di San Giovanni Battista. It's only open for Sunday-morning services, but if for a quick peek at other times you might ask locals if someone has a key to open the church. Just ask, "*Dov'è la persona che ci può far visitare la chiesa?*" For those who want to see churches in coastal villages, this may be the only way to gain entry. ✉ *Via Sant'Antonio.*

BEACHES

Conca dei Marini Beach. With its wonderful patches of emerald set in a blue-glass lagoon, Conca dei Marini's harbor is one of the most enchanting visions on the coast. Descend (and later ascend!) the scalinatelle past the Borgo Marinaro houses (a colony for off-duty celebrities) and down to the harbor of Santa Maria della Neve, set with cafés and a little chapel that seems to bless the picture-perfect beach. **Amenities:** food and drink; lifeguards; showers; toilets. **Best for:** snorkeling, swimming.

Lido Capo di Conca. Landmarked by its giant Saracen Tower, the Capo di Conca protects bathers from the western winds. Here at this privately run beach with a bar and restaurant, it is the water that compels: infinite shades of aquamarine, lapis, and amethyst shimmering in sunshine, glowing silver in moonlight, and becoming transparent in the rocky coves. **Amenities:** food and drink; lifeguards; toilets; showers. **Best for:** snorkeling; swimming. ✉ *Via Capo di Conca* ☎ *089/831512* 🌐 *www.capodiconca.it.*

WHERE TO STAY

$$$$ HOTEL **Grand Hotel Il Saraceno.** A gorgeous extravaganza with Gothic, Arabic, Oriental, and even Las Vegas influences, Il Saraceno occupies a cliff 3 km (2 miles) from Amalfi (its official address) and just steps from Conca dei Marini. **Pros:** ideal for living out your pirate fantasy; gorgeous garden terraces. **Cons:** distant from the action; a little too kitschy for some guests. $ *Rooms from: €350* ✉ *Via Augustariccio 33* ☎ *089/831148* 🌐 *www.saraceno.it* *56 rooms* *Closed Nov.–Mar.* *All meals.*

$$$ HOTEL **Hotel Belvedere.** One of the coast's most beloved hotels, the Belvedere is really not a hotel but a "home." **Pros:** local-flavored restaurant; a home away from home. **Cons:** busy Amalfi Drive entrance (be careful as you exit the doorway); no elevator to the beach. $ *Rooms from: €210* ✉ *Via Smeraldo 19* ☎ *089/831282* 🌐 *www.belvederehotel.it* *36 rooms* *Closed mid-Oct.–mid-Apr.* *All meals.*

The coast's leading hideaway for off-duty celebrities, Conca dei Marini is landmarked by its 16th-century watchtower.

$$$$ HOTEL Fodor's Choice ★ **Monastero Santa Rosa Hotel & Spa.** Set in a 17th-century monastery on the dramatic cliffs above the Amalfi Coast, this boutique resort is destined to become one of Italy's most exclusive retreats. **Pros:** excellent service; meticulously restored property; worth the splurge. **Cons:** out of reach for many budgets, some rooms could be more spacious. *Rooms from: €550 Via Roma 2 089/8321199 www.monasterosantarosa.com 12 rooms, 8 suites Closed Nov.–mid-Apr. Breakfast.*

AMALFI

18 km (11 miles) southeast of Positano, 32 km (20 miles) west of Salerno.

At first glance, it's hard to imagine that this resort destination, set in a verdant valley of the Lattari Mountains, with its cream-color and pastel-hue buildings tightly packing a gorge on the Bay of Salerno, was in the 11th and 12th centuries the seat of the Amalfi Maritime Republic, one of the world's great naval powers, and a sturdy rival of Genoa and Pisa for control of the Mediterranean. The harbor, which once launched the greatest fleet in Italy, now bobs with ferries and blue-and-white fishing boats. The main street, lined with leather shops and *pasticcerie,* has replaced a raging mountain torrent, and terraced hills where *banditti* (bandits) once roamed now flaunt the green and gold of lemon groves. Bearing testimony to its great trade with Tunis, Tripoli, and Algiers, Amalfi remains honeycombed with Arab-Sicilian cloisters and covered passages. In a way Amalfi has become great again, showing off its medieval glory days with sea pageants, convents-turned-hotels, ancient paper mills, covered streets, and its mosquelike cathedral.

> **WORD OF MOUTH**
>
> "Amalfi is really small but charming with cobblestone streets, alleys and passages that take the tourists back to ancient times. No steps or very little, we are happy of our selection of Amalfi as our base for this week."
>
> —jelopez33

Amalfi's origin is clouded. One legend says that a general of Constantine's army, named Amalfo, settled here in 320; another tale has it that Roman noblemen from the village of Melphi (in Latin, "a Melphi"), fleeing after the fall of the empire, were first in these parts, shipwrecked in the 4th century on their way to Constantinople. Myth becomes fact by the 6th century, when Amalfi is inscribed in the archives as a Byzantine diocese, and the historical pageant really begins. Its geographic position was good defense, and the distance from Constantinople made its increasing autonomy possible. Continuously hammered by the Lombards and others, in 839 it rose against and finally sacked nearby Salerno, to which its inhabitants had been deported. In the 10th century, Amalfi constructed many churches and monasteries and was ruled by judges, later called doges—self-appointed dukes who amassed vast wealth and power.

From the 9th century until 1101, Amalfi remained linked to Byzantium but also was increasingly independent and prosperous, perhaps the major trading port in southern Italy. Its influence loomed large, thanks to its creation of the *Tavola Amalfitana,* a code of maritime laws taken up by most medieval-era kingdoms. Amalfi created its own gold and silver coins—or *tari,* engraved with the cross of Amalfi—and ruled a vast territory. With trade extending as far as Alexandria and Constantinople—where a large colony of Amalfitan merchants resided—it became Italy's first maritime republic, ahead of rivals Pisa, Venice, and Genoa; the population swelled to about 100,000, many of them seafarers and traders.

But the days of wine and doges were about to end. In the 11th century Robert Guisgard of Normandy—in the duplicitous spirit of politicos to this day—first aided, then sacked the town, and the Normans from Sicily returned, after a short Amalfitan revolt, in the 12th century. Then, when the Republic of Pisa twice conquered it, Amalfi fell into decline, hastened by a horrific storm in 1343, then by an indirect blow from Christopher Columbus's discoveries, which opened the world beyond to competing trade routes. By the 18th century, the town had sunk into gloom, looking to its lemons and handmade paper for survival. After the state road was built by Ferdinand, the Bourbon king of Naples, in the 19th century, Amalfi evolved into a tourist destination, drawing Grand Tour–era travelers like Richard Wagner, Henry Wadsworth Longfellow, and Henrik Ibsen, all of whom helped spread Amalfi's fame.

GETTING HERE AND AROUND

By car, take the Statale 163 (Amalfitana) from outside Sorrento or Salerno, or take the Angri exit on the A3 motorway and cross the mountainous Valico di Chiunsi. Take the SITA bus from Sorrento–Salerno, or summer ferries from Naples–Sorrento–Salerno. The special express bus from Naples departs from Monday to Saturday at 9 am and 5:30 pm from the port; catching this bus makes for an easy and scenic ride back to the city, allowing you to bypass a transfer from the bus to the Circumvesuviana railway in Sorrento. Note, however, the Amalfi–Naples bus is at dawn!

In Amalfi you can purchase tickets prior to boarding at the Il Giardino delle Palma bar, a travel agency, or any tobacco shop displaying a SITA sticker; all SITA buses leave Amalfi from Piazza Flavio Gioia. One way to tour Amalfi and the surrounding area, including Ravello, is aboard an open-top City Sightseeing bus (⇨ *see The Amalfi Coast Planner, above*).

Amalfi's compact tourist center is split between the bustling *lungomare* (waterfront), with its public and private transportation hubs, and the piazza in front of the Duomo. Parking is a big problem, as the tiny lot on the seafront (€3 per hour) fills up fast. There is a huge car park in the rock 400 yards east of the town. Still, traveling here via ferry and bus or staying in a hotel with a parking garage are good ideas. Once you explore the main sights near the waterfront, take off and explore the souklike center, then escape to the outskirts and the terraced hills of the Valle dei Mulini, site of Amalfi's ancient paper mills. At a little waterfall at the very north of the town, beyond the Museo della Carta, look to the left for a set of *scalinatelle* and climb the 100-plus steps; follow a footpath to the right, where you're in the middle of a lemon grove. If you buy a fresh lemon along the way—its leaves will be intact and its taste sweeter than you're accustomed to—and down its slices with a pinch of salt, you'll be passing time as the locals have since the age of its republic.

VISITOR INFORMATION

Azienda Autonoma di Cura, Soggiorno e Turismo ✉ *Corso Reppubliche Marinare 27* ☎ *089/871107* 🌐 *www.amalfitouristoffice.it* 🕙 *Weekdays 8:30–1 (in summer also 2–6).*

EXPLORING

TOP ATTRACTIONS

Fodor's Choice ★ **Arsenale della Repubblica** (*Arsenal of the Republic*). From the middle of the 11th century, Amalfi's center of shipbuilding, custom houses, and warehouses was the Arsenale, today the only (partially) preserved medieval shipyard in southern Italy. Ships and galleys up to 80 feet long, equipped with up to 120 oars, were built at this largest arsenal of any medieval maritime republic. Two large Gothic halls here now host occasional exhibitions and display artifacts from Amalfi's medieval period, including paintings, ancient coins, banners, and jeweled costumes. The highlight is the original 66-chapter draft of the code of the Tavole Amalfitana, the sea laws and customs of the ancient republic, used throughout the Italian Mediterranean from the 13th to the 16th century. The Tavole established everything from prices for boat hires to procedures to be followed in case of a shipwreck. Long one of the treasures of the Imperial Library of Vienna, the draft was returned to Amalfi after more than 500 years. Ten of the arsenal's original 22 stone piers remain; the others were destroyed by storms and changes in the sea level on this ever-active coast. ✉ *South of Piazza dei Dogi, at Via Camera, by waterfront, Largo Cesareo Console 3* ☎ *089/871170* 🌐 *www.museoarsenaleamalfi.it* 🎫 *€2* 🕙 *Tues.–Sun. 11–6.*

Arsenale della Repubblica 1
Duomo di Sant' Andrea 4
Hotel Luna Convento 3
Maria Santissima Addolorata 6
Piazza Flavio Gioia 2
Porta della Marina 5
Rua Nova Mercatorum 8
Santa Maria Maggiore 7
Valle dei Mulini 9

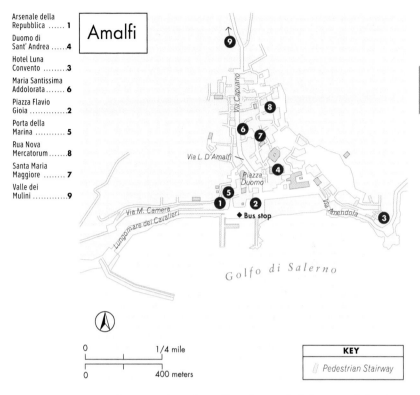

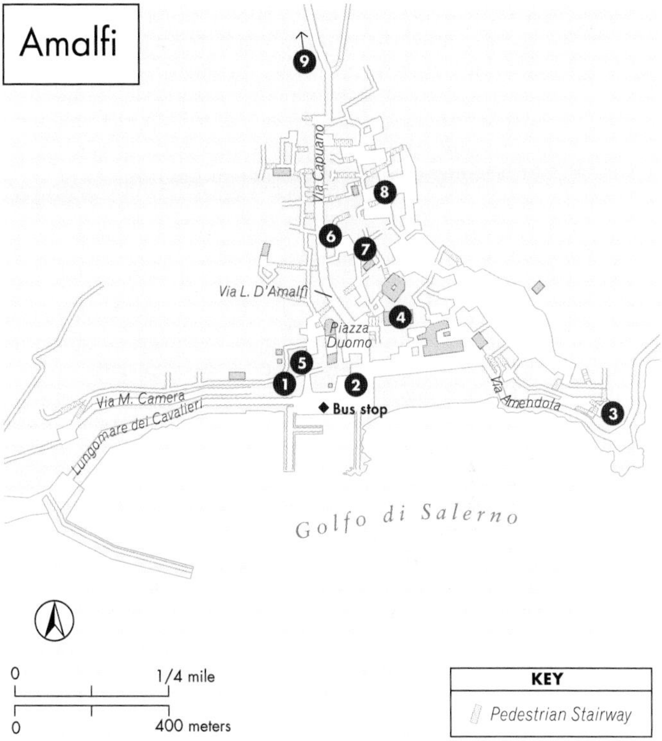

Fodor's Choice ★ **Duomo di Sant' Andrea.** Complicated, grand, delicate, and dominating, the 9th-century Amalfi cathedral has been remodeled over the years with Romanesque, Byzantine, Gothic, and baroque elements, but retains a predominantly Arab-Norman style. Cross and crescent seem to be wed here: the campanile, spliced with Saracen colors and the intricate tile work of High Barbery, looks like a minaret wearing a Scheherazadian turban, the facade conjures up a striped burnoose, and its **Chiostro del Paradiso** (Paradise Cloister) is an Arab-Sicilian spectacular. Built around 1266 as a burial ground for Amalfi's elite, the cloister, the first stop on a tour of the cathedral, is one of southern Italy's architectural treasures. Its flower-and-palm-filled quadrangle has a series of exceptionally delicate intertwining arches on slender double columns.

The chapel at the back of the cloister leads into the earlier (9th century) **basilica.** Romanesque in style, the structure has a nave, two aisles, and a high, deep apse. Note the 14th-century crucifixion scene by a student of Giotto. This section has now been transformed into a museum, housing sarcophagi, sculpture, Neapolitan goldsmiths' artwork, and other treasures from the cathedral complex.

Steps from the basilica lead down into the **Cripta di Sant'Andrea** (Crypt of Saint Andrew). The cathedral above was built in the 13th century to house the saint's bones, which came from Constantinople and supposedly exuded a miraculous liquid believers call the "manna of Saint Andrew." Following the one-way traffic up to the cathedral itself, you finally get to admire the elaborate polychrome marbles and painted, coffered ceilings from its 18th-century restoration. Art historians shake their heads over this renovation, as the original decoration of the apse must have been one of the wonders of the Middle Ages. ✉ *Piazza Duomo* ☎ *089/871324* 🌐 *www.diocesiamalficava.it* 🎫 *€3* ⏲ *Apr.–Sept., daily 9–7:45; Nov.–Jan. 6 and Mar., daily 9–5:45 (closed Jan. 7–Feb. except for daily services).*

Rua Nova Mercatorum. A tunnel-like passageway also known as Via dei Mercanti, the evocative Rua Nova was the main thoroughfare of medieval Amalfi, when the main road was a raging torrent. Still the town's most fascinating "street," it is especially wonderful when the light from alleys and windows plays on its white walls. Stretching almost the length of the main street, it ends at a medieval-era *contrada,* or neighborhood, with a fountain known as *Capo di Ciuccio* (donkey's head), where mules would refesh themselves after the climb down from the hills. ✉ *Adjacent to Via Pietro Capuano.*

FAMILY **Valle dei Mulini** (*Valley of the Mills*). Uphill from town, this was for centuries Amalfi's center for papermaking, an ancient trade learned from the Arabs, who learned it from the Chinese. Beginning in the 12th century, former flour mills were converted to produce paper made from cotton and linen. In 1211 Frederick II of Sicily prohibited this lighter, more readable paper for use in the preparation of official documents, favoring traditional sheepskin parchment. But by 1811 more than a dozen mills here, with more along the coast, were humming. Natural waterpower ensured that the handmade paper was cost-effective. Flooding in 1954, however, closed most of the mills for good, and many have been converted into private housing. The **Museo della Carta** (Museum of Paper) opened in 1971 in a 15th-century mill: paper samples, tools of the trade, old machinery, and the audiovisual presentation are all enlightening. You can also participate in a paper-making laboratory. ✉ *Via delle Cartiere 23* ☎ *089/8304561* 🌐 *www.museodellacarta.it* 🎫 *€4, including guided tour, laboratory €7* ⏲ *Mar.–Oct., daily 10–6:30; Nov.–Feb., Tues.–Sun. 10–2:30.*

WORTH NOTING

Hotel Luna Convento. The legendary St. Francis of Assisi founded this 13th-century former monastery that retains its original cloister, famous for its distinctive Arab-Sicilian arcaded columns and crypt with frescoes. Two centuries ago the property was transformed into the Amalfi Coast's earliest hotel. The many noteworthy guests include Henrik Ibsen, who wrote much of his play *A Doll's House* here. The hotel also owns the landmark Torre Saracena (Saracen Tower), now home to a bar and nightspot, which sits across the highway and stands guard over Amalfi's seaside promontory. ✉ *Via Pantaleone Comite 19* ☎ *089/871002* 🌐 *www.lunahotel.it.*

DID YOU KNOW?

Arab-Norman design can be seen throughout Amalfi, including in the Duomo di Sant' Andrea, where the style predominates over a mix of Gothic, Romanesque, Byzantine, and baroque influences.

> **WORD OF MOUTH**
>
> "Amalfi is quite magnificent. Scenically it is debatably even more beautiful than Big Sur, although if you like open, relatively wide, easy-to-navigate roads then Big Sur wins by a mile."
>
> —alisa_v

Maria Santissima Addolorata (*Our Lady of Sorrows*). This church is adjacent to the confraternity founded in 1765 to organize Amalfi's Good Friday celebrations. The entrance gate bears a late-Gothic bas-relief of the Crucifixion, once belonging to nobility from the nearby village of Scala and identified by its coat of arms at the foot of the cross. The interior is Neoclassical, with a coffered ceiling and a harmonious scale; note the 16th-century marble Madonna and Child in the sacristy. **TIP→ The church is only open on Saturday evening for 7 pm Mass (6:30 from November to March).** ✉ *Largo Santa Maria Maggiore* ⏲ *Open for Mass only, Apr.–Oct. 7 pm; Nov.–Mar. 6:30 pm.*

Piazza Flavio Gioia. A statue, set in an ironically disorienting traffic roundabout in front of the harbor, honors the Amalfitan credited with inventing the maritime compass in 1302. Many say it was the Chinese who invented the compass, passing the idea along to the Arabs, who traded with Amalfi; Gioia may have adapted it for sea use (for the record, some historians believe there was no such person as Gioia). ✉ *On waterfront.*

Porta della Marina. This gateway "door" to the harbor bears a huge, flaking ceramic panel, created by Renato Rossi in the 1950s, commemorating the trade routes of the republic during the Middle Ages. In one example, ships loaded with Italian timber sold the wood for gold in North Africa, then used the gold to buy gems, spices, and silks in Asia to trade back in Italy. Walk 200 feet along Corso delle Repubbliche Marinare, past the tourist office, to see the ceramic panel created by Diodoro Cossa in the 1970s. The scenes illustrate local historical highlights, among them Roman refugees establishing themselves in nearby Scala in the 4th century, the founding of Amalfi by these same Romans, Amalfi's commercial and diplomatic role in the Mediterranean, the arrival of St. Andrew's body, and the invention of the maritime compass. ✉ *Across from Piazza Flavio Gioia, next to arsenal.*

Santa Maria Maggiore. As inscribed on a capital at the entrance, one Duke Mansone I had this church constructed in 986. Though the layout is Byzantine, a 16th-century overhaul inverted the entrance and high altar, and the decoration is now mostly baroque. The campanile dates from the 12th century, and there's a noteworthy 18th-century crèche scene. **TIP→ The church is open only for Sunday services.** ✉ *Largo Santa Maria Maggiore, near Maria Santissima Addolorata.*

BEACHES

Santa Croce Beach. Named for the ruins of a chapel found in the beach's grotto, the rocky beach of Santa Croce is about 400 steps down from the village of Vettica Minore, west of Amalfi. Paradise for swimmers, the water is crystal clear and the surrounding coast is studded with emerald grottoes—stronger swimmers can admire a natural arch in

The piazza outside Amalfi's Duomo is a lively gathering place.

the rock, about 150 meters west (locals say that kissing your *bella* while swimming underneath ensures everlasting love). With a delightful restaurant and sun beds also here, this is the perfect beach experience. **Amenities:** food and drink; lifeguards; showers; toilets. **Best for:** snorkelling; swimming. ✉ *Amalfi*.

WHERE TO EAT

$$ SOUTHERN ITALIAN ✕ **Al Teatro.** Once a children's theater, this informal and charming white-stucco restaurant in the medieval quarter is 50 steps above the main drag. A house specialty is grilled squid and calamari with mint sauce, reflecting its position—suspended between sea and mountains. Try also the *Scialatielli al Teatro*, with tomatoes and eggplant. ■ **TIP→ The pizzas from the wood-fired oven are terrific.** *$ Average main: €15* ✉ *Via E. Marini 19* ☎ *089/872473* ⏲ *Closed Wed. and Jan.–mid-Feb.*

$$$ SOUTHERN ITALIAN ✕ **Da Gemma.** Diners in the know have sung the praises of this understated landmark since 1872. The kitchen glistens, the menu is printed on local handmade paper, and Italian foodies appreciate dishes such as *paccheri con burrata e scungilli* (large pieces of pasta with cheese and sea snails). For dessert try the local specialty: eggplant and chocolate. Tile floors, white tablecloths, and a terrace set above the main street create a soothing ambience. *$ Average main: €25* ✉ *Via Fra Gerardo Sasso 9* ☎ *089/871345* 🌐 *www.trattoriadagemma.com* ⏲ *Closed Wed. and mid-Jan.–Feb.*

$$$ SOUTHERN ITALIAN ✕ **Eolo.** One of the most sophisticated restaurants on the Amalfi Coast, Eolo is run by the owners of the Marina Riviera hotel. The decor is suavely tranquil—white-cove ceilings, Romanesque columns, mounted starfish—but the kitchen is anything but, tossing out superb

gastronomic delights patrons can accompany with one of more than 3,000 wines. Many dishes are fetchingly adorned with blossoms and other visual allures, but nothing compares to the view of Amalfi's harbor from one of the tables in Eolo's picture-window alcove. If you don't land one of these, don't fret—the entire room is pretty enough as it is. ⑤ *Average main: €25* ⊠ *Via Pantaleone Comite 3* ☎ *089/871241* ⊕ *www.eoloamalfi.it* ⊘ *Closed Tues. and Nov.–Mar.*

$

SOUTHERN
ITALIAN

✕ **Il Tari.** Locals highly recommend this little *ristorante* a few minutes' walk north of the Duomo. Named after the ancient coin of the Amalfi Republic, the restaurant occupies a former stable whose space has altered little outwardly since those equine days, though the white walls, appealing local art, crisp tablecloths, large panoramic photos, and tile floors make it cozy enough. Winning dishes on the vast menu include the wood-oven-baked thin-crust pizza and the *scialatielli alla Saracena* (long spaghetti-style pasta laden with tasty treats from the sea). ■TIP➜ **The prix-fixe options (from €20 to €40) are a great deal.** ⑤ *Average main: €12* ⊠ *Via P. Capuano 9–11* ☎ *089/871832* ⊕ *www. amalfiristorantetari.it* ⊘ *Closed Tues.*

$$$$

SOUTHERN
ITALIAN
Fodor'sChoice
★

✕ **La Caravella.** No wonder this is considered the most romantic restaurant in Amalfi, with lace-covered tables, *ciuccio* (donkey) ceramics, tall candles, and fresh floral bouquets in salons graced with frescoes and marble floors. Opened in 1959, it became the first in southern Italy to earn a Michelin star in 1966, and once drew a gilded guest list that included such fans as Andy Warhol and Federico Fellini. The menu maintains dishes favored 50 years ago: picture slices of fish grilled in lemon leaves marinated with an almond and wild fennel sauce. ■TIP➜ **A tasting menu is available, but don't miss the antipasti.** ⑤ *Average main: €40* ⊠ *Via Matteo Camera 12, near Arsenale* ☎ *089/871029* ⊕ *www.ristorantelacaravella.it* ⚖ *Reservations essential* ⊘ *Closed Tues. and Nov.–Feb.*

$$

SEAFOOD

✕ **Lo Smeraldino.** Open since 1949, this airy, popular fish restaurant on Amalfi's almost-emerald waterfront dishes out reasonably priced seafood and *cucina tipica Amalfitana* (Coast cuisine) such as the tasty penne with tomatoes, cream, eggplant, peppers, basil, and cheese, or excellent grilled fish. You can see the boats bringing in the day's catch, and at night pizza is served on the terrace amid the twinkling lights of hills, sea, and sky. ⑤ *Average main: €16* ⊠ *Piazzale dei Protontini 1* ☎ *089/871070* ⊕ *www.ristorantelosmeraldino.it.*

$$

SOUTHERN
ITALIAN

✕ **Stella Maris.** With its white awnings and prime location on the beach, Stella Maris is likely the first restaurant you'll encounter on arriving in Amalfi. Dining outdoors or in front of the glass walls, you can gaze at the fishing boats bobbing in the bay, or at the sun worshippers tanning on the small beach. The *risotto al pescespada* (rice with swordfish) is a treat, or try a pizza. If you haven't yet worked up an appetite, you can down an *aperitivo* or cocktail on the terrace. ⑤ *Average main: €15* ⊠ *Via della Regione 2* ☎ *089/872463* ⊕ *www.stella-maris.it* ⊘ *Closed Nov.–Mar.*

$$

SOUTHERN
ITALIAN

✕ **Taverna Buonvicino.** In the heart of medieval Amalfi, with outside seating occupying the small piazza outside the churches of Santa Maria Maggiore and the Maria Santissima Addolorata, this gastronomical treat is a testimony to the art of good food. Lovers of the craft prepare simple seasonal dishes using Grandma's recipes—try the grilled squid or the buffalo steak. The inside eating area is painted in vivid yellow and Pompeii red, reflecting the wheat and wine used in this fine restaurant and wine bar. *Average main: €18 Largo S. Maria Maggiore 1–3 089/8736385 www.tavernabuonvicino.it Closed Jan. and Feb.*

$$ SOUTHERN ITALIAN **Trattoria da Ciccia-Cielo-Mare-Terra.** Big windows overlook the sky, sea, and land, and there's ample free parking, so this modern seafood restaurant on the Amalfi Drive (approaching from Conca) is a good place to stop if you're driving. The young owner, Francesco Cavaliere, will give you a warm welcome. After some perfect pasta—the *spaghetti al cartoccio* (spaghetti with clams, olives, capers, and fresh tomatoes) has been a specialty for half a century—finish up with the ricotta-and-pear cake, designed to accompany a tiny glass of well-chilled limoncello. *Average main: €16 Via Giovanni Agustariccio 22 089/831265 www.ristorantedaciccio.com Closed Tues. and Nov.*

WHERE TO STAY

$ HOTEL Fodor's Choice ★ **Albergo Sant'Andrea.** Occupying one of the top spots in town this tiny, family-run *pensione* is just across from the magnificent steps leading to Amalfi's cathedral. **Pros:** on the main square; divine views of the Duomo; friendly staff. **Cons:** steep flight of steps to entrance; very simple rooms. *Rooms from: €100 Piazza Duomo 089/871145 www.albergosantandrea.it 8 rooms Closed Nov.–Mar. No meals.*

$$$$ HOTEL Fodor's Choice ★ **Grand Hotel Convento di Amalfi.** This fabled medieval monastery was lauded by such guests as Longfellow and Wagner, and though recent modernization has sacrificed some of its historic charm, it remains an iconic destination. **Pros:** a slice of paradise; iconic Amalfi. **Cons:** traditionalists will miss its old-world charm; a 10-minute walk to town. *Rooms from: €420 Via Annunziatella 46 089/8736711 www.ghconventodiamalfi.com 36 rooms, 17 suites Closed Nov.–Mar. Breakfast.*

$$ HOTEL **Hotel Amalfi.** Up a tiny side street not far from the Piazza Duomo, the unassumingly decorated Amalfi has small, somewhat characterless modern-style rooms (get one with a geranium-filled balcony if you can) without a great view. **Pros:** great central location; roof terrace. **Cons:** rooms are not very exciting; no access without negotiating steps. *Rooms from: €160 Via dei Pastai 3 089/872440 www.hamalfi.it 40 rooms All meals.*

$$ HOTEL **Hotel Aurora.** Regarded for its location near the beach, this well-run little hotel is a good deal for sand potatoes who prefer absorbing rays to hiking the highlands. **Pros:** away from the madding crowds; ideal for a beach-based trip. **Cons:** a bit of a walk to town; smaller rooms are a bit cramped. *Rooms from: €129 Piazzale dei Protontini 7, between Scalo d'Oriente and Lungomare dei Cavalieri 089/871209 www.aurora-hotel.it 29 rooms Closed Nov.–Mar. Breakfast.*

$$ HOTEL **Hotel Floridiana.** The one-time residence of Pisani (in the 12th century) and the surroundings bring you back to those times—look for the frescoed ceiling in the one-time ballroom, now dining room. **Pros:**

rooftop Jacuzzi; in the heart of the ancient marine town; friendly owners. **Cons:** the rooms face inward, no sea view. *Rooms from: €140* *Via Brancia 1* *089/8736373* *www.hotelfloridiana.it* *13 rooms* *Closed Nov.–Mar.* *Breakfast.*

$$$ HOTEL **Hotel Luna Convento.** Founded as a convent in 1222, allegedly by St. Francis of Assisi himself, the hotel has hosted Otto van Bismarck, Benito Mussolini, Ingrid Bergman, and Tennessee Williams, among other noted figures. **Pros:** staying in a convent: one of *the* Amalfi experiences, a 270-degree view. **Cons:** you need to cross the busy road to get to the pool, the food. *Rooms from: €270* *Via P. Comite 33* *089/871002* *www.lunahotel.it* *43 rooms* *Breakfast.*

$$$ HOTEL **Hotel Marina Riviera.** Once the site of fishermen's cottages—these structures are that close to the sea—this hotel graces a coastal promontory in Amalfi town itself. **Pros:** to-die-for views; wonderful pool; friendly owners; great breakfasts. **Cons:** entrance difficult to find; fronts busy road. *Rooms from: €250* *Via Panteleone Comite* *089/871104* *www.marinariviera.it* *34 rooms* *Closed Nov.–Mar.* *Breakfast.*

$$$$ HOTEL **Hotel Miramalfi.** High above the main coastal drive, this white-stucco hotel overlooks deep blue water and coastal ridges. **Pros:** incredible view; most rooms have balconies. **Cons:** a bit far from town; dining-room ceiling is unattractively low. *Rooms from: €350* *Via Quasimodo 3* *089/871588* *www.miramalfi.it* *49 rooms* *Breakfast.*

$$$$ HOTEL Fodor's Choice ★ **Hotel Santa Caterina.** When Elizabeth Taylor and Richard Burton wanted to escape, they headed here and little wonder. **Pros:** a treasure on the coast; wonderful view of the town. **Cons:** away from the main town; exhorbitant prices. *Rooms from: €425* *Strada Amalfitana 9* *089/871012* *www.hotelsantacaterina.it* *66 rooms* *All meals.*

NIGHTLIFE

Amalfi doesn't have many clubs for music or dancing. However, flyers and posters often go up announcing concerts and theatricals during the peak summer months.

SHOPPING

Leading off from Piazza Duomo is the main street of Amafli, Via Genova, which is lined with some of the loveliest shops on the coast. Be sure to take a lovely stroll along here at twilight.

BOOKS

La Scuderia del Duca Cartiera Amatruda. A publisher of fine books and postcards, La Scuderia sells desk accessories, objets d'art, and beautiful art tomes about Amalfi. *Largo Cesareo Console 8, near Arsenale* *089/872976* *www.carta-amalfi.it.*

Edicolé. If you're pining for English-language newspapers, wanting a book on Amalfi's history, or just looking for a suitable poolside novel, try this shop near the tourist office. *Via Repubbliche Marinare 17* *089/871180.*

FOOD AND CANDY

La Dolceria dell'Antico Portico. In the heart of Amalfi, this pasticceria boutique creates marvelous tortes, biscotti, and almond cakes. *Supportico Rua 10* *089/871143* *www.dolceria-amalfi.com.*

JEWELRY AND ACCESSORIES

Mostacciulo. A well-known and respected family of coral craftsmen has run this shop since 1930. ✉ *Piazza Duomo 22* ☎ *089/871552.*

LEATHER GOODS

Bazar Florio. Leather goods are popular items in small shops along the main streets; one good option is Bazar Florio, whose fair and friendly owner's stock includes handbags, wallets, and backpacks. ✉ *Via P. Capuano 5/7* ☎ *089/871980.*

ATRANI

1 km (½ mile) east of Amalfi, 5 km (3 miles) southwest of Ravello.

Fodor's Choice ★ In some respects this stage-set of a medieval town is a secret treasure: set atop a crag between cliffs overlooking the sea, this is the smallest municipality in Italy. Especially when viewed from the sea, the town looks like an amphitheater ready for a royal pageant. Its closely packed, dollhouse-scaled backstreets are filled with pastel-and-white houses and shops, fragrant gardens, arcaded lanes, and spiraling *scalinatelle.* But the hamlet's stellar attractions are its baroque-style churches, which dominate the skyline, and around which parish houses cluster in true medieval style.

Atrani is often overlooked by tourists, who drive right by it over the riverbed of the Torrente Dragone. It looks little changed from the days when it was closely linked to the Amalfitan republic, the residential choice of its aristocracy. In 1578 it gained its independence from Amalfi, with which it maintains a friendly rivalry; locals say the town holds its processions on its narrow inner streets to discourage Amalfitans from participating.

Pretty Piazza Umberto I, entirely enclosed by four-story houses, is the setting for the basics of Italian life for Atrani's less than 1,000 residents: general store, stationery store, coffee shop, bar, fruit stand, restaurants, barber, and tiny police station. An arcade to one side offers a glimpse of beach, fishing boats, and the sea beyond. At Christmas the whole town congregates here at dawn to drink cappuccino and share traditional cakes.

GETTING HERE AND AROUND

Atrani is a 10-minute walk from the western outskirts of Amalfi—take the seaside stairs off the drive, just after the tunnel. By car, take the Statale 163 (Amalfitana) from outside Sorrento or Salerno. There's SITA bus service from Sorrento, Positano, and Amalfi. The town itself is highly walkable; Piazza Umberto I is the town center.

EXPLORING

San Salvatore de Bireto. The bell of the 10th-century church of San Salvatore de Bireto tolled to announce the crowning of a new doge. The coronation ceremony was restricted to those wearing a *bireto,* the cloth cap that would be ceremoniously placed on the new doge's head, and someday worn attending his burial in the same church. The church was remodeled in 1810; the dome is beautifully tiled, and the paneled bronze doors cast in the 11th century came from Constantinople, as did the

The heart of the pretty town of Atrani looks for all the world just like an opera set.

doors in the Amalfi Duomo. Within is a 12th-century marble plaque showing two peacocks, one standing over a human head between two sirens, the other on a hare being attacked by two birds. Peacocks were considered immortal, but the symbolism of the two in this setting is open to interpretation.

Santa Maria Maddalena (*Church of Saint Mary Magdalene*). Sixteenth-century paintings attributed to Amalfi Coast artists adorn this church that was built in 1274 and given a neo-baroque facade in 1852. Majolica tiles cover the dome, and the bell tower has an octagonal belfry similar to the campanile of the Carmine church in Naples. Among the treasures here are the altar, with its richly colored marbles, and the aforementioned paintings, *St. Magdalen between St. Sebastian and St. Andrew* by Giovannangelo D'Amato of Maiori, and *The Incredulity of St. Thomas* by Andrea da Salerno.

WHERE TO EAT AND STAY

$$ SOUTHERN ITALIAN

A' Paranza. Atrani's best dining option can be found at the back of the piazza on the main walkway. White-cove ceilings reflect immaculate linen tablecloths in a place that is at once homely and quite formal. Entirely seafood-based, each day's fare depends on the catch. The tasting menu—antipasti ranging from marinated tuna to fried rice balls, with a helping of pasta and risotto, followed by a choice of dessert—is recommended, but if that sounds like too much, go for the *scialatielli ai frutti di mare* (spaghetti with seafood). Whatever you choose, leave room for the divine cakes. *Average main: €18* *Via Dragone 1/2* *089/871840* *Closed Dec. 8–26 and Tues. Sept.–July.*

$ SOUTHERN ITALIAN **Le Arcate.** A cave is not where you'd normally expect to find good food, but this simple, old restaurant, recently overhauled, changes the rules. Folks dig the *scialatielli Masaniello*—fresh pasta named after the local boy who became a revolutionary in Naples—as well as the pizza and grilled fish. **TIP→ Get a table on the large beach-view terrace, and you can lean over and see exactly where your meal has come from.** *Average main: €13 Via G. Di Benedetto 4, under arcades of roadway connecting Amalfi and Atrani 089/871367 www.learcate.net Closed mid-Jan.–mid-Feb. and Mon. mid-Sept.–mid-June.*

$$ HOTEL **Palazzo Ferraioli.** Occupying a 19th-century villa up the steps from Atrani's harbor, this hotel has an unrivaled view of the beach. **Pros:** the beauty center; the finest villa in town. **Cons:** all those steps; slightly removed from the action. *Rooms from: €175 Via Campo 16 089/872652 www.palazzoferraioli.it 25 rooms Breakfast.*

RAVELLO, PAESTUM, AND NEARBY

A few minutes west of Amalfi, perched atop a ridge of Monte Cerreto, and "closer to the sky than the sea"—according to French writer André Gide—the achingly lovely town of Ravello gazes down on the Bay of Salerno and the humbler villages surrounding it. This cloud-riding perch is just one reason why some travelers give Ravello the laurel as the Amalfi Coast's—some say Italy's—most beautiful town. Languor becomes Ravello's mood, a bit out of sync with the world below, and it makes this town a lovely place to catch your breath. Hearty souls trek between Atrani and Ravello by a path that climbs through the Valle del Dragone, or Dragon's Valley, a name inspired by the morning mists here (the descent is easier than the ascent!). Most Ravello-bound travelers, however, take the SITA or City Sightseeing bus from Amalfi's Piazza Flavio Gioia, which corkscrew their way up 1,000 feet along a road in the southern Monti Lattari (although the road is infrequently closed due to landslides). Cars follow the same route and really come in handy when driving farther south along Statale 163 to the towns rimming the Bay of Salerno, which have their off-the-beaten-track appeal. If you're based in Naples and have singled out Ravello for a day's sampling of the Amalfi Coast, by far the quickest route is via the mountain pass called the Valico di Chiunzi, easily reached via the A3 Naples–Salerno Autostrada from the exit at Angri.

After dropping down to sea level from Ravello or going eastward from Amalfi, the coast road, Statale 163, descends into Minori, known for its good beach and ancient Roman heritage. The road climbs up the cape by Torre Mezzacapo, then drops back down to sea level near the 15th-century church of San Francesco. Statale 163 then goes through the town of Maiori, with its much broader river valley producing another good beach, and passes Capo di Baia Verde, near the misleadingly named 17th-century Torre Normanna. The coast here becomes dramatic again, giving grand views of the sea as you climb past the promontory topped by Torre di Badia. Capo Tummolo and then Vallone di San Nicola, with the little village of Marina di Erchie, are ahead of you. The drive then descends to the fishing village of

Cetara, along a narrow inlet, continues along the coast, passing Torre de Fuenti and Vallone di Albori, and then faces the sea near Torre della Marina di Albori. At the junction of Raito, a lush little village, you cross the bridge over the Vallone Bonea to the town of Vietri, at which point traffic-light reality returns. Follow Statale 163 to the city of Salerno. Autostrada A3 south connects to E45, which leads to Battipaglia and the exit for the ancient temples of Paestum. Alternatively, hug the coast, driving along Salerno's *lungomare,* and continue along the fairly degraded coastline until you reach Paestum, 40 km (25 miles) from Salerno.

RAVELLO

6½ km (4 miles) northeast of Amalfi, 29 km (18 miles) west of Salerno.

Fodor's Choice ★ Positano may focus on pleasure, and Amalfi on history, but cool, serene Ravello revels in refinement. Thrust over Statale 163 and the Bay of Salerno on a mountain buttress, below forests of chestnut and ash, above terraced lemon groves and vineyards, it early on beckoned the affluent with its island-in-the-sky views and secluded defensive positioning. Gardens out of the *Arabian Nights,* pastel palazzos, tucked-away piazzas with medieval fountains, architecture ranging from Romano-Byzantine to Norman-Saracen, and those sweeping blue-water, blue-sky vistas have inspired a panoply of large personalities, including Wagner and Boccaccio, princes and popes, aesthetes and hedonists, and a stream of famous authors from Virginia Woolf to Tennessee Williams. Author and longtime resident Gore Vidal, not an easy critic, called the town's Villa Cimbrone panorama "the most beautiful view in the world." Today, many visitors flock here to discover this paradisiacal place, some to enjoy the town's celebrated music festival, others just to stroll through the hillside streets to gape at the bluer-than-blue panoramas of sea and sky.

The town itself was founded in the 9th century, under Amalfi's rule, until residents prosperous from cotton tussled with the superpower republic and elected their own doge in the 11th century; Amalfitans dubbed them *rebelli* (rebels).

When the plague cast its shadow in the 17th century, the population plummeted from upward of 30,000 to perhaps a couple of thousand souls, where it remains today. When Ravello was incorporated into the diocese of Amalfi in 1804, a kind of stillness settled in. Despite the decline of its power and populace, Ravello's cultural heritage and special loveliness continued to blossom. Gardens flowered and music flowed in the ruined villas, and artists, sophisticates, and their lovers filled the crumbling palazzos. Grieg, Wagner, D.H. Lawrence, Chanel, Garbo and her companion, conductor Leopold Stokowski, and then, slowly, tourists, followed in their footsteps. Today, at the Villa Rufolo, the noted Ravello Festival is held in its shaded gardens. Here, Wagnerian concerts are often held to pay homage to the great composer, who was inspired by these gardens to compose scenes of *Parsifal.*

With the exception of the Villa Rufolo concerts and the occasional event at the Auditorium Niemeyer, however, the hush lingers. Empty, narrow streets morph into whitewashed staircases rising into a haze of azure, which could be from the sea, the sky, or a union of both. About the only places that don't seem to be in pianissimo slow motion are Piazza Duomo, in front of the cathedral, during the evening passeggiata, or cafés at *pranzo* (luncheon) or *cena* (dinner). The town likes to celebrate religious festivals throughout the year—one of the nicest celebrations is the blossom-strewn celebration of Pentecost (usually the first week of June), when Piazza Duomo is ornamented with sidewalk pictures created with flower petals.

Although cars must park in the municipal lot, most arriving buses deposit their passengers near the hillside tunnel that leads to Piazza Duomo.

GETTING HERE AND AROUND

By car, take the hill road climbing just east of Atrani, or take the Angri exit on the A3 motorway and cross the mountainous Valico di Chiunsi. SITA and City Sightseeing buses make the run up and down the mountain between Ravello and Piazza Flavio Gioia in Amalfi, where you can catch the main Amalfi Drive bus to Sorrento. In Ravello, you can purchase tickets prior to boarding at Punto e Virgola (Via Roma 5) and Bar Calce (Via Boccaccio 11). There are about two buses every hour. Open-top City Sightseeing buses (⇨ *see The Amalfi Coast Planner, above*) make eight trips daily from Amalfi (and connect with the more modern beach towns of Minori and Maiori) for €3. Piazza del Duomo is the town's central point, with (as you face the Duomo) Via Roma to the left (north), Via San Giovanni del Toro straight ahead (east) up the steps of Via Wagner, and Via dei Rufolo to the right (south).

VISITOR INFORMATION

Azienda Autonoma Soggiorno e Turismo ✉ *Via Roma 18b* ☎ *089/857096* 📠 *089/857977* 🌐 *www.ravellotime.it* ⏲ *Daily 9:30–5 (Apr.–Oct. until 7).*

EXPLORING

TOP ATTRACTIONS

Fodor's Choice ★ **Auditorium Niemeyer.** Crowning Via della Repubblica and the hillside, which overlooks the spectacular Bay of Salerno, Auditorium Niemeyer is a startling piece of modernist architecture. Designed with a dramatically curved, all-white roof by the Brazilian architect Oscar Niemeyer (creator of Brasília), it was conceived as an alternative indoor venue for concerts, including those of the famed town music festival, and is now also used as a cinema. The subject of much controversy since its first conception back in 2000, it raised the wrath of some locals who denounced such an ambitious modernist building in medieval Ravello. They need not have worried. The result, inaugurated in 2010, is a design masterpiece—a huge, overhanging canopied roof suspended over a 400-seat concert area, with a giant eye-shape window allowing spectators to contemplate the extraordinary bay vista during performances. The terrace's lounge bar complements the experience. ✉ *Via della Repubblica* 🌐 *www.cinemaravello.it.*

Duomo. Ravello's first bishop, Orso Papiro, founded this cathedral, dedicated to San Pantaleone, in 1086. Rebuilt in the 12th and 17th centuries, it retains traces of medieval frescoes in the transept, an original mullioned window, a marble portal, and a three-story 13th-century bell tower playfully interwoven with mullioned windows and arches. The 12th-century bronze door has 54 embossed panels depicting Christ's life, and saints, prophets, plants, and animals, all narrating biblical lore. Ancient columns divide the nave's three aisles, and treasures include sarcophagi from Roman times and paintings by the southern Renaissance artist Andrea da Salerno. Most impressive are the two medieval pulpits: the earlier one (on your left as you face the altar), used for reading the Epistles, is inset with a mosaic scene of Jonah and the whale, symbolizing death and redemption. The more famous one opposite, used for reading the Gospels, was commissioned by Nicola Rufolo in 1272 and created by Niccolò di Bartolomeo da Foggia. It seems almost Tuscan in style, with exquisite mosaic work and bas-reliefs and six twisting columns sitting on lion pedestals. An eagle grandly tops the inlaid marble lectern.

A chapel to the left of the apse is dedicated to San Pantaleone, a physician beheaded in the 3rd century in Nicomedia. Every July 27 devout believers gather in hope of witnessing a miracle (similar to that of San Gennaro in Naples), in which the saint's blood, collected in a vial and set out on an inlaid marble altar, appears to liquefy and come to a boil. In the crypt is the **Museo del Duomo,** which displays treasures from about the 13th century, during the reign of Frederick II of Sicily. ✉ *Piazza del Duomo* ☎ *089/858311* 🌐 *www.chiesaravello.com* 🎟 *€3* ⏲ *Daily 9–7; between noon and 5:30, access to church is through museum, to right of steps.*

San Giovanni del Toro. Across the tiny piazza from the Hotel Caruso is the noted 11th-century church of San Giovanni del Toro. Its evocative interior has three high apses and a crypt with 14th-century frescoes of Christ and the apostles. A 12th-century *ambo* (pulpit) by Alfano da Termoli startles the eye with its blue Persian majolica and four columns topped with elaborate capitals. The chapel of the Coppola family in the left aisle has an exceptional 14th-century relief of St. Catherine of Alexandria. The small church's three porticos adorned with lunettes show an Arabian influence, and the tripartite back facade is exquisite. Restoration work on the church commenced in 2003, with no sign of being completed. ✉ *Piazza San Giovanni del Toro.*

Fodor's Choice ★ **Villa Cimbrone.** To the west of Ravello's main square, a somewhat hilly 15-minute walk along Via San Francesco brings you to Ravello's show-stopper, the Villa Cimbrone, whose dazzling gardens perch 1,500 feet above the sea. The ultimate aerie, this medieval-style fantasy was created in 1905 by England's Lord Grimthorpe and made world-famous in the 1930s when Greta Garbo found sanctuary from the press here. The Gothic *castello-palazzo* sits amid idyllic gardens that are divided by the grand Alleé of Immensity, leading in turn to the literal high point of any trip to the Amalfi Coast—the **Belvedere dell'Infinità** (Belvedere of Infinity). This grand stone parapet, adorned with amusing stone busts, overlooks the entire Bay of Salerno and frames a

Auditorium Niemayer 8
Duomo 5
Monastero di Santa Chiara .. 2
Museo del Corallo 6
San Giovanni del Toro 9
Santa Maria a Gradillo 7
Villa Cimbrone 1
Villa Episcopio ... 4
Villa Rufolo 3

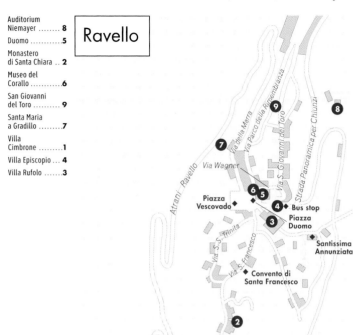

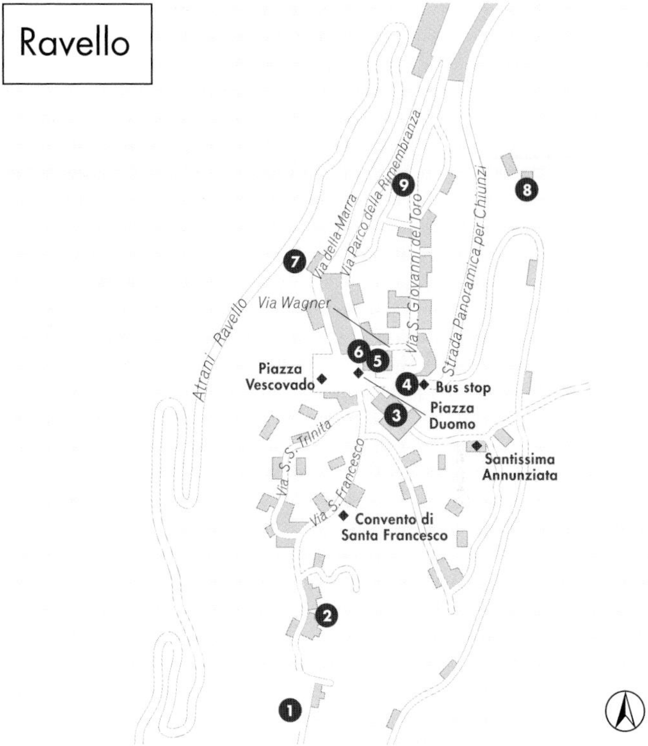

panorama the late writer Gore Vidal, a longtime Ravello resident, described as the most beautiful in the world. The name Cimbrone derives from the rocky ridge on which the villa stands, first colonized by the ancient Romans and hailed as Cimbronium back then. The villa itself is now a five-star hotel. ✉ *Via S. Chiara 26* ☎ *089/857459* 🌐 *www.villacimbrone.it* 🎫 *€7* ⏲ *Daily 9–half hr before sunset.*

Fodor's Choice ★ **Villa Rufolo.** Directly off Ravello's main piazza is the Villa Rufolo, home to some of the most spectacular gardens in Italy, many of which stunningly frame a Cinerama vista of the Bay of Salerno, often called the "bluest view in the world." If the master storyteller Boccaccio is to be believed, the villa was built in the 13th century by Landolfo Rufolo, whose immense fortune stemmed from trade with the Moors and the Saracens. Norman and Arab architecture mingle in a welter of color-filled gardens so lush the composer Richard Wagner used them as inspiration for Klingsor's Garden, the home of the Flower Maidens, in his opera *Parsifal.* Beyond the Arab-Sicilian cloister and the Norman tower lie the two terrace gardens. The lower one, the "Wagner Terrace," is often the site for Ravello Music Festival concerts, with the orchestra perched on a precarious-looking platform constructed over the precipice. Sir Francis Nevile Reid, a Scotsman, acquired the villa in 1851 and hired Michele Ruggiero, head of the excavations at

Pompeii, to restore the villa to its full splendor and replant the gardens with rare cycads, cordylines, and palms. Highlights of the house are its Moorish cloister—an Arabic-Sicilian delight with interlacing lancet arcs and polychromatic palmette decoration—and the 14th-century Torre Maggiore, the so-called Klingsor's Tower, renamed in honor of Richard Wagner's landmark 1880 visit. ✉ *Piazza Duomo* ☎ *089/857621* 🌐 *www.villarufolo.it* 🎫 *€5, extra charge for concerts* ⏲ *Daily 9–9; closes earlier when concert rehearsals are taking place; winter 9–sunset.*

WORTH NOTING

Monastero di Santa Chiara (*Monastery of St. Clare*). Along the path to the Villa Cimbrone lies this 13th-century monastery. The majolica flooring is one of its special elements, along with the matronaeum, or women's gallery, the only one left on the Amalfi Coast. Although only open to the public for the early-morning Sunday service, the wheel used to deliver food (and at one time unwanted children) to the nuns is just inside the entrance and can be seen anytime. ✉ *Via S. Chiara* 🌐 *www.sorelleclarisseravello.it.*

Museo del Corallo (*Coral Museum*). To the left of the Duomo, this private museum celebrates the venerable tradition of Italian workmanship in coral, harvested in bygone centuries from the gulfs of Salerno and Naples and crafted into jewelry, cameos, and figurines. The fascinating collection, not confined solely to coral work, includes a painting of Sisto IV from the 14th century and what may be an original Caravaggio. Look also in particular for a carved Christ from the 17th century, for which the J. Paul Getty Museum offered $525,000 in 1987 (the offer was refused) and a tobacco box covered in cameos, one of only two in the world. There is also a statue of the Madonna dating from 1532. Master craftsman in residence Giorgio Filocamo has crafted coral for Pope John Paul II, the Clintons, and Princess Caroline, as well as numerous Hollywood stars. ✉ *Piazza Duomo 9* ☎ *089/857461* 🌐 *www.museodelcorallo.com* 🎫 *Free* ⏲ *Mon.–Sat. 10–noon and 3–5.*

Santa Maria a Gradillo. A 13th-century church with a graceful dome, Santa Maria a Gradillo was where the town noblemen gathered to discuss civic issues; its atrium collapsed in the 18th century. The small Sicilian-Saracenic bell tower has two light mullion windows. **■ TIP→ The church's opening hours are erratic; inquire about them at the Duomo.** ✉ *Via Roma.*

Villa Episcopio. A bishop's residence that dates back to at least the 12th century, the villa was formerly called Villa di Sangro and is currently closed to the public with no sign of scheduled renovations commencing. Amid the gardens and ruins, Andre Gide found inspiration for his novel *The Immoralist,* Italy's King Vittorio Emanuele III abdicated in favor of his son in 1944, and Jackie Kennedy enjoyed breaks from her obligations as First Lady during a much-publicized 1962 visit. ✉ *Via Boccaccio.*

CLOSE UP

Walking Versus Hiking?

Throughout this entire region, walking *is* hiking, so be prepared. Amalfi, where streets usually take the form of staircases, is a resort where you may leave more fit than you were when you arrived. These towns are picturesque for a reason, and you've probably never seen so many flights of steps—those bothersome *scalinatelle*: thousands of them, leading down to beaches, up to churches, across the hills.

Getting around will take a healthy set of lungs, strong calves, comfortable footwear, time-outs for rest, and a big bottle of Ferrarelle water—slow and steady is the way to go. As for intentional hiking, mule paths and footpaths were the only land-means to get around before the car, and most remain in place for hikers' delight.

Local tourist offices have maps of hikes, and can organize a guide. Check out Julian Tippett's excellent walking book, *Landscapes of Sorrento and the Amalfi Coast* (Sunflower Press), often found at bookstores and newsstands in the area. Even if you're not in shape, you can still participate: take transportation uphill, and let gravity guide you down.

WHERE TO EAT

$ SOUTHERN ITALIAN Fodor's Choice ★

Cumpa' Cosimo. Lustier-looking than most Ravello spots, Cumpa' Cosimo is run devotedly by Netta Bottone, who tours the tables to ensure her clients are content. Her family has owned this cantina for more than 75 of its 300-plus years, and she has been cooking under the arched ceiling for more than 60 of them. You can't miss with any of the classic Ravellian dishes. A favorite (share it—it's huge) is a *misto* of whatever homemade pasta inspires her, served with a fresh, fragrant pesto. Meats, from Netta's own butcher shop next door, are generally excellent and local wines ease it all down gently. The *funghi porcini* mushroom starter is delicious and the house cheesecake or homemade gelato provide a luscious ending. *Average main: €13 ✉ Via Roma 46 ☎ 089/857156 ⏲ Sometimes closed Mon. in winter.*

$$ SOUTHERN ITALIAN

Da Salvatore. Adjacent to the Hotel Graal and sharing the same glorious view of the Bay of Salerno, this restaurant has a large terrace and room for dining just beyond its small garden. The classic Campanian cuisine prepared here includes *calzoncelli* (potatoes, mozzarella, and anchovies with grilled squid and cuttlefish) and *ndunderi* (ricotta gnocchi). The service is friendly, and "That View" is a real bargain at these prices (the same can be said for the six surprisingly upscale guest rooms found upstairs). *Average main: €18 ✉ Via della Repubblica 2 ☎ 089/857227 🌐 www.salvatoreravello.com ⏲ Sometimes closed Mon. in winter.*

$ SOUTHERN ITALIAN

Figli di Papà. The young chef-owners of this restaurant attempt to turn Campania classics into something more, and usually succeed. Past a fireplace that flickers in season and watercolors by Leo Kennedy, an Irish artist and past Ravello resident, you descend into a white, modernized 13th-century setting. The daily menu *turistica* may offer such dishes as *crespolini di pesce* (fish-stuffed crepes), and

The view from Villa Cimbrone's Belvedere of Infinity may be the finest on the coast.

lombo di agnello al rosmarino con spinaci all'uvetta (lamb cutlets with spinach and raisins). Tasting menus—to suit various appetites and wallet sizes—are even more creative, with unexpected combinations. To match the food, the owners provide a wine list featuring the best of the region, which can also be enjoyed on the outside terrace. *Average main: €12 Via della Marra 7 089/858302 www.ristorantefiglidipapa.it Closed 3 wks in Nov., 6 wks in Jan. and Feb., Tues. in winter.*

$ SOUTHERN ITALIAN **Giardini Caffè Calce.** A popular spot on a corner of Piazza Duomo, this café displays Irish painter Leo Kennedy's watercolors of Ravello. You can come here just for coffee, pastries, and ice cream, but sandwiches, salads, and a few entrées are also served. With an alfresco area and three guestrooms, this is a favorite of locals and visitors alike. *Average main: €10 Via Wagner 3 089/857152.*

$ PIZZA **Ristorante Pizzeria Vittoria.** Just south of the Duomo, this is a good place for a return to reality and an informal bite. Vittoria's thin-crust pizza with loads of fresh toppings is the star attraction, and locals praise it *molto*—it was a favorite of Gore Vidal. But also try the pasta, maybe fusilli with tomatoes, zucchini, and mozzarella. Vittoria is pretty, too, with arches and tile floors. All this adds up to crowds, so try to arrive on the early side. *Average main: €12 Via dei Rufolo 3 089/857947 www.ristorantepizzeriavittoria.it Closed Nov.–Mar., except Christmas.*

WHERE TO STAY

$$$$ HOTEL Fodor's Choice ★ **Hotel Caruso.** Set in a medieval palazzo on the highest point of Ravello (1,150 feet), overlooking an incomparable panorama of the Bay of Salerno, this has always been considered a corner of paradise. **Pros:** experience Ravello like a VIP; pure luxury; complimentary boat and shuttle services. **Cons:** out of most visitors' price range; loss of 19th-century charm from restoration. *Rooms from: €800 Piazza San Giovanni del Toro 2 089/858801 www.hotelcaruso.com 23 suites, 27 rooms Closed Jan. and Feb. All meals.*

$$ HOTEL **Hotel Graal.** The name comes from the Holy Grail, as in Wagner's opera *Parsifal,* but this inn is more an operetta. **Pros:** friendly staff; great views. **Cons:** rooms on the lower level are disappointing; the modern decor doesn't fit with the surroundings. *Rooms from: €145 Via della Repubblica 8 089/857222 www.hotelgraal.it 43 rooms Restaurant closed Mon. Oct.–Mar. Breakfast.*

$$$ HOTEL Fodor's Choice ★ **Hotel Palumbo.** This is the real deal—the only great hotel left in Ravello that's still a monument to the Grand Tour sensibility that first put the town on the map. **Pros:** impossibly romantic; wonderful coastal retreat; incredible Bay of Salerno views. **Cons:** with all this finery it can be difficult to relax; restaurant closed from November to March. *Rooms from: €245 Via S. Giovanni del Toro 16 089/857244 www.hotelpalumbo.it 10 rooms, 7 suites Some meals.*

$$ HOTEL **Hotel Parsifal.** In 1288 this diminutive property overlooking the coastline housed an order of Augustinian friars; today the intact cloister hosts travelers intent on enjoying themselves mightily. **Pros:** staying in a convent in Ravello; charming manager and his family dote on Americans. **Cons:** slightly removed from town; tiny rooms; restoration work ongoing in low season. *Rooms from: €130 Viale Gioacchino d'Anna 5 089/857144 www.hotelparsifal.com 17 rooms All meals.*

$$$ HOTEL **Hotel Rufolo.** D. H. Lawrence worked on *Lady Chatterley's Lover* during his 1926 visit (in Room 423), so it might be fun to revisit the novel's groundbreaking love scenes while at this hotel, run for generations by the Schiavo family. **Pros:** as close to La Rondinaia as mere mortals can get; beautiful views over Villa Rufolo; great pool. **Cons:** car park clutters the entrance; staff has been known to be unhelpful. *Rooms from: €290 Via San Francesco 1 089/857133 www.hotelrufolo.it 34 rooms Closed mid-Nov.–mid-Mar. All meals.*

$ HOTEL **Hotel Toro.** Two minutes from the Duomo, this little hotel with a garden and lots of antiques has been in the Schiavo family for three generations. **Pros:** a small piece of Ravello's artistic history; very central. **Cons:** long flight of steps to climb; space rather cramped. *Rooms from: €118 Via Roma 16 089/857211 www.hoteltoro.it 10 rooms Closed Nov.–mid-Apr. Breakfast.*

$$$$ HOTEL Fodor's Choice ★ **Hotel Villa Cimbrone.** Suspended over the azure sea and set amid legendary rose-filled gardens, this Gothic-style castle was once home to Lord Grimthorpe and a hideaway of Greta Garbo. **Pros:** gorgeous pool and grounds; stay where Garbo chose to "be alone." **Cons:** a longish hike from town center (porters can help with luggage); daily arrival of respectful day-trippers. *Rooms from: €530 Via Santa Chiara 26 089/857459 www.villacimbrone.com 19 rooms Closed Nov.–Mar. Breakfast.*

$$$$ HOTEL **Palazzo Avino.** In this 12th-century home of the aristocratic Sasso family, Wagner penned part of his opera *Parsifal* in the 1880s, and in the 1950s the palazzo hosted film star Ingrid Bergman and the director Roberto Rossellini. **Pros:** pure luxury; one of the region's finest restaurants. **Cons:** out of most travelers' price range; traditionalists, beware! *Rooms from: €470* ✉ *Via San Giovanni del Toro 28* ☎ *089/818181* *www.palazzoavino.com* *32 rooms, 11 suites* *Closed Nov.–Feb.* *No meals.*

$ HOTEL **Villa Amore.** A 10-minute walk from the Piazza Duomo, this charmingly secluded hotel with a garden is family-run and shares the same exhilarating view of the Bay of Salerno as Ravello's most expensive hotels. **Pros:** wonderful views; on-site restaurant has indoor and terrace seating. **Cons:** away from the main drag; basic rooms. *Rooms from: €100* ✉ *Via dei Fusco 5* ☎ *089/857135* *www.villaamore.it* *10 rooms* *All meals.*

$$$ HOTEL **Villa Maria Hotel.** Hued in glowing terra-cotta, adorned with gorgeous flowers, and fronted by a vast garden terrace, the Villa Maria offers more sunny warmth than most formal hotels in Ravello. **Pros:** friendly staff; convenient restaurant. **Cons:** most rooms face the valley, not the coast; pool is at the adjacent hotel. *Rooms from: €250* ✉ *Via Santa Chiara 2* ☎ *089/858400* *www.villamaria.it* *23 rooms* *All meals.*

NIGHTLIFE AND THE ARTS

Unless there's an event at the Auditorium Niemeyer, there's little nightlife activity other than the concerts offered by the Ravello Concert Society and the Ravello Music Festival. A few cafés and bars are scattered about, but the general peacefulness extends to evening hours. Hotels and restaurants may offer live music and can advise you about the few nightclubs, but around these parts the sound is soft and classical—or silence.

Fodor's Choice ★ **Ravello Concert Society.** The society runs a yearlong program at Villa Rufolo, with a few concerts also held in the neighboring town of Scala. Most evening concerts are held at 9:30, with occasional performances starting at 6:30. The 9:30 concerts begin well after sunset, so come earlier if you want to catch the evening glow. The society's website and Amalfi Coast tourist-information offices have schedules, and they're posted outside Villa Rufolo. ☎ *089/858149* *089/8424082* *www.ravelloarts.org.*

Mamma Agata. If you fancy learning how to make some of the things you've been eating, Mamma Agata, who has cooked for Elizabeth Taylor, Federico Fellini, Jackie Kennedy, and Marcello Mastroianni, will take you into her kitchen—with the almost obligatory stunning view—and take you through the preparation of the area's pasta dishes and sweets. A four-hour morning session is followed by lunch—that you yourself will have made. ✉ *Piazza San Cosma 9* ☎ *089/857845* *www.mammaagata.com.*

SHOPPING

ANTIQUES AND COLLECTIBLES

Bric-a-Brac. This shop carries antiques (mostly from the 19th century), including historic crèche scenes, and has a great selection of books about Ravello and antique prints of the city. ✉ *Piazza Duomo 4* ☎ *089/857153.*

BOOKS AND STATIONERY

Gruppo Petit Prince. This shop sells stationery, prints, and artworks. ✉ *Via San Francesco 9* ☎ *089/858033.*

CERAMICS

Ceramiche d'Arte Carmella. The store ships its Vietri-made and other hand-painted ceramics all over the world. Bargaining may reward you with a 10% discount, maybe more if you have a talent for it. There are also opportunities for gaining hands-on experience at the showroom and workshop, a three-minute walk away in a courtyard at Via Roma 20. ✉ *Via dei Rufolo 16* ☎ *089/857303.*

FOOD AND CANDY

Ravello Gusti & Delizie. Packed to the ceiling with basic foodstuffs, marvelous delicacies, and wines from all over Italy, this shop stocks intriguing lemon products—candies, candles, soaps, and even lemon honey. ✉ *Via Roma 28* ☎ *089/857716.*

JEWELRY AND ACCESSORIES

Gerardo Sacco. Jewelry maker Gerardo Sacco's theatrical earrings, necklaces, and bracelets may not be to everyone's taste, but their craftsmanship makes his shop worth a look. A brochure there shows Glenn Close, Elizabeth Taylor, Mel Gibson, and Princess Caroline of Monaco, among others, flashing his creations. ✉ *Piazza Duomo 8* ☎ *089/858125.*

WINE

Episcopio Winery. Wine merchants in Ravello have been cultivating grapes since 1860, and varieties of *rosso* (red) and *bianco* (white), as refined as their namesake town, can be purchased at this winery run by the nearby Hotel Palumbo. ✉ *Via Giovanni a Toro* ☎ *089/857244* 🌐 *www.hotelpalumbo.it.*

CETARA

3 km (2 miles) northeast of Erchie, 4 km (2½ miles) southwest of Vietri.

Tourists tend to take a pass on the village of Cetara. A quaint and quiet fishing village below orange groves on Monte Falerzo, it was held in subjugation to greater powers, like most of these coastal sites, throughout much of its history. From being a Saracen stronghold in the 9th century, it became the final holding of Amalfi at the eastern edge of the republic, which all through the 11th and 12th centuries tithed part of Cetara's fishing catch, *ius piscariae*—the town's claim to fame. It is rumored that the village's Latin name comes from this big catch—*cetaria* (tuna net), though Cetara is more renowned these days for its anchovies. Thousands of years ago, salted and strained, they became a spicy liquid called *garum,* a delicacy to the rich of ancient Rome. Garum, as well as the lighter *colatura di alici,* can be purchased at local

DID YOU KNOW?

Ravello's Villa Cimbrone, with some of the most heralded gardens along the Amalfi Coast, was where Greta Garbo chose to hide from the press in 1937.

grocery stores or at Cetarii, on the beachfront. After the Middle Ages, the village came under the dominion of the Benedictine abbey of neighboring Santa Maria di Erchie, and then became the port of the abbey of Cava, above the coast, which traded with Africa. In 1534 the Turks, led by the tyrant Sinan Pasha—on the invitation, no less, of Prince Ferdinando Sanseverino of Salerno—enslaved 300 Cetaran villagers, spiriting them away in 22 galleys and executing those who would not cooperate. A few survivors fled to Naples, which immediately ordered a watchtower to be raised in Cetara to ward off future raids. This is one of the many landmarks that remind tourists there were coastal perils previous to the one of driving on Statale 163. Beneath the tower is a rocky little beach, and a small park overlooks the harbor, where fishermen mend their nets and paint their boats. They often are away from home for months, fishing in deep waters. Other than the charmingly scenic waterfront, there are no sights of note, other than the church of San Pietro, near the harbor.

GETTING HERE AND AROUND

By car, take the Statale 163 (Amalfitana) from outside Sorrento or Salerno, or take the Angri exit on the A3 motorway and cross the mountainous Valico di Chiunsi. The SITA bus line runs here from Amalfi and Salerno. The town's only road leads to the beach.

EXPLORING

Back in the days of the Caesars, this little town ranked high on their menus, as it was said the most delectable tunas hailed from Cetara, thanks to the town's special *garum* recipe. Today, gourmands still flock here to eat like emperors, while others head here because the waterfront is so delightfully laid-back and "real."

BEACHES

Cetara. A medieval Norman tower provides a spectacular landmark for this beach on Cetara's picturesque marina. With blue-and-white boats lying on the sand, anchovy-fishing boats in the harbor, and children playing in the adjacent park, the beach is a hive of activity—stretch out your towel and enjoy the buzz. The water here is clean, and the lido has a cool bar and sun beds for rent. **■TIP→ The sun shines here until late afternoon, so if you stay long enough that hunger strikes, try the fried anchovies in the Cuopperia on the marina. Served in paper cones, they're the local fast food.** **Amenities:** food and drink; lifeguards; showers; toilets. **Best for:** snorkeling; swimming.

WHERE TO EAT AND STAY

$$ SEAFOOD ✕ **Acqua Pazza.** Locals along this part of the coast rave about this tiny restaurant a short stroll up from the harbor. The environment is modest—a spare interior with a few tables—but the seafood served here is remarkably fresh. Spaghetti with *colatura di alici* (anchovies) is also a specialty. *Ⓢ Average main: €15 ✉ Via Garibaldi 38 ☎ 089/261606 ⊕ www.acquapazza.it ⏲ Closed on Mon. mid-Oct.–mid-Mar.*

$ SOUTHERN ITALIAN ✕ **Al Convento.** Occupying part of a former convent, this restaurant receives glowing reviews for its varied and tasty preparations involving anchovies. For the adventurous there's the *spaghetti con colatura* (a modern version of the anchovy liquid known in Roman times as garum), but there are also straightforward but excellent pizzas from the wood-fired oven. The restaurant's ambience is low-key yet ethereal, with whitewashed walls, soaring arches, and a ceiling adorned with beautiful old frescoes. $ *Average main: €14* ⊠ *Piazza San Francesco 16* ☎ *089/261039* ⊕ *www.alconvento.net* ☉ *Closed Wed. mid-Oct.–mid-Mar.*

$$
SOUTHERN
ITALIAN
✕ **San Pietro.** At this pioneering restaurant just down from the bus stop, you can enjoy romantic outdoor seating overlooking the town square. The chef-owner, Franco, who has been here for about three decades, occasionally pops out of the kitchen to explain his original anchovy recipes—fried, marinated, *colatura,* and even in the bread. ■ **TIP→** **Book at least two days in advance, and Franco can prepare a typical menu from ancient Roman times.** $ *Average main: €15* ⊠ *Piazza San Francesco 2* ☎ *089/261091* ⊕ *www.sanpietroristorante.it* ☉ *Closed 6 wks in Jan. and Feb., Tues. in winter.*

$$$
HOTEL
🛏 **Cetus.** Cetara's leading hotel is set in a white-stucco building that seems to have grown right out of the living rock. **Pros:** amazing view floating above the sea; no better place in Cetara. **Cons:** 350 yards from town along Amalfi Drive; not ideal for walking; steep descent to beach. $ *Rooms from: €260* ⊠ *Corso Umberto I 1* ☎ *089/261388* ⊕ *www. hotelcetus.com* ⤶ *37 rooms* ⊙ *Breakfast.*

SHOPPING

Cetarii. Buy a bottle of the anchovy delicacy called *colatura di alici* and other local products such as lemon honey. ⊠ *Via Largo Marina 48/50* ☎ *089/261863* ⊕ *www.cetarii.it.*

PAESTUM

45 km (27 miles) southeast of Cetara, 42 km (25 miles) southeast of Salerno, 99 km (62 miles) southeast of Naples.

The ruins here are part of the ancient city of Poseidonia, founded by Greek colonists in the 7th century BC. When the Romans took over the colony in 273 BC and its name was latinized to Paestum, they changed the layout of the settlement, adding an amphitheater and a forum.

The S18 from the north has now been rerouted via the train station (Stazione di Paestum), which is about 800 yards from the ruins. Access can be gained through the perfectly preserved archway **Porta Sirena,** or—if motorized—through the northern gate of **Porta Aurea.**

GETTING HERE AND AROUND

By car, take the A3 motorway south from Salerno, take the Battipaglia exit to SS18. Exit at Capaccio Scala. Take a CSTP or SCAT bus hourly from Salerno or the State railway from Salerno.

VISITOR INFORMATION

Azienda Autonoma Soggiorno e Turismo ⊠ *Via Magna Grecia 887* ☎ *0828/811016* ⊕ *www.infopaestum.it* ☉ *May–Sept., daily 9–1 and 3–5; Oct.–Apr., daily 9–1 and 2–4.*

Paestum is the site of remarkably well-preserved Greek temples, including the Tempio di Cerere.

EXPLORING

Fodor's Choice ★ **Greek Temples.** One of Italy's most majestic sights lies on the edge of a flat coastal plain: the remarkably preserved Greek temples of Paestum. This is the site of the ancient city of Poseidonia, founded by Greek colonists probably in the 6th century BC. When the Romans took it over in 273 BC, they latinized the name to Paestum and changed the layout of the settlement, adding an amphitheater and a forum. Much of the archaeological material found on the site is displayed in the well-labeled **Museo Nazionale,** and several rooms are devoted to the unique tomb paintings—rare examples of Greek and pre-Roman pictorial art—discovered in the area.

At the northern end of the site opposite the ticket barrier is the **Tempio di Cerere** (Temple of Ceres). Built in about 500 BC, it is thought to have been originally dedicated to the goddess Athena. Follow the road south past the **Foro Romano** (Roman Forum) to the **Tempio di Nettuno** (Temple of Poseidon), a showstopping Doric edifice with 36 fluted columns and an entablature (the area above the capitals) that rivals those of the finest temples in Greece. Beyond is the so-called **Basilica.** The oldest of Paestum's standing structures, it dates from the early 6th century BC. The name is an 18th-century misnomer, though, since it was, in fact, a temple to Hera, the wife of Zeus. **■ TIP→ Try to see the temples in the late afternoon, when the light enhances the deep gold of the limestone and tourists have left them almost deserted.** ✉ *Via Magna Grecia* ☎ *0828/811023 museum, 0828/722654 ticket office* 🎫 *Site and museum €7, (€10 when there are exhibitions) museum only (after site closing time) €6* ⏲ *Excavations daily 8:45–2 hrs before sunset; museum daily 8:30–6:45; museum closed 1st and 3rd Mon. of month.*

WHERE TO EAT AND STAY

$ PIZZA **La Basilica Café.** Just off the main drag, this charming family-run café is set in a shady garden area and has a handy car park. The delicious pizzas are prepared in an oak wood stove—try the Zeus, made with fresh tomatoes, buffalo mozzarella, and rocket. The café uses top-quality local mozzarella in its pizzas. *Average main: €12 Via Magna Grecia 881 0828/811301 www.labasilicacafe.it Closed Jan. No dinner except summer weekends.*

$ B&B/INN **Azienda Agrituristica Seliano.** This working-farm-with-a-difference, about 3 km (2 miles) from Greek temples, consists of a cluster of 19th-century baronial buildings. **Pros:** a great taste of a working farm; a banquet every evening; transfers available from the station. **Cons:** confusing to find; not for non-dog fans. *Rooms from: €120 Via Seliano, about 1 km (½ mile) down dirt track west off main road from Capaccio Scalo to Paestum 0828/723634 www.agriturismoseliano.it 14 rooms Closed Nov.–Mar., will open for bookings All meals.*

SHOPPING

Tenuta Vannulo. If you want to visit a working farm, Tenuta Vannulo produces award-winning cheeses, yogurts, and ice cream. Say hello to the pen of buffaloes before sampling the sublime buffalo mozzarella—but get here early, it's often sold out by midday! *Via G. Galilei 0828/724765 to book products, 0828/727894 www.vannulo.it Daily 8–5.*

CAPRI, ISCHIA, AND PROCIDA

WELCOME TO CAPRI, ISCHIA, AND PROCIDA

TOP REASONS TO GO

★ **The living room of the world:** Pose oh-so-casually with the beautiful people sipping their Camparis on La Piazzetta, the central crossroads of Capri Town: a stage-set square that always seems ready for a gala performance.

★ **Spa-lendid Ischia:** Rebellious daughter of a distant volcanic eruption, Ischia was compensated for her rocky complexion with gorgeous spas famed for their seaweed soaks and fango mud cures.

★ **Marina di Corricella, Procida:** Lilliputian-size Procida has numerous harbors, but none will have you reaching for your paintbrush as quickly as this rainbow-hued, horizontal version of Positano.

★ **Anacapri's Siren Heights:** Be sure to be nice to the bus driver when you take the precipitously steep road up to Capri's bluff-top village—you're nearly a thousand feet above the Bay of Naples here.

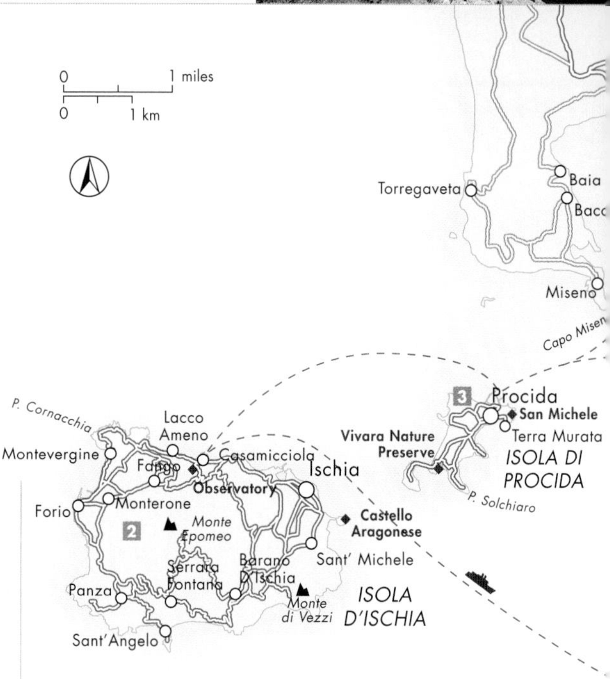

1 Capri. A tiny energy point in the universe with a magnetic pull far exceeding its size, Capri is a balmy and palmy never-never land that has been the darling of tourism for 2,500 years. Although its hotels rank among the priciest (and perchiest) around, its incomparable views and natural wonders—I Faraglioni and the Arco Naturale, to name but two—come with no price tags. Capri Town is the place to head for jet-setter glamour, while Anacapri—sitting high up on Monte Solaro—is noted for its understated charm, a fact that accounts for a disproportionate number of easel-toting visitors at the Villa San Michele, with its nonpareil bay view.

GETTING ORIENTED

Geological stepping-stones anchored in the Bay of Naples, the islands of Capri, Ischia, and Procida tip the two points of the bay's watery crescent. A mere drop in the blue Mediterranean with a popularity way out of proportion to its size, Capri is a *piccolo paradiso* often swamped by tidal waves of day-trippers. Happily, its more rustic sister islands in the archipelago offer something for escapists of every ilk.

2 Ischia. More than twice the size of Capri, lesser-known Ischia may have lost the beauty contest to its sister, but it has something Capri doesn't: paradisial white-sand beaches, thermal hot-spring spas, and many fewer day-trippers. Trekkers climbing Monte Epomeo can enjoy a 360-degree view of the gulf.

3 Procida. Although it's a short trip, 3 km (2 miles) from the mainland, this little volcanic outcropping remains a secret to many. Sun, cliffs, and sea combine to create the distinctive atmosphere so memorably immortalized in the film *Il Postino*. The town of Terra Murata is barnacled onto the hillside with its ancient baroque abbey of San Michele glittering amid the rocky terrain. The Vivara nature preserve is a paradise for bird lovers.

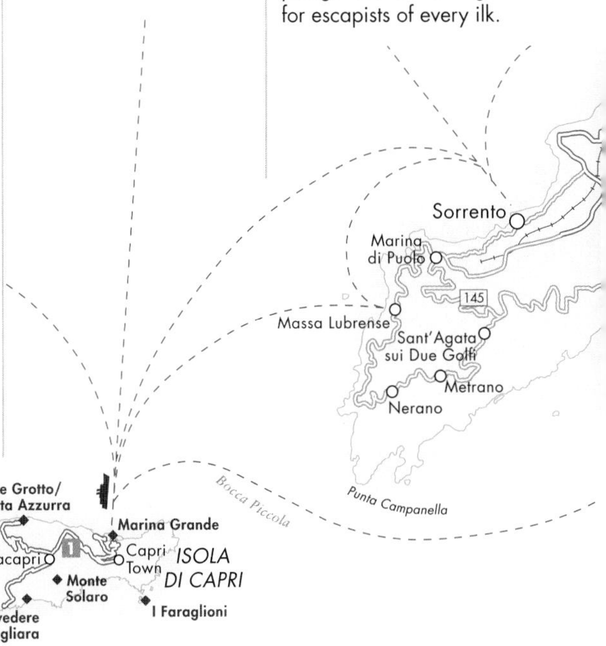

CAPRI IS FOR WALKERS

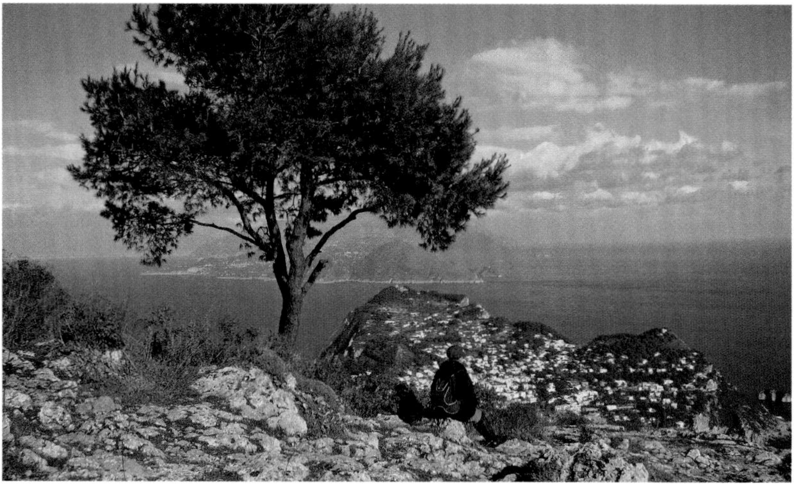

Although Capri may first conjure up chichi cafés and Gucci stores, it's also hiking heaven. Get ready for idyllic pathways running beside cactus-covered cliffs and whitewashed Arabian houses overlooking some of the bluest water on Earth.

(above) Atop Monte Solaro leading to the lovely Santa Maria a Cetrella lookout point (opposite top) The Lighthouse at Punta Carena from the Belvedere di Migliara (opposite bottom) Via Krupp

When Capri Town swarms with summer crowds and begins to feel like an ant farm, take to the hills—in a few minutes, you can find yourself atop a cliff without a trace of humanity in sight. Many trails here run past famous sights and they offer something for everyone. Novices will love the unique-in-all-the-world zigzag of Via Krupp—a work of art in itself—while pros will dare themselves with Il Passetiello, the ancient mule track that connected the island's two towns, from Via Capodimonte in Anacapri past 14th-century Carthusian pathways to stunning Santa Maria a Cetrella, plus some *very* steep cliff paths. On this trail, don't get too distracted by the amazing view of I Faraglioni as you descend into Capri Town or you may get there quicker than planned!

A SHORTCUT

The Monte Solaro chairlift, built in 1952 (and overhauled in 1998), hoists you to the peak in just more than 10 minutes, your feet dangling, at times, less than 100 feet above the houses and treetops. From here you can access some great hikes—namely one down to the famously scenic vista from Santa Maria a Cetrella. To save yourself a climb, remember to use the chairlift!

IL SENTIERO DEI FORTINI

One of the most beautiful coastal walks in the world, this "Path of the Forts" stretches along the western side of the island for 5.2 km (3.2 miles). Jaw-dropping views are accented by four Saracen fortresses (used mainly during the Napoleonic wars). Starting from the Grotta Azzura (Blue Grotto), you soon meet the first fort, Fortino di Orrico, set just 30 meters (100 feet) above the water. The path continues through rich Mediterranean maquis to Fortino di Mesola, with great views around this strategically placed fort. The path then rises past Fortino del Pino to the tiny Fortino del Tombosiello and then ends at the famous Faro lighthouse. Along the path, ceramic panels—inscribed with reflective haikus—describe your surroundings, the final touch to this unmissable open-air ecomuseum. This walk is not difficult, but lasts up to five hours, with no watering spots along the way, so bring lots of water!

BELVEDERE MIGLIARA TO PUNTA CARENA

The 40-minute walk along the paved Via Migliara from Anacapri to the Belvedere Migliara—with one of the most beautiful views on the island—and the Philosophy Park may be some folks' idea of a hike, but the blisters are truly worth it when you head on down the mountainside via the tiny path for 20 minutes to the Torre della Guardia, a Saracen tower once belonging to Axel Munthe. Stone steps take you down to Punta Carena, with its shell-shape rocky bay: perfect for a well-deserved swim!

SCALA FENICIA

Workout fans will have no hesitation in climbing (of course!) the 921 steps of the—probably—Greek (Phoenician)-built steps, once the main "road" from Capri to Anacapri. From Marina Grande follow the street (not the funicular) to Capri Town for five minutes until you see the signpost on your right. A paved residential path then takes you to the base of the stairway, with the next stop (apart from some time to catch your breath!) just under Villa San Michele, 290 meters (950 feet) above the sea. Take a break shortly before the top, just before passing under the main car road, to admire the 17th-century chapel of Sant'Antonio da Padova, dedicated to the patron saint of Anacapri.

GIRO DELL'ARCO NATURALE

Where else can you see the Arco Naturale, the Grotta di Matermaia, Villa Malaparte, and I Faraglioni in under two hours? *This walk, which is truly spectacular, along beauteous Via Pizzo Longo, is detailed in our box: "Classic Capri: A Good Walk."*

Updated by Fergal Kavanagh

The islands off Naples are so different from each other that you wonder how they can possibly be in the same bay—indeed, some would say that Capri, Ischia, and Procida are not true water mates, as they lie just beyond the bay's outer fringes. More tellingly, their contrasts go beyond mere geology and vegetation. They all occupy different niches in the traveler's mind.

Capri panders to the whims of the international great-and-good. Ischia serves the needs of a predominantly German and Italian clientele. Procida—the closest to the mainland—is more dependent on the weekend and summer influx of Neapolitans. But together, the islands of Capri, Ischia, and Procida—chosen by the Greeks, the supreme connoisseurs and aesthetes of antiquity, as their first base in Italy—combine a broad and delightful gamut of experiences.

Islandophiles, of course, have always had a special love for Capri (the first syllable is accented—"*Ca*-pri"). Pleasure dome to Roman emperors and still Italy's most glamorous seaside getaway, this craggy, whale-shape island has an epic beauty: cliffs that are the very embodiment of time, bougainvillea-shaded pathways overlooking the sea, trees seemingly hewn out of rock by the Greeks. Capri has always been a stage that lesser mortals could share with the Beautiful People, often an eclectic potpourri of duchesses who have left their dukes at home, fading French film actresses, pretenders to obscure thrones, waspish couturiers, and sleek supermodels.

Today Capri's siren song continues to seduce thousands of visitors. On summer days the port and *piazzetta* are often crammed, so if you can visit in spring or fall, do so. Yet even the crowds are not enough to destroy Capri's very special charm. The town itself is a Moorish stage set of sparkling white houses, tiny squares, and narrow medieval alleyways hung with flowers, while its hillsides are spectacular settings for luxurious seaside villas. The mood is modish but somehow unspoiled. The upper crust does its sun-baking in private villas, hinting that you, also, should retreat when the day-trippers take over—offering yourself to the sun at your hotel pool or exploring the hidden corners of the island. Even in the height of summer, you can enjoy a degree of privacy on one of the many paved paths that have been mapped out through species-rich Mediterranean maquis, winding around the island hundreds of feet above the sea.

Recent years have seen a diversification of the experiences offered on the three islands. Once entirely dependent on its thermal springs, Ischia is now the archaeological front-runner in the bay, thanks to its noted museum in Lacco Ameno. Procida has opened up to tourism, with some newer, smaller hotels remaining open throughout the year. All the islands are well served by road networks, with buses plying the main roads and a funicular on Capri reaching the main town from the Marina Grande, as well as a chairlift ascending to the top of Monte Solaro (1,932 feet) from Anacapri.

CAPRI, ISCHIA, AND PROCIDA PLANNER

WHEN TO GO

April, May, and early June is a good time to visit the islands; the weather is usually good, and hotels and restaurants have just reopened for the season. It gets terribly hot in summer, and visitors crowd the limited space available, particularly in August. Things quiet down in the early fall, and the weather is generally pleasant.

PLANNING YOUR TIME

Each of the three islands has its own individual charm—the chic resort of Capri, the volcanic spas of Ischia, and the rustic Procida. If you are unable to overnight, it is worth getting to Capri as early in the morning as possible to see the main sites before the human tsunami hits the island. Take a round-the-island boat trip and gaze at the natural beauty of the Fariglioni and the Blue Grotto, two of the unmissable sights on this fabled isle.

If archaeology and history are at the top of your list of priorities, choosing between Ischia and Capri can be difficult. Ischia has the added bonus of its natural thermal baths—if you want the gamut of natural saunas and access to a dreamy beach, head to Poseidon in Forio or landscaped Negombo in Lacco Ameno. The waters at Barano's Nitrodi (🌐 *www.fonteninfenitrodi.com*)—showers only—have been healing ailments since Roman times.

Moving around Capri to the main sites is generally easier—and can be done in a day if pushed—while Ischia calls for more chilling out at your destination. If time is limited, Procida and its magical waterfront, as immortalized in the Oscar-winning film *Il Postino,* can be tacked on to your stay as a day trip from Ischia or from the mainland.

GETTING HERE AND AROUND

BOAT TRAVEL

Lying equidistant from Naples (about 25 km [16 miles]), Ischia and Capri stand like guards at the main entrance to the Bay of Naples, with Ischia to the west and Capri to the south, while Procida is like a small stepping-stone halfway between Ischia and Capo Miseno (Cape Misenum), on the mainland. The islands can be reached easily from various points in and near Naples, and the port of Pozzuoli is the closest to Ischia and Procida. Nevertheless, most people head first to Capri using hydrofoils from the main port terminal in Naples—the Molo Beverello. Ferries are far less frequent, and leave from the nearby Calata Porta di Massa. There are also boat connections between the islands. *For details, see the "Getting Here and Around" sections for each island in this chapter.*

Schedules for many routes are listed every day in the local newspaper *Il Mattino*—buy a single ticket rather than a round-trip, which would tie you to the same line on your return journey. Day-trippers need to remember that the high-season crowds on the last ferries leaving the islands make this crossing riotously reminiscent of packed subways and buses back home; in addition, rough bay waters can also delay (and even cancel) these boat rides.

BUS TRAVEL

Once on the islands you can do without a car, as the bus service is good—the trip from Capri to Anacapri is breathtaking both for its views and the sheer drops just inches away. Tickets should be bought before boarding, and then stamped on the bus.

TAXI AND SCOOTER TRAVEL

For those with (much) deeper pockets, microtaxis are readily available to whiz you to your destination. Renting a scooter on Ischia gives you the freedom to explore at will, as well as giving you that real Italian experience.

RESTAURANTS

The islands' restaurants offer top-quality food, from Mamma's home cooking to Michelin-star dining experiences. Capri's eateries unsurprisingly cater to more sophisticated palettes, with innovative seafood creations, while less expensive, yet authentic spots are ubiquitous in Ischia and Procida. Ischia is renowned for its wild rabbit dishes.

Prices in the reviews are the average cost of a main course at dinner, or, if dinner isn't served, at lunch.

HOTELS

On Capri, hotels fill up quickly, so book well in advance to be assured of getting first-pick accommodations. Although island prices are generally higher than those on the mainland, it's worth paying the difference for an overnight stay. Once the day-trippers have left center stage and headed down to the Marina Grande for the ferry home, the streets regain some of their charm and tranquility.

Although Ischia can be sampled piecemeal on day excursions from Naples, given the size of the island, you'd be well advised to arrange a stopover. Ischia is known for its natural hot-water spas, and many hotels have a wellness or beauty center, meaning you may be tempted not to venture any farther than the lobby for the duration of your stay. Hotels in Procida tend to be family run and more down-to-earth. Note that booking is essential for the summer months, when half board may be required. Most hotels close from November to Easter, when the season is at its lowest.

Prices in the reviews are the lowest cost of a standard double room in high season.

TOURS

Vesuvius vs. Pompeii. There is a selection of tour operators in the area, one reputable company is Vesuvius vs. Pompeii, who offer guided walking tours and organize transfers. ✉ *Capri* ☎ *333/6409000 Mobile* 🌐 *www.vesuviusvspompeii.com.*

WORD OF MOUTH

"Capri is an unforgettable experience. I love the combination of sun, sea and history it offers. There are loads of things to see and do. From the Blue Grotto to Villa Jovis and people watching in the Piazzeta, it really is something else. Have a great time."
—francoisebelle

3

CAPRI

D.H. Lawrence once called Capri "a gossipy, villa-stricken, two-humped chunk of limestone, a microcosm that does heaven much credit, but mankind none at all." He was referring to its once rather farouche reputation as well as its unique natural beauty. Fantastic grottoes, soaring conical peaks, caverns great and small, plus villas of the emperors and thousands of legends brush the isle with an air of whispered mystery and an intoxicating quality as heady as its rare and delicious wines. Emperor Augustus was the first to tout the island's pleasures by nicknaming it *Apragopolis*—the City of Sweet Idleness—and Capri has drawn escapists of every ilk since. Ancient Greek and Roman goddesses were moved aside by the likes of Jacqueline Onassis, Elizabeth Taylor, and Brigitte Bardot, who made the island into a paparazzo's paradise in the 1960s. Today, new generations of glitterati continue to answer the island's call.

Of all the peoples who have left their mark on the island during its millennia of history, the Romans with their sybaritic wealth had the greatest effect in forming the island's psyche. Capri became the center of power in the Roman Empire when Tiberius scattered 12 villas around the island and decided to spend the rest of his life here, refusing to return to Rome even when, 10 years on, he was near death.

Life on Capri gravitates around the two centers of Capri Town (on the saddle between Monte Tiberio and Monte Solaro) and Anacapri, higher up (902 feet). The main road connecting Capri Town with the upper town of Anacapri is well plied by buses. On arriving at the main harbor, the Marina Grande, everyone heads for the famous funicular, which ascends (and descends) several times an hour. Once you're lofted up to Anacapri by bus, you can reach the island heights by taking the spectacular chairlift that ascends to the top of Monte Solaro (1,932 feet) from Anacapri's town center. Life on Capri gravitates around the two centers of Capri Town (on the saddle between Monte Tiberio and Monte Solaro) and Anacapri, higher up (902 feet). Within Capri Town and Anacapri foot power is the preferred mode of transportation, as much for convenience as for the sheer delight of walking along these gorgeous street and roads.

Capri is laced with spectacular walking paths.

GETTING HERE AND AROUND

Capri is well connected with the mainland in all seasons, though there are more sailings between April and October. However, you can't return to Naples after the last sailing (11 pm in high season, often 8 pm or even earlier in low season). Hydrofoils, Seacats, and similar vessels leave from Molo Beverello (below Piazza Municipio) in Naples, while far less frequent car ferries leave from Calata Porta di Massa, 1,000 yards to the east. There's also service to and from Sorrento's Marina Piccola. Much of Capri is pedestrianized, and a car is a great hindrance, not a help.

Several ferry and hydrofoil companies ply the waters of the Bay of Naples, making frequent trips to Capri. Schedules change from season to season; the most reliable source for departure times is *Il Mattino*, Naples's daily newspaper. There's little to be gained—sometimes nothing—from buying a round-trip ticket, which will just tie you down to the return schedule of one line. Book in advance in spring and summer for a Sunday return to the mainland.

Most of Capri's sights are reasonably accessible by either boat or bus, except for Villa Jovis and Cetrella, which require some walking (about 40 minutes). The bus service is relatively cheap (€1.80) and frequent, while taxis are likely to cost 10 to 20 times as much as public transport. Don't buy a *biglietto giornaliero* (day pass) for the bus and funicular unless you're thinking of covering almost every corner of the island—it costs €9.60, so you would need to make six separate trips to make it pay, and locals deem it a bit of a rip-off.

Alilauro. From Easter to October, Alilauro, through offshoot Alicost, offers three jet foils from Positano and Amalfi (approximately €20, travel time 50 minutes). ✉ *Capri* ☎ *081/4972238* 🌐 *www.alicost.it.*

Caremar. Caremar has up to seven ferry departures per day from Calata Porta di Massa (€12.70 slow, €17.80 fast with a travel time of 1 hour, 20 minutes). Three ferries leave daily from Sorrento (€14.70, travel time 25 minutes). ✉ *Capri* ☎ *892/123, 081/8370700* 🌐 *www.caremar.it.*

WORD OF MOUTH

"We spent three nights on Capri in May, and had a wonderful time. We did a lot of hiking, and I mean a lot. One must really walk to see this beautiful island."

—Tuscanlifeedit

Linee Marittime Partenopee. Linee Marittime Partenopee, also known as Gescab, has one to three hydrofoil departures every hour from Sorrento (€16.80, travel time 20 minutes) and one hydrofoil per day from Ischia (in the morning, €18, one hour). ✉ *Capri* ☎ *081/8781430, 081/8071812* 🌐 *www.consorziolmp.it.*

Navigazione Libera Del Golfo. From Naples, Navigazione Libera Del Golfo has roughly one hydrofoil departure per hour from Molo Beverello (€19, travel time 40 minutes). ✉ *Capri* ☎ *081/5520763* 🌐 *www.navlib.it.*

Rent a Scooter. Conveniently located at the traffic hub of the island, Rent a Scooter offers scooters from €25 for two hours (add €5 in August). ✉ *Via Roma 70, Capri Town* ☎ *081/8375863.*

SNAV. SNAV offers one or more hydrofoils every hour from Molo Beverello (€20.10, travel time 40 minutes). ✉ *Capri* ☎ *081/4285555* 🌐 *www.snav.it.*

CRUISE OUTFITTERS

Many outfitters provide boat tours of the island—you can also hire your own speedboat. If time is short, catch a tour on a larger, quicker, and sometimes more fun-packed boat—some operators offer guided tours, with a lively combination of anecdotes (and folk songs!) to accompany you throughout: Proffer a gratuity of a euro or two if you are happy with the trip.

Note: Giro passengers often have to purchase separate tickets (€12.50) to use the rowboats that tour the Blue Grotto. Check when signing up for your giro cruise.

Banana Sport. This popular outfitter offers speedboats starting at €90 for a minimum two-hour rental. A skipper can be requested if you don't wish to navigate. ✉ *Spiaggia Pontile Privato, Capri* ☎ *081/8375188.*

Capri Boats. Those wanting to experience the "Capri moon" over the Faraglioni, nighttime fishing expeditions, and an array of gozzo tours should contact this outfitter. ✉ *Via Largo Fontana 53, Marina Grande, Capri* ☎ *081/19726872* 🌐 *www.capriboats.com.*

Capri Relax Boats. One of the best and most stylish of the outfitters, Capri Relax has a really comprehensive range of tours. The island tour will take you into caves that larger boats can't reach, and their flexibility allows you to decide the itinerary. ✉ *Via Cristoforo Colombo 34, Marina Grande, Capri* ☎ *331/6084109* 🌐 *www.caprirelaxboats.com.*

3

Capri Sea Service. A wide panoply of options are offered, from gozzo tours to specialized diving trips. ✉ *Via Cristoforo Colombo 64, Marina Grande, Capri* ☎ *081/8378781* 🌐 *www.capriseaservice.com.*

Capri Time Boats. This suave operator not only offers island tours but goes beyond to the Amalfi Coast and islands in the bay. ✉ *Via Cristoforo Colombo 34, Marina Grande, Capri* ☎ *329/2149811* 🌐 *www.capritimeboats.com.*

Capri Whales. These tours are virtually living island history, as owner Gennarino Alberino was one of the divers who unearthed the ancient marble statues found in the Blue Grotto. Each of his boats is furnished with freshwater showers and iceboxes. Gennarino's knowledge of the island is encyclopedic, and few others can match it. ✉ *Via Cristoforo Colombo 17, Marina Grande, Capri* ☎ *081/8375833* 🌐 *www.caprinautica.it.*

Laser Capri. For those who want to make a tour on a larger, sturdier sightseeing boat, Laser has a fleet of larger ships that can take up to 100 people. Tickets cost €17 for a full-island tour (add €12.50 for the row boat to the Blue Grotto).Their ticket booth is just past the main funicular station landing. ✉ *Via Cristoforo Colombo 69, Marina Grande, Capri* ☎ *081/8375208* 🌐 *www.lasercapri.com.*

Leomar. Based on the beach at Marina Grande next to the bus stop, Leomar offers hourly and full-day speedboat rentals starting at €35–€45 per hour, six people maximum. They also have a 12-meter yacht at €800 per day. ✉ *Spiaggia Marina Grande, Capri.*

Motoscafisti Capri. With offices right on the dock at Marina Grande, this cooperative of gozzo boat owners offers three set tours that leave on the hour. Admission is €12–€14 depending on choice of tour; maximum number is 10 people per boat. Their "Blue" and "Yellow" tours include the Blue Grotto. ✉ *Via Provinciale 282, Capri* ☎ *081/8377714* 🌐 *www.motoscafisticapri.com.*

ESSENTIALS

Azienda Autonoma di Cura, Soggiorno e Turismo. The tourist office's excellent website has an English-language version. ✉ *Banchina del Porto, Marina Grande* ☎ *081/8370634* 🌐 *www.capritourism.com* ⏲ *Mon.–Sat. 9:30–1:30 and 3:30–45, Sun. 9–3 in high season; Mon.–Sat. 9:30–2:30 in winter* ✉ *Piazza Umberto I, Capri Town* ☎ *081/8370686* ✉ *Via G. Orlandi 59, Anacapri* ☎ *081/8371524.*

CAPRI TOWN AND NEARBY

This fantasy of white-on-white Capriote architecture, flower-filled window boxes, and stylish boutiques rests on a saddle between rugged limestone cliffs to the east and west, where huge herds of *capre* (goats) once roamed, hence the name of the island. Beyond Capri Town lies some of the island's most spectacular sights, including I Faraglioni and the Villa Jovis. As you disembark at the marina quay, note that unlike the other islands in the Bay of Naples, Capri is not of volcanic origin but was formed by marine deposits laid more than 100 million years ago and then uplifted during plate tectonic activity in the Pleistocene era (as recently as 1 to 2 million years ago); Monte Tiberio, to the south of the Marina Grande, and Monte Solaro, to the west, powerfully attest to these upheavals.

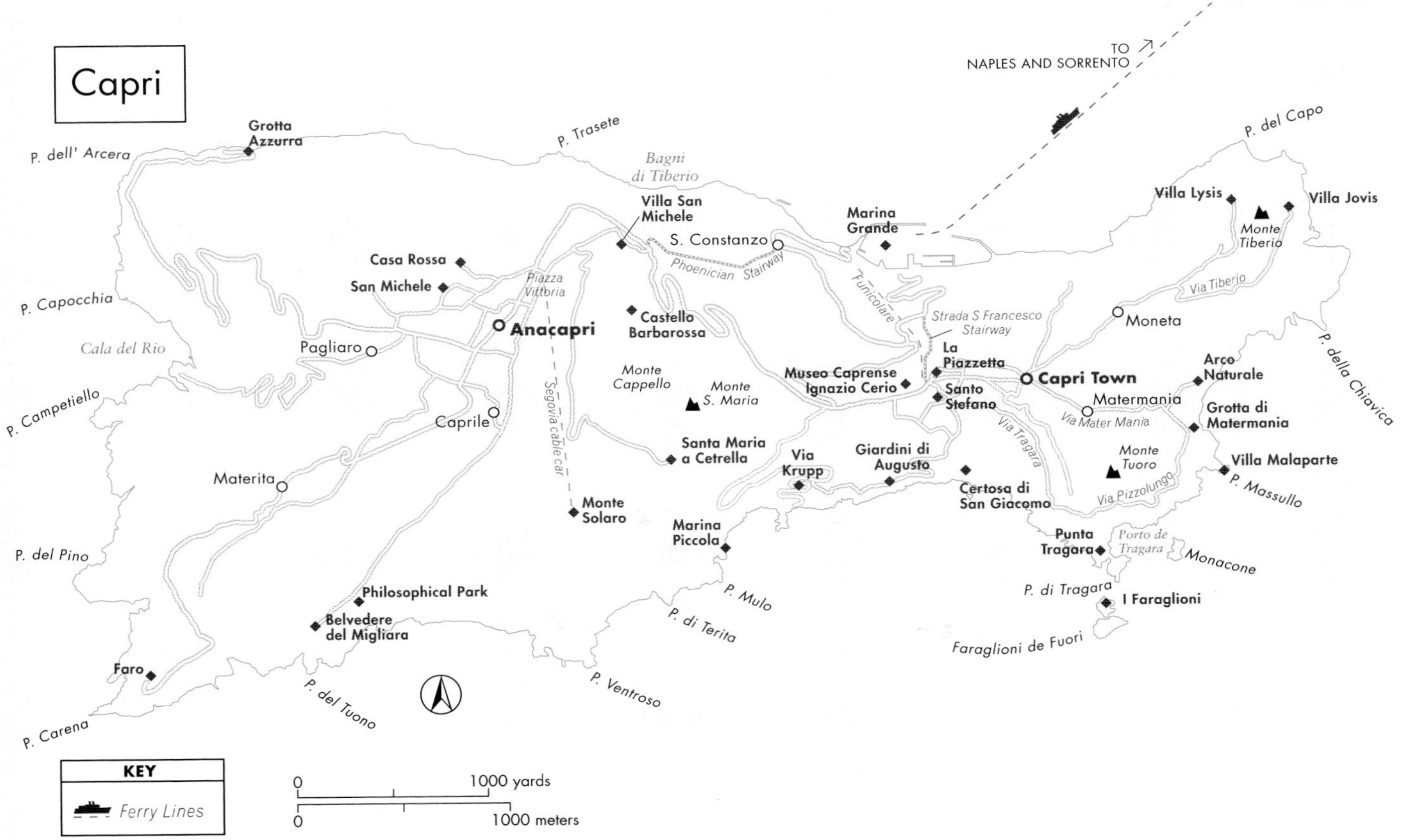
Capri
TO
NAPLES AND SORRENTO
P. dell' Arcera
Grotta Azzurra
P. Trasete
Bagni di Tiberio
P. del Capo
Villa Lysis
Villa Jovis
Monte Tiberio
Villa San Michele
S. Constanzo
Marina Grande
Casa Rossa
San Michele
Piazza Vittoria
Phoenician Stairway
Funicolare
Via Tiberio
P. Capocchia
Anacapri
Castello Barbarossa
Strada S Francesco Stairway
Moneta
Cala del Rio
Pagliaro
La Piazzetta
P. della Chiavica
Monte Cappello
Monte S. Maria
Museo Caprense Ignazio Cerio
Capri Town
Arco Naturale
Santo Stefano
Matermania
P. Campetiello
Caprile
Segovia cable car
Via Mater Mania
Grotta di Matermania
Via Tragara
Santa Maria a Cetrella
Via Krupp
Giardini di Augusto
Monte Tuoro
Villa Malaparte
Materita
Certosa di San Giacomo
Via Pizzolungo
P. Massullo
Monte Solaro
Marina Piccola
Punta Tragara
Porto de Tragara
Monacone
P. del Pino
P. di Tragara
I Faraglioni
Philosophical Park
P. Mulo
Belvedere del Migliara
P. di Terita
Faraglioni de Fuori
Faro
P. del Tuono
P. Ventroso
P. Carena
KEY
Ferry Lines
0
1000 yards
0
1000 meters

GETTING HERE AND AROUND

From the main harbor, Marina Grande, follow the crowds to the main ticket office for the famous funicular, located near where the pier juts out into the harbor. Look for the rounded arcadelike entrance set in the wall of stores and houses. The funicular heads up from the Marina Grande to the main attraction, Capri Town, the island's hub, which lies above in the saddle of the island. Across the way from the funicular office are ticket offices for many boat lines, near the small police station, plus for tickets to take buses up the hill to Capri Town and Anacapri.

EXPLORING

TOP ATTRACTIONS

Arco Naturale (*Natural Arch*). One of Capri's most famous natural wonders, this geologic arch framing Punto Massullo is all that remains of a large limestone cave that has suffered the erosive effects of wind and rain over the millennia. Once a cave that was likely hollowed out by wave action, it broke apart when lifted up to its present position, hundreds of feet above sea level, in relatively recent geological times (about 1–2 million years ago). ✉ *Via Arco Naturale, at the end of Via Matermania.*

Fodor's Choice ★ **Certosa di San Giacomo.** One of the true highlights of historic Capri and a base for the island's arts, this grand, palatial complex is nestled between the Castiglione and Tuoro hills, and was for centuries a Carthusian monastery dedicated to St. James. It was founded between 1371 and 1374, when Queen Giovanna I of Naples gave Count Giacomo Arcucci, her secretary, the land and the means to create it. The count himself then became devoutly religious and retired here until his death. After the monastery was sacked by the pirates Dragut and Barbarossa in the 16th century, it was heavily restored and rebuilt—thanks in part to heavy taxes exacted from the populace. The friars within were detested by many Capresi for refusing to open the gates to minister to the people when plague broke out.

You enter the complex via a grandly imposing entryway, which leads to the Biblioteca Comunale Popolare Luigi Bladier (public library—Capri's only free Internet point) and the spacious church of San Giacomo (built in 1690, reopened after renovations in 2010). After admiring the church's baroque frescoes, follow the signpost down toward the Parco, which leads down an avenue flanked by pittosporum and magnolia toward the magnificent monastery gardens and some welcome benches with stunning views. Take heed of the signs reminding you to watch your step, as the ground is uneven in places. Beyond a covered road lies the Chiostro Grande (Large Cloister)—originally the site of the monks' cells and now the home of a high school; nearby is the 15th-century Chiostro Piccolo (Small Cloister), both often the venues for summertime open-air concerts. The newly reopened (2010) Quarto del Priore hosts art exhibitions from international artists, but the showstopper here is the Museo Diefenbach, comprising a collection of restored large canvases by influential German painter K. W. Diefenbach, who visited Capri in 1900 and stayed until his death in 1913. For years, Diefenbach rivaled the Blue Grotto for sheer picturesqueness—he was given to greeting visitors replete with

CLASSIC CAPRI: A GOOD WALK

Pick up a decent map of Capri (the free one distributed to hotels is better than the €1 one at the information office on the main jetty) and start at Piazza Umberto I, better known locally as **La Piazzetta.** (Rather than taking the funicular up from the harbor area of **Marina Grande,** energetic foot soldiers will opt for the 15-minute climb on a former mule track starting from the small square on the quayside called Largo Fontana.)

Admire the majolica decoration of the clock tower dial and inspect the 17th-century church of **Santo Stefano,** then forge your way across to Via Le Botteghe; if you're thinking about a picnic lunch, you can stock up on provisions here. Take the small Via Madonna delle Grazie behind the fruit stall to see the Chiesa di Sant'Anna, with its restored 14th-century frescoes. The farther away you get from La Piazzetta, the quieter this pedestrianized road becomes. Via Le Botteghe becomes Via Fuorlovado and then Via Croce, developing gradually into an avenue fringed by bougainvillea and spreading oleander trees.

After about 10 minutes, at the Bar Lindos, the road to the Arco Naturale branches off to the right. Follow the ceramic signs for Arco Naturale along Via Matermania for about 15 minutes until the path forks (Arco Naturale, to the left; Grotta di Matermania, to the right).

Art and archaeology buffs (and less fervent hikers) will instead want to continue straight on at the bar and up Monte Tiberio.

A turnoff along the way takes you to the **Villa Lysis,** one of Capri's most legendary private homes, (look for the signpost off Via Tiberio). Return to Via Tiberio and continue onward—the full hike may take 45 minutes up the hill—to reach **Villa Jovis.**

Peer at the **Arco Naturale,** but remember the path is a cul-de-sac, so every step you go down has to be retraced. Then, knee joints permitting, take the hundreds of steps—and we mean hundreds (don't worry, you won't have to backtrack)—down to the **Grotta di Matermania,** an impressive natural cave where ancient Romans worshipped the goddess Cybele every dawn.

The path then levels out for one of the most beautiful seaside walks in the world—the Via Pizzolungo. This path continues south through fine Mediterranean maquis vegetation high above the shoreline, affording fine views of Punta Massullo where **Villa Malaparte** perches over the sea. Farther on is a panoramic point from which you can gaze at **I Faraglioni.**

At the end of the Giro dell'Arco Naturale (Natural Arch Circuit) is the **Punta Tragara,** another panoramic point, which marks your arrival back in Capri Town. From here take Via Tragara, until it joins with Via Camerelle. Look for a left turn down Via Cerio to the **Certosa di San Giacomo**, a former monastery that is Capri's grandest architectural set piece.

Retrace your steps until you get to Via Serena, a mere five-minute walk from the Piazzetta.

The walk will take between three and five hours. You'd be well advised to avoid the stickiest hours—weatherwise—from noon to 3 in summer.

DID YOU KNOW?

I Faraglioni, Capri's landmark rock formation, rises to a height of 350 feet. Plus, the rock farthest from shore, known as the Faraglione di Scopolo, is home to a blue-tinted lizard found nowhere else.

flowing white beard, monk's cowl, and primitive sandals. ✉ *Via Certosa, Capri* ☎ *081/8376218* 🌐 *www.polomusealenapoli.beniculturali.it* 🎫 *€4* 🕑 *Tues.–Sun. 9–2, summer also 5–8.*

Fodor's Choice ★ **I Faraglioni.** Few landscapes set more artists dreaming than that of the famous Faraglioni—three enigmatic, pale-ocher limestone colossi that loom out of the sea just off the Punta Tragara on the southern coast of Capri. Soaring almost 350 feet above the water, the Faraglioni have become for most Italians a beloved symbol of Capri and have been poetically compared to Gothic cathedrals or modern skyscrapers. The first rock is called Faraglione di Terra, since it's attached to the land; at its base is the famous restaurant and bathing lido Da Luigi, where a beach mattress may accompany the luncheon menu. The second is called di Mezzo or Stella, and little boats can often be seen going through its picturesque tunnel, which was caused by sea erosion. The rock farthest out to sea is Scopolo and is inhabited by a wall lizard species with a striking blue belly, considered a local variant by biologists although legend has it that they were originally brought as pets from Greece to delight ancient Roman courtiers. ✉ *End of Via Tragara.*

La Piazzetta. The English writer and Capriophile Norman Douglas called this square, officially known as Piazza Umberto I, "the small theater of the world." The rendezvous point for international crowds, this "*salone*" became famous as the late-night place to spot heavenly bodies—of the Hollywood variety, that is. Frank Sinatra, Rita Hayworth, Julie Christie, Julia Roberts, and Mariah Carey are just a few of the celebs who have made La Piazzetta the place where the rich and famous come to watch other rich and famous folk. These days, if the high flyers bother to make an appearance, they're likely to show up at 8 in the evening for an aperitif and some peppery *tarallucchi* bread sticks, with a possible return visit for a late-night limoncello.

In any event, the square is never less than picturesque and has been a natural crossroads and meeting point since Roman times. The religious complex of Santo Stefano was built around the square in the 17th century, but the clock tower and Municipio, or town hall (once the archbishop's palace) are the only remnants of its cathedral. Capri's version of Big Ben—the charming bell tower, or Torre dell'Orologio—is perched over the ancient gateway. ✉ *At intersection of vias Botteghe, Longano, and Vittorio Emanuele.*

Fodor's Choice ★ **Marina Piccola.** A 10-minute ride from the main bus terminus in Capri (Piazzetta d'Ungheria), Marina Piccola is a delightfully picturesque inlet that provides the Capresi and other sun worshippers with their best access to reasonable beaches and safe swimming. The entire cove is romantically lined with *stabilimenti*—elegant bathing lidos where the striped cabanas are often air-conditioned and the bodies can be Modigliani-sleek. The most famous of these lidos (there's a fee to use the facilities), found closest to the Faraglioni, is **La Canzone del Mare,** once presided over by the noted British music-hall singer Gracie Fields and for decades favored by the smart set, including Noël Coward and Emilio Pucci (who set up his first boutique here). La Canzone del Mare's seaside restaurant offers a dreamy view of the Faraglioni and a luncheon

THE ISLANDS THROUGH THE AGES

In terms of settlements, conquests, and dominion, the history of the islands echoes that of Campania's mainland. For eastern Mediterranean traders in the second and first millennia BC, Capri and Ischia were both close enough to the mainland to provide easy access to trade routes and impervious enough to afford natural protection against invaders.

Ischia, or Pithekoussai, as it used to be called—a word probably derived from the Greek term for a large earthenware jar (*pithos*) rather than the less plausible word, *pithekos,* meaning monkey—is renowned in classical circles as the first colony founded by the Greeks on Italian soil, as early as the 8th century BC.

Capri, probably colonized in the 7th century BC, a century or so later than Ischia, is amply described in the early years of the Roman Empire by authors such as Suetonius and Tacitus, as this was the island where Tiberius spent the last 10 years of his life.

After the breakup of the Roman Empire, the islands, like many other parts of the Mediterranean, suffered a succession of incursions. Saracens, Normans, and Turks all laid siege to the islands at some stage, between periods of relative stability under the Swabians, the Angevins, the Aragonese, and the Spanish.

After a short interregnum under the French at the beginning of the 19th century, a period of relative peace and prosperity ensued. Over the next century, from the opening of its first hotel in 1822, Capri saw an influx of visitors that reads like a who's who of literature and politics, especially in the first decades of the 20th century. Ischia and Procida established themselves as holiday resorts much later, with development taking place from the 1950s onward.

here, although pricey, can serve as an iconic Capri moment. Jutting out into the bay at the center of the marina is the **Scoglio delle Sirene,** or Sirens' Rock—a small natural promontory—which the ancients believed to be the haunt of the Sirens, the mythical temptresses whose song seduced Odysseus in Homer's *Odyssey.* This rock separates the two small beaches: Pennaulo, to the east, and Marina di Mulo, site of the original Roman harbor, to the west. The small church, **Chiesa di Sant'Andrea,** was built in 1900 to give the local fishermen a place of worship. ✉ *Via Marina Piccola.*

Punta Tragara. The "three sons of Capri" can be best seen from the famous lookout point at Punta Tragara at the end of gorgeous Via Tragara. At this point, a path—marked by a plaque honoring the poet Pablo Neruda, who loved this particular walk—leads down hundreds of steps to the water and the feet of I Faraglioni, and perhaps to a delightful lunch at one of the two lidos at the rock base: Da Luigi, a household name in the Bay of Naples, or La Fontelina, an exclusive sun-drenched retreat nearby. After lunch, habitués then hire a little boat to ferry them back to nearby Marina Piccola and the bus back to town. Near the start of the Neruda path turn left to find the most gorgeous seaside walk in Capri—the Via Pizzolungo. Another place to drink in

Villa Jovis was the home of Emperor Tiberius during the final years of his rule over ancient Rome.

the view of I Faraglioni, which is most romantic at sunset, is the Punta Del Cannone, a hilltop belvedere reached beyond the Certosa di San Giacomo and the Giardini di Augusto. ✉ *End of Via Tragara.*

Fodor's Choice ★ **Villa Jovis.** Named in honor of the ancient Roman god Jupiter, or Jove, the villa of the emperor Tiberius is riveted to the towering Rocca di Capri like an eagle's nest overlooking the strait separating Capri from Punta Campanella, the tip of the Sorrentine peninsula. Lying near the easternmost point of the island, Villa Jovis is a powerful reminder of the importance of the island in Roman times. What makes the site even more compelling are the accounts of the latter years of Tiberius's reign from Capri, between AD 27 and 37, written by authors and near-contemporaries Suetonius and Tacitus. This villa was famous for its sybaritic living, thus sounding a leitmotif whose echo can be heard at the luxurious hotels of today.

There are remarkably few discrepancies between the accounts of the two historiographers. Both point to Tiberius's mounting paranoia in Rome, while Tacitus outlines his reason for choosing Capreae (Annals, Book IV). "Presumably what attracted him was the isolation of Capreae. Harborless, it has few roadsteads even for small vessels; sentries can control all landings. In winter the climate is mild, since hills on the mainland keep off gales. In summer the island is delightful, since it faces west and has open sea all round. The bay it overlooks was exceptionally lovely, until Vesuvius's eruption transformed the landscape." Capri in Roman times was the site of 12 spacious villas, but Villa Jovis is both the best preserved and must have been the largest, occupying nearly 23,000 square feet.

The entrance to the site lies just beyond the *pharos* (lighthouse) built under Tiberius and used until the 17th century to warn ships away from the narrows between Capri and the mainland. Pick up a site map at the ticket office, which gives a useful breakdown of the various areas of the villa to be visited. Nearby, you can find the Salto di Tiberio (Tiberius's Leap), the place where ancient gossips believed Tiberius had enemies, among them his discarded lovers and even unfortunate cooks, hurled over the precipice into the sea some 1,000 feet below. After taking stock of this now-harmless viewing platform and its information panels, take the upper path past the baths complex around the palace residential quarters to view the heavily restored Chapel of Santa Maria del Soccorso and its large bronze statue of the Madonna, a gift to the island from the Caprese painter Guido Odierna in 1979. The walk around the perimeter of the site gives an idea of the overall layout of the palatial residence, which in places rose to five stories in height. From here descend some steps and then a ramp to the *ambulatio* (walkway), which offers additional spectacular views and plenty of shade, as well as a *triclinium* (dining room) halfway along. The center of the site is a complex devoted to cisterns. Unlike in Pompeii, there was no aqueduct up here to provide fresh running water, so the cisterns next to the bath complex were of prime importance. From La Piazzetta allow 45 minutes each way for the walk alone. ✉ *Via A. Maiuri, Capri* ☎ *081/8374549* 🎫 *€2* ⏲ *Daily 9–1; closed 1st two Tues. and last two Sun. of month.*

Fodor's Choice ★ **Villa Lysis.** Opened to the public in 2003, this legendary domain looms large in Capri's consciousness. The island's Xanadu, Manderlay, and San Simeon, it was originally known as the Villa Fersen, after Baron Jacques d'Adelsward-Fersen, the builder. Fleeing to the island from a scandal involving Parisian schoolboys, the French aristocrat had this white-stucco pile designed by Edouard Chimot in 1903 in shimmering Belle Epoque style, replete with gilded-mosaic columns and floors looted from the island's ancient Roman sites. Past the impressive columned entrance, inscribed in stone with "Amori et Dolori Sacrum" (A Shrine to Love and Sorrow), the baron would retire to write poems and paint pictures in his Liberty Style (art nouveau) salons. Sadly all the furnishings are gone, but you can still gasp at the ballroom open to the sea and the large smoking room in the basement, where, in a titled pool, Fersen committed suicide by ingesting a lethal mix of opium and champagne in 1923. Outside are magical terraces with views to rival the adjacent Villa Jovis. ✉ *Via Lo Capo* ☎ *081/8386111 Capri municipal office* 🎫 *Free* ⏲ *Apr.–mid-Oct., Tues.–Sun. 10–6.*

WORTH NOTING

Giardini di Augusto (*Gardens of Augustus*). From the terraces of this beautiful public garden, you can see the village of Marina Piccola below—restaurants, cabanas, and swimming platforms huddle among the shoals—and admire the steep, winding Via Krupp, actually a staircase cut into the rock. Friedrich Krupp, the German arms manufacturer, loved Capri and became one of the island's most generous benefactors. If you find the path too challenging you can reach the beach by taking a bus from the Via Roma terminus down to Marina Piccola. ✉ *Via Matteotti, beyond monastery of San Giacomo, Capri* 🎫 *€1* ⏲ *Summer daily 9–7:30, winter daily 9–5:30.*

DID YOU KNOW?

After being off limits for 32 years, winding Via Krupp was reopened in 2008, complete with a plaque unveiled by Italian president Giorgio Napolitano proclaiming the road a symbol of liberty and an homage to beauty.

Grotta di Matermania. Set in the bowels of Monte Tuoro, this legend-haunted cave was dedicated to Cybele, the Magna Mater, or Great Mother of the gods—hence the somewhat corrupted name of the cave. A goddess with definite Eastern origins, Cybele did not form part of the Greek or Roman pantheon: worship of her was introduced to Italy in 204 BC at the command of the Sibylline oracle, supposedly for the purpose of driving Hannibal out of Italy. At dawn the cave is touched by the rays of the sun, leading scholars to believe it may also have been a shrine where the Mithraic mysteries were celebrated. Hypnotic rituals, ritual sacrifice of bulls, and other orgiastic practices made this cave a place of myth, so it's not surprising that later authors reported (erroneously) that Emperor Tiberius used it for orgies. Nevertheless, the cave was adapted by the Romans into a luxurious *nymphaeum* (small shrine), but little remains of the original structure, which would have been covered by tesserae, polychrome stucco, and marine shells. If you want to see the few ancient remains, you have to step inside the now-unprepossessing cavern. ⊠ *Giro del'Arco Naturale.*

Marina Grande. Besides being the main harbor gateway to Capri and the main disembarkation point for the mainland, Marina Grande is usually the starting point for round-island tours and trips to the Blue Grotto. The marina has faded in the glare of neon since the days when it was Sophia Loren's home in the 1958 film *It Started in Naples.* Originally a conglomeration of fishermen's houses built on ancient Roman foundations, it's now an extended hodgepodge of various architectural styles, with buildings that almost exclusively service the tourist industry. Warehouses and storerooms in which fishermen once kept their boats and tackle are now shops, restaurants, and bars, most either tacky or overpriced. To the west, however, lie three sights worth exploring: the historic 17th-century church of **San Costanzo,** the ruins of the **Palazzo a Mare** (the former palace of emperor Augustus), and the chic **Baths of Tiberius beach.** ⊠ *Marina Grande.*

Museo Caprense Ignazio Cerio. Former mayor of Capri Town, designer of the island's most ravishing turn-of-the-20th-century villas, author of delightfully arcane books, and even paleontologist par excellence, Edwin Cerio was Capri's leading genius and eccentric. His most notorious work was a Capri guidebook that all but urged tourists to stay away. His most beautiful work was the Villa Solitaria—once home to famed novelist Compton Mackenzie and set over the sea on the Via Pizzo Lungo path. He also set up this small but interesting museum, which conserves finds from the island. Room 1 displays Pleistocene fossils of pygmy elephant, rhino, and hippopotamus, which all grazed here 200,000–300,000 years ago, when the climate and terrain were very different. Although most of the important archaeological finds—such as the statues found in the Blue Grotto—have been shipped off to Naples, Room 4 displays the leftovers, a scantily labeled collection of vases, mosaics, and stuccowork from the Greek and Roman periods. ⊠ *Piazzetta Cerio 5* ☎ *081/8376681* 🖷 *081/8370858* 🌐 *www.centrocaprense.org* 🎟 *€2.50, guided tours by appointment €15.50* ⏲ *Tues.–Sat. 10–1.*

CLOSE UP

Active Capri

Unsurprisingly, these islands are a haven for fans of water sports. Apart from the ample opportunities for swimming in crystal clear water (but if it's sandy beaches you want, avoid Capri), all three islands have long-established scuba-diving centers (although the prices on Capri are exorbitant). Windsurfers should head to Ischia, while Procida is the ideal place to rent a yacht for short or long trips. Boat and canoe rental is available on all three islands. You might prefer, however, to just avail yourself of the thermal baths for which Ischia is renowned.

With their high peaks, both Capri and Ischia offer spectacular trekking opportunities. Ischia's Monte Epomeo, at 2,582 feet, is somewhat more challenging than the 1,932 feet of Monte Solaro in Capri, especially as on the latter you can choose to use the chairlift for one leg (if not both) of the trip.

The path from Capri Town to the Faraglioni is one of the most beautiful seaside walks in the world, although a strong competitor is the five-hour trek past four Napoleonic towers on the island's west coast.

Santo Stefano. Towering over La Piazzetta, with a dome that is more sculpted than constructed and with *cupolettas* that seem molded from frozen zabaglione, Capri's mother church is a prime example of *l'architettura barocchеggiante*—the term historians use to describe Capri's fanciful form of baroque architecture. Often using vaulting and molded buttresses (because there was little wood to be found on such a scrubby island to support the ceilings), Capri's architects became sculptors when they adapted Moorish and Grecian styles into their own "homemade" architecture. Sometimes known unglamorously as the ex-cathedral, the church was built in 1685 by Marziale Desiderio of Amalfi on the site of a Benedictine convent (founded in the 6th century), whose sole relic is the clock tower campanile across the Piazzetta. As in so many churches in southern Italy, there has been a good deal of recycling of ancient building materials: the flooring of the high altar was laid with polychrome marble from Villa Jovis, while the marble in the Cappella del Sacramento was removed from the Roman villa of Tragara. Inside the sacristy are some of the church treasures, including an 18th-century large silver bust of San Costanzo, the patron saint of Capri, whose holy day is celebrated every May 14. Opposite the church on the tiny Piazzetta I. Cerio are the Palazzo Cerio Arcucci, with its Museo Caprense Ignazio Cerio; the Palazzo Farace, which houses the Biblioteca Caprense I. Cerio (I. Cerio Library); and the Palazzo Vanalesti, the executive offices of the Capri tourist board. ✉ *Piazza Umberto I* ☎ *081/8370072* ⏲ *Daily 7–1, 5–end of evening service.*

Villa Malaparte. Nicknamed the *Casa Come Me* (House Like Myself) and perched out on the rocky Punta Massullo, this villa is considered by some historians to be a great monument of 20th-century architecture. Built low to be part of the ageless landscape, the red-hue villa was designed in Rationalist style by the Roman architect Adalberto

Libera in the late 1930s for its owner Curzio Malaparte (author of the novel *La Pelle,* which recounts various World War II experiences in Naples). Unfortunately, the aesthetic concerns of the villa are inextricably entailed with political ones: Curzio Malaparte was a full-blown Fascist, and the only reason why this house was allowed to be built along this otherwise unsullied stretch of coast was by special fiat from none other than Mussolini. Malaparte was unhappy with the design and made a number of alterations during the construction phase, including the famous trapezoidal staircase that seems to grow out of the roof. The villa is private, but if you want to see it up close, it was featured as a suitably striking backdrop for Brigitte Bardot in Jean-Luc Godard's underrated film *Contempt* (1963). ✉ *Giro dell'Arco Naturale.*

ANACAPRI AND NEARBY

One of the most breathtaking bus rides anywhere follows the tortuous road from Capri Town 3 km (2 miles) up a dramatic escarpment to Anacapri. At 902 feet over the bay, Anacapri is the island's only other town and leading settlement on the island's peaks, poetically referred to as the Monte Sirene (Siren Heights). Crowds are thickest around the square, which is the starting point of the chairlift to the top of Monte Solaro and close to Villa San Michele, the main magnet up here for tour groups. Allow plenty of time when traveling to or from Anacapri, as space on the local buses is usually at a premium. Alternatively, the athletically inclined can hike from close to Marina Grande up to Anacapri by taking the 921 steps of the Scala Fenicia (the Phoenician Stairway, more likely to have been built by the Greeks than the Phoenicians) to Villa San Michele. Needless to say, most people will want to tackle the Scala Fenica going down, not up. As a fitting finale to a visit to Anacapri, take the convenient bus down the hill to the water's edge and the fabled Blue Grotto.

GETTING HERE

There's regular bus service to Anacapri from Marina Grande or Capri Town (Piazzetta d'Ungheria).

EXPLORING

TOP ATTRACTIONS

Fodor's Choice ★ **Casa Rossa** (*Red House*). Capri is famous for its villas built by artists, millionaires, and poets who became willing prisoners of Capri during the Gilded Age. Elihu Vedder, Charles Coleman, Lord Algernon, and the Misses Wolcott-Perry were some of the people who constructed lavish Aesthetic Movement houses. Built by the American colonel J. C. MacKowen, this particular villa, near the center of Anacapri, was erected between 1876 and 1899. With walls hued in distinctive Pompeian red, the villa incorporates a noted 15th-century Aragonese tower. A historian and archaeologist, MacKowen wrote a guide to Capri and brought to light marble fragments and statues inside the Blue Grotto, thus revealing and validating its importance as a nymphaeum in Roman times. Local legend says that Anacapri's menfolk locked their women in Casa Rossa when they went to work in Naples, but the villa now houses a permanent exhibition called "The Painted Island," featuring 32 canvases from masters such as Brancaccio and Carelli, depicting images of Capri in the 19th and 20th centuries.

Continued on page 118

CAPRI BY BOAT

To savor Capri to the fullest you must sail its blue waters as well as wander through its squares and gardens. Happily, the famous "giro" cruises around the island allow you to enjoy the perfect sailing safari.

Sooner or later, the beautiful coastline of Capri will lure you to its shores, where you'll be in good company: ancient heroes, emperors, Hollywood divas, and legions of mere mortals have been answering the same siren call from time immemorial. Fact is, you haven't fully experienced Capri until you've explored its rocky shoreline, a veritable Swiss cheese of mysterious grottoes tucked into its myriad inlets and bays. As you'll learn, the Blue Grotto may be world famous, but there's also a Green Grotto, a Yellow Grotto, a Pink, and a White. And unless you possess fins, the only way to penetrate many of these secret recesses is to book yourself on one of the island's giro (tour) cruises—they have been an iconic Caprese experience since the 19th century. Offered by a flotilla of companies ranging from bare-bones to high luxe, these roundabout tours—many last only two hours but you can also sign on for daylong cruises—give you the chance to travel the island's "highway," marvel at sights immortalized in 1,001 travel posters, and, for one magical afternoon, take possession of one of the horseshoe-shape inlets where movie stars are as much at home as dolphins.

above, Capri's iconic Faraglioni rock formation

A "GIRO" TOUR AROUND CAPRI

An aquatic version of the famous Italian *passeggiata* (stroll), the Capri giro cruise is offered on two main types of boat. The classic craft is a *gozzo*—once the traditional fishing boat of the Bay of Naples, it now varies in comfort from luxe (shower, lunch, aperitif) to basic (BYO *panino*). Or opt for a *gommone*, a speedboat: this gives you a chance to create your own itinerary—but watch out for gas prices. Coastal highlights are outlined below, but you can always opt to follow your instincts, take an inviting side lagoon, and Robinson Crusoe the day away in one of the innumerable small inlets.

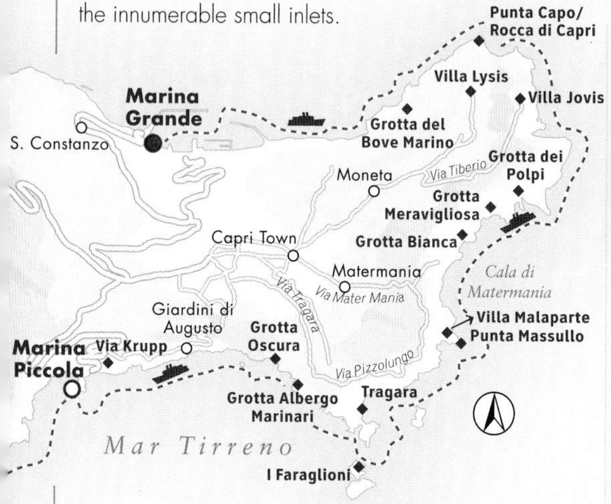

Grotta Bianca

STARTING YOUR ROUNDS

Capri's gateway harbor, the **Marina Grande**, is where most giro cruises start. Time, budget, weather, and confidence will determine your choice of tour—long or short, cheap or ritzy, guided or independent—but the more extensive ones should cover the following sites. East of the marina lies the **Grotta del Bove Marino** (Sea Lion's Cave). Listen for the distinctly mammalian howl, amplified naturally by the cave walls: local fishermen may tell you the creature is still in residence, but what you're hearing is the wail of the wind and sea. You soon reach **Punta Capo**, marked by its welcoming statue of the Madonna del Soccorso. Here, atop the **Rocca di Capri**—Capri's own Gibraltar—catch a glimpse of the **Villa Lysis**, a 19th-century Xanadu that clings like a wasps' nest to the cliff and, perched atop the looming peak, the ruins of Emperor Tiberius's fabled **Villa Jovis**.

Villa Jovis

SEA FOR YOURSELF

Rounding Capri's eastern coast you arrive at the **Grotta dei Polpi**, originally named for its abundance of octopus and cuttlefish; recently fished dry, it is now called the Coral Cave. Past a gorge, you'll arrive at **Grotta Meravigliosa**—the "cave of marvels," as its innumerable stalagmites and stalactites prove (look, as most people do, for one that is said to resemble the Madonna). You'll need a sweater and even a scarf in here—it's glacial even in peak summer.

Farther along is the **Grotta Bianca** (White Grotto), whose opal waters—their

Marina Grande

color is due to the mix of seawater and deep-spring water—shimmer against a spectacularly jagged white backdrop; past the entrance a large crevice has produced a natural swimming pool, known as the Piscina di Venere (Pool of Venus). Entering the **Cala di Matermania**, spot the distant square-shaped sea rock known as Il Monacone, once home to a hermit-monk who kept a net hanging off its side (woe betide any fisherman who did not throw in some fish!). Astride the promontory of **Punta Massullo** is that modernist eyeknocker, the red-hued **Villa Malaparte**.

Past the ancient Roman port of **Tragara** lies the famed **Faraglioni**, the earthen powerhouse of three massive rocks rising from the sea that remain the scenic masterpiece of Capri. The "Faraglione di Terra" is linked to land and nestles two famous lido restaurants, Da Luigi and La Fontelina. The next rock monolith out is the "Faraglione di Mezzo" (Middle)—this one has the tunnel that is so much fun to sail through—while the farthest one out is the Scopolo, or "Faraglione di Fuori" (External). If you have an expert guide ask him to take you into the little blue grotto—a small cave illuminated by an underwater window of aquamarine light—tucked behind the Faraglioni.

Faraglioni

Villa Malaparte

Cala di Matermania

WATER COLORS

Farther on sits the **Grotta Albergo Marinari**. Despite its name, there is no hotel here; the cave was used by sailors as shelter from sudden sea storms. Next lies the **Grotta Oscura**, whose deceptively narrow entrance opens up to reveal the largest cave on the island, its two large oval caverns a showplace of stunning light reflections. Drifting up the southern coast of Capri, the zigzagging drama of **Via Krupp** threads its way over the hillside to chic **Marina Piccola**. It was here on the Scoglie delle Sirene (Siren's Rock), immortalized in Canto XII of the *Odyssey*, that mermaids tried to lure Odysseus, the world's first tourist, onto its hazardous shoals.

Faro

Just after **Punta Ventroso** look for the Cala di San Costanzo, where a "face" in the rock presumably resembles St. Costanzo, the patron saint of Capri. A few hundred meters farther on is the **Grotta Verde** (Green Grotto), whose waters resemble an enormous deep-sea daiquiri, and which in turn is followed by the **Grotta Rossa**, whose red hue is caused by algae buildup. A little way beyond

Marina Piccola

is the **Grotta dei Santi** (Saints' Cave), whose rocky outcrop resembles human figures at prayer. Take some time to enjoy the truly stunning waters of **Cala Marmolata**, which you'll sail through before coming to the lighthouse, or **Faro**. Sail the length of the west coast to the cape landmarked by the Torre Damecuta. From the Gradola shore you will find your spectacular finale, the **Grotta Azzurra** (Blue Grotto).

MAKING THE MOST OF THE GROTTA AZZURA

Today, many travelers visit Capri's fabled Grotta Azzurra (Blue Grotta) using tour boats departing either from Capri's Marina Grande or from the small embarkation point below Anacapri (reached by bus from Anacapri Town). This approach can prove frustrating: you have to board one boat to get to the grotto, then transfer to a smaller one to pass through the 3-foot-high cave opening, and then are allowed—due to the midday traffic jam of boats—disappointingly little time once inside the cave. Instead, in late afternoon—not midday—take the bus from Anacapri's Piazza Vittoria to the Strada della Grotta Azzurra. Interested in protecting the early-afternoon hours for their traditional siesta, many native Capresi insist that the optimum time to see the unearthly blue is between 10 AM and 1 PM. However, more objective observers advise that the best time is around 4 PM or 5 PM, when the raking light of the sun is most brilliant. At this hour, many—though not all—of the boatmen have departed along with the tour buses, so you may have the Blue Grotto pretty much to yourself.

- €26 from Marina Grande, €12.50 by rowboat from Grotta Azzurra
- 9–1 hr before sunset, closed if sea is even minimally rough

Grotta Azzurra

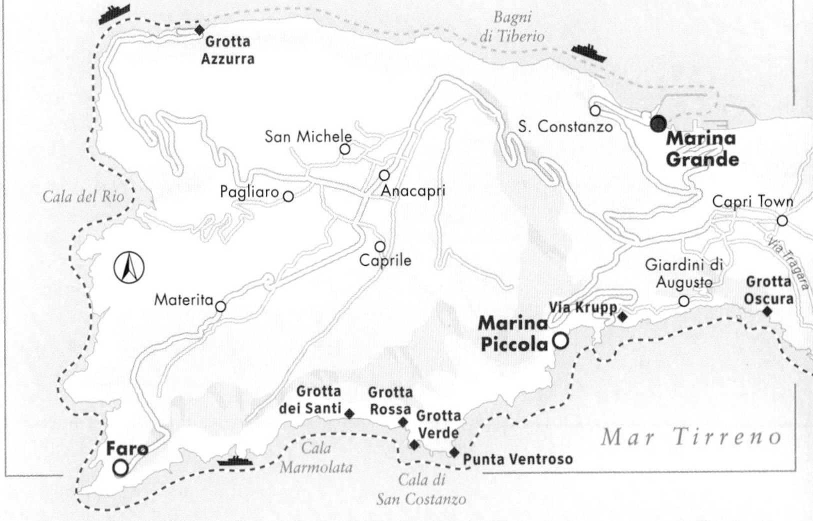

Don't miss the views from the highest roof terrace in central Anacapri, taking in Monte Solaro and Ischia. ✉ *Via G. Orlandi* ☎ *081/8382193* 🎫 *€2* ⏲ *May–Sept., Tues.–Sun. 10:30–1:30 and 6:30–9.*

Fodor's Choice ★ **Grotta Azzurra.** Only when the Grotta Azzurra was "discovered" in 1826 by the Polish poet August Kopisch and Swiss artist Ernest Fries, did Capri become a tourist haven. The watery cave's blue beauty became a symbol of the return to nature and revolt from reason that marked the Romantic era, and it soon became a required stop on the Grand Tour. In reality, the grotto had long been a local landmark. During the Roman era—as testified by the extensive remains, primarily below sea level, and several large statues now at the Certosa di San Giacomo—it had been the elegant, mosaic-decorated nymphaeum of the adjoining villa of Gradola. Historians can't quite agree if it was simply a lovely little pavilion where rich patricians would cool themselves or truly a religious site where sacred mysteries were practiced. The water's extraordinary sapphire color is caused by a hidden opening in the rock that refracts the light. At highest illumination the very air inside seems tinted blue.

The Grotta Azzurra can be reached from Marina Grande or from the small embarkation point below Anacapri on the northwest side of the island, accessible by bus from Anacapri. If you're pressed for time, however, skip this sometimes frustrating and disappointing excursion. You board one boat to get to the grotto, then transfer to a smaller boat that takes you inside. If there's a backup of boats waiting to get in, you'll be given precious little time to enjoy the gorgeous color of the water and its silvery reflections. ✉ *Capri* 🎫 *€26 from Marina Grande, €12.50 by rowboat from Grotta Azzurra near Anacapri* ⏲ *9–1 hr before sunset; closed if sea is even minimally rough.*

Monte Solaro. An impressive limestone formation and the highest point on Capri (1,932 feet), Monte Solaro affords gasp-inducing views toward the bays of both Naples and Salerno. A 12-minute chairlift ride will take you right to the top (refreshments available at the bar), where you can launch out on a number of scenic trails on the western side of the island. Picnickers should note that even in summer it can get windy at this height, and there are few trees to provide shade or refuge. ✉ *Piazza Vittoria* ☎ *081/8371428* 🎫 *€7.50 one-way, €10 round-trip* ⏲ *Daily 9:30–5. Closed Jan. 7–Feb. 7 and in adverse weather conditions.*

Fodor's Choice ★ **Santa Maria a Cetrella.** Scenically perched on the slopes of Monte Solaro, this small sanctuary in late-Gothic style—with its older parts dating to the late 14th century—offers a truly picturesque frame for a panorama that takes in much of the island. It also marks the top of the second access route (Il Passetiello) used in ancient times, which linked Capri Town with Anacapri. Steep, slippery, and in spots still dangerous, this is the pathway that the Carthusian monks of San Giacomo would have used to reach their properties in the upper part of the island. Congregants were mainly fisherfolk whose boats were moored in the Marina Piccola directly below; they also used this cliff-top aerie as a lookout against Saracen pirates. The church was substantially rebuilt

AROUND ANACAPRI: A GOOD WALK

From Anacapri's main square of Piazza Vittoria, take Via Capodimonte opposite the *Seggiovia* (chairlift) to **Villa San Michele,** about a five-minute walk, past a formidable array of garish boutiques, bars, and liqueur factories, all vying to ensnare passersby.

As with many sites on the island, it's best to get to the villa shortly after it opens, or in the early evening when the day-trippers have moved through.

After browsing through its rooms and strolling through the gardens and the ecomuseum, retrace your steps to Piazza Vittoria and make for the lower station of the Seggiovia to **Monte Solaro.** You'll soon be whisked out of town over whitewashed houses and carpets of spring-flowering broom and rockrose to the viewing platform at the top of Solaro.

From here a path leads north downhill toward the sublimely picturesque church of **Santa Maria a Cetrella** through some of the most beautiful wooded countryside on Capri.

In spring and autumn watch for migrating birds. A splash of yellow combined with an undulating flight could be the golden oriole; the multicolor bee-eater also migrates via Capri in May and September.

On the way back down from Cetrella, follow the signs to Anacapri along Via Monte Solaro (downhill), passing close to the ruins of the **Castello Barbarossa** and then emerging close to the Villa San Michele.

If you have time and energy left over, make for Via Orlandi, a useful street for stocking up on provisions.

Pass the impressive **Casa Rossa** (Red House), on your right, and then take the next right turn (Via San Nicola) to Piazza San Nicola and the church of **San Michele.** Climb to the organ loft to savor its magnificent majolica-tile floor depicting the Garden of Eden, then head back to the Piazza Vittoria.

At this point choose between the Belvedere di Migliara and the Grotta Azzurra. A 40-minute walk to **Belvedere di Migliara** is rewarded with an iconic view as well as the world's first **Philosophical Park.** By mid- to late afternoon, the crowds will have vanished from the **Grotta Azzurra** (Blue Grotto), at the sea below Anacapri.

Catch the convenient bus that links the town with the grotto and enjoy this fabled sight around 4 pm or 5 pm, when connoisseurs swear that the light is best.

TIMING

The walk takes approximately four hours, allowing at least one hour for the visit to Villa San Michele and its gardens, and a further two hours' leisurely amble on the round-trip. Add a half hour if visiting the Belvedere di Migliara, as it is off the beaten track.

If armed with a packed lunch, you're most likely to find a picnic site near Cetrella—in attempts to discourage low-spending day-trippers from the mainland, consumption of picnics is made fairly difficult on Capri.

by Franciscan monks in the early 17th century, when a sacristy was added. To reach Santa Maria, you can climb a path leading off Viale Axel Munthe (an hour-long walk); an alternative is to descend a path leading from the Monte Solaro chairlift. The church has erratic opening times; ask at the chairlift for further information. Mass is celebrated at dawn every Sunday in September, but the site remains unforgettable year-round. ✉ *Monte Solaro.*

Fodor's Choice ★ **Villa San Michele.** From Anacapri's Piazza Vittoria, picturesque Via Capodimonte leads to Villa San Michele, the charming former home of Swedish doctor and philanthropist Axel Munthe (1857–1949) that Henry James called "the most fantastic beauty, poetry, and inutility that one had ever seen clustered together." At the ancient entranceway to Anacapri at the top of the Scala Fenicia, the villa is set around Roman-style courtyards, marble walkways, and atria. Rooms display the doctor's varied collections, which range from bric-a-brac to antiquities. Medieval choir stalls, Renaissance lecterns, and gilded statues of saints are all part of the setting, with some rooms preserving the doctor's personal memorabilia. A spectacular pergola path overlooking the entire Bay of Naples leads from the villa to the famous Sphinx Parapet, where an ancient Egyptian sphinx looks out toward Sorrento: you cannot see its face—on purpose. It is said that if you touch the sphinx's hindquarters with your left hand while making a wish, it will come true. The parapet is connected to the little Chapel of San Michele, on the grounds of one of Tiberius's villas.

Besides hosting summer concerts, the Axel Munthe Foundation has an ecomuseum that fittingly reflects Munthe's fondness for animals. Here you can learn about various bird species—accompanied by their songs—found on Capri. Munthe bought up the hillside and made it a sanctuary for birds, and today this little realm is still an Eden. ✉ *Viale Axel Munthe 34* ☎ *081/8371401* 🌐 *www.villasanmichele.eu* 🎫 *€7* 🕓 *Nov.–Feb., daily 9–3:30; Mar., daily 9–4:30; Apr. and Oct., daily 9–5; May–Sept., daily 9–6.*

WORTH NOTING

Castello Barbarossa. The foundation of this ruined castle, almost clinging to the side of the cliff above Villa San Michele, dates to the late 10th century, when Capri was ruled by the ancient maritime republic of Amalfi. Named after the admiral of the Turkish fleet, Khair-Eddin, or Barbarossa (Redbeard), who stormed and took the castle in 1535, much of the original layout has been changed over the centuries. The castle is part of the Swedish-run Axel Munthe Foundation, which organizes weekly, guided visits on Thursday afternoons from May to October (call the foundation to reserve a place) besides carrying out ornithological research in the surrounding area. ✉ *Axel Munthe Foundation* ☎ *081/8371401* 🌐 *www.villasanmichele.eu* 🎫 *Free.*

Fodor's Choice ★ **Philosophical Park.** Frustrated by Capri's ongoing commercial overdevelopment, Swedish professor Gunnar Adler-Karlsson acquired the land around the Belvedere Migliara with the intention of maintaining an ecologically pure area. Covering 11,000 square meters (36,000 square feet), paths lead through rich Mediterranean maquis with over sixty

A chairlift makes ascending Monte Solaro a breeze.

ceramic panels lining the way with quotes from great thinkers from Aristotle to Einstein. Allegedly the first of its kind in the world, just feet away from one of the most gorgeous views in the world, this park is devoted to peace and reflection. A complete guide, called "Meditation Upon Western Wisdom," hangs from the trees (and is also available free from the adjacent Da Gelsomino restaurant). ✉ *Via Migliara* 🌐 *www.philosophicalpark.org* 🎫 *Free.*

San Michele. In the heart of Anacapri, the octagonal baroque church of San Michele, finished in 1719, is best known for its exquisite majolica pavement designed by Solimena and executed by the *maestro-riggiolaro* (master tiler) Chiaiese from Abruzzo. A walkway skirts the depiction of Adam and a duly contrite Eve being expelled from the Garden of Eden, but you can get a fine overview from the organ loft, reached by a winding staircase near the ticket booth (a privileged perch you have to pay for). ✉ *Piazza San Nicola* ☎ *081/8372396* 🌐 *www.chiesa-san-michele.com* 🎫 *€2* 🕒 *Apr.–Oct., daily 9–6.45; Nov and Mar., daily 10–2.*

WHERE TO EAT

IN AND AROUND CAPRI TOWN

$$ SOUTHERN ITALIAN

✕ **Al Grottino.** This small and friendly family-run restaurant, which is in a 14th-century building handy to the Piazzetta, has arched ceilings and lots of atmosphere; autographed photos of famous customers cover the walls. House specialties are *scialatielli ai fiori di zucchine e gambaretti* (homemade pasta with zucchini flowers and shrimps) and linguine *ai scampi*, but the owner delights in taking his guests through the menu of regional dishes. $ *Average main: €16* ✉ *Via Longano 27, Capri Town* ☎ *081/8370584* 🌐 *www.ristorantealgrottino.net* 🕒 *Closed Nov.–mid-Mar.*

$$$ SOUTHERN ITALIAN

Aurora. Though often frequented by celebrities—whose photographs adorn the walls inside and out—this restaurant offers courtesy and *simpatia* irrespective of your star status. The oldest restaurant on the island, now in its third generation, it has a sleekly minimalist interior, but if you want to see and be seen, book a table outside on one of Capri's chicest thoroughfares. The cognoscenti start by sharing a pizza *all'Acqua*: thin, with mozzarella and a sprinkling of *peperoncino* (chili). Also try the *gnocchetti al pesto con fagiolini croccanti e pinoli* (dumplings with pesto, beans, and pine nuts)—but leave room for the homemade sweets. Often open until 2 am, the newly opened Aurora Bar across the way serves *aperitivi* and light meals. *Average main: €25 Via Fuorlovado 18/22, Capri Town 081/8370181 www.auroracapri.com Closed Jan.–mid-Mar.*

$$ SOUTHERN ITALIAN

Capri's. With an unrivaled view over the bay, this sleek restaurant is just feet away from the Piazzetta. Since it is on one of the island's most congested streets, you'll find passersby often gathering to watch the sushi chef preparing *Capri crudo* (raw Capri) in one window or to study the gallery of celebrity diners in another— Kanye West got engaged here. Result: Groups of "street traffic" do come in for a quick bite. You can't blame them: Across the threshold two all-window, no-wall dining terraces (one uncovered in good weather) afford spectacular vistas across to Procida and Ischia—the only restaurant on the island that can boast this. But the food here deserves hours to savor such treats as the Mediterranean sushi or *scialatielli con aragosta* (homemade pasta with lobster) or *paccheri al coccio* (pasta with shellfish). Open all year, the owner also runs the whitewashed Capricorno restaurant on Via Longano. *Average main: €20 Via Roma 38, Capri Town 081/8377108 www.capris.it Open all year.*

$$$ SOUTHERN ITALIAN

Edode. When you've had enough of florid, flowery Caprese decor, head here to this sleek entry among the island's restaurants. The name may come from the ancient Greek for food, the seats may have been imported from Austria, the peach-on-white columns hail from Paris, but the ambience conjures up New York's hot–cool Meatpacking district. From the menu, you can't go wrong with the fresh fish, the specialty being *paccheri con gamberi e crema di zucchini* (large pasta with shrimp and cream of zucchini). The wine list has more than 700 choices from all over the world. Enjoy a fine bottle and settle in for some nice people-watching. *Average main: €30 Via Camerelle 81/83, Capri Town 081/8388252 www.edodecapri.com Closed mid-Oct.–Mar.*

$$ SOUTHERN ITALIAN

Il Geranio. Take the steps up to the right just before the Giardini di Augusto to find this romantic spot, where outdoor seating is staggered on the layered terraces, commanding a fine view of the Faraglioni. The menu depends on the season, but combines the best of local and international cooking, specializing in both meat and seafood dishes. Try the *scialatielli con vongole e funghi porcini* (clams and porcini mushrooms). *Average main: €16 Via Matteotti 8, Capri Town 081/8370616 www.geraniocapri.com Closed mid-Oct.–Mar.*

DID YOU KNOW?

Villa San Michele's original owner and guiding spirit, Axel Munthe, did not actually live in his ornate complex. He called the Torre di Materita, set higher on the island, his true home.

$$$$ SOUTHERN ITALIAN

La Canzone del Mare. Although it's not primarily a restaurant, luncheon in the covered pavilion of this legendary bathing lido of the Marina Piccola is Capri at its most picture-perfect. The set menus change every year, but a favorite main dish is *paccheri con gamberi e peperoncini verdi* (with shrimp and green peppers). With two seawater pools, a rocky beach, and the Faraglioni in the distance, it was the erstwhile haunt of Gracie Fields, Emilio Pucci, Noël Coward, and any number of 1950s and '60s glitterati. The VIPs may have departed for more private beaches, but this setting is as stellar as ever. You need to pay a fee (€20 for a sun bed, €30 with umbrella) to actually use the bathing *stabilimento* (club), but why not make a day of it? There are five suites available, too, in case a day is not enough. Boats also depart from here for Da Luigi, the lido/restaurant at the base of the Fariglioni. *Average main: €55 ✉ Via Marina Piccola 93, Capri Town ☎ 081/8370104 www.lacanzonedelmare.com Closed Oct.–Mar. No dinner.*

$$ SOUTHERN ITALIAN Fodor's Choice ★

La Capannina. For decades one of Capri's most celebrity-haunted restaurants, La Capannina is near the busy social hub of the Piazzetta, and the discreet flower-decked covered veranda is ideal for dining by candlelight—or you can join the regulars in the outdoor covered area. Specialties, aside from an authentic Capri wine with the house label, are ravioli *capresi* and linguine *con lo scorfano* (flat spaghetti with scorpion fish), squid stuffed with caciotta cheese and marjoram, and an exquisite "Pezzogna" (sea bream cooked whole in a copper casserole, topped with a layer of potatoes). The wine cellar is open for perusal, and their nearby gourmet store ships worldwide. The small late-night bar across the side alleyway is under the same ownership. *Average main: €20 ✉ Via Le Botteghe 12b, Capri Town ☎ 081/8370732 www.capanninacapri.com Closed Nov.–mid-Mar. and Wed. in Mar. and Oct.*

$$$ SOUTHERN ITALIAN

La Fontelina. Given its position right on the water's edge, seafood is almost de rigueur here, but for a slightly different starter, try the *polpette di melanzane* (eggplant fritters); then dip into the vegetable buffet. The house sangria is a highly recommendable, blissful mix of white wine and fresh fruit. La Fontelina also functions as a lido, with steps and ladders into fathoms-deep blue water, and this location—accessible by boat from Marina Piccola or on foot from Punta Tragara (10 minutes)—makes it a good place to spend a delightfully comatose day. Only lunch is served and reservations are recommended during high season. *Average main: €25 ✉ Via Faraglioni 2, Capri Town ☎ 081/8370845 Closed mid-Oct.–Easter. No dinner.*

$$$ SOUTHERN ITALIAN

Le Grottelle. This extremely informal trattoria enjoys a distinctive setting: it's built up against limestone rocks not far from the Arco Naturale, with the kitchen in a cave at the back. Whether you stumble over it (and are lucky enough to get a table) or make it your destination after an island hike, Le Grottelle will prove memorable, thanks to that ambience and sea views encompassing the Amalfi Coast's Li Galli islands. The food? Oh, that . . . the menu includes ravioli and local rabbit, but go for the seafood, with linguine *con gamberetti e rucola* (pasta with shrimp and arugula) being one of the more interesting specialties. *Average main: €25 ✉ Via Arco Naturale 13, Capri ☎ 081/8375719 Closed Nov.–mid-Mar.*

IN AND AROUND ANACAPRI

$ NEAPOLITAN **Barbarossa.** This ristorante-pizzeria is the first you'll see if you arrive in Anacapri by bus. A shabby staircase leads to the covered terrace with panoramic views of the Barbarossa castle on the hill as well as the sea. The no-frills ambience belies the quality of the *cucina*: besides *pizze* they specialize in local dishes—be sure to try the risotto *con gamberi a limone* (shrimp with lemon). *Average main: €14 Piazza Vittoria 1 081/8371483 www.caprirestaurant.it.*

$$ SOUTHERN ITALIAN Fodor's Choice ★ **Da Gelsomina.** Amid its own terraced vineyards with inspiring views to the island of Ischia and beyond, this is much more than just a well-reputed restaurant. The owner's mother was a friend of Axel Munthe and he encouraged her to open a kiosk serving hot food, which evolved into Da Gelsomina. Specialities include *Pollo a mattone*, chicken grilled on bricks, and locally caught rabbit. It has an immaculately kept swimming pool, which is open to the public for a small fee—a buffet is served as you lounge here. Close to one of the island's finer walks as well as the Philosophy Park, it's an excellent base for a whole day or longer. There's also a five-room *pensione*, with free transfer service by request from Anacapri center. *Average main: €18 Via Migliara 72 081/8371499 www.dagelsomina.com Closed Jan.–Feb. and Tues. in winter. No dinner in winter.*

$$ SOUTHERN ITALIAN **Il Cucciolo.** Nestling in thick maquis high above the Blue Grotto and a five-minute walk from the Roman site of Villa Damecuta, this must be one of the most romantic locations in Capri, perfectly placed to catch the setting sun. The cucina is refreshingly inventive with fish being a specialty: ask for *pasta fresca con zucchini e gamberi* (fresh pasta with zucchini and shrimp). There's a free evening chauffeur service to and from Anacapri. Reservations are essential in the evening. *Average main: €23 Via La Fabbrica 52 081/8371917 Reservations essential Closed Nov.–mid-Jan.*

$$ SOUTHERN ITALIAN **La Rondinella.** This is an airy ristorante–pizzeria opening onto the main road on one side and Anacapri's pedestrianized street on the other. In summer make sure you reserve a table out on the popular terrace. If you have difficulty choosing from the extensive menu, ask for advice or opt for one of their best pasta dishes, linguine *macchiavelle* (with capers, olives, and cherry tomatoes). The name of the anchovy-based linguine *ciammurra* refers to the town's inhabitants. *Average main: €15 Via Orlandi 295 081/8371223 Closed Nov.–Feb. and Thurs. Oct.–May.*

WHERE TO STAY

IN AND AROUND CAPRI TOWN

$$$$ HOTEL Fodor's Choice ★ **Capri Tiberio Palace.** Luxury hotels abound here, but this one goes just that little further to impress, with a style that evokes the golden age of 1950s Capri, and a scene-stealing, timeless view. **Pros:** friendly staff; luxurious touches; luggage collected at the port. **Cons:** no port-to-door guest shuttle; some rooms are not as large as expected in a five-star. *Rooms from: €390 Via Croce 11–15, Capri 081/9787111 www.capritiberiopalace.it 35 rooms, 20 suites Closed mid-Oct.–mid-Apr.*

$$$ HOTEL **Il Gatto Bianco.** Once the spot where Jacqueline Kennedy famously sought refuge when hounded by paparazzi, this is still a favorite destination to channel Capri's Sunset Boulevard-y ghosts. **Pros:** central location; wonderful atmosphere. **Cons:** perhaps too close to the action; no sea view. *Rooms from: €201 Via Vittorio Emanuele 32, Capri Town 081/8370203 www.gattobianco-capri.com 40 rooms Closed Nov.–mid-Mar. Breakfast.*

$$$$ HOTEL Fodor's Choice ★ **J. K. Place.** As the most supremely stylish and glamorous hotel in southern Italy, occupying an 1876 villa above Marina Grande harbor, this almost makes other accommodations on Capri seem dowdy and dull. **Pros:** exquisite pool; very close to chic Tiberio beach; free shuttle to town. **Cons:** expensive; only for high rollers; pool visible from main road. *Rooms from: €700 Via Provinciale Marina Grande 225, Capri 081/8384001 www.jkcapri.com 22 rooms Closed mid-Oct.–mid-Apr. Breakfast.*

$$ HOTEL **La Minerva.** A one-time private home, this has become a favorite in Capri, with the same family presiding here, three generations later, offering a friendly welcome. **Pros:** those views; that swimming pool; family-welcome. **Cons:** a 10-minute climb to the Piazzetta. *Rooms from: €140 Via Occhio Marino 8, Capri 081/8377067 www.laminervacapri.com 18 Closed Nov.–Mar.*

$$ HOTEL **La Palma.** Though the oldest on Capri (1822), this attentively run hotel has not rested on its laurels—at the front door you're immediately given a blast of island glamour, with the gleaming lobby, and majolica-tile rooms providing a delightful contrast to the hustle at street level outside (this is just down the street from La Piazzetta). **Pros:** the most central of Capri's luxury hotels; real island glamour. **Cons:** perhaps too central; rather far from the sea. *Rooms from: €190 Via V. Emanuele 39, Capri Town 081/8370133 www.lapalma-capri.com 70 rooms Closed Nov.–Easter Some meals.*

$$$$ HOTEL **La Scalinatella.** If you're bronzed and beautiful, or just bronzed, or even just beautiful, this is your kind of hotel. **Pros:** all rooms have a sea view; his-and-her bathrooms. **Cons:** a bit removed from the center; main pool visible from main road. *Rooms from: €470 Via Tragara 10, Capri Town 081/8370633 www.scalinatella.com 5 rooms, 24 junior suites, 1 suite Closed Nov.–Mar. Breakfast.*

$$ HOTEL **La Tosca.** It may be hard to find in the warren of side streets in Capri Town, but quiet La Tosca is worth all the trouble, with an unassuming vibe, terrace views, and reasonable rates. **Pros:** simple unadorned charm; pleasant owner. **Cons:** not all rooms have good views; it gets booked up early. *Rooms from: €150 Via Birago 5, Capri 081/8370989 www.latoscahotel.com 11 rooms Closed Nov.–Feb.*

$$$$ HOTEL Fodor's Choice ★ **Punta Tragara.** The most beautiful hotel on Capri—originally a private villa designed by Le Corbusier and site of a secret wartime meeting between Churchill and Eisenhower—was opened in the 1970s by Count Manfredi. **Pros:** a taste of the good life; the entire staff seems to have graduated from the finest finishing schools. **Cons:** a 10-minute walk from the center; some find the style dated, although others find it a plus. *Rooms from: €570 Via Tragara 57, Capri Town*

081/8370844 www.hoteltragara.com 27 rooms, 11 junior suites, 6 suites Closed mid-Oct.–mid-Apr. Breakfast.

$$$$ HOTEL Fodor's Choice ★ **Quisisana.** Some say there are three villages on Capri: Capri Town, Anacapri, and this celebrated landmark hotel, which looms large in the island's mythology, drawing "didn't-I-meet-you-in-Saint-Tropez?" from guests who wouldn't *dream* of staying anywhere else. **Pros:** luxe atmosphere on a large scale. **Cons:** not for all pockets; convention-size and far from cozy. *Rooms from: €360 Via Camerelle 2, Capri Town 081/8370788 www.quisisana.com 132 rooms, 15 suites Closed Nov.–mid-Mar. Breakfast.*

$$ B&B/INN **Villa Krupp.** Occupying a beautiful house overlooking the idyllic Gardens of Augustus, this historic hostelry was once the home of Maxim Gorky, whose guests included Lenin. **Pros:** direct access to the Gardens of Augustus, stunning views. **Cons:** a lot of steps to be negotiated; rooms are simple. *Rooms from: €140 Viale Matteotti 12, Capri Town 081/8370362 www.villakrupp.com 12 rooms Closed Nov.–Mar. Breakfast.*

$$$ HOTEL **Villa Sarah.** Few hotels offer such a quintessentially Caprese spirit as this; located in one of the island's most pleasant residential quarters, you'll feel like a guest in a private villa. **Pros:** gorgeous pool; lush gardens. **Cons:** a long and steep climb from the Piazzetta; some rooms are small. *Rooms from: €220 Via Tiberio 3/a, Capri Town 081/8377817 www.villasarah.it 19 rooms Closed Nov.–Mar. Breakfast.*

IN AND AROUND ANACAPRI

$$ HOTEL **Biancamaria.** This tastefully refurbished hotel with its pleasing facade and whitewashed spreading arches lies in a traffic-free zone close to the heart of Anacapri. **Pros:** friendly staff; Anacapri literally at your doorstep. **Cons:** on the main pedestrian road; no gardens. *Rooms from: €170 Via G. Orlandi 54 081/8371000 www.hotelbiancamaria.com 25 rooms Closed mid-Oct.–Easter Breakfast.*

$$$$ HOTEL Fodor's Choice ★ **Caesar Augustus.** A continuing favorite of the Hollywood set, this landmark has long been considered a Caprese paradise thanks to its breathtaking perch atop an Anacapri cliff. **Pros:** possibly the most glamorous place on earth; summer concerts on site. **Cons:** a bit far from the action for some; noisy road. *Rooms from: €460 Via G. Orlandi 4 081/8373395, 081/8371421 reservations www.caesar-augustus.com 55 rooms Closed Nov.–mid-Apr. Breakfast.*

$$$$ RESORT Fodor's Choice ★ **Capri Palace Hotel & Spa.** This Anacapri icon has grown both physically and conceptually over the years, amassing a noted art collection, launching a fashion and home line (including a line of Capri Touch shoes, custom made for each client), and working with some of Italy's top names on unique design touches. **Pros:** noted art collection; stunning (and sometimes surprising) design; postcard views; award-winning spa and dining; five-star service. **Cons:** all that glam comes at a price; some may find the quiet Anacapri location removed from the action (and water). *Rooms from: €360 Via Capodimonte, 14, Anacapri 39 081/9780111 www.capripalace.com 65 rooms, 13 suites Closed mid-October to mid-April Breakfast.*

$$ **San Michele.** Surrounded by luxuriant gardens, in a large cream villa,
HOTEL the San Michele offers solid comfort and good value, along with spectacular views from sky-high Anacapri. **Pros:** large pool; spectacular views. **Cons:** some rooms are tiny; the staff is not the friendliest. *Rooms from: €169 ✉ Via G. Orlandi 5 ☎ 081/8371427 🌐 www.sanmichele-capri.com 61 rooms ⊗ Closed Nov.–Mar. Some meals.*

NIGHTLIFE AND THE ARTS

As would be expected, Capri offers a fair spread of evening entertainment, especially on weekends and during the busier months of July and August, when many upper-crust Italians from the mainland occupy their holiday homes on the island. For music that's fairly gentle on the ears, try one of the traditional *taverne,* which are peculiar to Capri Town. There are also a number of discos and piano bars from which to choose, but the nightlife is more laid-back than Naples or even Ischia. On summer nights the place to be seen showing off your tan and sipping your extra-dry martini is the Piazzetta. Capri Town's Via Camerelle has the island's most popular late-night spots, often found in underground cellars.

BARS

Pulalli. Under the shadow of the Piazzetta's clock tower, this is a pleasant spot to enjoy tapas-style snacks while sipping wine on the open terrace. *✉ Piazza Umberto I, 4 ☎ 081/8374108.*

DISCOS

Celeste. Frequented by the same crowd who flock to Anema e Core, house music and hip-hop are the order of the night at this Camerelle hot spot. *✉ Via Camerelle 63, Capri Town ☎ 081/8377308.*

Number Two. If you are looking for the nightlife edge, try Number Two, open until the small hours in the centre of Capri Town. *✉ Via Camerelle 1, Capri Town ☎ 081/8377078.*

Red. For 360-degree music almost any night of the year, Red is the clubbing spot for cognoscenti of various ages. Unlike most other discos in Italy, no admission fee is charged, though you're expected to knock back the odd drink (about €15 each). A new "wine corner" is pulling in the thirtysomethings. This is the only club open all year. On Thursday in July and August, make a point of going down to Antonio Beach near the Faro, where Red arranges open-air discos by the water's edge beginning at 10:30 pm. *✉ Via Orlandi 259 ☎ 081/8373605.*

TAVERNE

Anema e Core. Anema e Core means "soul and heart" in Caprese dialect. This popular place is tucked down a quiet side street, a two-minute walk from the Piazzetta. Admission (€40) includes an eclectic range of lightish live music after 11 pm and a drink from the bar. No food is served, so come well-sated. There's no dancing here officially, though some patrons—including celebrities—occasionally take to the tables. The spot is closed Monday and is usually open 9 pm to 3 am. Reservations are essential on weekends. *✉ Via Sella Orta 1, Capri Town ☎ 081/8376461 🌐 www.anemaecorecapri.it.*

DID YOU KNOW?

La Piazzetta, Capri Town's main square, is the place to see and be seen on the island—never more so than on New Year's Eve, when a night of dancing culminates with a fireworks display.

THE ARTS

Culturally speaking, Capri has a fairly long hibernation, awakening briefly for the New Year celebrations. Recitals and other low-key cultural events are held in October and January in the Centro Caprense Ignazio Cerio, though from June through September the island comes alive with various events, including an outdoor concert season. It's a magical experience to see works performed at Anacapri's Villa San Michele (on Friday evenings) or on the spectacular terrace of the Hotel Caesar Augustus. In general, for information about cultural events and art exhibitions, ask at the local tourist information office or scan the posters in shop windows.

The Certosa di San Giacomo is the cultural heart of the island, hosting events throughout the year. Concerts are held in the two attractive cloisters from June through September. July sees the Certosa International Arts Festival, hosting film screenings, recitals, and readings while the New Year's Eve festivities are eclipsed by the film festival Capri Hollywood (🌐 *www.caprihollywood.com*).

Capri also caters to the literati, with Le Conversazioni (🌐 *www.leconversazioni.it*) presenting well-known authors reading from their works in Piazzetta di Tragara. Held at the beginning of July, previous editions have featured David Byrne, Martin Amis, and Ethan Coen.

SPORTS AND THE OUTDOORS

Although there are several tennis courts on the island, most have restricted access, so the vast majority of people looking to burn excess energy do so at sea level or below. For naturalists, bird-watching is particularly good in spring and autumn as Capri lies on a migration pathway, and botany lovers will be thrilled by the island's various nature trails, especially from April to June.

Capri Gym Fitness Center. For a simple workout, the Capri Gym Fitness Center allows one-off visits. ✉ *Via Roma 10, Capri* ☎ *081/8375430.*

La Fontelina. Rather than visiting public beaches, many sun worshippers opt to enjoy the fabled *stabilimenti balneari* (private bathing lidos) scattered around the island, some of which offer real relaxation and unbelievable views. One of the most famous is La Fontelina, open from April to October. At the foot of the Faraglioni rocks, the lido has a magical setting. There's no beach here, so the lido isn't suitable for children. You can get to La Fontelina by using a rocky path that begins at the end of Via Tragara; others prefer to take a ferry (€5) from the more accessible Marina Piccola during the afternoon. The excellent but pricey restaurant is only open for lunch. ✉ *Località Faraglioni, Via Faraglioni 2, Capri Town* ☎ *081/8370845* 🎫 *€20 admission includes locker and sun chair; €10 for beach umbrella.*

Lido del Faro. The Lido del Faro, on the Anacapri side of the island, is set amid rocks with a natural basin as a seawater swimming pool and is open from April to October during daylight hours. The sun usually beats down on this westerly headland all day, while on summer nights the restaurant provides a unique setting for enjoying the freshest fish. The lido is easily accessible by bus from Anacapri. Note that many other stabilimenti are set on the enchanting Marina Piccola, particularly the famous Canzone del Mare (⇨ *see Where to Eat*). ✉ *Località*

Punta Carena ☎ *081/8371798* 🌐 *www.lidofaro.com* 💳 *€20 admission includes locker and sun bed, €6 beach umbrella.*

Marina Piccola. Sorry—Capri is not noted for fine beaches. "Strand-ed" habitués cram onto Marina Piccola, generally considered to have the best beach on the island. It's certainly the most historic: Homer believed this to be the legendary spot where the Sirens nearly snared Odysseus. Social go-getters seem to prefer the less picturesque Bagni di Tiberio beach near Marina Grande. Expect to pay about €14 per person for the use of showers, lockers, and a sun chair/sun bed. It's definitely worth investing in snorkeling gear, as the sea is rich in marine life, and visibility is often excellent. **Amenities: showers; toilets; food and drink. Best for: swimming; snorkelling.**

SHOPPING

Although Capri is unlikely to be a bargain-hunter's paradise, shopping here is almost an experience in its own right. Frustratingly though, goods are often displayed without price tags, which means you have to shop Italian-style: decide whether you like an article first and then inquire about its price, rather than vice versa.

ART

Franco Senesi Fine Art. In the heart of Capri town, this gallery is a favorite for collectors and enthusiasts of contemporary art, with paintings by local and international artists availabe to buy. ✉ *Via V. Emanuele 50, Capri Town* ☎ *081/8378828* 🌐 *www.francosenesifineart.com.*

BOOKSTORES

La Conchiglia. An antiquarian's delight and one of the most elegant bookstores in Italy, La Conchiglia not only offers the largest selection of books on Capri and the Bay of Naples islands but publishes many sumptuous tomes through its own imprint. In addition to their own books, an attractive array of 19th-century prints, gouaches, and vintage editions of English books on Capri and the south of Italy is offered at their art gallery–cum–store on Via Camerelle, although a greater variety of titles is offered at their Via Le Botteghe location. There's also a branch in Anacapri. ✉ *Via Camerelle 18, Capri Town* ☎ *081/8378199* 🌐 *www.laconchigliacapri.com* ✉ *Via Le Botteghe 12, Capri Town* ☎ *081/8376577* ✉ *Via Orlandi 205* ☎ *081/8372646.*

GIFTS

La Capannina Più. With a selection of over 1,000 wines, including kosher varieties, as well as marmalades and local Capri "stone" sweets (chocolate covered almonds), this is not to be missed. It's an ideal place to purchase gifts for the connoisseur of fine food. ✉ *Via Le Botteghe 79, Capri Town* ☎ *081/8378899.*

JEWELRY

Chantecler. The extra security of being on a virtually crime-free island means that you can actually wear the expensive items you might want to buy. Some tax-free "bargains" might be possible from that Capri institution, Chantecler, where you can find a miniature replica of the Bell of Good Fortune, from the church of San Michele in Anacapri, presented to President Roosevelt at the end of World War II. ✉ *Via Vittorio Emanuele 51, Capri Town* ☎ *081/8370544* 🌐 *www.chantecler.it.*

La Campanina. Try La Campanina for a distinctive locally crafted brooch or some cuff links displaying ancient Roman coins. ✉ *Via Vittorio Emanuele 18/20, Capri Town* ☎ *081/8370643* 🌐 *www.capridream.com/linacapri.*

PERFUME

Carthusia. If you're looking for something that's easily portable to take back from Capri, then eau de toilette, a potpourri, or perfumed soap might be just the thing. Carthusia has been making perfumes since 1948, but—as they will proudly tell you—the tradition of perfumery on the island stretches back hundreds of years to the days of Queen Giovanna of Anjou. The factory, close to the Certosa di San Giacomo, is open for visits and a limited range of purchases, although there are no official guided tours of the premises. ✉ *Factory: Via Matteotti 2d, Capri Town* ☎ *081/8370368* 🌐 *www.carthusia.com* 🖂 *Via Camerelle 10, Capri Town* ☎ *081/8370529* 🖂 *Via Capodimonte 26* ☎ *081/8373668.*

RESORTWEAR

Da Costanzo. Da Costanzo has been the "king" of Caprese sandalmakers since Jackie O, Sophia Loren, and Grace Kelly all purchased pairs here in the good old days. ✉ *Via Roma 49, Capri Town* ☎ *081/8378077.*

Emilio Pucci. Emilio Pucci's stores throughout the world carry his colorful fashion creations, as well as shoes, bags, and accessories. It all started here in 1950 in this boutique store. ✉ *Via Camerelle 65, Capri Town* ☎ *081/8388200* 🌐 *www.emiliopucci.com.*

La Parisienne. Capri's main shopping streets—the Via Vittorio Emanuele and Via Camerelle, down the road from the island's main square, La Piazzetta—are crammed with world-famous names (Fendi, Gucci, Prada, Dolce & Gabbana, Ferragamo, Hermès). But if you're overwhelmed by the choice and are looking for something stylish but Capri-distinctive—in an astonishing range of colors—then check out the bright hand-block prints on clothes, bags, and shoes by Capri-local Livio De Simone at La Parisienne; here, too, you can purchase copies of the original capri pants. ✉ *Piazza Umberto I 7, Capri Town* ☎ *081/8370283* 🌐 *www.laparisiennecapri.it.*

Mariorita. Lovers of fashion, both Italian and international, appreciate this hip boutique at the Capri Palace Hotel, selling Versace, Valentino, Missoni, Trussardi, and Hugo Boss among other big labels. They also deal in fine ceramics and have a children's section. ✉ *Piazza Vittoria* ☎ *081/8371426* 🌐 *www.mariorita.com.*

Russo Uomo. The boutiques of Roberto Russo are favored by fashion folk. Russo Uomo has one of the largest selections. ✉ *Piazzetta Quisisana, Capri Town* ☎ *081/8388200.*

Vincenzo Faiella. Sandals are a Capri specialty. With a family business stretching back to 1917, Vincenzo Faiella is justifiably proud of his made-to-measure footwear. Expect to pay €60 to €110 for a carefully handcrafted pair. ✉ *Via Le Botteghe 21, Capri Town* ☎ *347/6780079.*

ISCHIA

Although Capri leaves you breathless with its charm and beauty, Ischia (pronounced EES-kee-ah, with the stress on the first syllable), also called the *Isola Verde* (Green Island)—not, as is often believed, because of its lush vegetation, but for its typical green tuff rock—takes time to cast its spell. In fact, an overnight stay is definitely not long enough for the island to get into your blood. Here you have to look harder for the signs of antiquity, the traffic can be reminiscent of Naples—albeit on a good day—and the island displays all the hallmarks of rapid, uncontrolled urbanization. Ischia does have its jewels, though. There are the wine-growing villages beneath the lush volcanic slopes of Monte Epomeo, and unlike Capri, the island enjoys a life of its own that survives when the tourists head home.

Ischia is volcanic in origin. From its hidden reservoir of seething molten matter come the thermal springs said to cure whatever ails you. Today the island's main industry, tourism, revolves around the more than 100 thermal baths; most of them are attached to hotels. In the height of summer, the island's population of 60,000 swells more than sixfold, with considerable strain placed on local water resources and public transport facilities and with decibel counts rising notably. However, most of the *confusione* is concentrated within the island's six towns and along its main roads, and it's relatively easy to find quiet spots even close to the beaten path.

Much of the 23 miles (37 km) of coastline are punctuated with a continuum of *stabilimenti balneari* (private bathing establishments) in summer (there are also lots of public beaches), set against the scenic backdrop of Monte Epomeo and its verdant slopes. Most port traffic to the island—mainly ferries and hydrofoils from the mainland—is channeled into Ischia Porto with some arrivals at Casamicciola and Forio, burgeoning resorts and busy spa centers. Buses between the main towns are frequent and cheap, though somewhat overcrowded.

GETTING HERE AND AROUND

Ischia is well connected with the mainland in all seasons. The last boats leave for Naples and Pozzuoli at about 8 pm (though in the very high season there is a midnight sailing), and you should allow plenty of time for getting to the port and buying a ticket. Ischia has three ports—Ischia Porto, Casamicciola, and Forio (hydrofoils only)—so you should choose your ferry or hydrofoil according to your destination. Non-Italians can bring cars to the island relatively freely.

Ischia's bus network reaches all the major sites and beaches on one of its 18 lines. The principal lines are CD and CS, circling the island in clockwise and counterclockwise directions—in the summer months runs continue until after midnight. The main bus terminus is in Ischia Porto at the start of Via Cosca, where buses run by the company EAV (☎ *081/19800119* 🌐 *www.eavbus.it*) radiate out around the island. There are also convenient *fermate* (stops) at the two main beaches—Citara and Maronti—with timetables displayed at the terminus. Tickets cost €1.90 for 90 minutes, €6 for 24 hours; note that conditions can get hot and crowded at peak beach-visiting times.

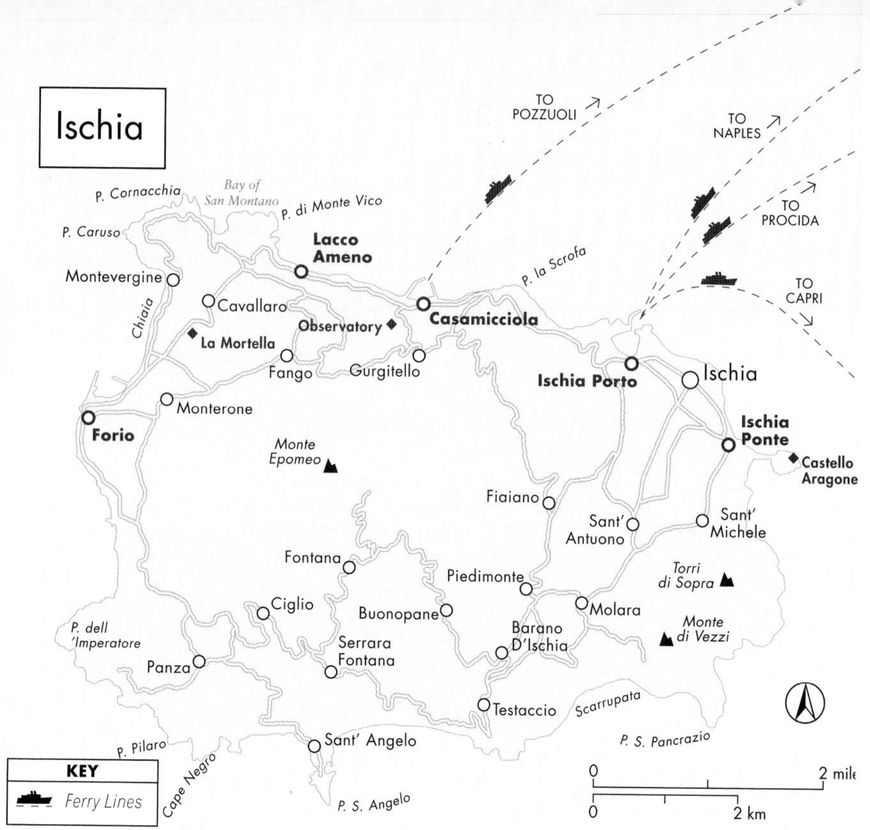

A number of car and scooter rental facilities are available. Note that police are vigilant about seat-belt and parking violations.

Autonoleggio IN Scooter. Behind the main bus stop, and with a branch also in Forio, this has a fleet of new scooters from €25 per day and cars from €40. ✉ *Piazzale Trieste 9, Ischia Porto* 🌐 *www.autonoleggioinscooter.it.*

Alilauro. Alilauro has roughly one hydrofoil per hour traveling from Beverello, Naples, to Ischia Porto (€19.90, travel time 40 minutes). From May through September, up to seven hydrofoils per day depart for Forio (€19.70, travel time 50 minutes). ☎ *081/991888* 🌐 *www.alilauro.it.*

Caremar. Caremar has six hydrofoil departures from Molo Beverello, Naples, to Ischia Porto (€16.40), travel time between 45 minutes and 1 hour) and eight ferry departures per day, from Calata Porta di Massa, Naples (€11.20, travel time 1 hour, 30 minutes). Ferry departures are also available from Pozzuoli (€8.50, travel time 1 hour). ☎ *081/984818* 🌐 *www.caremar.it.*

MedMar. MedMar has up to six daily departures from Calata Porta di Massa, Naples (€11.30, travel time 1 hour, 30 minutes), and up to ten ferries daily departing from Pozzuoli, sometimes docking at Casamicciola (€11.55, travel time 1 hour). ☎ *081/992803* 🌐 *www.medmargroup.it.*

SNAV. SNAV offers up to eight hydrofoils daily from Molo Beverello, Naples, to the marina of Casamicciola (€18.60, travel time 50 minutes). ☎ *081/4285555* 🌐 *www.snav.it.*

Del Franco. About 200 yards from Ischia Porto's ferry terminal, Del Franco, opposite Hotel Jolly, has a fair range of sturdy bicycles, both traditional (€15 per day) and electric (€25). ✉ *Via Alfredo De Luca 127, Ischia Porto* ☎ *081/991334* 🌐 *www.noleggiodelfranco.it.*

EuroScooterCar. Closer to the port, facing the marina, EuroScooter-Car offers cars from €35 daily and scooters from €30 (add €5 in August). ✉ *Via Iasolino 45, Ischia Porto* ☎ *081/982722* 🌐 *www.islandcenterischia.it.*

VISITOR INFORMATION

Azienda Autonoma di Cura, Soggiorno e Turismo. The information office is housed in the historic municipal bath building. It is also the information point for Procida. ✉ *Via Iasolino 7, Ischia Porto* ☎ *081/5074231* 📠 *081/5074230* 🌐 *www.infoischiaprocida.it* ⏲ *Mon.–Sat. 9–2 and 3–8.*

ISCHIA PORTO

4 km (3 miles) east of Casamicciola.

Ischia Porto is the largest town on the island and the usual point of debarkation. It's no workaday port, however, but a pretty resort with plenty of hotels and low, flat-roofed houses on terraced hillsides above the water. Known by the Romans as Villa dei Bagni, its villas and gardens are framed by umbrella pines and locals mingle with German tourists in the narrow streets.

GETTING HERE AND AROUND

Ferries and hydrofoils bring you here from Naples and Pozzuoli.

EXPLORING

Ischia Porto's harbor area was originally a landlocked lake in a volcanic crater: the Bourbon king Ferdinand II had a channel cut to create an opening seaward, and then created a sheltered port (1854). As you walk into the town along the waterfront, note the grandiose facade of the municipal baths (where Ferdinand II used to take the waters), now used for town council offices and occasional art exhibitions.

Ciccio. While exploring Ischia Porto, be sure to stop by Ciccio, near the ferry piers, for the best gelato on Ischia. ✉ *Piazza Antica Reggia 5* ☎ *081/991314* 🌐 *www.bardaciccio.it.*

WHERE TO EAT AND STAY

$$ SOUTHERN ITALIAN

✕ **Gennaro.** The oldest restaurant on the island has been a favorite of the stars, including Tom Cruise and Sophia Loren. Family-run, it opened on the seafront overlooking the boats in 1965 and continues to serve excellent fish in a convivial atmosphere. Specialties include risotto *alla pescatore* (rice with shellfish) and linguine *all'aragosta* (with lobster). In perfect English, friendly owner Gennaro will happily take you through the celebrity-laden wall of photos. $ *Average main: €16* ✉ *Via Porto 59* ☎ *081/992917* 🌐 *www.ristorantegennaro.it* ⏲ *Closed Nov.–mid-Mar.*

$$$$ HOTEL **Hotel Aragona Palace.** Dominating the entrance to the Riva Destra, Ischia's restaurant strip overlooking the port, this is the closest luxury hotel to the arriving hydrofoils. **Pros:** a hop, skip, and jump from the port; ferry-watching from the roof garden. **Cons:** rooms have only showers with no baths; rather far from the nearest beach. *Rooms from: €320 ✉ Via Porto 12 ☎ 081/3331229 ⊕ www.hotelaragona.it 52 rooms.*

$$$ HOTEL **Hotel La Villarosa Terme.** Part of a family-run chain of four hotels in the town of Ischia, this is set in a villa and garden, with a thermally heated pool. **Pros:** view from roof garden; wonderful pool. **Cons:** maybe too close to the town; some rooms are more attractive than others. *Rooms from: €222 ✉ Via Giacinto Gigante 5, Ischia ☎ 081/991316 ⊕ wwww.dicohotels.it 37 rooms ⏲ Closed Nov.–Mar. Some meals.*

NIGHTLIFE AND THE ARTS

Nightlife on Ischia starts late in the evening and you should be prepared to stay the course until the early hours. In some private gardens, occasional concerts and cultural events are offered during the summer months, with one of the highlights being the **Piano & Jazz Festival** (⊕ *www.pianoejazz.it*) at the end of August.

Blue Jane. Offering live music and DJ sets, Blue Jane, shaped like a boat, has a spectacular setting on the port's entry overlooking the bay. The club is a landmark, and visitors have included Mick Jagger and Gianni Agnelli. ✉ *Pagoda Beach.*

Valentino Club. In the center of Ischia Porto, this is the focal point for all but the gel-and-scooter set, with clientele in its early twenties and above. Admission varies between €16 and €25, depending on what's on offer. ✉ *Corso Vittorio Colonna 97* ☎ *081/982569* ⊕ *www.valentinoischia.eu.*

ISCHIA PONTE

2 km (1 mile) southeast of Ischia Porto.

The spectacular Castello Aragonese, towering atop an islet just off the main shore, landmarks Ischia Ponte. The town's name (Ischia Bridge) refers to the striking causeway built in the mid-15th century to connect it with the rest of Ischia. Although it has an amazing history, the castle also looms large in today's Ischia, as it becomes the appropriately cinematic setting for the Ischia Film Festival every July, with occasional exhibitions held in the Chiesa dell'Immacolata.

GETTING HERE AND AROUND

Take Bus No. 7 from Ischia Porto. If arriving by car or scooter, bear in mind that the access to the town is pedestrianized during peak hours (there is, however, a large car park).

EXPLORING

Castello Aragonese. The spectacular Castello Aragonese, towering atop an islet just off the main shore, landmarks Ischia Ponte. The town's name (Ischia Bridge) refers to the striking causeway built in the mid-15th century to connect it with the rest of Ischia. The little island was settled as early as the 5th century BC, when the tyrant Hiero of Syracuse came to the aid of Cumae in its power struggle against the Etruscans.

Ischia's Castello Aragonese sits on its own island, just offshore from Ischia Ponte.

This was his reward: an almost unassailable natural islet more than 300 feet high, on which he erected high watchtowers to monitor movements across the Bay of Naples. The island changed hands in the succession of centuries, with Greeks from Neapolis, Romans, Visigoths, Vandals, Ostrogoths, Saracens, Normans, Swabians, and Angevins successively modifying the fortifications and settlements. Ischia Ponte was where the population of Ischia sought refuge in 1301, when Epomeo's last eruption buried the town of Geronda on the other side of the causeway. The new influx of inhabitants led to a flurry of building activity, most notably the **Cattedrale dell'Assunta,** built above a preexisting chapel that then became its crypt. In the following century the Angevin castle was rebuilt by Alfonso of Aragon (1438), who gave it much of its present form. However, its turbulent history continued well into the 19th century, when it was seriously damaged by the English in their attempts to dislodge the French during the Napoleonic Wars (1809).

Two hours should be enough to give you a feel of the citadel, stroll along its ramparts, and visit its key religious sites. Don't miss the frescoed 14th-century crypt beneath the cathedral (Giotto school), although the ruined cathedral itself, with its noticeable 18th-century additions—such as the baroque stucco work—is quite atmospheric. Occasional exhibitions are held in the Chiesa dell'Immacolata, and there are two bars. Access to the citadel is via an elevator from the base, and the various walks at the top are clearly signposted. While taking in the whole site, enjoy the stunning views from the various vantage points. ✉ *Castello Aragonese* ☎ *081/992834* 🌐 *www.castelloaragonese.it* 🎫 *€10* 🕒 *June–Sept., daily 9–7:30; Mar.–May, Oct.–Jan. 8, daily 9–5. Closed Jan. 9–Mar. 1.*

Museo del Mare Ischia. Housed in the Palazzo dell' Orologio, the town's Museo del Mare Ischia is dedicated to the daily life of fishermen. Ship models, archaeological finds, nautical instruments, and the stray modern art show make up the small holdings. ✉ *Via Giovanni Da Procida 3* ☎ *345/2305766* 🌐 *www.museodelmareischia.it* 🎟 *€2.50, children under 12 free* ⏲ *Tues.–Sun, July and Aug. 10:30–12:30 and 7–11; Sept and Oct., Apr.–June, daily 10:30–12:30 and 3–7; Nov.–Jan. and Mar., daily 10:30–12:30; closed Feb.*

WHERE TO EAT AND STAY

$$ SOUTHERN ITALIAN

✕ **Ristorante Cocò.** This inviting restaurant with its outside terrace sits on the causeway linking the Aragonese castle to the rest of Ischia and is renowned for its fresh fish, which is highly prized by the Ischitani. Try the linguine *ai calamaretti* (with squid); a good starter in winter months is the vegetable-based *zuppa di fagioli e scarola* (bean and escarole soup). $ *Average main: €24* ✉ *Via Aragonese 1* ☎ *081/981823* 🌐 *www.ristorantecocoischia.com* ⏲ *Closed Jan. and Feb.*

$$ HOTEL Fodor's Choice ★

Albergo Il Monastero. The Castello Aragonese, on its own island, is the unrivaled location for this unique hotel, where a peaceful ambience and simple but comfortable rooms overlooking the Mediterranean far below add to the fairy-tale impression, and the friendly management adds to the magic. **Pros:** stunning views; how often do you get to stay in a castle? **Cons:** a long way from the entrance to your room; some consider it too far from the town's action. $ *Rooms from: €135* ✉ *Castello Aragonese 3* ☎ *081/992435* 🌐 *www.albergoilmonastero.it* 🛏 *22 rooms, 1 suite* ⏲ *Closed Nov.–Mar.* 🍴 *Breakfast.*

$ HOTEL

Villa Antonio. With a superlative panoramic view over the Bay of Cartaromana, with the Castello Aragonese posing front and center, the Antonio offers a quiet haven five minutes from the crowds. **Pros:** attractive price; lovely seaside location. **Cons:** many steps to negotiate before elevator; guest rooms' small windows don't do justice to the view. $ *Rooms from: €90* ✉ *Via S. Giuseppe della Croce* ☎ *081/982660* 🌐 *www.villantonio.it* 🛏 *18 rooms* 💳 *No credit cards* ⏲ *Closed Nov.–mid-Mar.* 🍴 *Breakfast.*

NIGHTLIFE AND THE ARTS

Bar Calise. Midway between Ischia Porto and Ischia Ponte, Bar Calise is allegedly "the biggest bar in Europe." Here is all you need for a good night out in one garden—you can choose between live music, a nightclub ('O Spasso), a piano bar, a restaurant-pizzeria, or a more traditional café. And if you have a hankering for a *cornetto* late at night, this is the only place on the island to find such pastry delicacies after midnight. Vetern Emiddio Calise runs this complex as well as three other bars and *pasticcerie* (try their specialty Monte Epomeo) around the island. ✉ *Piazza degli Eroi, Ischia* ☎ *081/991270* 🌐 *www.barcalise.com* ⏲ *Nov.–Easter, Thurs.–Tues. 7–1.*

Feast of Sant'Anna. There's a rich tradition in Ischian local festivals, with the Feast of Sant'Anna (July 26) holding pride of place with its skillful choreography and floating procession in the marina at Ischia Ponte below the Aragonese Castle.

Ischia Film Festival. The free Ischia Film Festival takes over the Castello Aragonese for a week each July, focusing—appropriately, given its unbeatable location—on films with stunning landscapes. ✉ *Ischia* ☎ *081/0100098* 🌐 *www.ischiafilmfestival.it.*

SHOPPING

Imagaenaria. A bookshop from times almost long gone, it has a large selection of rare volumes and limited editions, as well as the latest novels and a large English-language selection. ✉ *Via Luigi Mazzella 68* ☎ *081/985632* 🌐 *www.imagaenaria.com.*

CASAMICCIOLA

2 km (1 mile) east of Lacco Ameno.

Known properly as the spa town of Casamicciola Terme, with the largest concentration of thermal baths on the island, the lower town revolves around the busy Piazza Marina with its large bust of the Italian king Vittorio Emanuele II and its marble plaque honoring Henrik Ibsen, who was inspired by the beauty of the area to write *Peer Gynt* here. Although much of the town was destroyed in an 1883 earthquake, it has retained some charming examples of 19th-century architecture.

GETTING HERE AND AROUND

Take Bus No. 1/CD/CS from Ischia Porto. Bus No. 3 climbs to the upper part of the town.

EXPLORING

Other than a small 19th-century geophysical observatory, there are few sights in town, but that doesn't bother most visitors, who have headed here to enjoy the famous spa hotels. Note the stunning, although now derelict, building on the left as you approach the town from Ischia: it is Pio Monte della Misericordia, opened in 1604 as a hospital that is in the history books because it housed Europe's first spa.

WHERE TO EAT AND STAY

$$ HOTEL **Albergo L'Approdo.** Near Casamicciola's port, spas, and town center, this is a small hotel with a fine array of facilities. **Pros:** wonderful elevated views; pool perched above bay. **Cons:** the beach is across a busy road; showers are tiny. *Rooms from: €160* ✉ *Via Eddomade 29* ☎ *081/994077* 🖷 *081/980185* 🌐 *www.fidihotels.it* *39 rooms* *Some meals.*

$$$ HOTEL Fodor's Choice ★ **Terme Manzi.** Dating from the mid-19th century, it was at this hotel that so-called "thermal tourism" began, in one of the largest spas in the south of Italy—the bath where Giuseppe Garibaldi bathed is conserved in a corner. **Pros:** some say five stars is not enough; wonderful indoor pool. **Cons:** located in a nondescript square; very far from beach. *Rooms from: €250* ✉ *Piazza Bagni 4* ☎ *081/994722* 🖷 *081/900311* 🌐 *www.manziterme.it* *55 rooms, 3 suites* *Breakfast.*

LACCO AMENO

6 km (4 miles) west of Ischia Porto, 3 km (2 miles) north of Forio.

Lacco Ameno was colonized by the Greeks as early as the 8th century BC, and the landscape here has remained epic: it was used as the backdrop for the barge scene in Elizabeth Taylor's *Cleopatra.* For all its famous visitors, the town does not have a jet-setty vibe and looks lackluster on first impression. But take a walk down the main road, which turns into the Corso Rizzoli along the seafront and you will find a pedestrianized heaven: flanked by low-key shops, cafés, and restaurants and lined with cobblestones, the promenade runs for several idyllic blocks with the bay rarely out of sight. The Bay of San Montano, a brilliant blue-sapphire buckle along the coast, is the setting for the Giardini Negombo, the most stylish of the thermal complexes on the island. At sunset, Corso Rizzoli becomes a romantic's heaven.

GETTING HERE AND AROUND

Take Bus No. 1/CD/CS from Ischia Porto.

EXPLORING

Museo Archeologico di Pithecusae. Lacco Ameno's archaeological importance—it rests below the first Greek settlement on Italian soil on the island, at Monte Vico to the west—is amply reflected by the finds displayed in Ischia's top museum, the Museo Archeologico di Pithecusae, and the ancient site beneath the church of Santa Restituta. The museum occupies much of the Villa Arbusto, built by Carlo d'Aquaviva in 1785 on top of a Bronze Age settlement. Inaugurated in 1999, with the directors of both the British Museum and the Louvre in attendence, its eight rooms house a wide range of Greek pottery unearthed at the ancient necropolis site near the Baia di San Montano, much of it dating to the earliest years of the Greek colony (late 8th century BC), including Nestor's Cup, the oldest known kotyle vase in existence. There is also a room dedicated to internationally renowned filmmaker Angelo Rizzoli, who once lived in the villa, as well as a section devoted to dolphins. Villa Arbusto combines musical *serate,* or evening soirées, in summer months with visits to the antiquities museum. ✉ *Villa Arbusto, Corso Angelo Rizzoli 210* ☎ *081/996103* 📠 *081/3330288* 🌐 *www.pithecusae.it* 🎟 *€5, gardens free* ⏲ *Daily 9:30–1, Apr.–Oct. also 4–8.*

Museo e Scavi Santa Restituta. Beside the nearby church of Santa Restituta, almost completely rebuilt following a catastrophic earthquake in 1883, you can gain access to the underground excavations at the Museo e Scavi Santa Restituta, which are a memorable lesson in stratigraphy. Discovered in 1950 when the old majolica pavement above was removed, the underground site shows the building activities of several different periods (archaic Greek, Hellenistic, Roman, and Early Christian), faithful reconstructions of an ancient loom and a miller's workshop, and the various finds discovered in situ. Although the structures are poorly labeled, and it takes an expert eye to discern which buildings belong to which periods, this gives you a good idea of historical continuity on the island. ✉ *Piazza Santa Restituta* ☎ *081/980161* 🎟 *€3* ⏲ *Apr.–Oct., Mon.–Sat. 9:30–12:30 and 4.30–7. Closed Nov.–Mar.*

WHERE TO EAT AND STAY

$ SOUTHERN ITALIAN **O' Padrone Dò Mare.** A gorgeous seaside location, just off the pedestrian stretch, this is the ideal place to enjoy fresh fish—the name, "owner of the sea" says it all. An institution on the island, now in its seventh decade, locals and visitors crowd the terrace, which shares the view with the Regina Isabella hotel. Franco, the *padrone*, is justifiably proud of his shellfish-filled *spaghetti misto mare.* $ *Average main: €12* ✉ *Corso A. Rizzoli* ☎ *081/900244* ⏲ *Nov.-Mar.*

$ PIZZA **Ristorante Pizzeria Acquasalata.** Just behind the baffling-named Topless Bar (it isn't), and still popularly known by its orginal name, Antico Pizzeria del Corso, the lush gardens here are a haven from the bustle of Casamicciola's main thoroughfare. Staff are not the friendliest, but the authentic Neapolitan pizzas make up for it. Fresh fish, grilled meat, and, of course, Ischitan rabbit are also on the menu. $ *Average main: €10* ✉ *Corso Luigi Manzi 107, Casamicciola* ☎ *081/995481* 🌐 *www.acquasalata.it.*

$$$$ HOTEL **Albergo della Regina Isabella.** Built in the early 1960s, and home to Elizabeth Taylor and Richard Burton while they filmed *Cleopatra*, Ischia's largest luxury hotel is tucked away in an exclusive corner of the beach in Lacco Ameno. **Pros:** central location; considered by locals the top hotel on the island. **Cons:** not the most elegant of facades; rooms are fairly spartan for a hotel in this price category. $ *Rooms from: €605* ✉ *Piazza Santa Restituta 1* ☎ *081/994322* 🌐 *www.reginaisabella.com* *128 rooms, 8 suites* ⏲ *Closed Nov.–mid-Apr.* *Breakfast.*

$$$$ HOTEL Fodor's Choice ★ **Mezzatorre Resort & Spa.** Far from the madding, sunburned crowds that swamp Ischia, this luxurious getaway sits in splendid isolation on the extreme promontory of Punta Cornacchia. **Pros:** tranquil retreat; wonderful views; shuttle provided from Lacco Ameno. **Cons:** very isolated. $ *Rooms from: €450* ✉ *Via Mezzatorre 23, Forio d'Ischia* ☎ *081/986111* 🌐 *www.mezzatorre.it* *57 rooms* ⏲ *Closed Nov.–Apr.* *Breakfast.*

THE ARTS

Ischia Global Film & Music Festival. Since its inception in 2002, the Ischia Global Film & Music Festival (🌐 *www.ischiaglobal.com*) has become an important festival, attracting such stars as Burt Bacharach, Dennis Hopper, Val Kilmer, Harry Belafonte, Naomi Watts, and Jean-Claude Van Damme. Hosted in July by the luxurious Regina Isabella Hotel in Lacco Ameno, the event is pleasingly informal. ✉ *Piazza Santa Restituta 1* 🌐 *www.ischiaglobal.com.*

SPORTS AND THE OUTDOORS

If you visit one of Ischia's many *terme*, or spa baths, you will not only be following a well-established tradition stretching back more than 2,000 years but also sampling one of the major contemporary delights of the island. You should allow at least half a day for this experience, but the better value is to get there early and indulge until sunset. If you do decide to restrict yourself to half a day, then go in the afternoon, when the hefty entrance fees are slightly lowered. The larger establishments have a plethora of pools offering natural hydromassage at different temperatures and in different settings, with a complement of bars and restaurants to enable customers to stay on the premises right through the day. Most terme are equipped with beauty centers, offering an unbelievably broad range of services, from mud-pack treatments and manicures to bioenergetic massage.

Giardini Negombo. For the ultimate Ischian spa escape, try the stylishly landscaped park of Giardini Negombo. Designed around a beach of the finest sand, by the scenic bay of San Montano, it was created decades ago by Duke Luigi Camerini, a passionate botanist (who named his resort in honor of its resemblance to a bay in Sri Lanka). There are 12 saltwater or thermal pools here, plus facilities for hydromassage, a beauty center with sauna and Turkish bath, sports facilities for diving, windsurfing, volleyball, yoga, a bar, restaurant, and, according to the brochure, "a boutique for irresponsible purchases." All this is set in gardens with 500 species of Mediterranean plants and several panoramic views. Everything here—modern stone waterfalls, elegant poolside tables with thatched-leaf umbrellas, sensitive landscaping—is in the finest taste. At night, the outdoor arena often hosts big-name concerts. The Hotel della Baia ($) is also on-site. ✉ *Baia di San Montano* ☎ *081/986152* 🌐 *www.negombo.it* 🎫 *€30 all day, €25 after 1pm, €15 after 3:30pm; add €1–3 to prices in Aug.* ⏲ *Mid-Apr.–mid-Oct., daily 8:30–7.*

FORIO

9 km (6 miles) west of Ischia Porto.

Lying close to the main wine-producing area of the island, Forio is a busy seaside resort with beaches barely a minute's walk from its town center. Farther along are the small San Francesco and the larger Citara, two of the island's better-known beaches. At first glance, the town seems to provide sad evidence of suburban sprawl (there are more houses without planning permits here than with), and its natural setting of flat coastline is not the most alluring.

GETTING HERE AND AROUND

Take Bus No. 1/CS/CD from Ischia Porto. Bus No. 2 continues to Citara beach and the popular Poseidon Gardens.

EXPLORING

Fodor's Choice ★ **La Colombaia.** A crenelatted white fortress, La Colombaia was once the summer residence of noted film director Luchino Visconti, and now houses a permanent exhibition of photographs outlining the history of cinema and theater, as well as promoting art and cultural activities on the island. The Visconti Foundation, based here, awards an international prize in the director's name, and plans to host contemporary art exhibitions. The villa itself, unchanged since the director's death in 1976, boasts stunning views over the Baia San Montano. The official address is the town of Forio but the site is actually closer to Lacco Ameno. ✉ *Via Francesco Calise 142* ☎ *348/5127762* 🌐 *www.fondazionelacolombaia.it* 🎫 *€5* ⏲ *Tues.–Sun. 10–1 and 4–8.*

Fodor's Choice ★ **La Mortella.** Two kilometers (1 mile) north of Forio is one of the most famous gardens in Mediterranean Italy, La Mortella. The garden was a labor of love designed in 1956 by the landscape architect Russell Page

The Santuario del Soccorso in Forio is Ischia's most picturesque church.

for Sir William Walton and his Argentine-born wife, Susana. The garden was created within a wide, bowl-shaped, rocky valley, originally not much more than a quarry, overlooking the Bay of San Francesco and with spreading views toward Monte Epomeo and Forio. Lady Walton, who passed away in 2010, was a talented gardener in her own right, and first planted the trees of her childhood here: jacaranda and the rare bromeliad. Native wild plants were encouraged in the upper reaches of the gardens, with dainty vetches and orchids as well as myrtle, from which the garden got its name, La Mortella. Considering the volcanic valley out of which the gardens were sculpted, they are appropriately threaded with pathways of rocks hewn from Vesuvius. In homage to the hot springs of the island, the centerpiece is an elliptical pond with three small islands adorned with the immense boulders that once littered the grounds. Below, underground cisterns were excavated to catch natural drinking water.

Besides some soothing strolls among the well-labeled flower beds and landscaped rock gardens, try to spend some time in the museum dedicated to the life and works of the late English composer, William Walton. The gardens have excellent facilities, including a shop selling Sir William's music and Lady Walton's lively biography of her husband, *Behind the Facade,* as well as light, homemade refreshments. A theater was opened in 2006, and hosts a concert series on most weekends. Book well in advance for these tickets. ✉ *Via Francesco Calise 39* ☎ *081/986220* 🌐 *www.lamortella.org* 🎫 *€12, €20 for concert, including visit to garden* ⏲ *Apr.–Oct., Tues., Thurs., and weekends 9–7.*

Fodor's Choice ★ **Santuario del Soccorso.** A good spot for a sunset stroll, the island's most picturesque church is here: the 14th-century whitewashed church of Santa Maria della Neve, down at the harbor, better known as the Santuario del Soccorso. Check out the wooden crucifix in the chapel on the left; it was washed up on the shore below the church in the 15th century. Restored in 2013, this is the oldest statue on the island. For an overview of the town go to the Torrione, one of 12 towers built under Aragonese rule in the 15th century to protect Forio's inhabitants from the ever-present threat of pirate raids. *Daily 9 am–11 pm.*

WHERE TO EAT

$ SOUTHERN ITALIAN **Bar-Ristorante Bagno Teresa.** This is an unpretentious restaurant on Citara Beach (no dress code) that offers a range of fresh seafood at reasonable prices served with lively local wine. If you want to stay light for the afternoon swim, this is the place to come—there's no need to order a full Mediterranean splurge. *Average main: €10* *Baia di Citara* *081/908517* *No dinner Mon.; closed mid-Nov.–Mar.*

$$$ SOUTHERN ITALIAN **Umberto a Mare.** This iconic eatery has occupied the space below the Santuario del Soccorso since 1936, when the original Umberto began to grill the local catch on the seafront. Grandson Umberto now presides over the kitchen, conjuring up gourmet dishes such as *crudo di ricciola marinata* (marinated raw Mediterranean amber jack) and *paccheri dolcemare*, a sweet pasta dish with squid, sultanas, pine nuts, and a touch of cinnamon. The setting is divine, with a terrace overlooking the Bay of Citara and the green tuff *scogli innamorati* (lovers' rocks). Round off your meal with the delicious eggplant and chocolate supreme. There are also 11 guest rooms, all with a sea view. *Average main: €25* *Via Soccorso 2* *081/997171* *www.umbertoamare.it* *Closed Nov.–Mar.*

WHERE TO STAY

$$ HOTEL **Hotel Semiramis.** A quiet family-run hotel, this is within three minutes' walk of Citara Beach and the crowded Giardini Poseidon spa. **Pros:** great views; friendly staff. **Cons:** a bit of a climb from the beach; not much action in the evening. *Rooms from: €128* *Via G. Mazzella 236, Spiaggia di Citara* *081/907511* *081/907511* *www.hotelsemiramisischia.it* *33 rooms* *Closed Nov.–Mar.* *Breakfast.*

$$ HOTEL **Il Gattopardo.** Surrounded by verdant Ischian maquis and a vineyard, this modern-style hotel is in the most striking and quiet area of Forio. **Pros:** the outdoor pool under the olive trees; friendly staff. **Cons:** the entrance is more akin to a sports club than hotel; some rooms are too close to the action. *Rooms from: €180* *Via G. Mazzella 146* *081/997714* *www.ilgattopardo.com* *72 rooms* *Closed Nov.–Mar.* *Some meals.*

$$$ HOTEL **La Bagattella.** Run by the Lauro family, also responsible for Alilauro hydrofoils, this high-style oasis has a white wedding-cake, Arabesque ambience, with flower-covered balconies, sleek illuminated pool, exotic plants, and palm trees. **Pros:** wonderful grounds; lovely pool. **Cons:** the newer wing lacks atmosphere; a bit kitschy for some. *Rooms from: €300* *Via Tommaso Cigliano 8* *081/986072* *www.labagattella.it* *52 rooms* *Closed Nov.–Mar.* *Some meals.*

SPORTS AND THE OUTDOORS

Giardini Poseidon Terme. The largest spa on the island, with the added boon of a natural sauna hollowed out of the rocks, is the Giardini Poseidon Terme. Here you can sit like a Roman senator on two stone chairs recessed in the rock and let the hot water cascade over you. With countless thermally regulated pools, promenades, and steam pools, plus lots of toga-clad kitschy statues of the Caesars, Poseidon exerts a special pull on Germans, many of them grandparents shepherding grandchildren. On certain days, the place is overrun with people, so be prepared for crowds and wailing babies. ✉ *Citara Beach* ☎ *081/9087111* 🌐 *www.giardiniposeidon.it* *€32 all day, €27 after 1pm; add €2 to prices in Aug., €5 for visitors (no bathing) between 6 pm and 7 pm. There is also a €5 deposit for the keyband.* ⏱ *Apr.–Oct., daily 9–7.*

WORD OF MOUTH

"Procida is really worth a visit, a lovely, lovely place, still gritty and down-to-earth and filled with real Italians. Corricella, especially." —Julia1

SHOPPING

Ischia Thermae Cosmetici Naturali. With all the beauty farms on Ischia, it's enjoyable to visit the main cosmetics factory on the island, Ischia Thermae, which occupies an 18th-century palazzo in the town center of Forio. Besides poring over some of the formidably named articles in their retail outlet (such as Thermal Mud Purifying Mask Exfoliator), guided tours of the factory (call for times) are on offer, with the bonus of a free sample of their products. ✉ *Via Schioppa 17* ☎ *081/997745* 🌐 *www.ischiathermae.com* ⏱ *Daily 10–1 and 4–7.*

PROCIDA

Lying barely 3 km (2 miles) from the mainland and 10 km (6 miles) from the nearest port (Pozzuoli), Procida is an island of enormous contrasts. It's the most densely populated island in Europe—just more than 10,000 people crammed into less than 3½ square km (2 square miles)—and yet there are oases like Marina Corricella and Vivara, which seem to have been bypassed by modern civilization. The inhabitants of the island—the *Procidani*—have an almost symbiotic relationship with the Mediterranean: many join the merchant navy, others either fish or ferry vacationers around local waters. And yet land traffic here is more intense than on any other island in the Bay of Naples.

In scenic terms this is the place to admire what the Italians call "Spontaneous," or folkloric Mediterranean, architecture: look for the tall archways on the ground floor, which signal places where boats could be stowed in winter, the outside staircases providing access to upper floors without cramping interior living space, and the delicate pastel colors of the facades contrasting with the deeper, bolder blues of the sea. Picturesquely scenic, it's no surprise that Procida has strong artistic traditions and is widely considered the painters' island par excellence.

The Giardini La Mortella was built by British composer Sir William Walton and his wife, Lady Susana.

GETTING HERE AND AROUND

Procida's ferry timetable caters to the many daily commuters who live on the island and work in Naples or Pozzuoli. The most frequent—and cheapest—connections are from the Port of Pozzuoli. After stopping at Procida's main port, Marina Grande (also called Sancio Cattolico), many ferries and hydrofoils continue on to Ischia, for which Procida is considered a halfway house. As with the other islands, buy a single ticket rather than a round-trip (there's virtually no saving on a round-trip ticket, which is usually twice the single fare, and it ties you down to one operator on your return). There are four main bus routes that will take you to practically every corner of the island as well as a fleet of microtaxis operating round island tours and plying the route between the port and the Marina di Chiaiolella, on the southwest of the island. To get to Vivara, a road climbs westward out of Chiaiolella, and motorized access is barred shortly before reaching the bridge linking the two islands. This island is closed to visitors, but accompanied tours can be arranged through the Comune (☎ *081/8101941* 🌐 *www.comune.procida.na.it*).

The bus terminus in Procida is at the disembarkation point in Via Roma. Provided there's no traffic gridlock along the island's narrow streets, the buses run by the company SEPSA (☎ *081/991808* 🌐 *www.eavbus.it*) will get you to most destinations within about 10 minutes for €1.10. Chiaiolella is the most frequently served destination (about every 15 minutes) and timetables are displayed—and tickets bought—at a newsstand next to the hydrofoil ticket office.

In summer the bus service runs until about 1 in the morning. Tickets can be bought for €1.40 from the bus driver. Keep in mind that on-the-spot checks and hefty fines are frequently imposed on riders without a ticket.

Although Procida has fewer hills than either Ischia or Capri, cycling is really only feasible when the roads are closed to motorized traffic (evenings in summer). Most islanders get around on mopeds and scooters, which means the streets between the port and the center of the island are both noisy and loaded with pollutants, making casual strolling and window-shopping stressful.

Beaches can be reached by sea or land, with fishermen improvising as water-taxi drivers.

Caremar. Caremar has four hydrofoils departing from Molo Beverello, Naples (€13.20, travel time 35 minutes), and up to seven ferry departures per day from Calata Porta di Massa, Naples (€9.70, travel time 1 hour). There are three ferries per day from Pozzuoli (€8.20, travel time 40 minutes). ☎ *081/8967280* 🌐 *www.caremar.it.*

SNAV. Four daily hydrofoils leave from Molo Beverello, Naples (€14.90, travel time 35 minutes). ☎ *081/4285555.*

VISITOR INFORMATION

Mi.Ra.Tour. The official tourist office of Procida is in Ischia, but this travel agency distibrutes free maps of the island and accepts left luggage. It's open daily from 9 to 8 in summer (winter 10–1 and 4–8). ✉ *Via Roma 109, Procida* ☎ *081/8968089* 🌐 *www.procidaisola.it.*

TERRA MURATA AND ABBAZIA DI SAN MICHELE

Boats pull into the main port, **Marina Grande** (or **Sancio Cattolico** the local dialect for "safe place"), which is fetchingly adorned with pastel-hued houses and the church of Santa Maria della Pietà (1760). For your introductory look, hike up to the Piazza di Martiri on your way up to the **Castello**. Magnificent views can be enjoyed from the piazza in front of the castle, including the enchanting fishing village of the Marina della Corricella. For a fascinating glimpse of the traditional architecture, once you reach the piazza turn left and walk about 600 feet until you come to a tiny passageway that leads to the **Casale Vascello,** originally a gated area of tumbling-down cottages. After exploring on your way to the Cascale Vascello district, continue along Via San Michele to the highest point on the island, the old town of **Terra Murata**—a fascinating cluster of ancient buildings, including a church, palazzi, fortifications, ancient walls, and gateways, mostly in yellow-gray tuff stone. A Benedictine abbey was founded here in the 11th century, safely tucked away from mainland marauders, and the area became the focal point for the inhabitants of the island.

GETTING HERE AND AROUND

Take Bus C2 to get to this popular town.

EXPLORING

Abbazia di San Michele. Within Terra Murata is the Abbazia di San Michele. San Michele (St. Michael) is the island's patron saint and a key figure in its history and traditions. Legend has it that in 1535, when the sultan of Algeria's admiral laid siege to the island, San Michele appeared above the pirate force and put them to flight (the 17th-century painting depicting the scene is in the choir of the abbey's 17th-century church; one of the invaders' anchors can also be viewed). On the wall close to the richly coffered ceiling of the church is another depiction of San Michele, attributed to the grandmaster Luca Giordano (1699). As you walk around the church, note the holes in marble flagstones on the floor, which were in effect trapdoors through which bodies could be lowered to the underground crypt below. Children will be fascinated by the skulls still lurking in the maze of catacombs leading to a secret chapel. The cultural association Millennium offers guided tours for a small fee. ✉ *Terra Murata, Procida* ☎ *081/8967612* 🌐 *www.abbaziasanmichele.it* 🎫 *Free* ⏲ *Apr.–Oct., Mon.–Sat. 9–1 and 3–6, Sun. 9–1; Nov.–Mar., call for times* ☞ *Guided tours, €2 per person to museum and catacombs available on request at bookstore at entrance to abbey.*

ex-convent of Santa Margherita Nuova. Perched precariously at the top of a cliff facing the small bay of Corricella is the 16th-century ex-convent of Santa Margherita Nuova, recently renovated. ✉ *Terra Murata, Procida.*

Palazzo d'Avalos. The easily distinguishable and now abandoned Palazzo d'Avalos, built at the same time—confusingly, sometimes called Palazzo Reale or Il Castello—was the 17th-century residence of Innico d'Avalos, cardinal and mayor of Procida, and used as a prison from the 1830s until 1987. Rumor has it that its inmates were a little miffed at having to abandon the sun-drenched island of Procida. Now it is for sale for a cool €28 million. ✉ *Terra Murata, Procida.*

SHOPPING

Procida's best shopping area is at the port, with stores open year-round.

Fine House. Specializing in ceramics from Procida, this store near the port is also a treasure trove for other gift ideas. ✉ *Via Roma 116, Procida* ☎ *081/8969593.*

Noi Due. If you are looking for fine ceramics, stop off here. They also stock elegant minimalist linen clothing for women. ✉ *Via Roma 51, Procida* ☎ *081/8967661.*

Rosso Corallo. Watch artisan Luisa Izzo transforming coral into fine jewelry, such as brooches, bracelets, and necklaces. ✉ *Via Vittorio Emanuele 6, Procida* ☎ *081/8969356.*

CORRICELLA

This sleepy fishing village, used as the setting for the waterfront scenes in the Oscar-winning film *Il Postino*, has been relatively immune to life in the limelight. Apart from the opening of an extra restaurant and bar, there have been few changes. The **Graziella** bar at the far end of the seafront offers the island's famous lemons squeezed over crushed ice to make an excellent granita.

Procida is famed for its Good Friday procession.

GETTING HERE AND AROUND

Take Bus C2 from Marina Grande Sancio Cattolico to Terra Murata, then proceed on foot.

EXPLORING

Fodor's Choice ★ **Marina di Corricella.** Perched under the citadel of the Terra Murata, the Marina di Corricella is Procida's most iconic sight. Singled out for the waterfront scenes in *Il Postino* (*The Postman*, the 1995 Oscar winner for Best Foreign Film—the bar in the film is now a restaurant), this fishermen's cove is one of the most eye-popping villages in Campania—a rainbow-hued, horizontal version of Positano, comprising hundreds of traditional Mediterranean-style stone houses threaded by numerous *scalatinelle* (staircase streets). This is the type of place where even those with failing grades in art class feel like reaching for a paintbrush to record the delicate pink and yellow facades. ✉ *Corricella, Procida.*

WHERE TO EAT

$ NEAPOLITAN ✕ **Graziella.** This atmospheric restaurant sits right on the waterfront down at Corricella. It's family run and as rustic as they come, with food served on plastic tables outside. For starters try the *bruschette* and the seafood specialty, a selection of shellfish, octopus, and anchovies big enough for two. The *impepata di cozze* (mussels in pepper) is a must, and top it all off with a homemade *granita di limone* (lemon crushed ice), made freshly everyday here, and undoubtedly the best on the island. Leave space for the locally made cakes. $ *Average main: €12* ✉ *Via Marina Corricella 14* ☎ *081/8967479* ▭ *No credit cards* ⊙ *Closed Dec.–Feb.*

$$ SOUTHERN ITALIAN **La Conchiglia.** A meal here on the Chiaia beach really offers an appreciation for the magic of Procida. Coricella is a picture-postcard on your left and Capri twinkles in the distance beyond the lapping waves. The seafood is divinely fresh and the pasta dishes usually soul-warming. Access here is either on foot down the steps from Via Pizzaco or by the orange boat every two hours from the Corricella harborfront—phone owner Gianni for times (it's free for diners). *Average main: €16 Via Pizzaco 10 081/8967602 www.laconchigliaristorante.com Closed mid-Nov.–Mar.*

WHERE TO STAY

$ HOTEL Fodor's Choice ★ **La Casa sul Mare.** One of Procida's best boutique hotels, this charmer overlooks the fishing village of Corricella and the bay. **Pros:** stunning views; wonderful atmosphere. **Cons:** tiny bathrooms; guests have complained about the service. *Rooms from: €90 Via Salita Castello 13 081/8968799 www.lacasasulmare.it 10 rooms Jan Breakfast.*

$$ HOTEL **La Tonnara.** In one of Procida's cutest corners, this inviting new hotel option (take the Bus L1/L2 from Marina Grande Sancio Cattolico to the Marina di Chiaiolella) has been renovated from a former warehouse for tuna fishers. **Pros:** lovely setting; on the beach. **Cons:** constant stream of beachgoers outside the gate. *Rooms from: €150 Via Marina Chiaiolella 51b, Corricella, Procida 081/8101052 www.latonnarahotel.it 14 rooms Breakfast.*

4

SORRENTO AND THE SORRENTINE PENINSULA

WELCOME TO SORRENTO AND THE SORRENTINE PENINSULA

TOP REASONS TO GO

★ **"Torna a Surriento":** Sorrento's old town quarter is one of the most romantic places in Italy—be sure to dine in front of the Sedile Dominova, a 16th-century frescoed loggia that is a colorful backdrop for cafés and serenading waiters warbling "Come Back to Sorrento."

★ **A view with a room:** Give in to suite temptation and splurge on Sorrento's grand hotels perched by the Bay of Naples. The best are Belle Epoque extravaganzas with enough gilded salons to make even a Proust heroine swoon.

★ **Shopping along Via San Cesareo:** Sorrento's regional trifles are world famous, and this charming street is just the place to find embroideries, inlaid wooden intarsia, music boxes, leather items, and lemon products.

★ **Passeggiare:** Join the *passeggiata* (evening strolling ritual) at Piazza Tasso and follow the locals as they make the rounds of Sorrento's historical center to gossip, strut, and see and be seen.

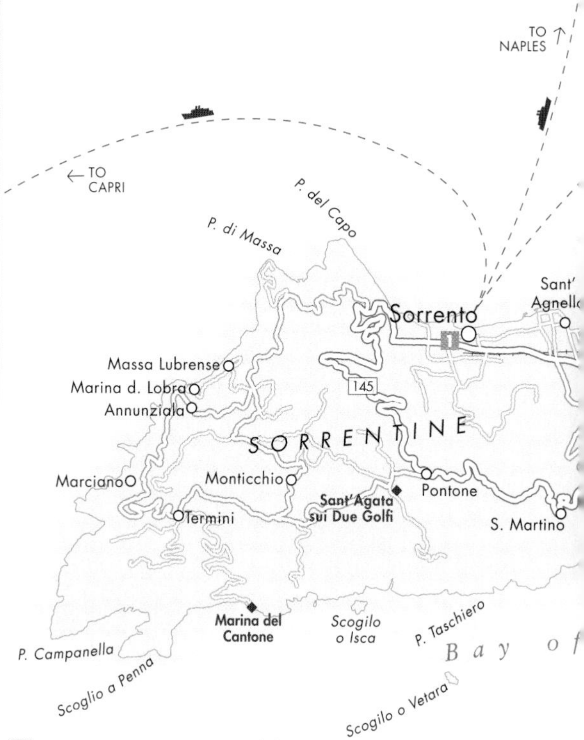

1 Sorrento. When literati sang Sorrento's praises in the Grand Tour era, palatial hotels went up to accommodate the titled lords who rushed to visit. The English, especially, left their stamp on the city, which is still notably civil and genteel. Perched on a cliff across the bay from Naples—with Vesuvius front and center—it has no major tourist attractions; the Belle Epoque city itself, with its enchanting sherbet-hued *palazzi* and bouquets of villas, is the draw. The charming historic quarter is centered on Piazza Tasso. Follow Via San Cesareo through a labyrinth of alleys to the Chiesa di San Francesco (with a gorgeous, bougainvillea-draped cloister) and the Villa Comunale, where you get a Cinerama view of the bay.

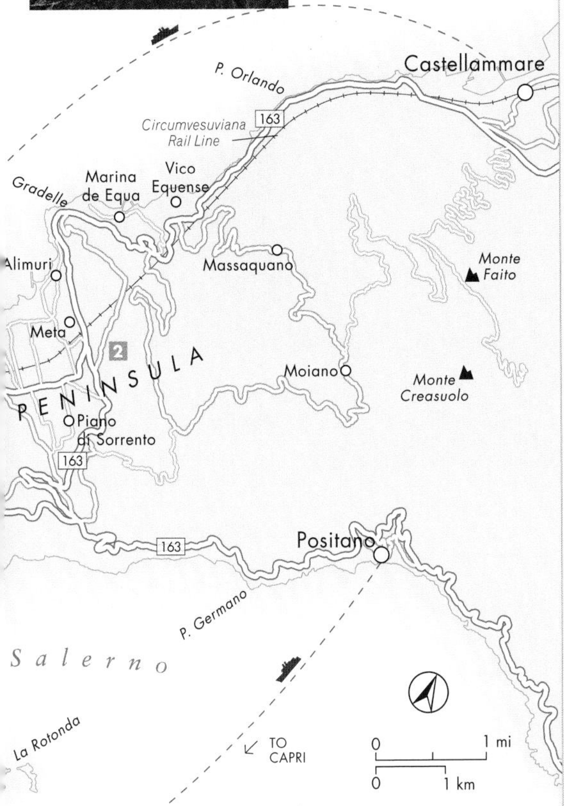

GETTING ORIENTED

Connected to Naples via the famous Circumvesuviana train, to Capri and Amalfi via the ferries and hydrofoils that depart its Marina Piccola, and set equidistant from Pompeii and the Amalfi Coast, Sorrento is a convenient home base for visiting the region. Set high atop a bluff on the peninsula created by the Lattari Mountains, it has a stunning view of the Bay of Naples. Beyond the town lies a scenery-rich peninsula famous for fabulous restaurants, Edenic parks, and a famously popular beach at Marina del Cantone.

2 The Sorrentine Peninsula. When the crowds of Sorrento get too much, you can always get out of town. Northeast of the city, the route leads to Sant'Agnello, an aristocratic beauty spot hallowed by two historic hotels, the Cocumella and the Parco dei Principi (the latter with a famous botanical park). South of Sorrento, Sant'Agata sui Due Golfi crowns a peak that overlooks both the Bay of Naples and the Bay of Salerno. Travel south down the peninsula to reach the delightfully festive beach at Marina del Cantone.

CAMPANIA'S WINE RENAISSANCE

Two thousand years ago, wine from Campania was considered some of the best in the Roman Empire. But in recent centuries, the region's wine production—and quality—declined precipitously, only to be raised from mediocrity in the past 20 years. Now Campanian wine is once again arousing the passions and palates of wine connoisseurs.

A vinous renaissance is underway: traditional grape varieties like Aglianico and Piedirosso (reds), and Fiano and Falanghina (whites) have halted the southward expansion of "foreign" (i.e., northern Italian) intruders like Sangiovese and Trebbiano. There is a new spirit of pride and achievement in the region, evidenced by the rapid increase in production of DOC (Controlled Denomination of Origin) wines, meaning they are recognized by Italy's system for ensuring quality wines. Like those in Tuscany to the north, wineries are increasingly opening their doors to the public.

LABEL TERMS

Italian wine laws are complex. Fortunately wine labels feature some indications of quality and style. The most rigorous classification—with restrictions on geographic zone, grape variety, and production methods—is DOCG (*Denominazione di Origine Controllata e Garantita*), followed by DOC (*Denominazione di Origine Controllata*), and IGT (*Indicazione Geografica Tipica*), which has the fewest restrictions. Other wine label terms to look out for: *vino di tavola* means basic table wine; *riserva* indicates the wine was aged longer than usual; *classico* signifies a well-respected, traditional style; *secco* means dry; *frizzante* indicates sparkling; and *dolce* is sweet.

AGLIANICO (TAURASI)
The most renowned regional red variety is Aglianico, which makes Taurasi near Avellino, the first-ever southern Italian wine to receive a DOCG label in 1993. The varietal has been called "the Barolo of the south" for its structure and ability to age. Aglianico produces full-bodied red wines with crisp acidity, robust tannins, and complex flavors of plum and spice. These wines are excellent with grilled steak, pizza, and pasta with meat ragù.

CODA DI VOLPE
An ancient full-bodied white grape grown near Naples. Until recently, it was used as a blending grape with Falanghina and Greco (in the white Vesuvio DOC) or Fiano. Now it is possible to find the crisp, medium-bodied Coda di Volpe bottled by itself. The varietal is excellent with gently prepared (not grilled) shellfish dishes or panfried fish, as it is fairly neutral and can be overwhelmed by strongly flavored foods.

FALANGHINA
An ancient white grape that may have been a base for the fabled Falernum, the most highly prized wine of the Roman period. This varietal has experienced a revival in recent years. It is a full-bodied, fresh-tasting white wine with fruity notes. Falanghina can be found in many DOC wines by itself,

and is blended with Greco and Biancolella to make Capri Bianco, the DOC white wine from the island of Capri. Falanghina is acidic enough to pair well with grilled and fried seafood dishes.

FIANO (FIANO DI AVELLINO)
This classical white grape shows best in the volcanic soils of Avellino, where it has garnered DOCG status. The wine expresses strong flavors of honey, spices, and nuts. It is excellent as an aperitivo, and pairs well with tough-to-match artichokes, as well as seafood linguine and most fish dishes.

GRECO (GRECO DI TUFO)
Greco is a Campanian variety that does best around the village of Tufo, where it has DOCG status. The soil there is a sulfurous soft rock called *tufo* (*tuffeau* in French). Greco is a light white wine that expresses ripe stone fruits, like peaches, with notes of almond and citrus. It is great served as an aperitivo and matched with cold antipasto.

PIEDIROSSO (AKA PER'E PALUMMO)
This late-ripening red grape variety produces a fruity wine with notes of cherries and herbs. It is the main grape in the red wines of Vesuvio DOC and Capri DOC. Piedirosso pairs well with pizza, cured meats, and grilled vegetables.

Updated by Fiorella Squillante

As a hub for a banquet of must-see sites—Pompeii and Naples to the north, Capri to the west, and the Amalfi Coast to the south—the beautiful, Belle Epoque resort town of Sorrento is unequaled. The rest of the Sorrentine Peninsula, with plains and limestone outcroppings, watchtowers and Roman ruins, groves and beaches, monasteries and villages, winding paths leading to isolated coves and panoramic views of the bays of both Naples and Salerno, remains relatively undiscovered.

Like the familiar song "Come Back to Sorrento," with its long, mournful closing notes (listen to the Pavarotti version and you may shed a few tears), Sorrento is tinged with melancholy. Its streets seem like 19th-century sepia photographs, vestiges of the Roman Empire's ruins are strewn about, and tiers of votive offerings of hopeful Sorrentines flicker in the crypt of the basilica of Sant'Antonino. Vesuvius, as always, looms in the distance. And with the sun's heart-stopping descent into the Bay of Naples, the isle of Capri fades into the purple twilight, as if to disappear forever.

Gently faded, in the manner of a stereopticon image, Sorrento still exudes a robust appeal. For anyone suffering "nostalgia di Napoli"—a longing for tarantellas, strumming mandolines, and *dolce far niente*—this is the ideal place, because it's relatively free of the urban grit found in the real Naples. Sorrento's tourist industry that began centuries ago is still dominant, although the lords and ladies of bygone days have been replaced with (mainly English, German, and Japanese) tour groups.

The Sorrentine Peninsula was first put on the map by the ancient Romans. Emperors and senators, who knew a good thing when they saw it, claimed the region for their own, crowning the golden, waterside cliffs of what was then called "Surrentum" with palatial villas. Modern resorts now stand where emperors once staked out vacation spots. Reminders of the Caesars' reigns—broken columns, capitals, marble busts—lie scattered among the area's orange trees and terraces. Sorrento goes as far back as the Samnites and the Etruscans, the *bons viveurs* of the early ancient world, and for much of Sorrento's existence it has remained focused, in fact, on pleasure. The Sorrentine Peninsula became a major stop on the elite's Grand Tour itineraries beginning in the late 18th century, thanks to glowing reports from Goethe, Lord Byron, Shelley, and Richard Wagner, Keats, Scott, Dickens, and Ibsen. By the mid-19th century, grand hotels and wedding-cake villas had sprung up to welcome the flow of princes, khans, and tycoons.

Eons ago, when sea levels dropped during the glaciations, the peninsula's tip and Capri were joined by an overland connection, and today it still seems you can almost make it in a single jump. Separating Sorrento from the Amalfi Coast, this hilly, forested peninsula provides the famed rivals breathing space, along with inviting restaurants and an uncrowded charm all its own.

SORRENTO AND THE SORRENTINE PENINSULA PLANNER

WHEN TO GO

Guess what? Summer months may, in fact, be the new "off-season"—horror stories of torrid days and humungous crowds have driven even more people to travel here during May/June and September/October, and the region is packed to the gills with travelers during those months. That doesn't mean that this region isn't crowded during July and August.

Let's not forget that summer is filled with festivities and offers the best weather for sunning and swimming, bringing dense crowds and higher prices, especially during the middle two weeks of August, when Italians vacation en masse. But no time is perfect: although April and May are sublime, Italian students are then on break and can overrun major sites.

The news is usually wonderful for the weather. Sheltered by the Lattari Mountains arcing east to west across the peninsula and inland from the Amalfi Coast, and exposed to cool breezes from two bays, the Sorrentine Peninsula enjoys a climate that is among the mildest in Italy; the temperature rarely falls below 10°C (50°F) in winter, or climbs above 31°C (90°F) in summer. In winter many hotels close from November to March. As for rain, or what the locals call *passione di Pasqua* ("tears of passion" at Easter), it's rare although weeklong storms can strike.

PLANNING YOUR TIME

Sorrento has plenty of appeal in its own right, but its greatest virtue is its central location—it makes a fine base, putting you within day-trip distance of Pompeii, the Amalfi Coast, and the islands of the bay.

You should spend a day taking in Sorrento itself and the surrounding area, plus another leisurely day exploring the Sorrentine Peninsula, enjoying the best beaches and restaurants in the area or taking a rural hike. For day trips, an excursion along the Amalfi Drive is a rise-early, full-day excursion. You can easily get from Sorrento to the Amalfi Coast by bus, or ferry around the peninsula in the summertime. Other day-trip alternatives include an excursion to the archaeological sites around the Bay of Naples. The train from Sorrento will deposit you right in front of Pompeii, Villa Oplontis, or a short distance from Herculaneum. Boat, ferry, and hydrofoil services also connect you with Naples and the surrounding area, plus the islands of Capri and Ischia, all valid day-trip alternatives.

Keep in mind that if you're driving, and you wind up not heading back to Sorrento until after dark, you should stick to the main roads. It's easy to get lost on back roads at night.

GETTING HERE AND AROUND

BOAT TRAVEL

Many commercial ferries and hydrofoils run year-round (with more trips in high season). To get to smaller towns or to take private boats, you can make arrangements with private boat companies or independent fishermen. Seek out people who are recommended by the tourist office or your hotel.

Ferries and hydrofoils go to and from Sorrento, with connections to Naples, Capri, Positano, and Amalfi.

Contacts Alilauro ☎ *081/8781430, 081/4972222* 🌐 *www.alilauro.it.* **Caremar** ☎ *081/8073077* 🌐 *www.caremar.it.* **Linee Maritime Partenopee** ☎ *081/8781430* 🌐 *www.consorziolmp.it.* **SNAV** ☎ *081/4285555* 🌐 *www.snav.it.*

BUS TRAVEL

At €2.50 for a one-way *extraurbano* bus ticket from Sorrento to other locations on the peninsula—and some lines with departures every 20 minutes—the bus is a good way to get around quickly and cheaply. Municipal EAV buses radiate out from the Circumvesuviana station to most major destinations on the peninsula, while SITA buses go farther afield to Positano, Amalfi, and Naples.

Inform the driver of your destination when boarding to avoid missing your stop. If traveling up from the port of Sorrento at Marina Piccola, or the waterfront at Marina Grande, you'll need to get an EAV orange bus. The main orange bus stop in Sorrento is on Piazza De Curtis.

Tickets must be purchased in advance. Time-stamp your ticket in the machine at the front of the bus as you board. You can buy tickets at cafés, bars, tobacco shops, and newsstands area-wide.

Bus Contact SITA ☎ *089/405145* 🌐 *www.sitasudtrasporti.it.*

CAR TRAVEL

All traffic from Naples to Sorrento is ultimately channeled onto the Statale 145, which must be one of the slowest state highways in southern Italy.

The road is single lane all the way from the A3 Autostrada turnoff at Castellammare di Stabia.

Though you'll get some scenic vistas as you inch along the peninsula, it's only when you get beyond Sorrento, on the road to Massa Lubrense or Sant'Agata, that a car becomes more of a benefit than a liability. Don't expect excellent driving standards in the Sorrento area, and be especially careful of scooters, which tend to take considerable liberties. Avoid traveling from Naples to Sorrento on Saturday evenings and on fine Sunday mornings in summer. The same applies to the Statale 145 late on a Sunday afternoon, when immense numbers of day-trippers and weekenders return home to the Naples area.

If you make a stop in Sorrento by car, head for the large parking lot called Ulisse (after the hotel of which it is a part): take a left turn into Via degli Aranci when you meet the "no entry" signs as you enter Sorrento, pass under the railway bridge, and turn right at the roundabout.

This road skirts the town center (to the right). At the stop sign on Corso Italia take a right turn, and turn right immediately down toward the Marina Grande.

Contacts Ulisse Parking. On your left after the road bridge, this is within easy walking distance of the town center and Marina Grande. ✉ *Via Del Mare 22* ☎ *081/8774923* 🎫 *€2 per hr.*

4

TRAIN TRAVEL

The train stations on the Circumvesuviana line serving the Sorrentine Peninsula are Meta, Piano di Sorrento, Sant'Agnello, and Sorrento, in order of increasing distance from Naples. The main transport hub for cheap, efficient bus services radiating to destinations along the coast and inland is the Circumvesuviana station in Sorrento.

If heading to Sorrento from Naples, use the Stazione Centrale (Piazza Garibaldi), which is the second stop on the Circumvesuviana line as it departs from Naples. Follow the *Circumvesuviana* signs, which will take you through the ticket barriers down into the train stations.

Trains to Sorrento run every half hour from Naples; some trains are *direttissimo* (express), only stopping at major stations; they take half the time of local trains. Round-trip fares are €8.20 for Naples to Sorrento (if traveling round-trip on the weekend, purchase a day pass good for unlimited stops on the line) and €3.50 for Pompei Scavi–Sorrento. In Sorrento the train station is opposite Piazza Lauro and a five-minute walk from Piazza Tasso.

Contacts Circumvesuviana 🌐 *www.eavcampania.it.*

RESTAURANTS

Having much higher levels of tourism than Naples, the area around Sorrento has fewer cheap and cheerful restaurants for locals, but you are more likely to find waiters who speak some English, *trattorie*, which stay open right through August, and generally higher levels of cuisine. As a rule of thumb, avoid set menus (often called *menu turistico*) and go for whatever looks freshest to you. Remember that fish and steak prices on menus are often indicated by a price per 100 grams. Look carefully if it seems suspiciously cheap!

Prices in the reviews are the average cost of a main course at dinner, or, if dinner isn't served, at lunch.

HOTELS

Sorrento has a plethora of upper-range hotels with fin de siècle charm, perched on top of impressive tuff cliffs, with balconies and terraces giving an immediate this-is-it sensation.

> **WORD OF MOUTH**
>
> "Sorrento is a fine place to spend a few days. Easy to catch ferries to islands. Convenient to Naples, Pompeii, etc."
>
> —Julia1

If traveling on a tighter budget, you can choose between a three-star accommodation or a B&B in the town center or a quieter hotel farther from Sorrento's hub and from the sea.

If staying on the peninsula, don't assume you'll be a stone's throw from the shoreline: at times access to the sea is lengthy and arduous, and most of the coastline is rocky.

Hotel prices listed in the guide are for two people in a standard double room in high season.

TOURS

City Sightseeing Sorrento. A much better sightseeing alternative to driving yourself around (and driving yourself crazy in the process) is the double-decker tour bus operated by City Sightseeing Sorrento. ✉ *Via degli Aranci 172* ☎ *081/8774707* 🌐 *www.sorrento.city-sightseeing.it.*

Vesuvius vs Pompeii. For guided tours of the Sorrentine Peninsula (but also departing from Sorrento to Capri, Pompeii, and the Naples area) check out the knowledgeable and passionate team of Vesuvius vs. Pompeii. They can also arrange private transfers and vehicles for people with disabilities. ☎ *333/6409000* 🌐 *www.vesuviusvspompeii.com.*

VISITOR INFORMATION

Tourist Information **Azienda Autonoma di Soggiorno Sorrento-Sant'Agnello.** Besides dispensing a wealth of information, the tourist office also has a useful booking service for hotels, B&Bs, and vacation apartments throughout the peninsula. ✉ *Via L. De Maio 35* ☎ *081/8074033* 📠 *081/8773397* 🌐 *www.sorrentotourism.com* 🕒 *Weekdays 8:30–4:15 (also Sat. in summer).*

SORRENTO

Sorrento may have become a jumping-off point for visitors to Pompeii, Capri, and Amalfi, but you can find countless reasons to love it for itself. The Sorrentine people are fair-minded and hardworking, bubbling with life and warmth. The tuff cliff on which the town rests is like a great golden pedestal spread over the bay, absorbing the sunlight in deepening shades through the mild days, and orange and lemon trees waft a luscious perfume in spring.

Winding along a cliff above a small beach and two harbors, the town is split in two by a narrow ravine formed by a former mountain stream. To the east, dozens of hotels line busy Via Correale along the cliff—many have "grand" included in their names, and some indeed still are. To the west, however, is the historic sector, which still enchants. It's a relatively flat area, with winding, stone-paved lanes bordered by

DID YOU KNOW?

The Sedile Dominova, an open-air loggia decorated with baroque trompe l'oeil frescos, has been a meeting place for Sorrento residents since the 16th century.

balconied buildings, some joined by medieval stone arches. The central piazza is named after the poet Torquato Tasso, born here in 1544. This part of town is a delightful place to walk through, especially in the mild evenings, when people are out and about, and everything is open. Craftspeople are often at work in their stalls and shops and are happy to let you watch; in fact, that's the point. Music spots and bars cluster in the side streets near Piazza Tasso.

GETTING HERE AND AROUND

From downtown Naples, take a Circumvesuviana train from Stazione Centrale (Piazza Garibaldi), SITA bus from the Port (Varco Immacolatella), or hydrofoil from Molo Beverello. If you're coming directly from the airport in Naples, pick up a direct bus to Sorrento. By car, take the A3 Naples–Salerno highway, exiting at Castellammare, and then following signs for Penisola Sorrentina, then for Sorrento.

Parcheggio de Curtis. This car park is conveniently close to the Circumvesuviana train station. ✉ *Via de Curtis, Sorrento* 🎫 *€2 per hr.*

EXPLORING

TOP ATTRACTIONS

Basilica di Sant'Antonino. Gracing Piazza Sant'Antonino and one of the largest churches in Sorrento, the Basilica di Sant'Antonino honors the city's patron saint, St. Anthony the Abbot. The church and the portal on the right side date from the 11th century. Its nave and side aisles are divided by recycled ancient columns, and the interior is baroque style, with fine paintings, including one on the nave ceiling painted by Giovan Battista Lama in the mid-16th century. Directly opposite across the piazza is the turn-of-the-20th-century *Municipio* (town hall). ✉ *Piazza Sant'Antonino* ☎ *081/8781437* 🎫 *Free* ⏲ *Daily 7–noon and Mon.–Sat. 5–7.*

Convento di San Francesco. Near the Villa Comunale gardens and sharing its view over the Bay of Naples, the convent is celebrated for its 14th-century cloister. Filled with greenery and flowers, the Moorish-style cloister has interlaced pointed arches of tufa rock, alternating with octagonal columns topped by elegant capitals, supporting smaller arches. The combination makes a suitably evocative setting for summer concerts and theatrical presentations. The church portal is particularly impressive, with the original 16th-century door featuring intarsia (inlaid) work. The interior's 17th-century decoration includes an altarpiece, by a student of Francesco Solimena, depicting St. Francis receiving the stigmata. The convent is now an art school, where students' works are often exhibited. ✉ *Piazza S. Francesco* ☎ *081/8781269* 🎫 *Free* ⏲ *Daily 8–1:30, 3:30–8.*

Duomo dei SS Filippo e Giacomo. Ancient, but rebuilt from the 15th-century right up to 1924, the town's cathedral follows a Latin-cross design; its nave and two side aisles are divided by thick piers with round arches. A Renaissance-style door and artworks, including the archbishop's 16th-century marble throne and ceiling paintings attributed to the 18th-century Neapolitan school, are easily viewable. Outstanding 19th- and 20th-century marquetry ornaments a magnificent choir loft, entrance panels, and representations of the Stations of the Cross. Look for the unusual 10th-century marble slab used as a gravestone,

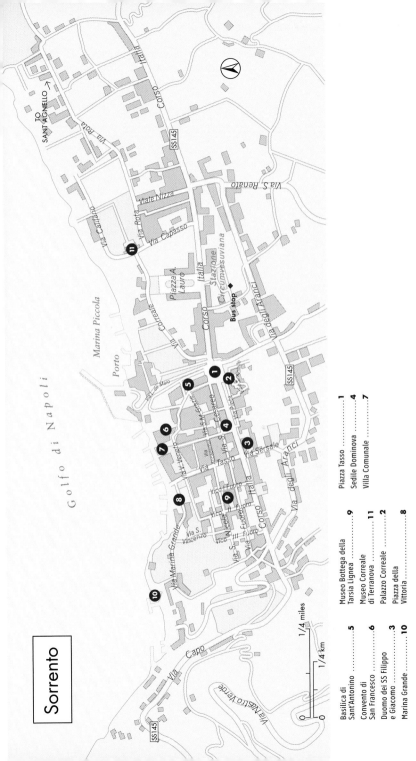

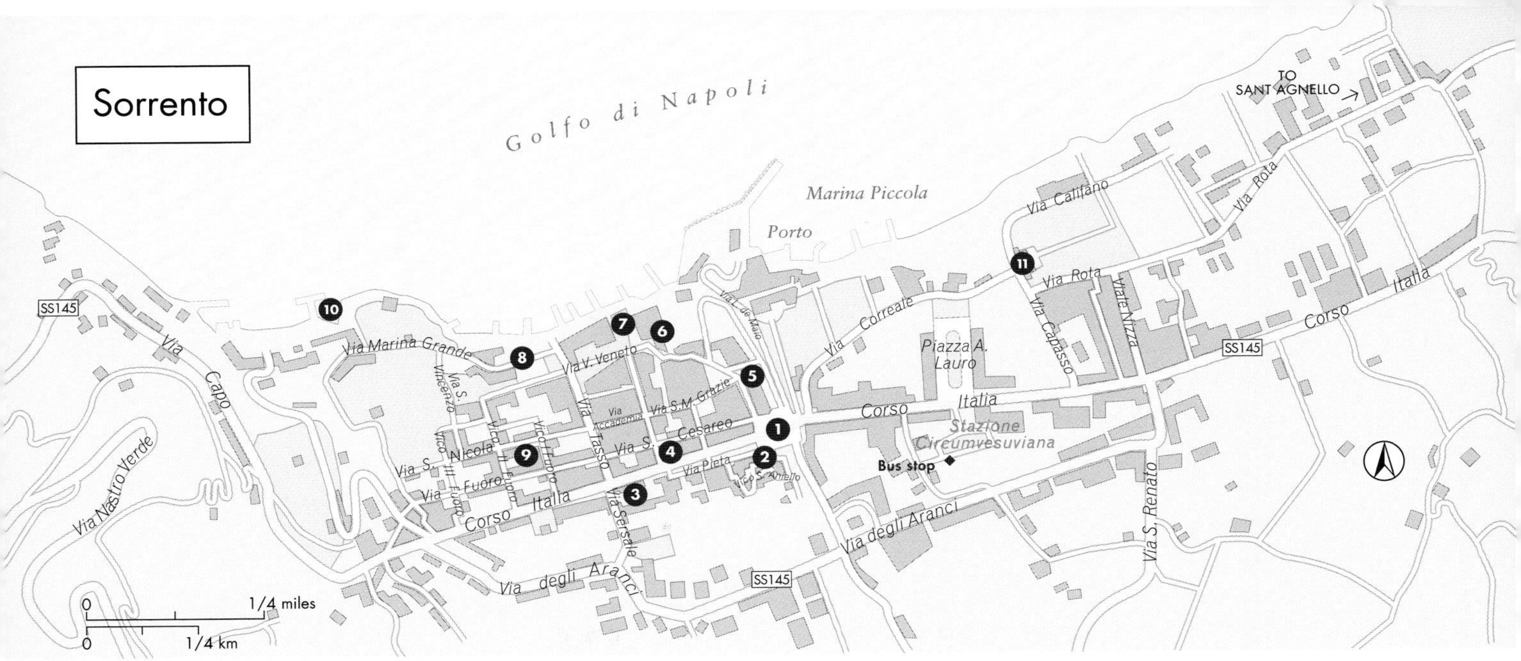

Basilica di Sant'Antonino **5**

Convento di San Francesco **6**

Duomo dei SS Filippo e Giacomo **3**

Marina Grande **10**

Museo Bottega della Tarsia Lignea **9**

Museo Correale di Terranova **11**

Palazzo Correale **2**

Piazza della Vittoria **8**

Piazza Tasso **1**

Sedile Dominova **4**

Villa Comunale **7**

with a lioness on the front and a depiction of the deceased on the back. The delightfully florid three-story campanile, topped by a clock and a belfry, has an open, arcaded base and recycled Roman columns. ✉ *Largo Arcivescovado, at Corso Italia and Via S. Maria della Pietà 44* ☎ *081/8782248* 🌐 *www.cattedralesorrento.it* 🎫 *Free* 🕑 *Daily 7:30–noon and 4–7.*

Museo Correale di Terranova. In an 18th-century villa with a lovely garden, on land given to the patrician Correale family by Queen Joan of Anjou in 1428, this museum is a highlight of Sorrento and a must for connoisseurs of the *seicento* (Italian 17th century). It has an eclectic private collection amassed by the count of Terranova and his brother—one of the finest devoted to Neapolitan paintings, decorative arts, and porcelains. Magnificent 18th- and 19th-century inlaid tables by Giuseppe Gargiulo, Capodimonte porcelains, and Rococo portrait miniatures are reminders of the age when pleasure and delight were everything. Also on view are regional Greek and Roman archaeological finds, medieval marble work, glasswork, old-master paintings, 17th-century majolicas—even the poet Tasso's death mask. The building itself is fairly charmless, with few period rooms, but the garden offers an allée of palm trees, citrus groves, floral nurseries, and an esplanade with a panoramic view of the Sorrento coast. ✉ *Via Correale 50* ☎ *081/8781846* 🌐 *www.museocorreale.it* 🎫 *€8* 🕑 *Apr.–Oct. Tues.–Sat. 9:30–6:30; Nov.–Mar. Tues.–Sun. 9.30–1:30.*

Sedile Dominova. Enchanting showpiece of the Largo Dominova—the little square that is the heart of Sorrento's historic quarter—the Sedile Dominova is a picturesque open loggia with expansive arches, balustrades, and a green-and-yellow-tile cupola, originally constructed in the 16th century. The open-air structure is frescoed with 18th-century trompe-l'oeil columns and the family coats of arms, which once belonged to the *sedile* (seat), the town council where nobles met to discuss civic problems as early as the Angevin period. Today Sorrentines still like to congregate around the umbrella-topped tables near the tiny square. ✉ *Largo Dominova, at Via S. Cesareo and Via P.R. Giuliani* 🕑 *Daily 9–1 and 4–8.*

Villa Comunale. The largest public park in Sorrento sits on a clifftop overlooking the entire Bay of Naples. It offers benches, flowers, palms, and people-watching, plus a seamless vista that stretches from Capri to Vesuvius. From here steps lead down to Sorrento's main harbor, the Marina Piccola. ✉ *Adjoining church of San Francesco.*

NEED A BREAK?

Bar Villa Comunale. The unassuming Bar Villa Comunale, closed mid-November to March, is the perfect spot to sit with Sorrento's cardplayers or just gaze across the Bay of Naples at the perfect scenery. ✉ *Villa Comunale* ☎ *081/8074090.*

Davide. For an afternoon delight, why not head across the road to Davide to indulge in a gelato? For something with a local twist, try *profumi di Sorrento,* the in-house citrus fruit sorbet, or a cream-laden *semifreddo al delizie a limone*. Davide is closed November through March. ✉ *Via Giuliani 39* ☎ *081/8781337.*

Marina Grande is Sorrento's main fishing harbor, as well as a popular tourist hangout.

WORTH NOTING

Marina Grande. Close to the historic quarter (but not that close—many locals prefer to use the town bus to shuttle up and down the steep hill), the port, or *borgo*, of the Marina Grande is Sorrento's fishing harbor. In recent years it has become unashamedly touristy, with outdoor restaurants and cafés encroaching on what little remains of the original harbor. Most establishments down here are geared to the English-speaking market—expect a *Good evening* rather than a *Buona sera* as you enter, and menu listings that may make you think you've been teleported into a British fish-and-chip shop. The Marina still remains a magical location for an evening out on the waterfront, but if you're interested in a dip—given the dubious seawater quality here and the cramped conditions—head out instead toward Massa Lubrense and Nerano. Don't confuse this harbor with Marina Piccola, at the base of the cliff, below Piazza Tasso and the Hotel Excelsior Vittoria; that's the area where ferries and hydrofoils dock. ✉ *Via del Mare.*

Museo Bottega della Tarsia Lignea (*Museum of Intarsia Work*). The 18th-century Palazzo Pomaranci Santomasi houses an assorted collection of the celebrated Sorrentine decorative art of intarsia, or *intarsi* (inlays), comprising mainly 19th-century furniture and some modern artistic creations. Also on view are 19th-century paintings, prints, and photographs of the Sorrentine Peninsula. One-day workshops can also be booked. ✉ *Via San Nicola 28* ☎ *081/8771942* 🎫 *€8* 🕓 *Daily 10–6:30.*

Palazzo Correale. Just off the southeast corner of Piazza Tasso, this palazzo was built in the 14th century in Catalan style but transformed into a Rococo-era showstopper, thanks to its exquisite **Esedra Maiolicata**

A GOOD WALK

Divinely picturesque, the old town of Sorrento is like a Belle Epoque stage set—festooned with palazzi, charming streets, and gorgeous landmarks, it is custom-tailored for one of the most enjoyable promenades you will ever take.

Begin at Sorrento's historic center, **Piazza Tasso,** watched over by statues of the namesake poet. Avoid busy Corso Italia to head instead to the southwest corner of the piazza to Via Santa Maria della Pietà to take a look at the noted **Palazzo Correale** (No. 24), whose 18th-century majolica courtyard, now a flower shop, overflows with charm. Follow this street until you reach the Largo Arcivescovado, site of the **Duomo dei SS Filippo e Giacomo.**

After viewing the cathedral, head for its wedding-cake campanile, then make a right off Corso Italia down Via Giuliani to enter Sorrento's most picturesque quarter.

Here, on Via San Cesareo, is the beautifully frescoed **Sedile Dominova,** the ancient, open-air site of civic discourse (at night illuminated for café sitters); one of your best "big exhale" hours will be spent here. Return to Piazza Tasso along Via San Cesareo, lit with 19th-century lanterns and the main shopping drag. When you arrive at the edge of Piazza Tasso, go left toward the bay, a block or so along Via De Maio, to pretty Piazza Sant'Antonino, the site of the 11th-century **Basilica di Sant'Antonino.** Past this piazza take Via Santa Maria delle Grazie and Via Donnorso to the church of **San Francesco** to feast your eyes on its legendary 14th-century "Paradise" cloister.

Relax in the adjoining **Villa Communale** gardens and enjoy the Cinemascope-wide view of the Bay of Naples. Continue on Via Veneto to the **Piazza della Vittoria** to see the faded "Casa di Tasso" sign that marks the birthplace of the town's revered poet. Cross the piazza to the aristocratic Hotel Bellevue Syrene, whose fabulous garden belvedere is the most beautiful place to have drinks. Pass the hotel to exit the walls near the Porta Greca (Greek Gate) and take the stairway down to **Marina Grande** for dinner at a festive seafood restaurant. Catch a bus on the Via del Mare to return.

(Majolica Courtyard, 1772). This was one of the many examples of majolica and faienceware created in this region, a highlight of Campanian craftsmen. (Another notable example is the Chiostro delle Clarisse at Naples's Santa Chiara.) In 1610 the palazzo became the Ritiro di Santa Maria della Pietà and today remains private, but you can view the courtyard beyond the vestryway. Its back wall—a trompe l'oeil architectural fantasia, entirely rendered in majolica tile—is now a suitably romantic setting for the Ruoppo florist shop. Buy a rose here and bear it through the streets of old Sorrento, an emblem of your pleasure in the moment. As you leave the palazzo, note the unusual arched windows on the palace facade, a grace note also seen a few doors away at **Palazzo Veniero** (No. 14), a 13th-century structure with a Byzantine-Arab influence. ✉ *Via Pietà 24.*

Piazza della Vittoria. Tree-shaded Piazza della Vittoria is book-ended by two fabled hotels, the Bellevue Syrene and the Imperial Hotel Tramontano, one wing of which was home to famed 16th-century writer Torquato Tasso. Set by the bay-side balcony, the facade of the Casa di Tasso is all the more exquisite for its simplicity and seems little changed since his day. The poet's house originally belonged to the Rossi family, into which Tasso's mother married, and was adorned with beautiful gardens (Tasso wove gardens into many of his poems). The piazza itself is supposedly the site where a temple to Venus once stood, and the scattered Roman ruins make it a real possibility. ✉ *Via Veneto and Via Marina Grande.*

Piazza Tasso. This was the site of Porta Catello, the summit of the old walls that once surrounded the city. Today it remains a symbolic portal to the old town, overflowing with apricot-awninged cafés, Stile Liberty (Italian art nouveau) buildings, people who congregate here day and night, and horse-drawn carriages clip-clopping by. In the center of it all is Torquato Tasso himself, standing atop a high base and rendered in marble by sculptor Giovanni Carli in 1870. The great poet was born in Sorrento in 1544 and died in Rome in 1595, just before he was to be crowned poet laureate. Tasso wrote during a period when Italy was still recovering from devastating Ottoman incursions along its coasts—Sorrento itself was sacked and pillaged in 1558. He is best known for his epic poem *Jerusalem Delivered,* which deals with the conquest of Jerusalem during the First Crusade. At the northern edge of the piazza, where it merges into Corso Italia, is the church of Maria del Carmine, with a Rococo wedding-cake facade of gleaming white-and-yellow stucco. Step inside to note its wall of 18th-century tabernacles, all set, like a jeweler's display, in gilded cases, and the fine ceiling painting of the Virgin Mary. ✉ *Western end of Corso Italia and above Marina Piccola, at eastern edge of historic district.*

Capo di Sorrento and the Bagno della Regina Giovanna. Just 2 km (1 mile) west of Sorrento, turn right off Statale 145 toward the sea, and then park and walk a few minutes through citrus and olive groves to get to Capo di Sorrento, the craggy tip of the cape, with the most interesting ancient ruins in the area. They were identified by the Latin poet Publius Papinius Statius as the ancient Roman villa of historian Pollio Felix, patron of the great authors Virgil and Horace. Next to the ruins is Bagno della Regina Giovanna (Queen Joan's Bath). A cleft in the rocks allows the sea to channel through an archway into a clear, natural pool, with the water turning iridescent blue, green, and violet as the sunlight changes angles. The easiest way to see all this is to rent a boat at Sorrento; afterward, sailing westward will bring you to the fishermen's haven of Marina di Puolo, where you can lunch on fresh catch at a modest restaurant.

WHERE TO EAT

$$ SOUTHERN ITALIAN

✕ **Camera & Cucina.** The large kitchen opens onto the modern and stylish dining area, hung with well-selected photo collections by international artists. The outdoor bar area is a lovely spot to enjoy their signature *mojito mediterraneo,* in which Russian vodka meets local lemon, tomatoes, and basil. Among the specialties of this gallery-restaurant: *paccheri* with tuna and anchovies from Cetara and *ravioli di spigola* (with sea bass). Private cooking classes are also on offer. [$] *Average main: €16* ✉ *Via Correale 19* ☎ *081/8773530* 🌐 *www.cameraecucina.it.*

$$ SOUTHERN ITALIAN ✕ **Da Emilia.** Near the Marina Grande, and not the most visually prepossessing place in Sorrento, this spot has the advantage of having Signora Emilia herself in the kitchen (and often out front as well). The rickety wooden tables and red-check tablecloths are a refreshing change from the town's (occasionally pretentious) elegance. Go for a plate of honest spaghetti with clams, wash it down with a carafe of the slightly acidic white wine, and watch the fishermen mending their nets. *Average main: €18 ✉ Via Marina Grande 62 ☎ 081/8072720 ⊙ Nov.–Feb., closed Tues.*

$$$ MODERN ITALIAN ✕ **Il Buco.** In the spirit of "Slow Food," this restaurant just off Piazza Sant'Antonino uses only local and seasonal ingredients of the highest quality in its nouvelle creations. Dine on inventive sea and land dishes like *fedelini* pasta seasoned with Sorrento walnuts and anchovies. Round off the meal with a balsamic vinegar *tiramisu* with wild strawberries and ginger *granita*. Reservations are recommended for dinner. *Average main: €30 ✉ Seconda Rampa di Marina Piccola, 5 ☎ 081/8782354 ⊕ www.ilbucoristorante.it ⊙ Closed Wed. and Jan. and Feb.*

$$ SOUTHERN ITALIAN ✕ **Il Delfino.** Right on the sea, this restaurant is attached to a *stabilamento* (beach club). You can eat in the sunshine or in a glassed-in nautical-motif dining area. Though you won't see many locals here—they're unlikely to be impressed by the four-language menus—seafood platters are fresh and flavorful, and this informal, economical venue also has a snack bar for light meals. You can even swim off the pier—but please: wait two hours after eating! *Average main: €20 ✉ Via Marina Grande 216 ☎ 081/8782038 ⊕ www.ristorantebagnidelfino.it ⊙ Closed Nov.–Mar.*

$$ SOUTHERN ITALIAN ✕ **La Basilica.** Under the same ownership as the Ristorante Museo Caruso, this budget alternative to its famous brother has no cover or service charges, but offers the same wine list (about 1,700 labels) plus a bountiful choice of hearty Italian dishes. In a tiny alley between piazzas Tasso and St. Antonino, its main salon is decorated with modern paintings of an erupting Vesuvius, but for a more romantic setting, the smaller room on the opposite side of the road has a tiny balcony overlooking the tortuous road to the harbor. There is also outside seating. Try the *strozzapreti* (priest-chokers) pasta with scampi and cherry tomatoes or the fabulous rice cake on zucchini sauce. *Average main: €16 ✉ Via S. Antonino 28 ☎ 081/8774790 ⊕ www.ristorantelabasilica.com.*

$$ SOUTHERN ITALIAN Fodor's Choice ★ ✕ **La Favorita—'O Parrucchiano.** This restaurant is in a sprawling, multilevel, high-ceiling greenhouse and orchard, with tables and chairs set amid enough tropical greenery to fill a Victorian conservatory. The effect is enchantingly 19th century. Opened in 1868 by an ex-priest ('*O Parrucchiano* means "the priest's place" in the local dialect), La Favorita continues to serve classic Sorrentine cuisine. The shrimp baked in lemon leaves, cannelloni, homemade Sorrentine pasta, chocolate and hazelnut cake, and lemon profiteroles are all excellent, but they can't compete with the unique interior. *Average main: €15 ✉ Corso Italia 71 ☎ 081/8781321 ⊕ www.parrucchiano.com ⊙ Closed Wed. from mid-Nov.–mid-Mar.*

The Majolica Courtyard is a highlight of the Palazzo Correale.

$$$ ITALIAN **La Lanterna.** On the site of ancient Roman thermal baths (you can still see ruins under a glass section in the floor), this is a historic venue as well as a beloved eatery. Whether dining outdoors under the lanterns, or indoors under the beamed ceiling and stucco arcades, you'll enjoy *cucina tipica, locale e nazionale,* traditional local and national dishes, including old favorites such as *calamaro ripieno* (stuffed calamari) or *zuppa di pesce* (fresh fish soup). *Average main: €30* *Via S. Cesareo 25* *081/8781355* *www.lalanternasorrento.it* *Nov.–Apr., closed Wed.*

$$ SOUTHERN ITALIAN **L'Abate.** With tables outside on the pretty Piazza Sant' Antonino and a charming atmosphere inside, this is a great place to try Sorrento classics such as spaghetti with zucchini, *paccheri* in seafood sauce and beef fillet dressed with *provolone del monaco*. The *buffet della casa* offers a wide choice of vegetables and fresh appetizers to start with, while mixed sautéed shellfish, pizza, and a delicious homemade parfait round things off. Cooking classes are organized in the private upstairs dining room. *Average main: €20* *Piazza S. Antonino 25, Sorrento* *081/8072304* *www.labatesorrento.it* *Nov. and Jan.–Mar.; Wed. year-round.*

$$$ SOUTHERN ITALIAN Fodor's Choice ★ **Ristorante Museo Caruso.** Sorrentine favorites, including *acquerello* (fresh fish appetizer) and ravioli with crab and zucchini sauce, are tweaked creatively here. The staff is warm and helpful, the singer on the sound system is the long-departed "fourth tenor" himself, and the operatic memorabilia (including posters and old photos of Caruso) is viewed in a flattering blush-pink light. This elegant restaurant deserves its longtime popularity. It is open from noon to midnight and has five-course tasting menus from €50. *Average main: €25* *Via S. Antonino 12* *081/8073156* *www.ristorantemuseocaruso.com.*

WHERE TO STAY

$$$$ HOTEL Fodor's Choice ★ **Bellevue Syrene.** This retreat, magnificently set on a bluff high over the Bay of Naples is one of Italy's legendary hotels, once a gentle fantasia of Venetian chandeliers, Louis-Phillipe rugs, and Belle Epoque murals, it has been renovated to resemble something right out of sizzling South Beach. **Pros:** impeccable design elements; elegant common areas; half board available. **Cons:** very expensive; parking is €25 a day. *Rooms from: €450 ✉ Piazza della Vittoria 5 ☎ 081/8781024 ⊕ www.bellevue.it ⇨ 49 rooms ⊙ Closed Jan.–Mar. ¶ Some meals.*

$ HOTEL **Del Corso.** This centrally located, family-run hotel close to Sorrento's major hub, Piazza Tasso, is homey and comfortable, with pleasant common areas and basic, clean rooms. **Pros:** open year-round; pleasant, accommodating staff; only 100 meters from the station. **Cons:** no pool; some rooms are small; no parking. *Rooms from: €120 ✉ Corso Italia 134 ☎ 081/8071016 ⊕ www.hoteldelcorso.com ⇨ 27 rooms ⊙ Closed Nov.–Feb. ¶ Breakfast.*

$$$$ HOTEL Fodor's Choice ★ **Excelsior Vittoria.** Overlooking the Bay of Naples, this luxurious Belle Epoque dream has been in the same family since 1834; the public salons are virtual museums, with Victorian love seats and *stile liberty* ornamentation. **Pros:** beyond the protected gates you're in the heart of town; gardens buffer city noise. **Cons:** not all rooms have sea views; some rooms are rather small; front desk can be cold. *Rooms from: €350 ✉ Piazza Tasso 34 ☎ 081/8071044, 800/980053 in Italy only ⊕ www.exvitt.it ⇨ 92 rooms ¶ Breakfast.*

$$ HOTEL **Hotel Antiche Mura.** Classically elegant and family-run, this four-star is a great find, with the added bonus of a swimming pool in a citrus garden where sections of the ancient city walls are still visible. The lobby's marble columns and ceramic tiling give a lasting first impression, while the bright pastel rooms, facing inland, are airy and comfortable. **Pros:** central location; garden swimming pool. **Cons:** no views from the guest rooms. *Rooms from: €190 ✉ Via Fourimura 7 (Piazza Tasso) ☎ 081/8073523 ⊕ www.hotelantichemura.com ⇨ 46 rooms, 5 suites.*

$$ HOTEL **Hotel Astoria.** In the heart of Sorrento's historical center, down a quiet pedestrian-only narrow street, this charming hotel has a light and gracious Mediterranean style. **Pros:** central location; friendly staff. **Cons:** no views. *Rooms from: €150 ✉ Via Santa Maria delle Grazie 24 ☎ 081/8074030 ⊕ www.hotelastoriasorrento.com ⇨ 43 rooms ⊙ Closed Jan. and Feb. ¶ Breakfast.*

$$$$ HOTEL **La Favorita.** The glamorous lobby may be a white-on-white extravaganza of Caprese columns, tufted sofas, shimmering crystal chandeliers, ecclesiastical silver objects, and gilded baroque mirrors, but the charming staff ensure the vibe is elegantly casual. **Pros:** central location; beautiful terrace; idyllic garden. **Cons:** no views from the guest rooms. *Rooms from: €450 ✉ Via T. Tasso 61 ☎ 081/8782031 ⊕ www.hotellafavorita.com ⇨ 85 rooms ⊙ Closed Nov. and Jan.–Mar. ¶ Breakfast.*

$ B&B/INN **Relais Palazzo Starace.** There is no lobby and no view, but this B&B does boast a gentle price tag in a central part of town, and that's a winning combo for summertime Sorrento. **Pros:** great location; helpful owner; competitive prices; discounted parking at nearby

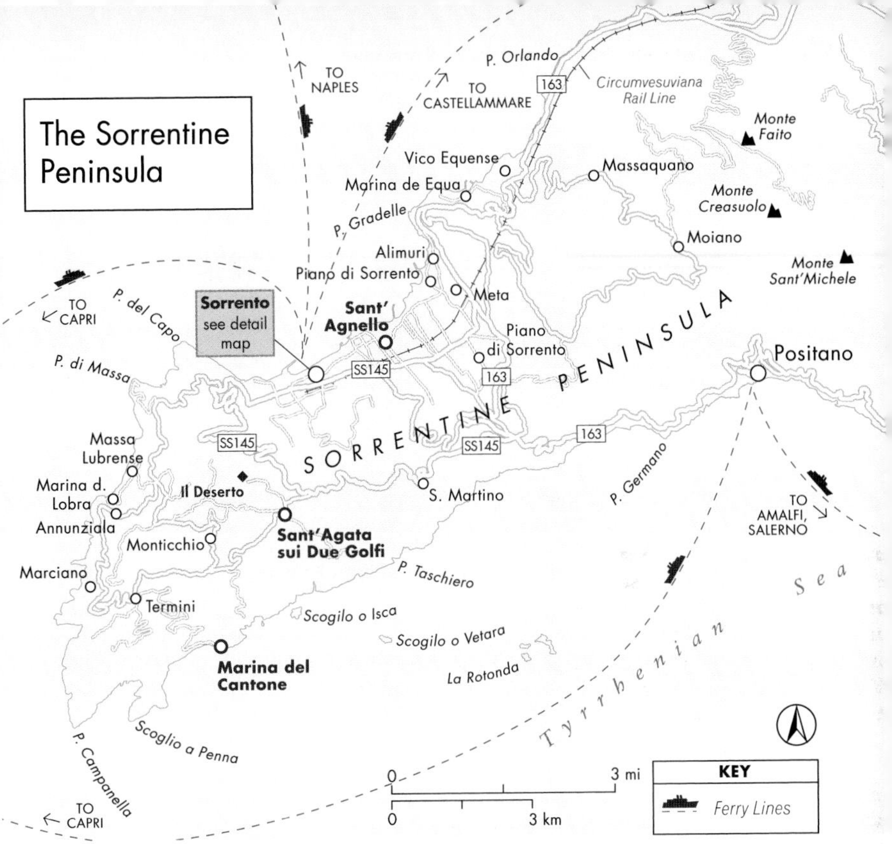

garage. **Cons:** no views; room with the air conditioner on balcony is noisy. *Rooms from: €120 Via Santa Maria della Pietà 9 081/8784031 www.palazzostarace.com 5 rooms Closed Jan. and Feb. Breakfast.*

$$$$ HOTEL **Royal.** Lush, landscaped gardens surround this hotel, an oasis of quiet and cool, with an elevator to sea level and a private beach. **Pros:** centrally located; spacious lounge; friendly staff. **Cons:** minimum three-night stay in high season; some first floor rooms have obstructed views. *Rooms from: €450 Via Correale 42 081/8073434 www.royalsorrento.com 96 rooms Closed mid-Nov.–Easter Breakfast.*

$$ HOTEL Fodor's Choice ★ **Settimo Cielo.** Even if your wallet won't allow a stay at one of Sorrento's grand hotels, you can still find lodgings overlooking the water, and this hotel on the road to Capo Sorrento is an excellent choice for budget travelers. **Pros:** plenty of parking; excellent views. **Cons:** no-frills decor, long walk along busy road into Sorrento. *Rooms from: €140 Via Capo 27 081/8781012 www.hotelsettimocielo.com 20 rooms Breakfast.*

NIGHTLIFE AND THE ARTS

Music spots and bars cluster in the side streets near Piazza Tasso, among them Fauno Notte Club and Artis Domus. Ask at your hotel about clubs that might interest you and to get the latest news.

Feste (*religious festivals*). Traditional festivities include an atmospheric procession in the thick of Thursday night before Easter, with locals donning eerie white hoods, followed by a less awesome "black" procession on Good Friday evening. Christmas has its usual accompaniment of crèches, while further celebrations are held on February 14—not St. Valentine's Day, but St. Anthony's Day; he's the patron saint of Sorrento.

Incontri Musicali Sorrentini. Incontri Musicali Sorrentini is the main cultural event of the year, offering a bevy of concerts and theatrical entertainments from the last week of August to the end of September, many held in the famous Moorish-style cloister of the church of San Francesco. There are several outdoor venues in Sant'Agnello nearby. Check with your hotel or the Sorrento tourist office (🌐 *www.sorrentotourism.com*) for schedules and information. ✉ *Cloister of Chiesa di San Francesco* ✉ *Piazzetta Angri and Largo Annunziata in Sant'Agnello.*

Tarantella Show. The Tarantella Show presents tarantella dances with masks, costumes, and tambourines, as well as classic Neapolitan folklore performances complete with *pulcinelle* (comedic prankster figures in Neapolitan theater) and *pazzarielli* (jesters). ✉ *Fauno Notte Club* ☎ *081/8781021* 🌐 *www.faunonotte.it.*

Teatro Tasso. Catch a performance of traditional Neapolitan music, folk dancing, and dinner shows, in which performers wear 19th-century Sorrentine costumes. ✉ *Piazza S. Antonino 25, 80067* ☎ *081/8075525* 🌐 *www.teatrotasso.com.*

SHOPPING

The main shopping street is Via San Cesareo—along this pedestrian thoroughfare, lined with dozens of shops selling local and Italian crafts, the air is pungent with the perfume of fruit and vegetable stands. Corso Italia has more modern boutique offerings, among which are Benetton, Max Mara, Paul & Shark. Various shops are in the portico of piazza Lauro. Wood inlay (*intarsia*) is the most-sought-after item, but you'll be surprised by the high quality of embroidery, leather items, corals, cameos, and metalwork. Local crafts, but in line with a contemporary art spirit, can be found in Via Fuoro, while some classic antique dealers are in Via P. R. Giuliani.

BOOKS

Libreria Tasso. A browse-worthy stock of English books and maps means you'll never run out of holiday reads. ✉ *Via S. Cesareo 96* ☎ *081/8071639* 🌐 *www.libreriatasso.com.*

CLOTHING AND PERFUME

Aromi di Sorrento-Mezzo Kilo. Far from the tourist streets, this little shop is crammed with Sorrento's best soaps and essences, delicious *confetti* and sweets. It's also worth hunting down to delight in Giuseppina Gambardella's ingenious Christmas decorations made with peppers. ✉ *Via Fuoro 62/A* ☎ *333/3718544.*

Autori Capresi. Capri tailors produce high-class linen clothes for adults and children at this beautiful atelier. Nothing is left to chance in the handmade finishing on the classic white-and-beige linen, and colorful creations. ✉ *Via Padre Reginaldo Giuliani 21* ☎ *081/19173242.*

Capua. The voguish cashmere clothes and accessories for women and men are renewed annually to keep up with new trends without forgetting the classics. This shop is a good choice for quality cashmere at reasonable prices. ✉ *Piazza A. Lauro 14* ☎ *081/8073353.*

Corium. Choose the leather design from the hundreds on display and the cobbler will knock up a pair of unique sandals for you. ✉ *Via degli Archi 20* ☎ *081/8071567.*

Nonna Cristina. The wearability and lovely style of these children's clothes in soft and extra-fine materials will have the little ones dressed in true Made-in-Italy fashion. ✉ *Piazza A. Lauro 13* ☎ *081/8072492.*

CRAFTS

Arte e Dimora. Right in the *centro storico*, but not easy to find, the tiny store of Arte e Dimora might be just the place to fall in love with a unique *souvenir de voyage*. With no e-mail or telephone, the extravagant Michele tends his tiny space full of hundreds of different kinds of bric-à-brac, including watercolors, frames, old tin boxes, and one-of-a-kind vintage items. ✉ *Vico 1, Fuoro 9 bis.*

Gargiulo Salvatore. A visit to this inlaid-wood shop, now in its third generation of Sorrentine craftsmen, takes you back in time. Jewelry, musical boxes, and wooden pictures are particularly fine. ✉ *Via Fuoro 33* ☎ *081/8782420.*

La Conchiglia. You choose one of the hundreds of designs and one of the resident *maestri* creates your own made-to-measure sandals on the spot—a less expensive option than you might think. ✉ *Via Fuoro 29* ☎ *081/8774605.*

Terrerosse. At this atelier-shop two artists make unusual creations, such as lamps, vases, and paperweights from shell, ceramic, glass, wood, stone, and other natural materials. ✉ *Via Fuoro 73* ☎ *349/7542872.*

JEWELRY

Gioielleria di Somma. Tired of Sorrento's coral and cameos? A trendier alternative is this jewelry shop with classics by Pomellato, DoDo, Bulgari, and many others. ✉ *Corso Italia 114* ☎ *081/8073213.*

Leonard Jewels. Vincenzo and his son Nicholas make distinguished jewels with both coral and lava at Leonard Jewels; for those famous carved Sorrentine cameos head to the mezzanine floor. ✉ *Via S. Cesareo 24* ☎ *081/8772923.*

Vincenzo Piscopo. With a good selection of cameos, rings, necklaces, bracelets, and pendants,this shop makes good use of silver and coral in its jewelry. ✉ *Corso Italia 210 d* ☎ *081/8771777.*

KITCHENWARE

Casa Mia. The ideal stop for home-decorating ideas and useful kitchen utensils in classic or stylishly designed forms. ✉ *Piazza A. Lauro 5, Sorrento* ☎ *081/0203991.*

LIQUEUR

Limonoro. The lovely local lemon liqueur, limoncello is made and sold here. You can observe the production process in the back of this tiny white shop, and watch the owners paint designs on the pretty bottles. ✉ *Via S. Cesareo 49/53* ☎ *081/8785348* 🌐 *www.limonoro.it.*

SANT'AGNELLO, MARINA DEL CANTONE, AND NEARBY

Grand monasteries, the finest beach along the Gulf of Positano, an Edenic botanical park, and southern Italy's finest restaurant are just a few of the discoveries that await the traveler willing to leave Sorrento's Belle Epoque splendor behind and take to the scenic hills and coasts of the Sorrentine Peninsula. As it turns out, many people do just that—the towns here get crowded with weekenders from Naples and Rome, and the two-lane state roads 145 and 163 are often congested. The sights here, however, are worth the bother. For those without a car, SITA buses run regularly throughout the peninsula, with most routes stopping in Sorrento. Bus stops are frequent along the peninsula roads, but it's always best to be armed with a local timetable to avoid long waits at stops. Buses stop by request and only at official stops, so flag them down when you would like to get picked up and on boarding request the desired stop.

SANT'AGNELLO

2 km (1 mile) east of Sorrento.

Back in the 18th and 19th centuries, the tiny hamlet of Sant'Agnello was an address of choice. To escape Sorrento's crowds, Bourbon princes and exiled Russian millionaires vacationed here, some building sumptuous villas, others staying at the Hotel Cocumella, the oldest hotel on the Sorrentine Peninsula. On the quieter coastal side of town, Sant'Agnello still possesses a faintly ducal air. The 15th- to 16th-century parish church, Chiesa Parrocchiale di Sant'Agnello, is as lyrical as its name: swirls of lemon yellow and white, decorated with marble-gloss plasterwork. Nearby is a spectacular belvedere, the Terrazza Punta San Francesco, complete with café, which offers a hold-your-breath view of the Bay of Naples.

GETTING HERE AND AROUND

Take the A3 Napoli–Salerno highway to the Castellammare di Stabia exit. Take Statale 145 south and follow signs for "Penisola Sorrentina" and Sant'Agnello. By train, take the Circumvesuviana to the Sant'Agnello stop. There is regular municipal bus service from downtown Sorrento.

EXPLORING

Sant'Agnello's two most famous estates sit side by side. In the early 19th century, the Jesuit **Cocumella monastery** was transformed into a hotel, welcoming the rich and famous. Today, only lucky guests can enjoy its gardens. Next door is the **Parco dei Principi,** a hotel built by Gio Ponti in 1962 surrounded by a botanical park laid out in 1792 by the Count of Siracusa, a cousin to the Bourbons. Traversed by a diminutive Bridge of Love, this was a favorite spot for Désireé, Napoléon's first *amour,* who came here often. Shaded by horticultural rarities, this park leads to the count's Villa di Poggio Siracusa, a Rococo-style iced birthday cake of a house perched over the bay. Green thumbs and other circumspect visitors can stroll through the romantic park, now part of the Hotel Parco dei Principi.

WHERE TO STAY

$$$$ HOTEL **Cocumella.** In a cliff-top garden overlooking the Bay of Naples, the Cocumella occupies a baroque monastery, complete with frescoed ceilings, antique reliquaries, and a marble cloister. **Pros:** quiet location; elegant and romantic. **Cons:** far from off-site restaurants; car a necessity; many rooms and areas of hotel need renovation. *Rooms from: €385 Via Cocumella 7 081/8782933 www.cocumella.com 50 rooms Closed Nov.–Mar. Breakfast.*

$$$$ HOTEL **Grand Hotel Parco dei Principi.** Inside, this chic 1960s Moderne hotel is all white walls and blue-glass accents; outside blooms the fabled Parco dei Principi, the lush *giardino* laid out in the early 19th century. **Pros:** stunning garden; grand bay views; fun '60s decor; exquisite pool area. **Cons:** rooms in roadside wing fall short of those in main bay-side building. *Rooms from: €400 Via Rota 44, Sorrento 081/8784644 www.grandhotelparcodeiprincipi.net 96 rooms Breakfast.*

$$$ HOTEL **Hotel Mediterraneo.** With its understated old-world charm, sweeping bay views, and impeccable service, Hotel Mediterraneo is the logical choice for a four-star hotel experience in Sant'Agnello. **Pros:** spectacular views; free shuttle into town; bright and spacious rooms. **Cons:** not all rooms have sea views; decor in some rooms could be spruced up. *Rooms from: €250 Via Crawford 85 081/8781352 www.mediterraneosorrento.com 70 rooms Closed Nov.–Mar. Breakfast.*

SANT'AGATA SUI DUE GOLFI

7 km (4½ miles) south of Sorrento, 10 km (6 miles) east of Positano.

Because of its panoramic vistas, Sant'Agata was an end-of-the-line pilgrimage site for beauty lovers through the centuries, especially before the Amalfi Drive opened up the coast to the southeast. As its name suggests, this village 1,300 feet above sea level looks out over the bays of Naples and Salerno (Sant'Agata refers to a Sicilian saint, honored here with a 16th-century chapel), and it found its first fame during the Roman Empire as the nexus of merchant routes uniting the two gulfs. Now that the town has become slightly built up, you have to head to its outskirts to take in the vistas.

GETTING HERE AND AROUND

By car, take the A3 Napoli–Salerno highway to the Castellammare di Stabia exit. Take Statale 145 south and follow signs for "Penisola Sorrentina." Once you reach Piano di Sorrento, take Statale 163 (direction Positano) and after about 3 km (2 miles), turn back onto Statale 145, following signs for Sant'Agata sui Due Golfi. By public transport, take the Circumvesuviana to Sorrento, then a SITA bus to Sant'Agata sui Due Golfi.

4

EXPLORING

Il Convento di San Paolo al Deserto. Sant'Agata's most famous vantage point is on the far north side of the hill, where an ancient Greek sanctuary is said—somewhat fancifully—to have been dedicated to the Sirens of legend. That choice location became Il Convento di San Paolo al Deserto, a monastery built by the Carmelite fathers in the 17th century and now occupied by an order of nuns. Partly crumbling and partly restored, the monastery's famed belvedere—with panoramic views of the blue waters all around, and of Vesuvius, Capri, and the peninsula—was a top sight for Grand Tour–era travelers. To access the belvedere's tower, ring the bell at the monastery and ask for the key to open the gate. To get to the Deserto from the center of Sant'Agata, take the main road (Corso Sant'Agata) past the church of Santa Maria delle Grazie on your right, and keep walking uphill on Via Deserto for a little more than half a mile. If traveling by car, park in the raised lot opposite the hotel O Sole Mio. ✉ *Via Deserto* ☎ *081/8780199* 🎫 *Donations welcome* 🕒 *Oct.–Mar., daily 10–12 and 3–5; Apr.–Sept., daily 8:30–12 and 5–7.*

Santa Maria delle Grazie. Today's travelers head to Sant'Agata less for the sublime beauties of Il Deserto than for its lodging options and to dine at Don Alfonso 1890, the finest restaurant in Campania. Across the way from Don Alfonso on the town square is the beautiful 16th-century Renaissance church of Santa Maria delle Grazie. The shadowy, evocative interior features an exceptional 17th-century altar brought from the Girolamini church in Naples in the 19th century. Attributed to Florentine artists, it's inlaid with lapis, malachite, mother-of-pearl, and polychrome marble.

WHERE TO EAT AND STAY

$$$$ SOUTHERN ITALIAN Fodor's Choice ★

✕ **Antico Francischiello da Peppino.** Overlooking rows of olive trees that seem to run into the sea, this eatery is away from the throng, halfway between Sant'Agata and Massa Lubrense. Two huge, beamed dining rooms with brick archways, old chandeliers, antique mirrored sideboards, hundreds of mounted plates, and tangerine tablecloths make for quite a sight. Specialties at this fourth-generation establishment include *baccalà* (cod) in olive oil with a sweet-and-sour vegetable dish in pear sauce, or swordfish rolls. The towering dessert trolley is full of goodies, and you can taste as many as you like. 💲 *Average main: €40* ✉ *Via Partenope 27, halfway between Sant'Agata and Massa Lubrense, Sorrento* ☎ *081/5339780* 🌐 *www.francischiello.com* 🕒 *Closed Wed. Nov.–Mar.*

$$$$ SOUTHERN ITALIAN Fodor's Choice ★

✕ **Don Alfonso 1890.** The late R. W. Apple, the *New York Times*' famous traveling epicure, once declared Don Alfonso the best restaurant in Italy, and it remains a gastronomic giant. The restaurant, a sort of southern Italian Chez Panisse—pioneer in upscale farm-to-table cuisine—grows all its own produce on a small farm nearby. The operation is a family affair, with mama (Livia) in the dining room and papa (former chef Alfonso Iaccarino) these days tending to the organic plot. And now their sons have moved into the business—one as head chef, the other maitre'd. The menu reflects this generational shift, with classic dishes listed beside more edgy inventions. Delicate cheese ravioli topped with a ragu of house-grown tomatoes, might give way to more contemporary fare like fried lobster nuggets or sea urchin ice cream with rose *fettuccine.* *Average main: €50* ✉ *Corso Sant'Agata 13, Sorrento* ☎ *081/8780026* *www.donalfonso.com* *Closed Nov.–Mar, and Mon. No lunch Tues. June–Sept.; Apr., May, and Oct. closed Tues.*

$ HOTEL **Sant'Agata.** If you wish to stay in hilltop Sant'Agata sui Due Golfi, this efficiently run hotel provides airy and pleasant lodging and a good bed to fall into after a meal at Don Alfonso 1890 or a walk to the Deserto belvedere. **Pros:** recently renovated; easily accessible by SITA bus; free Wi-Fi; quiet location. **Cons:** far from the beach. *Rooms from: €110* ✉ *Via dei Campi 8/A* ☎ *081/8080800* *081/5330749* *48 rooms* *Closed Nov.–Feb.* *Breakfast.*

4

MARINA DEL CANTONE

5 km (3 miles) southwest of Sant'Agata sui Due Golfi.

As the largest (pebble) beach on the Sorrentine Peninsula, Marina del Cantone attracts weekend sun worshippers and foodies drawn by the seaside restaurants here. To get to the beach, usually dotted with dozens of festive umbrellas, a slender road winds down to the sea through rolling vineyards and the small town of Nerano, ending at the Gulf of Positano near the Montalto watchtower. While enjoying Marina del Cantone's wonderful beach and kick-back village vibe, it also offers a front-row seat to the haunting geological spectacle that is the islets of **Li Galli,** which seems to follow you around as you drive up and down the Amalfi Coast. Other than Positano, Marina del Cantone is the best place to hire a boat to visit these tiny islands—Gallo Lungo, Castelluccia, and La Rotonda—which sit on the horizon to the east of the beach. They're also called Isole Sirenuse (Isles of the Sirens), after the mythical girl group that lured unwitting sailors onto the rocks.

GETTING HERE

By car, take the A3 Napoli–Salerno highway to the Castellammare di Stabia exit. Take Statale 145 south and follow signs for "Penisola Sorrentina." Once you reach Piano di Sorrento, take Statale 163 (direction Positano) and after about 3 km, turn back onto Statale 145, following signs for Sant'Agata sui Due Golfi, then Metrano, then Nerano-Marina del Cantone. By public transport, take the Circumvesuviana to Sorrento, then a SITA bus to Nerano-Marina del Cantone.

EXPLORING

Nautica O Masticiello. Nautica O Masticiello runs daily trips to Capri from June to September, and regular tours along the Amalfi Coast including Li Galli, Amalfi, and Positano, weather permitting. They also offer a wide selection of boat rentals, with or without a captain. ✉ *Waterfront* ☎ *081/8081443* *www.masticiello.com.*

WHERE TO EAT AND STAY

$$$ SOUTHERN ITALIAN **Maria Grazia.** A great story lies behind this area favorite. Signora Maria was running this little waterfront trattoria between the world wars when an aristocrat came round unexpectedly to eat with the

marina fishermen; Maria cooked up the best she had on hand—spaghetti with stuffed zucchini blossoms. Through the well-satisfied aristocrat, the dish and the restaurant became famous. You can still enjoy it, even without a noble title, in season. *Average main: €25* ✉ *Spiaggia di Marina del Cantone* ☎ *081/8081011* ⊙ *Closed Dec., Jan., mid-Nov. and Feb., except on weekends.*

$$$ SOUTHERN ITALIAN **Taverna del Capitano.** The fascinating cuisine here is based on old recipes from the various cultures—Norman and Moorish among them—that loom large in the history of the region. Extravagant recipes such as *cornetti di pasta-farciti con gamberi e conditi con frutti di mare* (homemade croissant pasta filled with shrimps in seafood sauce) are worth trying. You can rely on the knowledgeable maître d' for an absorbing commentary on the various dishes and advice on the right wine from a siege-ready cellar. For dessert, opt for candied eggplant filled with ricotta and topped with chocolate sauce. Above the restaurant area is a select 10-room hotel—called La Locanda del Capitano—run by the same family, with the best rooms overlooking the waterfront. Lodging prices ($$) include full beach facilities. *Average main: €25* ✉ *Piazza delle Sirene 10/11, Massa Lubrense, Marina del Cantone* ☎ *081/8081028* 🌐 *www.tavernadelcapitano.com* ⊙ *Closed Jan. and Feb. and Mon. and Tues., except in summer.*

$ HOTEL **Quattro Passi.** The focus at this hotel and Italian-nouvelle restaurant is on relaxation and fine food, but the comfortable environs also make it a pleasure to fall into bed. **Pros:** close to the beach; truly exceptional restaurant; cooking lessons on request. **Cons:** grounds can be a bit buggy in summer; no sea view. *Rooms from: €30* ✉ *Via A. Vespucci 13N, Massa Lubrense, Nerano* ☎ *081/8082800* 🌐 *www.ristorantequattropassi.com* *7 rooms* ⊙ *Closed Wed. and Nov.–mid-Mar.* *Breakfast.*

5

THE BAY OF NAPLES

WELCOME TO THE BAY OF NAPLES

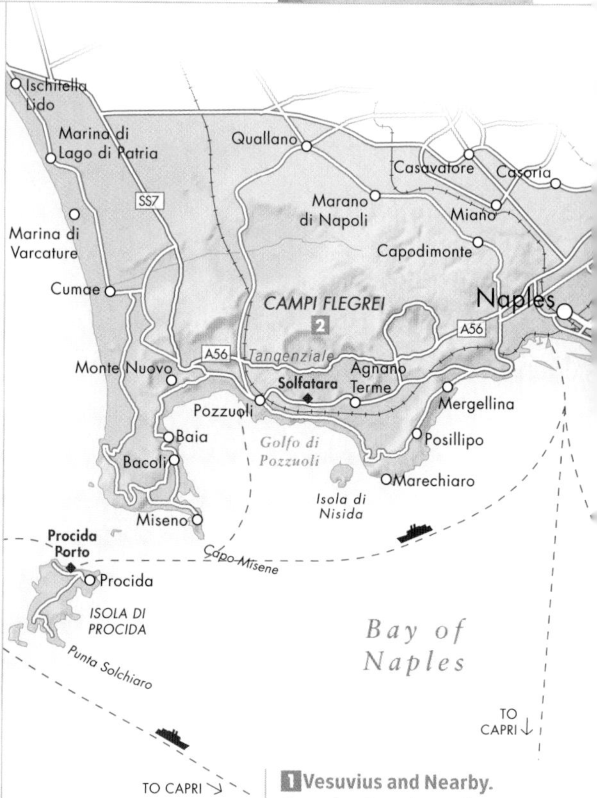

TOP REASONS TO GO

★ **Archaeological treats:** Thanks to the destructive yet preserving powers of Vesuvius, you can visit Pompeii and Herculaneum for a glimpse of ancient Roman life.

★ **Sweeping views:** Look seaward from the Acropolis at ancient Cumae and imagine you're a Greek colonist just arrived on the Italian mainland in the 8th century BC.

★ **A gastronomic splurge:** See how the Romans have revived their reputation as *bons viveurs* in restaurants at modern Pompeii, or enjoy the day's catch on the waterfront at Pozzuoli.

★ **Home to Mr. and Mrs. Nero:** As an alternative to the tourist bustle at other sites, head for Oplontis, a Roman villa with astoundingly well-preserved frescoes that ooze charm and tranquility.

★ **The dream volcano:** Geothermal energy has been trapped since time immemorial under the cone of Vesuvius—as you'll experience on a hike around the peak.

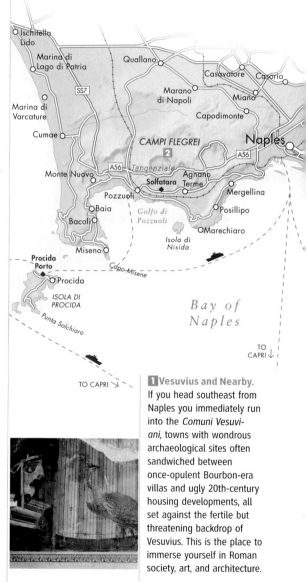

1 Vesuvius and Nearby. If you head southeast from Naples you immediately run into the *Comuni Vesuviani,* towns with wondrous archaeological sites often sandwiched between once-opulent Bourbon-era villas and ugly 20th-century housing developments, all set against the fertile but threatening backdrop of Vesuvius. This is the place to immerse yourself in Roman society, art, and architecture.

2 West of Naples. Starting from the western suburbs of Naples, the Phlegrean Fields stretch in a coastal belt all the way to the coast at Cumae. Pockmarked with volcanic craters, this was where Rome's senators and emperors came to spend the summer, tapping the geothermal energy to enhance their downtime with steam baths and swims. It is no coincidence that this remains a favorite excursion for Neapolitans in the 21st century.

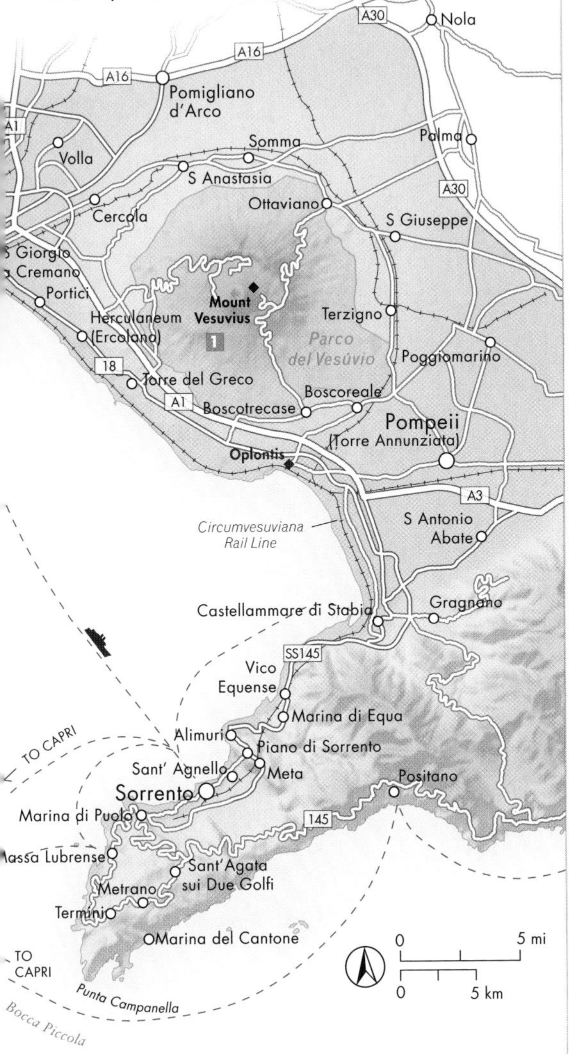

GETTING ORIENTED

The Bay of Naples chapter includes two main areas: southeast of Naples, the famous region dominated by Vesuvius and home to the spectacular ancient sites of Pompeii and Herculaneum; and, along the coast west of Naples, the Campi Flegrei region, also home to many ancient wonders. The Circumvesuviana railway serves the Vesuvian area from Naples and Sorrento, the major bases for day trips. Naples is the obvious base for the Campi Flegrei, but public transportation from Naples to the main sites beyond Pozzuoli is sporadic. If you're visiting Cumae and Baia, you'll disembark the train at Fusaro and take a bus the rest of the way. If you want to stay in the region for a few days, you can overnight at one of several fetching country-style hotels.

CAMPANIA'S ANCIENT TREASURES

AN ARCHAEOLOGICAL "DISNEYLAND"

As so often happens in history, other people's catastrophes are an archaeologist's dream: Pompeii, Herculaneum, and nearby ancient sites were remarkably preserved for posterity courtesy of Vesuvius's biggest eruption.

(above) The Castle at Baia is home to the Museo Archeologica dei Campi Flegrei. (opposite top) Roman temple at Pozzuoli (opposite bottom) Temple of Venus, Baia

Pompeii, Herculaneum, Baia, Cumae, Oplontis . . . no wonder the regions to the west and east of Naples are considered two of the world's greatest treasure troves of Greek and Roman antiquity. The area surrounding Naples has a Greco-Roman history that makes the big city itself look like the new kid on the block. The Greeks first Hellenized Italy's boot in the 6th century BC at Cumae. From the 1st century AD, the Romans made the region a vast playground. Favored by upper-middle-class Romans, Pompeii and Herculaneum were like French Riviera towns of today. And when emperors wanted to indulge in sybaritic living they headed west instead, from Puteoli to Baia, to build palatial residences for indulging in vices that would have been unseemly in Pompeii or (just read Petronius's *Satyricon*) Rome.

THE EMPRESS'S DUGOUT

The gigantic villa at Oplontis is attributed to Mrs. Nero, the Empress Poppaea. When Vesuvius erupted, the villa was probably empty, suggesting that it was undergoing restructuring. The villa does, though, have ravishing Roman murals done in the ultimate 2nd and 3rd Pompeiian styles.

POMPEII

When it comes to Campania's overflowing basket of treasures of the ancient world, everyone starts with Pompeii, and rightly so. Rome's Forum might be more majestic, but for a cross-section of Roman everyday life Pompeii is UNESCO World Heritage site "*Numero I.*"

Not only are everyday people commemorated, but in the Orchard of the Fugitives they are also preserved as death left them. In the Thermopolium, the day's takings were found in the till. Graffiti abounds (one, the Latin version of "House done," advice from one thief to another).

Over at the Villa dei Casti Amanti, excavations uncovered the skeleton of a mule used to work the flour mill. In the Domus of Julius Polybus, the past reemerges via virtual technology: missing pieces were put back to re-create the house while the original owner is given an eerie voice-over. To carry historical continuity further, inspired by Pompeii's Cave Canem mosaic, you can even adopt a local dog. On the day you visit, some sections of Pompeii may be closed for restoration, but the place is so large that there's always more than enough to see.

HERCULANEUM

The excavations here are more compact than in Pompeii. The mix of mud and pyroclastic matter left much

organic material eerily intact, down to a carbonized Roman boat given its own pavilion, along with spectacular frescoes and mosaics. To see it all come alive, visit the spectacular MAV Museum, whose exhibits include a computer re-creation of the fateful day in 79 AD when Vesuvius blew.

BAIA

With its thermal springs, this bay of bays boasted antiquity's most extensive bath complex, where Rome's Great and the Good headed for leisure purposes. Much of the complex remains on the slopes, though part of one pleasure palace—Emperor Claudius's Nymphaeum—lies submerged, the highlight of a submarine area you can view on a glass-bottomed boat.

CUMAE

Here Greeks established their first foothold on Italy's mainland, introducing the cult of Apollo whose priestess, the Cumaean Sibyl, prophesied for Aeneas the founding of Rome. Eight centuries later she was still in business, predicting, at least according to Robert Graves, to a young Claudius his future emperorship. Her "cave," one of the ancient wonders of the world, is actually part of a Roman military tunnel.

Updated by
Martin Bennett

If you're lucky enough to travel to Naples by water, a peacock's tail of splendor unfolds before you as you enter the vast Golfo di Napoli, the Bay of Naples. Enshrined in 1,001 travel posters, this pulse-tingling vista offers a turquoise-rimmed crescent of isles, hills, azure sea, ancient cities, and modern villas, all arrayed around the bay to the east and west of Naples.

But on each side of the city the earth fumes and grumbles, reminding us that all this beauty was born of cataclysm. Along the coast to the west are the Campi Flegrei, the Phlegrean Fields of the ancients, where the crater of the Solfatara spews satisfyingly Dante-esque gases and where hills like Monte Nuovo have a habit of emerging overnight. Nearby are the dark, deep waters of Lago d'Averno (Lake Avernus), the lake that was allegedly the ancient doorway to the Underworld, realm of the pagan afterlife ruled over by the god Hades. To the southeast of Naples slumbers Vesuvius, the mother of all mounts, looking down from its 4,000-foot height at the coastal strip stretching from modern and ancient Pompeii all the way to Naples. With potential destruction ever at hand, it is small wonder that southern Italians—and in particular Neapolitans—obey to the letter Horace's precept *carpe diem:* "seize the day."

Even with the world's most famous volcano looming over the scene like a perpetual standby tombstone, visitors should feel relatively safe. The observatory on Vesuvius's slopes keeps its scientific finger on the subterranean pulse and will warn when signs of misbehavior become evident, so you need not worry about becoming an unwilling exhibit in some encore of Pompeii. You can simply concentrate on the memorable sights that fringe the spectacularly blue bay. The entire region is rife with legend and immortal names. Sixteen kilometers (10 miles) to the west of Naples lies an area where the emperors Claudius and Nero schemed and plotted in their villas, Virgil composed his poetry, and where, at Puteoli (now Pozzuoli), the Apostle Paul landed to spread the Gospel. Here, in and around what was called the Phlegrean (burning) Fields, are ancient sites, such as the Greeks' first colony in mainland Italy, the city of Cumae, home of the famed Cumaean Sibyl; the luxury-loving Baia, whose hot springs made it ancient Rome's most fashionable pleasure dome; and the amphitheater of Pozzuoli, whose subterranean galleries are better preserved than even those at Rome's Colosseum. Here are the Campi Flegrei—inspiration for Dante's *Inferno*—and the sulfur-bound Solfatara, the "Little Vesuvius." Leapfrogging over Naples and spread out east along the bay are the ancient noble villa at Oplontis and, in the shadow of Vesuvius, Herculaneum and Pompeii—among the largest archaeological sites in Europe. Nowhere else in Italy is there a comparable mingling of natural vigor with the remains of antiquity.

BAY OF NAPLES PLANNER

WHEN TO GO

This part of the Mediterranean is at its best in spring and fall, though you may encounter hordes of schoolchildren at archaeological sites. The weather is often chilly in winter, and roads on the upper slopes of Vesuvius can become dangerously icy. Spectacular summertime events take place at the ancient Roman baths at Baia and the ancient Roman theaters at Pompeii. The verdant Campi Flegrei becomes a floral feast at springtime, and as late as June and July the north-facing slopes of Vesuvius remain awash with color.

PLANNING YOUR TIME

Allow two full days for visiting the major sites of Herculaneum, best combined with a visit to Vesuvius. Likewise for Pompeii, which pairs well with a side trip to the more rarefied Oplontis. To learn more about what you've seen, spend some time at the Herculaneum's MAV museum where, via cutting-edge computer technology, ruins are virtually restored to their original glory. For several buildings in Pompeii you must make Internet reservations (🌐 *www.arethusa.net*) at least 24 hours before you visit. In the Campi Flegrei, your top priorities should be the sites in Pozzuoli, the outlying site of Cumae, or the monumental archaeological park in Baia, all of which you can visit on a single ticket.

GETTING HERE AND AROUND

BOAT TRAVEL

Metro del Mare ferries provide a scenic seasonal option for getting around the bay. The ferries, which serve all the main ports, are more expensive and slower than ground transportation but deliver spectacular views. Line 1 stops in Bacoli (Baia), Pozzuoli, Naples, Ercolano, Torre del Greco, Torre Annunziata, Castellammare di Stabia, and Sorrento. Line 2 connects Pozzuoli and Sorrento. Consult the website for departure times, which vary with the season. The company recently introduced a variation on the glass-encased *bateau mouche* vessels that travel the Seine in Paris.

Contact **Metro del Mare** ☎ *199/600700* 🌐 *www.metrodelmare.it.*

BUS TRAVEL

All the main tourist sights east of Naples are well served by rail from the city, with more frequent departures and trips that take far less time than by bus. Travel west of Naples is best started by train, though for Baia and Cumae you will transfer to buses at either Fusaro or Lido Fusaro.

CAR TRAVEL

Pompeii is a short distance off the A3 Naples–Salerno Autostrada (toll from Naples or Nocera: €1.60), but this major highway with only two lanes in each direction is often congested. A car can be useful for exploring the Campi Flegrei region, especially for sites like Cumae and Lake Avernus where public transportation is infrequent or nonexistent. From Naples, travel toward Pozzuoli on the Tangenziale—the Naples bypass (toll €0.65)—exiting at the appropriate junction.

Most archaeological sites are accessible by car. Use a *parcheggio custodito* (attended parking lot), particularly at Pompeii and Herculaneum, and avoid on-street unattended parking. Metered parking (look for the blue lines on the street) is scarce in most places.

Off the main highways, signposting is sometimes poor, with road signs competing with advertising placards. The westbound Tangenziale (Napoli–Pozzuoli) should be avoided on Saturday evenings and on Sunday in summer (crowds heading out of Naples for nightlife or beaches). Road conditions are usually good, though surfaces near the top of Vesuvius can become icy in winter.

TRAIN TRAVEL

Stazione Centrale, in Naples's Piazza Garibaldi, is the hub for public transportation both east and west of Naples. The Circumvesuviana connects Naples, Herculaneum, Torre del Greco, Torre Annunziata, Vesuvius, Pompeii, and Sorrento. FS Metroplitana Linea 2 serves Pozzuoli (⇨ *see Pozzuoli, below*). For the Phlegrean Fields to the west of Naples, take the Cumana line, run by SEPSA, from the terminus at Piazza Montesanto near Montesanto Metropolitana station. **TIP→ Confusion can be avoided by not taking every route map at face value. Baia, for instance, appears on some maps even though the station here vanished years ago. To reach Baia one needs to get down from the train at Fusaro and take a small red bus, waiting outside; likewise to get to Cumae.**

Contacts Circumvesuviana railway ☎ *800/053939* 🌐 *www.vesuviana.it.* **SEPSA** ☎ *800/001616* 🌐 *www.sepsa.it.*

RESTAURANTS

Volcanoes might wreak disaster every millennium or so, but on a day-to-day basis they also guarantee the most fertile of soils. Wine, olives, vegetables—Naples and environs produce prize specimens, and in the cases of mozzarella and pizza can claim pride of origin. And, of course, there's the fruit of the sea, from the tiny and taste-packed anchovy to swordfish nearly a table long. Nowhere does the pride in tradition show more clearly than at Pompeii's Il Principe. The restaurant's menu is in Latin, and the historically accurate (and marvelous) dishes served here hark back to the era when Vesuvius was still the intact Monte

Summa, the abode of the wine god Dionysus, whose image, fittingly, graces the wine list. *Prices in the reviews are the average cost of a main course at dinner or, if dinner is not served, at lunch.*

HOTELS

Though much of the Vesuvian area is embraced by the Vesuvius National Park, don't expect well-appointed *agriturismi,* or rustic lodgings—or, for that matter, hotels that have you sighing with pleasure when you throw open the shutters. But don't fear. East of Naples there are some great bets for hotels, with two of them found along Herculaneum's Miglio D'Oro. *Prices in the reviews are the lowest cost of a standard double room in high season.*

TOURS

Balla in Style runs tours to Vesuvius, Pompeii, Herculaneum, and other sights east and west of Naples. Melody Travel (⇨ *see Naples Planner, in Chapter 6)* arranges all-day trips of Bay of Naples sights, or you can combine a daily tour of Naples with the Herculaneum ruins or another sight outside the city.

Contact Balla in Style ☎ *081/8074328* 🌐 *www.ballainstyle.com.*

VISITOR INFORMATION

In addition to the tourist offices listed in the various towns this chapter covers, the EPT office in Naples (⇨ *see Naples Planner, in Chapter 6)* is a good resource for touring and other information. Also invaluable, particularly for events and itineraries, is the InCampania website of the official regional tourism bureau.

Contact InCampania ☎ *081/2301614* 🌐 *www.incampania.com.*

5

VESUVIUS AND NEARBY

Though barely more than a third as tall as the perennially active Mt. Etna, its Sicilian counterpart, Vesuvius, with its relatively modest 1,277-meter (4,189-foot) height, has achieved unparalleled status in the collective consciousness. For centuries this intermittently active volcano had offered a spectacle to visitors who flocked to the Bay of Naples to marvel at its small-scale eruptions, ever-present plumes of smoke, and thundering fumaroles. In the mid-18th century, the entire court of Naples set up shop in Portici, at the foot of the mountain, building summer villas that served as ringside seats to the volcano's hypnotic pyrotechnics.

Artists painted the mountain in eruption, streams of lava rendered in lurid hues of blood. Romantic poets climbed the peak under the full moon to create odes extolling its sublime and terrible power. Duchesses would hire chair porters to bear them up to the rim, where, down below, rainbow mounds of sulfurous ash, vents of hissing steam, lunar-like boulders—everything, it seems, but little imps dashing about with long Luciferian pitchforks—presented a hellish sight.

Vesuvius's eruptions—from the ancient era through the 18th century—had long been legendary, but the volcano's lethal handiwork only became apparent to modern minds when the Roman towns of Pompeii and Herculaneum were discovered by accident and then excavated in the late 18th century. As it turned out, having been buried since the famous AD 79 eruption, these towns promptly became the most celebrated archaeological sites in Europe, offering up untold artistic treasures, the finest of which are on display at Naples's incredible Museo Archeologico Nazionale.

Today, thousands of visitors arrive every day to sites around the bay, most with one eye monitoring *'O Vesuvio*, just a few miles away. About 30 eruptions of various magnitudes have occurred in the past 2,000 years, the most recent of which took place in 1944. This might be construed as good news, but many volcanologists think it's ominous when a living volcano is so silent—only two eruptions happened in the 20th century—and they now maintain a constant watch.

HERCULANEUM (ERCOLANO)

12 km (8 miles) southeast of Naples, 40 km (25 miles) northwest of Salerno.

Fodor's Choice ★ A visit to the archaeological site of Herculaneum neatly counterbalances the hustle of its larger neighbor, Pompeii. Although close to the heart of busy Ercolano—indeed, in places right under the town—the ancient site seems worlds apart. Like Pompeii, Herculaneum was buried by Vesuvius's eruption in AD 79. Unlike Pompeii, it was submerged in a mass of volcanic mud that sealed and preserved wood and other materials including food (at Pompeii, most organic matter rotted away over time). Several villas have inlaid marble floors that evoke the same admiration as the mosaics in Naples's Museo Archeologico. Elsewhere it's possible to gauge how the less privileged lived: more remains of the upper stories than in Pompeii, so you can view the original stairs to the cramped, poorly lighted rooms that gave onto the central courtyard. Here there's more of a sense of a living community than Pompeii conveys.

GETTING HERE AND AROUND

To get to Herculaneum by car, take the A3 Naples–Salerno highway and exit at Ercolano. Follow signs for the "*Scavi*" (excavations). The Circumvesuviana railway *(⇨ Bay of Naples Planner, above, for contact info)* connects Herculaneum to Naples, Portici, Torre del Greco, Torre Annunziata, Pompeii, and Sorrento. City buses No. 157 and 255 depart Naples's Piazza Municipio for Herculaneum, via Portici, regularly. No. 255 continues on to Torre del Greco as well.

VISITOR INFORMATION

The friendly staffers at the tourist-information office, which is near the MAV Museum, provide advice and distribute copies of a helpful pamphlet and map of the ruins.

Ufficio Turistico ✉ *Via IV Novembre 82, Ercolano* ☎ *081/7881243*
🕒 *Mon.–Sat. 8–6.*

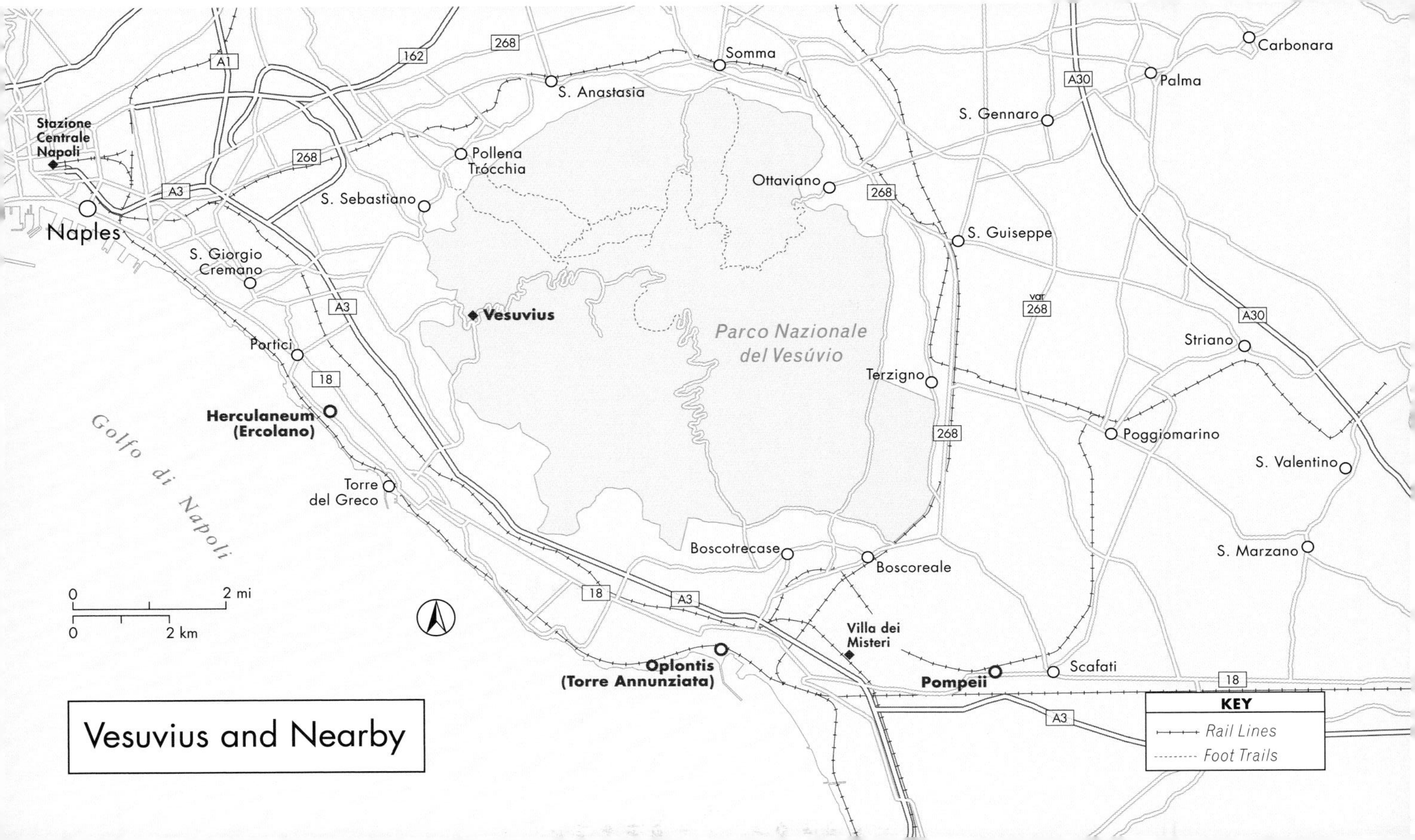
Vesuvius and Nearby
Naples
Stazione Centrale Napoli
S. Giorgio Cremano
Portici
Herculaneum (Ercolano)
Torre del Greco
Golfo di Napoli
S. Sebastiano
Pollena Trócchia
S. Anastasia
Somma
Vesuvius
Parco Nazionale del Vesúvio
Ottaviano
S. Gennaro
Palma
Carbonara
S. Guiseppe
Terzigno
Striano
Poggiomarino
S. Valentino
S. Marzano
Boscotrecase
Boscoreale
Villa dei Misteri
Oplontis (Torre Annunziata)
Pompeii
Scafati
A1
A3
A30
162
268
var 268
18
0
2 mi
0
2 km
KEY
Rail Lines
Foot Trails

THE BAY OF NAPLES THROUGH THE AGES

Rich archaeological and literary evidence reveals a continuous human presence in Campania for millennia. Used as an outpost probably by the Minoans and Mycenaeans in the second millennium BC, the area was first colonized by Greeks from Euboea in the 8th century BC; they settled on the island of Pithekoussai (modern-day Ischia) and later on the mainland at Cumae. The Greek geographer Strabo (64 BC–after AD 21), who appears to have traveled extensively in the area, provides further documentation to the area's history. The early Greeks traded widely with the Etruscans and local Italic peoples, eventually extending their sphere of influence to Neapolis and southward and northward along the shores of the Tyrrhenian Sea.

Greek civilization flourished for hundreds of years along this seaboard, but there was nothing in the way of centralized government until centuries later, when the Romans extended their domain southward and began to set up colonies of their own for added protection, especially after incursions led by such flamboyant figures as Pyrrhus and Hannibal in the 3rd century BC.

The Romans transformed Pompeii and Herculaneum into posh getaways, but all their merrymaking was stilled in AD 79 by a jolt from Vesuvius, believed by few at the time to harbor any danger for those living at its base. We are fortunate to have Pliny the Younger's memorable description of his uncle being overwhelmed by fumes and dying of asphyxiation in Stabiae, now Castellammare di Stabia. Although written some years after the event, Pliny's letter to Tacitus is a unique and moving account of the disaster, and now the basis of the film commentary on the eruption in Herculaneum's MAV Museum.

EXPLORING

TOP ATTRACTIONS

Fodor's Choice ★ **Herculaneum Ruins.** Lying more than 50 feet below the present-day town of Ercolano, the ruins of Herculaneum are set among the acres of greenhouses that make this area one of Europe's principal flower-growing centers. In AD 79 the gigantic eruption of Vesuvius, which also destroyed Pompeii, buried the town under a tide of volcanic mud. The semiliquid mass seeped into the crevices and niches of every building, covering household objects, enveloping textiles and wood—and sealing all in a compact, airtight tomb. Excavation began in 1738 under King Charles of Bourbon, using the technique of underground tunnels. Digging was interrupted but recommenced in 1828, continuing into the following century. Today less than half of Herculaneum has been excavated. With contemporary Ercolano and the unlovely Resina Quarter—famous among bargain hunters for its secondhand-clothing market—sitting on top of the site, progress is limited. From the ramp leading down to Herculaneum's well-preserved edifices, you get a good overall view of the site, as well as an idea of the amount of volcanic debris that had to be removed to bring it to light.

About 5,000 people lived in Herculaneum when it was destroyed, many of them fishermen, craftsmen, and artists. Though Herculaneum had only one-third the population of Pompeii and has been only partially excavated, what has been found is generally better preserved. In some cases you can even see the original wooden beams, staircases, and furniture. Do not miss the **Villa dei Papiri** (Villa of Papayri), an excavation in a corner of the site, built by Julius Caesar's father-in-law. The building is named for the 1,800 carbonized papyrus scrolls dug up here in the 18th century, leading scholars to believe that this may have been a study center or library. You can view full-color virtual reproductions in the nearby MAV museum. Also worth special attention are the carbonized remains within the **Casa del Tramezzo di Legno** (House of the Wooden Partition ⇨ *below*).

Be sure to stock up on refreshments beforehand, as there is no food at the archaeological site. At the entrance, pick up a map showing the grid-like layout of the dig, which is divided into numbered blocks, or insulae. Splurge on an audio guide (€6.50 for one, €10 for two), and then head down the tunnel to start the tour at the old shoreline. Most of the houses are open and a representative cross-section of domestic, commercial, and civic buildings can be seen. Decorations are especially delicate in the **Casa del Nettuno ed Anfitrite** (House of Neptune and Amphitrite ⇨ *below*), named for the subjects of a still-bright mosaic on the wall of the *nymphaeum* (a recessed grotto with a fountain). North of this house is the **Casa del Bel Cortile** (House of the Beautiful Courtyard). One of its inner rooms displays a cast taken of three skeletons found in the storerooms down at the old seafront, where almost 300 inhabitants sought refuge from the eruption and were ultimately encapsulated for posterity. Both the **Casa dei Cervi** (House of the Stags) and the **Terme Suburbane** (Suburban Baths) are closed for restoration. As an alternative, you can head to the House of the Ship, which contains a small Roman vessel whose wood and equipment has survived very much intact. **■TIP→ At the entrance you can pick up a copy of "Pianta degli Scavi Archeologici di Ercolano," the excellent free pamphlet and map about the site that's as good as most of the guides you must pay for.** ✉ *Corso Resina 6, Ercolano* ☎ *081/8575347* 🌐 *www.pompeiisites.org* 🎫 *€11 for Herculaneum only; €20 for biglietto cumulativo ticket to 5 sites (Pompeii, Herculaneum, Boscoreale, Oplontis, and Stabiae) valid for 3 days; admission free for visitors under 18* ⏲ *Nov.–Mar., daily 8:30–5, last entrance at 3:30; Apr.–Oct., daily 8:30–7:30, ticket office closes at 6.*

FAMILY Fodor's Choice ★ **Museo Archeologico Virtuale (MAV).** Dazzling "virtual" versions of Herculaneum's streets and squares, computerized re-creations of the House of the Faun, even a multi-D simulation of Vesuvius erupting: Herculaneum's 1st-century-meets-the-21st-century museum extravaganza has it all. After stopping at the ticket office for the headset audio tour (€3), you descend, as in an excavation, to a floor below. Passing ancient faces that have now been given a name, the "percorso" path inserts you inside a re-creation of Herculaneum's first dig. You'll experience Herculaneum's Villa dei Papiri before and—even more dramatically—during the eruption, courtesy of special effects; enter "the burning cloud"

5

Much better preserved than Pompeii, Herculaneum boasts houses with frescoes whose colors remain much more vivid.

of 79 AD (actually vaporized water); then emerge, virtually speaking, inside Pompeii's House of the Faun, which can be seen both as it is and as it was for two centuries BC. The next re-creation—complete with rippling grass and moving cart and oxen—is again Villa dei Papirii. Then comes a stellar pre- and post-flooding view of Baia's *nymphaeum,* the now-displaced statues arrayed as they were in the days of Emperor Claudius, who commissioned them.

Visitors here are invited to take a front-row seat for "Day and Night in the Forum of Pompeii," with soldiers, litter-bearing slaves, and toga-clad figures moving spectrally to complete the spell; or to make a vicarious visit to the "Lupari" brothels, their various pleasures illustrated in virtual and graphic frescoes along the walls. There are holograms of jewelry of the earthquake fugitives and a touch-and-browse section of the Papyrii's 1,800 scrolls, too. Recent installations include, beside a wooden model of Herculaneum's theater, its virtual recreation. It was here that a local farmer, while digging a well, first came across what proved to be not merely a single building, but a whole town. The farmer reputedly removed some statues; here their virtual equivalents stand in their niches by daylight as an actor learns his lines. A dove flies skyward, and then, with night, the torches ignite. Equally fascinating are the virtual baths, where the mysteries of Roman plumbing come alive before your eyes. For an extra €4 and the most spectacular of all, is the Sensurround film of Vesuvius erupting. The words of Pliny the Elder provide a timeless commentary while the floor vibrates before your feet. "Wisdom begins in wonder," said Socrates, and this museum nobly proves the ancient philosopher correct. ✉ *Via IV Novembre 44, Ercolano* ☎ *081/19806511* 🌐 *www.museomav.it* 🎟 *€11.50 (€7.50 museum only, €5 eruption simulation only)* ⏲ *Tues.–Sun. 9:30–5.*

WORTH NOTING

Casa del Nettuno ed Anfitrite (*House of Neptune and Amphitrite*). The house takes its name from the mosaic in back that still sports its bright blue coloring and adorns the wall of the small, secluded *nymphaeum*, or shrine with fountains. According to legend, in the time-honored fashion of the Olympians, Neptune (or Poseidon) saw Amphitrite dancing with the Nereids on the island of Naxos, carried her off, and married her. The adjacent wall, in similar mosaic style though less well preserved, has a hunting scene of a stag being pursued by a dog. Annexed to the same house is a remarkably preserved wine shop, where amphorae still rest on carbonized wooden shelves. ✉ *Insula V, on Cardo IV parallel to Cardo V (close to Forum Baths).*

5

Casa del Tramezzo di Legno (*House of the Wooden Partition*). An outstanding example of carbonized remains is in the Casa del Tramezzo di Legno, as it has been prosaically labeled by archaeologists. Following renovation work in the mid-1st century AD, the house was designed to have a frontage on three sides of Insula III and included a number of storerooms, shops, and second-floor habitations. This suggests that the owner was a wealthy *mercator*, a member of the up-and-coming merchant class that was starting to edge the patricians out of their privileged positions. The airy atrium has a lovely garden. Look closely at the *impluvium* (a channel to collect rainwater), and you'll see the original flooring below, which was later replaced with marble, perhaps after a change of owners. Next to the *impluvium* is an elegant marble table, or *cartibulum*, while behind is the *tablinum* (reception room), partially screened off by a bronze-studded wooden partition, the central part of which is missing, that would also have had hooks for hanging *lucernae* (lamps). ✉ *Insula III, 11–12.*

Palaestra. No town would have been complete without its sports facilities, and Herculaneum was no exception. Just opposite the *thermopolium*, on Cardo V, is the entrance to the large Palaestra, where a variety of ball games and wrestling matches took place. Only three of more than 20 peristyle columns here have been excavated, a reminder of how much of the ancient town remains buried under solidified volcanic mud. ✉ *Insula Orientalis II.*

Taberna di Priapo (*Priapus's Tavern*). The tavern's intricate warren of private chambers—not to mention its name (Priapus was a god of fertility)— suggests that more than just food and drink was on offer here. Be sure to wander back to the waiting room, on the right. ✉ *Insula IV.*

Terme del Foro (*Forum Baths*). Stories of Roman licentiousness are belied by the Terme del Foro, which contained separate sections for men and women. Here you see most of the architectural ingredients of *thermae* (baths). But besides the mandatory trio in the men's section (a round *frigidarium*, a cool swimming pool; a *tepidarium*, a semi-heated pool; and a *calidarium*, or heated pool), there's also an *apodyterium*, or changing room, with partitioned shelves for depositing togas and a low podium to use as seating space while in line to use the facilities. For more attractive mosaics—particularly a spectacular rendition of

Neptune—go around into the women's baths, which apparently had no frigidarium. The heating system in the tepidarium was also different—no hot air piped through or under, only braziers. Note the steam vents ingeniously built into the bath's benches, and the small overhead cubbies in which bathers stored their togas. All these fascinating features plus waterwheels and the intricacies of Roman plumbing are splendidly reproduced in a room of the MAV museum, as near to experiencing a Roman bath as one is likely to get. ✉ *Insula VI.*

Palazzo Reale (*Royal Palace*). Now in a state of distinctly dilapidated grandeur, painted off-yellow, complete with the occasional graffito, Portici's royal palace stands at the foothills of Vesuvius. In the 1730s, the area was chosen by the first Bourbon king of the Two Sicilies, Charles III, as the site for a royal palace that would be sufficiently close to Naples for him to be able to return to the capital at a moment's notice, yet far enough away for him and his entourage to indulge in hunting, one of the main Bourbon pursuits. Exhibitions are sometimes mounted on the *piano nobile* (main floor), but even if the rooms aren't open, you can usually still climb the monumental staircase, at the top of which a fading fresco supplies an inkling of the Palazzo Reale's past glory. ■ **TIP→ The No. 255 tram bus stops in the courtyard between the northern and southern wings. The monumental staircase is on the seaward side.** ✉ *Via Università 100, 1 km (½ mile) northwest of Ercolano, Portici* ☎ *081/7754850* *Palace free, exhibition admission fee varies* ⊙ *Sept.–July, weekdays 9–6.*

WHERE TO EAT AND STAY

$ SOUTHERN ITALIAN **A' Cantinella do Cunvento.** A short walk down Via Università from the Royal Palace of Portici brings you to this unpretentious ristorante–pizzeria, known to the locals as Da Peppino after its owner-manager, Giuseppe. Crowded at lunchtime with staff from the nearby college, this spot has great pizzas, down-to-earth service, and prices that are hardly donnish. ■ **TIP→ The prix-fixe option—an incredibly good value—includes pasta or rice, a main (octopus salad is a specialty), and fruit for €10.** $ *Average main: €10* ✉ *Via Università 64, Portici* ☎ *081/7755301* ▭ *No credit cards* ⊙ *Closed Sun.*

$ SOUTHERN ITALIAN **La Fornacella.** Doing a brisk trade with both *stranieri* and locals—always a good sign—this restaurant and pizzeria on the roundabout near the Circumvesuviana station is a 10-minute walk from the excavations of Herculaneum. Dishes vary according to season but always draw on local recipes: pasta *e fagioli* (with beans) is a winter favorite, and richly garnished *schiaffoni* (flat tube pasta) with seafood is a summer stalwart. Limoncello is offered for free. ■ **TIP→ If you're sensitive to traffic noise, avoid sitting at the outside tables.** $ *Average main: €10* ✉ *Via IV Novembre 90–92, Ercolano* ☎ *081/7774861* ⊕ *www.lafornacella.it* ⊙ *Closed Mon.*

$ B&B/INN **Hotel Ercolano.** Across the road from the Herculaneum archaeological site, this bed-and-breakfast inn has views of the ruins and the sea beyond. **Pros:** convenient location; multiple meal plans, from breakfast-only to full board; free parking. **Cons:** rooms are on the smallish side. $ *Rooms from: €80* ✉ *Corso Resina 230, Ercolano* ☎ *081/7771357* *10 rooms* *Multiple meal plans.*

$$$ HOTEL Fodor's Choice ★ **Miglio d'Oro Park Hotel.** The grand Vesuvian villas lined up along "the golden mile" are normally just for visits, but you can actually stay in the Miglio d'Oro. **Pros:** five-minute walk from the Herculaneum ruins; rare "villa" experience; friendly reception; cheaper rooms a good find. **Cons:** some rooms pricey. *Rooms from: €225 ✉ Corso Resina 296, Ercolano ☎ 081/7399999 🌐 www.migliodoroparkhotel.it 40 rooms, 7 suites No meals.*

WORD OF MOUTH

"I didn't think it was possible to be more impressed than Pompeii, but the state of preservation of Herculaneum is indeed something special. Being able to go into so many buildings and having the opportunity to see a Roman town frozen in time is something I will never forget."

—stanbr

VESUVIUS

16 km (10 miles) east of Naples, 8 km (5 miles) northeast of Herculaneum, 40 km (25 miles) northwest of Salerno.

Fodor's Choice ★ Vesuvius may have lost its plume of smoke, but it has lost none of its fascination—especially for those who live in the towns around the cone. They've now nicknamed it the "Sterminator." In centuries gone by, their predecessors would study the volcano for signs of impending destruction. *Napoli fa i peccati e la Torre li paga,* the residents of nearby Torre del Greco used to mutter—"Naples sins and the Torre suffers." When reports of depraved behavior circulated about Neapolitans across the bay, chastisement was only to be expected. Today, the world continues to watch *'O Vesuvio* with bated breath.

GETTING HERE AND AROUND

Busvia del Vesuvio's guided tours (€22) depart from opposite the info point that's adjacent to Pompeii's Villa dei Misteri Circumvesuviana station. About halfway up to Vesuvius, passengers transfer to a 4x4 eco-vehicle that passes through wooded parkland. The route is scenic in every sense of the term, the last stretch being a 20-minute climb on foot to the edge of the cone itself. EAVBUS provides public-bus service to Mt. Vesuvius (€10.60 return from Pompeii Piazza Anfiteatro, €9.60 from the Ercolano Circumvesuviana station). Vesuvio Express operates 10-seat minibus service (€10) from Ercolano Circumvesuviana station. The vehicles thread their way rapidly up back roads, reaching the top in 20 minutes. Allow at least 2½ hours for the journey, including a 30-minute walk to the crater on a soft cinder track. A shorter, also scenic option is the red-and-white Vesuvio Tour tram bus from the entrance of Camping Zeus, near the Villa dei Misteri train station, which proceeds directly to the Large Cone, where you descend and then pay another ticket for access to the crater. An adult round-trip ticket costs €12.

To arrive by car, take the A3 Napoli–Salerno highway exit "Torre del Greco" and follow Via E. De Nicola from the tollbooth. Follow signs for the Parco Nazionale del Vesuvio (Vesuvius National Park). Circumvesuviana railway (⇨ *Bay of Naples Planner, above,*

You'll be amazed at how Vesuvius looms over the entire region—even in Naples, 10 miles away, it remains a totally commanding presence.

for contact info) serves the main archaeological sites at the foot of Vesuvius. Trains leave from the Porta Nolana–Corso Garibaldi station in Naples and stop at the main terminal at Piazza Garibaldi 10 blocks away, taking in all the main archaeological sites on route. There are about two trains per hour, with a cost of €1.80 to Ercolano and Torre Annunziata, and €2.40 to Pompei Scavi–Villa dei Misteri).

Busvia del Vesuvio. ☎ *340/9352616* 🌐 *www.busviadelvesuvio.com.*

EAVBUS ☎ *081/19805000, 800/211388 toll free* 🌐 *www.eavcampania.it.*

Vesuvio Express ✉ *Piazzale Stazione Circumvesuviano 7* ☎ *081/7393666* 🌐 *www.vesuvioexpress.it.*

Vesuvio Tour ✉ *Camping Zeus, Via Villa dei Misteri 3* ☎ *081/8615320* 🌐 *www.campingzeus.it.*

EXPLORING

Mt. Vesuvius. Although its destructive powers are undoubtedly diminished, Vesuvius's threat of an eruption is ever present. Seen from the other side of the Bay of Naples, Vesuvius appears to have two peaks: on the northern side is the steep face of Monte Somma, possibly part of the original crater wall in AD 79; to the south is the present-day cone of Vesuvius, which has actually formed within the ancient crater. The AD 79 cone would have been considerably higher, perhaps peaking at more than 6,000 feet. The upper slopes bear the visible scars left by 19th- and 20th-century eruptions, the most striking being the lava flow from 1944 lying to the left (north side) of the approach road from Ercolano on the way up.

As you tour the cities that felt that wrath, you may be overwhelmed by the urge to explore the volcano itself, and it's well worth the trip. The view when the air is clear is magnificent, with the curve of the coast and the tiny white houses among the orange and lemon blossoms. When the summit becomes lost in mist, though, you'll be lucky to see your hand in front of your face. If you notice the summit clearing—it tends to be clearer in the afternoon—head for it. If possible, see Vesuvius after you've toured the ruins of buried Herculaneum to appreciate the magnitude of the volcano's power. Admission to the crater includes a compulsory guide, usually a young geologist who speaks a smattering of English. At the bottom you'll be offered a stout walking stick (a small tip is appreciated when you return it). **■TIP→ The climb can be tiring if you're not used to steep hikes. Because of the volcanic stone you should wear athletic shoes, not sandals.** ☎ *081/7775720* 🎫 *€8* ⏲ *Daily 9 am–2 hrs before sunset.*

Museo dell'Osservatorio Vesuviano (*Museum of the Vesuvius Observatory*). In bygone ages the task of protecting the local inhabitants from Vesuvius fell to the patron saint of Naples, San Gennaro, whose statue was often paraded through city streets to placate the volcano's wrath, but since the mid-19th century the Osservatorio Vesuviano has attentively monitored seismic activity. The original 1841 observatory, conspicuous with its Pompeian-red facade, has survived unscathed on the volcano's upper slopes and now serves as a conference center and small museum whose exhibits include a mineralogical display, landscape gouaches, and early seismographs. Informational panels describe the contributions of the observatory's directors and other staff to the development of volcano-monitoring instrumentation. ✉ *Via Osservatorio, Ercolano* ☎ *081/7777149, 081/6108483* 🌐 *www.ov.ingv.it* 🎫 *Free guided tours* ⏲ *Sept.–Mar. weekdays 9–2, weekends 10–2; Apr.–July weekdays 9–4, weekends 10–4* ⏲ *Closed Aug. and several days in Dec. and Jan.*

OPLONTIS (TORRE ANNUNZIATA)

20 km (12 miles) southeast of Naples, 5 km (3 miles) west of Pompeii.

Fodor's Choice ★

Surrounded by the fairly drab 1960s urban landscape of Torre Annunziata, Oplontis justifies its reputation as one of the more mysterious archaeological sites to be unearthed in the 20th century. The villa complex has been imaginatively ascribed—from a mere inscription on an amphora—to Nero's second wife, Poppaea Sabina. Her family was well known among the landed gentry of neighboring Pompeii, although, after a kick in the stomach from her emperor husband, she died some 15 years before the villa was overwhelmed by the eruption of 79. As Roman villas go, Poppaea's Villa, or Villa A, as it's called by archaeologists, is way off the top end of the scale.

GETTING HERE AND AROUND

By car, take the A3 Napoli–Salerno highway to the "Torre Annunziata" exit. Follow Via Veneto west, then turn left onto Via Sepolcri for the excavations. By train take the Circumvesuviana railway *(⇨ Bay of Naples Planner, above, for contact info)* to Torre Annunziata, the town's modern name (€3.70 round-trip from Naples).

EXPLORING

Oplontis. For those overwhelmed by the throngs at Pompeii, a visit to the site of Oplontis offers a chance for contemplation and intellectual stimulation. What has been excavated so far of the Villa of the Empress Poppaea covers more than 7,000 square meters (75,000 square feet), and because the site is bound by a road to the west and a canal to the south, its full extent may never be known. Complete with porticoes, a large peristyle, a pool, baths, and extensive gardens, the villa is thought by some to have been a school for young philosophers and orators.

Unlike Herculaneum and Pompeii, no skeletons were found here, leading scholars to conclude that the villa had been abandoned after the earthquake of 62 AD and was undergoing restructuring pending sale to another owner. With many of the frescoed houses in Pompeii closed for restoration or open only for limited viewing, you have to come here to appreciate the full range of Roman wall paintings. One highlight is found in Room 5, a sitting room once overlooking the sea. Here a painted window depicts the sanctuary of Apollo, while off to the left a photogenic peacock perches next to a theatrical mask. Owing to the second Pompeian style, the walls, with their frescoed arches and columns, seem to open out onto a scene beyond, as seen in the paintings in the *triclinium* (dining room; Room 6) and the *cubiculum* (bedroom; Room 7). At the back, through a cooling garden newly planted with bay trees as in antiquity, is an Olympic-size swimming pool. The adjacent guest rooms, or hospitalia, display murals of the fourth Pompeian Style, dating them from 50 AD onward. With painted fruits and flowers, vegetation was guaranteed to flourish all year, and in the open *viridarium* (pleasure garden; Room 16) guests could compare painted flora and the odd bird with the real things. Room 21 is a Roman latrine, its ancient fittings clearly on view. **■ TIP→ Works by ancient Greek and Roman playwrights are sometimes performed (in Italian) at Oplontis between June and September. Tickets can be bought at the Proloco in Torre Annunziata, close to the Oplontis site at Via Sepolcri 16.** ✉ *Via Sepolcri 1* ☎ *081/8575347* 🌐 *www.pompeiisites.org* 🎫 *€5.50 includes Boscoreale; €20 includes 3-day ticket for Herculaneum, Pompeii, and Boscoreale* ⏲ *Apr.–Oct., daily 8:30–7:30 (ticket office closes at 6); Nov.–Mar., daily 8:30–5 (ticket office closes at 3:30).*

POMPEII

Mention Pompeii and most travelers will think of ancient Roman villas, prancing bronze fauns, writhing plaster casts of Vesuvius's victims, and the fabled days of the emperors. Mention Pompeii to many southern Italians, however, and they will immediately think of Pompei (to use the modern-day Italian spelling, not the ancient Latin), home to the Santuario della Madonna del Rosario, the 19th-century basilica in the center of the new town, with the archaeological ruins taking second place. Although millions of culture seekers worldwide head for ancient Pompeii every year, the same number of Italian pilgrims converge on

Another of the bay area's archaeological treasures is the Villa of the Empress Poppaea, so vast it dwarfs the residences in Pompeii.

Pompei's basilica as a token of faith—joining processions, making *ex-voto* offerings, or just honoring a vow. Wealthy Neapolitans come to make their donations to help the church carry out its good deeds. New-car owners come to get their vehicles blessed—and given driving standards in these parts of the world, insurance coverage from on high is probably a sensible move.

Caught between the hammer and anvil of cultural and religious tourism, the modern town of Pompei has shaken off its rather complacent approach and is now endeavoring to polish up its act. In attempts to ease congestion, parts of the town have been made pedestrian-friendly and parking restrictions tightened. Departing from the rather sleazy reputation of previous years, several hotels have filled the sizable niche in the market for quality deals at affordable prices. As for recommendable restaurants, if you deviate from the archaeological site and make for the center of town, your choices will include two restaurants specializing in ancient Roman recipes, historically accurate but no less delicious for that. The modern town may be a circus but the center ring is always the splendors and wonders of ancient Pompeii itself (*see our special photo feature, "Ancient Pompeii: Tomb of a Civilization," for a suggested tour of the fabulous site*).

GETTING HERE AND AROUND

To get to Pompeii by car, take the A3 Napoli–Salerno highway to the "Pompei" exit and follow signs for the nearby "Scavi" excavations. There are numerous guarded car parks near the Porta Marina, Piazza Essedra, and Anfiteatro entrances where you can leave your vehicle for a fee.

Pompeii has two central Circumvesuviana railway (⇨ *Bay of Naples Planner, above, for contact info*) stations served by two separate train lines. The Naples–Sorrento train stops at "Pompei Scavi-Villa dei Misteri," 100 yards from the Porta Marina ticket office of the archaeological site, while the Naples–Poggiomarino train stops at Pompei Santuario, more convenient for the Santuario della Madonna del Rosario and the hotels and restaurants in the modern town center. A third FS (state) train station south of the town center is only convenient if arriving from Salerno or Rome.

WORD OF MOUTH

"We also joined a group formed by a licensed guide outside Pompeii, and were very glad we did. He was a wealth of information, and as we were not planning to be there for several hours, think we made a good decision."
—Socaltraveler

VISITOR INFORMATION

At the infopoint booth, just to the right of the Villa dei Misteri Station entrance, you can pick up a good, free map, and get audio guides to the ruins. You can also arrange for personally guided group tours (€12), and there's an Internet point. You can also pick up a free map at the Ufficio Informazione booth, outside the archaeological site. The welcoming staffers can tell you which sites can't be visited on the day you've arrived, saving you unnecessary walking.

infopoint ✉ *Piazza Porta Marina Inferiore 1* ☎ *0815369869* 🌐 *www.pompeiholiday.com.*

Ufficio Informazione ✉ *Piazza Porta Marina* ☎ *081/8575347* 🌐 *www.pompeiisites.org* 🕓 *Daily 9–5.*

WHERE TO EAT

$$$$ NEAPOLITAN

✕ **Il Principe.** This is the closest you'll get to experiencing the tastes of ancient Pompeii. Il Principe's owner, Marco Carli, and his wife, Pina, have spent decades researching ancient Roman cuisine and can boast of having fed, if not Roman emperors, at least three U.S. presidents. Try the *pasta vermiculata garo,* otherwise known as spaghetti with *garum pompeianum,* a fish-based sauce consumed widely in Roman times. Round off the meal with the *cassata di Oplontis* (a sweet made with ricotta cheese and honey), inspired by a still-life fresco found in a triclinium at the site of Oplontis. The restaurant occasionally arranges banquets at the surrounding archaeological sites, complete with music played on ancient Roman instruments. The events are worth attending both for the food and the chance to commune with the locals. **■TIP→ If the restaurant's grandiose interior overwhelms you, opt for the more informal outdoor dining area.** [$] *Average main: €50* ✉ *Piazza B. Longo 8* ☎ *081/8505566* 📠 *081/8633342* 🌐 *www.ilprincipe.com* 🕓 *Closed Sun. dinner, Mon. (except lunch in summer), and 3 wks in Aug.*

Continued on page 209

ANCIENT POMPEII
TOMB OF A CIVILIZATION

The site of Pompeii, petrified memorial to Vesuvius's eruption on the morning of August 24, AD 79, is the largest, most accessible, and probably most famous of excavations anywhere.

A busy commercial center with a population of 10,000–20,000, ancient Pompeii covered about 160 acres on the seaward end of the fertile Sarno Plain. Today Pompeii is choked with both the dust of 25 centuries and more than 2 million visitors every year; only by escaping the hordes and lingering along its silent streets can you truly fall under the site's spell. On a quiet backstreet, all you need is a little imagination to sense the shadows palpably filling the dark corners, to hear the ancient pipe's falsetto and the tinny clash of cymbals, to envision a rain of rose petals gently covering a Roman senator's dinner guests. Come in the late afternoon when the site is nearly deserted and you will understand that the true pleasure of Pompeii is not in the seeing but in the feeling.

A FUNNY THING HAPPENS ON THE WAY TO THE FORUM

as you walk through Pompeii. Covered with dust and decay as it is, the city seems to come alive. Perhaps it's the familiar signs of life observed along the ancient streets: bakeries with large ovens just like those for making pizzas, tracks of cart wheels cut into the road surface, graffiti etched onto the plastered surfaces of street walls. Coming upon a *thermopolium* (snack bar), you imagine natives calling out, "Let's move on to the am-phitheater." But a glance up at Vesuvius, still brooding over the scene like an enormous headstone, reminds you that these folks—whether

The beautiful **Porta Ercolano** (Herculaneum Gate) was a main gate that led to Herculaneum and Naples, one of seven gates in the ancient city walls.

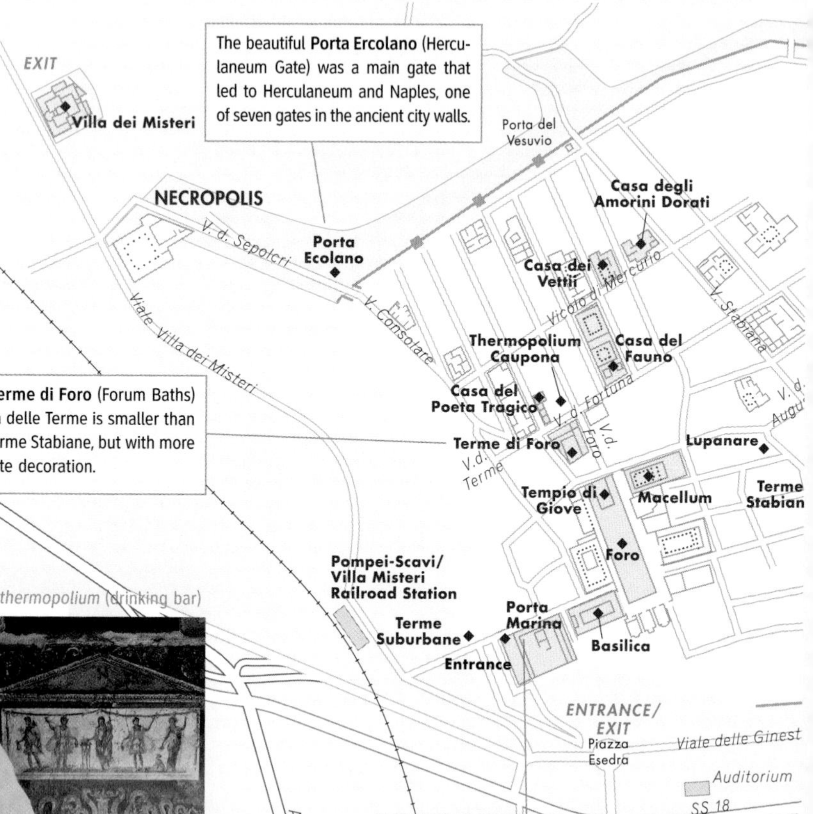

The **Terme di Foro** (Forum Baths) on Via delle Terme is smaller than the Terme Stabiane, but with more delicate decoration.

A *thermopolium* (drinking bar)

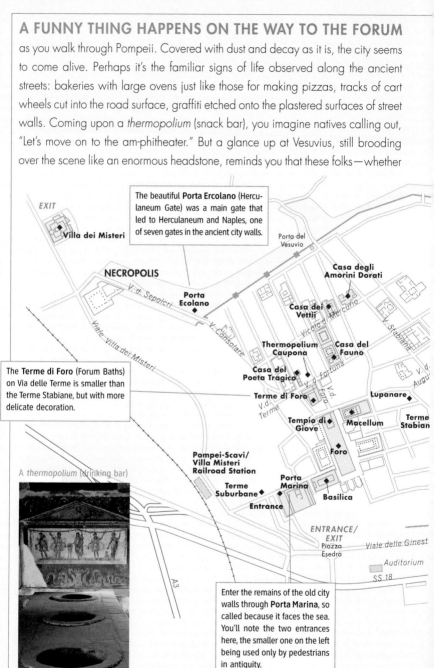

Enter the remains of the old city walls through **Porta Marina**, so called because it faces the sea. You'll note the two entrances here, the smaller one on the left being used only by pedestrians in antiquity.

Pompeii's cemetery, or Necropolis

imagined in your head or actually wearing a mantle of lava dust—have not taken a breath for centuries. The town was laid out in a grid pattern, with two main intersecting streets. The wealthiest took a whole block for themselves; those less fortunate built a house and rented out the front rooms, facing the street, as shops. There were good numbers of *tabernae* (taverns) and *thermopolia* on almost every corner, and frequent shows at the amphitheater.

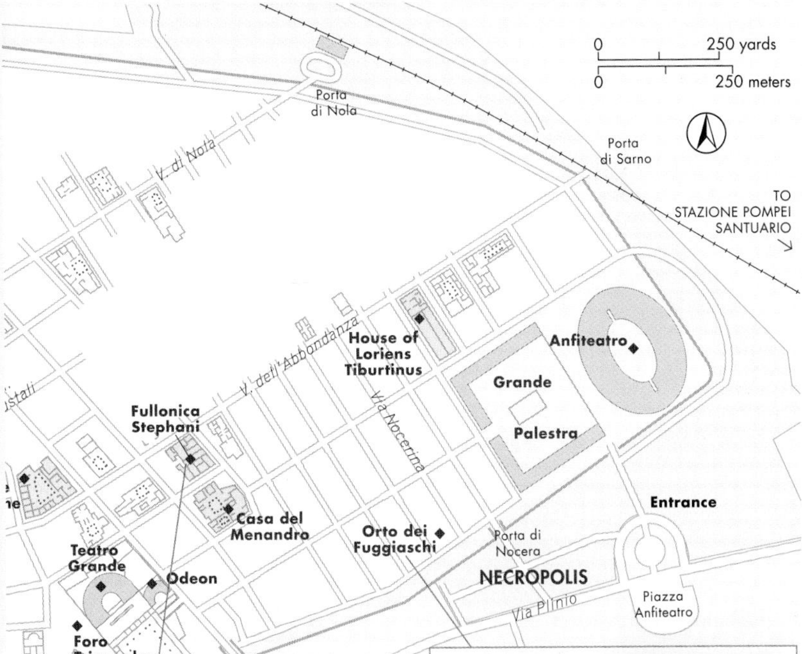

Togas, the required Roman attire, were washed and wool was dyed at **Fullonica Stephani**. Urine was used to bleach and clean garments.

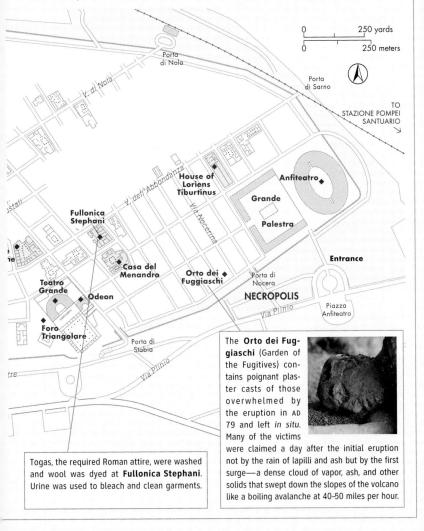

The **Orto dei Fuggiaschi** (Garden of the Fugitives) contains poignant plaster casts of those overwhelmed by the eruption in AD 79 and left *in situ*. Many of the victims were claimed a day after the initial eruption not by the rain of lapilli and ash but by the first surge—a dense cloud of vapor, ash, and other solids that swept down the slopes of the volcano like a boiling avalanche at 40–50 miles per hour.

PUBLIC LIFE IN ANCIENT POMPEII

Forum

THE CITY CENTER

As you enter the ruins at Porta Marina, make your way uphill to the **Foro** (Forum), which served as Pompeii's cultural, political, and religious center. You can still see some of the two stories of colonnades that used to line the square. Like the ancient Greek *agora* in Athens, the Forum was a busy shopping area, complete with public officials to apply proper standards of weights and measures. Fronted by an elegant three-column portico on the eastern side of the forum is the **Macellum**, the covered meat and fish market dating to the 2nd century BC; here vendors sold goods from their reserved spots in the central market. It was also in the Forum that elections were held, politicians let rhetoric fly, speeches and official announcements were made, and worshippers crowded around the **Tempio di Giove** (Temple of Jupiter), at the northern end of the forum.

Basilica

On the southwestern corner is the **Basilica,** the city's law court and the economic center. These rectangular aisled halls were the model for early Christian churches, which had a nave (central aisle) and two side aisles separated by rows of columns. Standing in the Basilica, you can recognize the continuity between Roman and Christian architecture.

THE GAMES

The **Anfiteatro** (Amphitheater) was the ultimate in entertainment for Pompeians and offered a gamut of experiences, but essentially this was for gladiators rather than wild animals. By Roman standards, Pompeii's amphitheater was quite

Amphitheater

small (seating 20,000). Built in about 80 BC, making it the oldest permanent amphitheater in the Roman world, it was oval and divided into four seating areas. There were two main entrances—at the north and south ends—and a narrow passage on the west called the Porta Libitinensis, through which the dead were probably dragged out. A wall painting found in a house near the theater (now in the Naples Museum) depicts the riot in the amphitheater in AD 59 when several citizens from the nearby town of Nocera were killed. After Nocerian appeals to Nero, shows were suspended for three years.

Fresco of Pyramus and Thisbe in the House of Loreius Tiburtinus

BATHS AND BROTHELS

In its day, Pompeii was celebrated as the Côte d'Azur, the seaside Brighton, the Fire Island of the ancient Roman empire. Evidence of a Sybaritic bent is everywhere—in the town's grandest villas, in its baths, and especially in its rowdiest *lupanaria* (brothels), murals still reveal a worship of hedonism. Satyrs, bacchantes, hermaphrodites, and acrobatic couples are pictured indulging in hanky-panky.

The first buildings to the left past the ticket turnstiles are the **Terme Suburbane** (Suburban Baths), built—by all accounts without permission—right up against the city walls. The baths have eyebrow-raising frescoes in the *apodyterium* (changing room) that strongly suggest that more than just bathing and massaging went on here.

On the walls of **Lupanare** (brothel) are scenes of erotic games in which clients could engage. The **Terme Stabiane** (Stabian Baths) had underground furnaces, the heat from which circulated beneath the floor, rose through flues in the walls, and escaped through chimneys. The water temperature could be set for cold, lukewarm, or hot. Bathers took a lukewarm bath to prepare themselves for the hot room. A tepid bath came next, and then a plunge into cold water to tone up the skin. A vigorous massage with oil was followed by rest, reading, horseplay, and conversation.

GRAFFITI

Thanks to those deep layers of pyroclastic deposits from Vesuvius that protected the site from natural wear and tear over the centuries, graffiti found in Pompeii provide unique insights into the sort of things that the locals found important 2,000 years ago. A good many were personal and lend a human dimension to the disaster that not even the sights can equal.

At the baths: **"What is the use of having a Venus if she's made of marble?"**

At the entrance to the front lavatory at a private house: **"May I always and everywhere be as potent with women as I was here."**

On the Viale ai Teatri: **"A copper pot went missing from my shop. Anyone who returns it to me will be given 65 bronze coins."**

In the Basilica: **"A small problem gets larger if you ignore it."**

PRIVATE LIFE IN ANCIENT POMPEII

The facades of houses in Pompeii were relatively plain and seldom hinted at the care and attention lavished on the private rooms within. When visitors arrived they passed the shops and entered an open peristyle, from which the occupants received air, sunlight, and rainwater, the latter caught by the *impluvium*, a rectangular-shaped receptacle under the sloped roof. In the back was a receiving room, the *tablinum*, and behind was another open area, the atrium. Life revolved around this uncovered inner courtyard, with rows of columns and perhaps a garden with a fountain. Only good friends ever saw this part of the house, which was surrounded by *cubicula* (bedrooms) and the *triclinium* (dining area). Interior floors and walls usually were covered with colorful marble tiles, mosaics, and frescoes.

House of Paquius Proculus

Several homes were captured in various states by the eruption of Vesuvius, each representing a different slice of Pompeiian life.

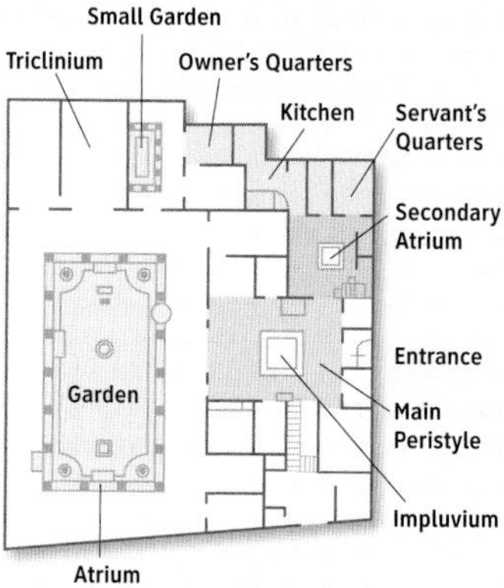

The **Casa del Fauno** (House of the Faun) displayed wonderful mosaics, now at the Museo Archeologico Nazionale in Naples. The **Casa del Poeta Tragico** (House of the Tragic Poet) is a typical middle-class house. On the floor is a mosaic of a chained dog and the inscription *cave canem* ("Beware of the dog"). The **Casa degli Amorini Dorati** (House of the Gilded Cupids) is an elegant, well-preserved home with original marble decorations in the garden. Many paintings and mosaics were executed at **Casa del Menandro** (House of Menander), a patrician's villa named for a fresco of the Greek playwright. Two blocks beyond the Stabian Baths you'll notice on the left the current digs at the **Casa dei Casti Amanti** (House of the Chaste Lovers). A team of plasterers and painters were at work here when Vesuvius erupted, redecorating one of the rooms and patching up the cracks in the bread oven near the entrance—possibly caused by tremors a matter of days before.

CASA DEI VETTII

The **House of the Vettii** is the best example of a house owned by wealthy *mercatores* (merchants). It contains vivid murals—a magnificent *pinacoteca* (picture gallery) within the very heart of Pompeii. The scenes here—except for those in the two wings off the atrium—were all painted after the earthquake of AD 62. Once inside, cast an admiring glance at the delicate frieze around the wall of the *triclinium* (on the right of the peristyle garden as you enter from the atrium), depicting cupids engaged in various activities, such as selling oils and perfumes, working as goldsmiths and metalworkers, acting as wine merchants, or performing in chariot races. Another of the main attractions in the Casa dei Vettii is the small cubicle beyond the kitchen area (to the right of the atrium) with its faded erotic frescoes now protected by Perspex screens.

UNLOCKING THE VILLA DEI MISTERI

Villa dei Misteri

There is no more astounding, magnificently memorable evidence of Pompeii's devotion to the pleasures of the flesh than the frescoes on view at the **Villa dei Misteri** (Villa of the Mysteries), a palatial abode 400 yards outside the city gates, northwest of Porta Ercolano. Unearthed in 1909, this villa had more than 60 rooms painted with frescoes; the finest are in the *triclinium*. Painted in the most glowing Pompeiian reds and oranges, the panels relate the saga of a young bride (Ariadne) and her initiation into the mysteries of the cult of Dionysus, who was a god imported to Italy from Greece and then given the Latin name of Bacchus. The god of wine and debauchery also represented the triumph of the irrational—of all those mysterious forces that no official state religion could fully suppress.

Pompeii's best frescoes, painted in glowing reds and oranges, retain an amazing vibrancy.

The Villa of the Mysteries frescoes were painted circa 50 BC, most art historians believe, and represent the peak of the Second Style of Pompeiian wall painting. The triclinium frescoes are thought to have been painted by a local artist, although the theme may well have been copied from an earlier cycle of paintings from the Hellenistic period. In all there are 10 scenes, depicting children and matrons, musicians and satyrs, phalluses and gods. There are no inscriptions (such as are found on Greek vases), and after 2,000 years historians remain puzzled by many aspects of the triclinium cycle. Scholars endlessly debate the meaning of these frescoes, but anyone can tell they are the most beautiful paintings left to us by antiquity. In several ways, the eruption of Vesuvius was a blessing in disguise, for without it, these masterworks of art would have perished long ago.

PLANNING FOR YOUR DAY IN POMPEII

GETTING THERE

The archaeological site of Pompeii has its own stop (Pompei–Villa dei Misteri) on the Circumvesuviana line to Sorrento, close to the main entrance at the Porta Marina, which is the best place from which to start a tour. If, like many visitors every year, you get the wrong train from Naples (stopping at the other station "Pompei"), all is not lost. There's another entrance to the excavations at the far end of Piazza Immaculata, just a seven-minute walk to the Amphitheater.

ADMISSION

Single tickets cost €11 and are valid for one full day. The site is open Apr.–Oct., daily 8:30–7:30 (last admission at 6), and Nov.–Mar., daily 8:30–5 (last admission at 3:30). For more information, call 081/8575347 or visit www.pompeiisites.org.

WHAT TO BRING

The only restaurant inside the site is both overpriced and busy, so it makes sense to bring along water and snacks. If you come so equipped, there are some shady, underused picnic tables outside the Porta di Nola, to the northeast of the site.

MAKING THE MOST OF YOUR TIME

Visiting Pompeii does have its frustrating aspects: many buildings are blocked off by locked gates, and enormous group tours tend to clog up more popular attractions. But the site is so big that it's easy to lose yourself amid the quiet side streets. To really see the site, you'll need four or five hours.

Certain buildings within Pompeii (Suburbane and Casa del Menandro) are open for restricted viewing. Reservations must be made on-line at www.arethusa.net, where you can find information on opening times.

TOURS

To get the most out of Pompeii, rent an audio guide (€6.50 for one, €10 for two; you'll need to leave an ID card) and opt for one of the three itineraries (2 hours, 4 hours, or 6 hours). If hiring a guide, make sure the guide is registered for an English tour and standing inside the gate; agree beforehand on the length of the tour and the price, and prepare yourself for soundbites of English mixed with dollops of hearsay. For a higher quality (but more expensive) full-day tour, try Context Travel (🌐 www.contexttravel.com).

MODERN POMPEI

Caught between the hammer and anvil of cultural and religious tourism, the modern town of Pompei (to use the modern-day Italian spelling, not the ancient Latin) is now endeavoring to polish up its act. In attempts to ease congestion and improve air quality at street level, parts of the town have been pedestrianized and parking restrictions tightened. Several hotels have filled the sizable niche in the market for excellent deals at affordable prices. As for recommendable restaurants, if you deviate from the archaeological site and make for the center of town, you will be spoiled for choice.

IF YOU LIKE POMPEII

If you intend to visit other archaeological sites nearby during your trip, you should buy the *biglietto cumulativo* pass, a combination ticket with access to four area sites (Herculaneum, Pompeii, Oplontis, Boscoreale). It costs €20 and is valid for three days. Unlike many archaeological sites in the Mediterranean region, those around Naples are almost all well served by public transport; ask about transportation options at the helpful Porta Marina information kiosk.

CLOSE UP

Pompeii Prep

Pompeii inspires under any circumstances, but it comes alive if you do some preparation before your visit.

First, read up—there are many good books on the subject, including these engaging, jargon-free histories: *Pompeii: The Day a City Died*, by Robert Etienne; *Pompeii: Public and Private Life*, by Paul Zanker; *The Lost World of Pompeii*, by Colin Amery; and *Pompeii: Life of a Roman Town*, by Mary Beard. For accurate historical information woven into the pages of a thriller, pick up *Pompeii: A Novel*, by Robert Harris.

Second, be sure to visit the Museo Archeologico Nazionale in Naples, where most of the finest art from Pompeii now resides. The highlights include the epic Alexander fresco, which once decorated the House of the Faun, and, in the Museum's "Gabinetto Secreto," louche frescoes advertising services on offer in the Lupari brothels. The museum is a rewarding stop even if Pompeii isn't in your plans. Over at the Herculaneum MAV Museum, through virtual reconstructions, ancient structures come alive before your eyes, and even the occasional animated figure to match.

5

$$$$ SOUTHERN ITALIAN **Ristorante President.** Carrying on a tradition of top-quality cuisine started by their father, chef Paolo Gramaglia and his sister Laila—the pastry chef and sommelier—run this restaurant that consistently ranks among Campania's best. This is a place where customers sigh with satisfaction after every course. For something different, try the *aragosta ubriacata* ("drunken" lobster cooked in white wine), accompanied by imaginative side dishes such as *sfoglie di zucca in agrodolce* (sweet-and-sour pumpkin strips). The presentation is never short of beautiful, and the service is impeccable. **TIP→ Ristorante President sometimes hosts Roman-inspired banquets with musical accompaniment; they're worth checking out if one is occurring when you are in Pompeii.** *Average main: €40 Piazza Schettini 12 081/8507245 081/8638147 www.ristorantepresident.com Closed Mon. Nov.–Mar.*

WHERE TO STAY

$ HOTEL **Hotel Amleto.** Connoisseurs of historical furnishings will find the Hotel Amleto an absolute treat. **Pros:** near sites and restaurants; attentive service. **Cons:** books up in high season; rooms facing street are noisy. *Rooms from: €90 Via B. Longo 10 081/8631004 081/8635585 www.hotelamleto.it 25 rooms Breakfast.*

$ HOTEL **Hotel Diana.** This small family-run hotel is a good base for budget travelers wishing to be within striking distance of Pompeii's ruins. **Pros:** quiet setting; charming garden; helpful staff; near Pompeii's archaeological site; convenient location for evening strolls; good for travelers using public transportation. **Cons:** no pool; noisy when fully booked; smallish rooms. *Rooms from: €80 Vico Sant'Abbondio 12 081/8631264 www.pompeihotel.com/en 32 rooms Breakfast.*

$ HOTEL **Villa Diomede Hotel.** A practical choice (especially for families) near Pompeii's archaeological site, this hotel run by a friendly staff has spacious, ultramodern rooms, five with kitchens and cooking utensils. **Pros:** good for families; rates include breakfast and free parking; location convenient to the archaeological site; hotel affiliated with nearby Vesuvio Tours tram bus to Mt. Vesuvius. **Cons:** decor is pleasant but not luxurious; some train noise can be heard. *Rooms from: €72* *Via Diomede 9* *081/5362753* *www.hotelvilladiomede.it* *16 rooms* *Breakfast.*

WEST OF NAPLES

Extinct volcanoes, steaming fumaroles, bubbling mud, natural spasms, and immortal names, all steeped in millennia of history, are the basic ingredients of the Campi Flegrei, or Phlegrean Fields (from the ancient Greek word *phlegraios,* or burning). Pompeii and Herculaneum, to the east of Naples, may be the most celebrated archaeological sites in Campania, but back in the days of the emperors they were simple middle-class towns compared to the patrician settlements to the west of Naples. Here, at Baia, famed figures like Cicero, Julius Caesar, Claudius, Nero, and Hadrian built sumptuous leisure villas (*villae otiorum*) and ports for their gigantic pleasure barges; here St. Paul arrived at Puteoli (to use Pozzuoli's ancient Latin moniker) on board an Alexandrian ship; here the powerful came to consult the oracles of the Cumaean Sibyl; and here Virgil visited Lago d'Averno—Lake Avernus, the legendary entrance to the Underworld—to immortalize it in his *Aeneid.* Although several villas have now sunk beneath the sea, there are many archaeological sites still extant: the Flavian Amphitheater, which, if not as imposing aboveground as the Colosseum at Rome, is far better preserved in the galleries and cages below the arena in which wild beasts, gladiators, and stage props were kept in readiness; the ancient acropolis area of Puteoli now known as Rione Terra, the ruins of the Sibyl's cave in Cumae; and the ancient baths of Baia.

POZZUOLI

8 km (5 miles) west of Naples.

Fodor's Choice ★ Legendary spirits populate Pozzuoli. St. Paul stepped ashore at the harbor here in AD 61 en route to Rome: his own ship had been wrecked off Malta, and he was brought here on the *Castor and Pollux,* a grain ship from Alexandria that was carrying corn from Egypt to Italy. Not far from the harbor esplanade, San Gennaro, patron saint of Naples, earned his holy martyrdom by being thrown to the lions at an imperial gala staged in the town's enormous amphitheater, constructed by the Flavian emperors (the wild beasts were said to have torn the rags from Gennaro's body but to have left him unharmed—at which point he was taken to the Solfatara and decapitated). More recently, that latter-day goddess Sophia Loren was raised in a house still standing on a backstreet.

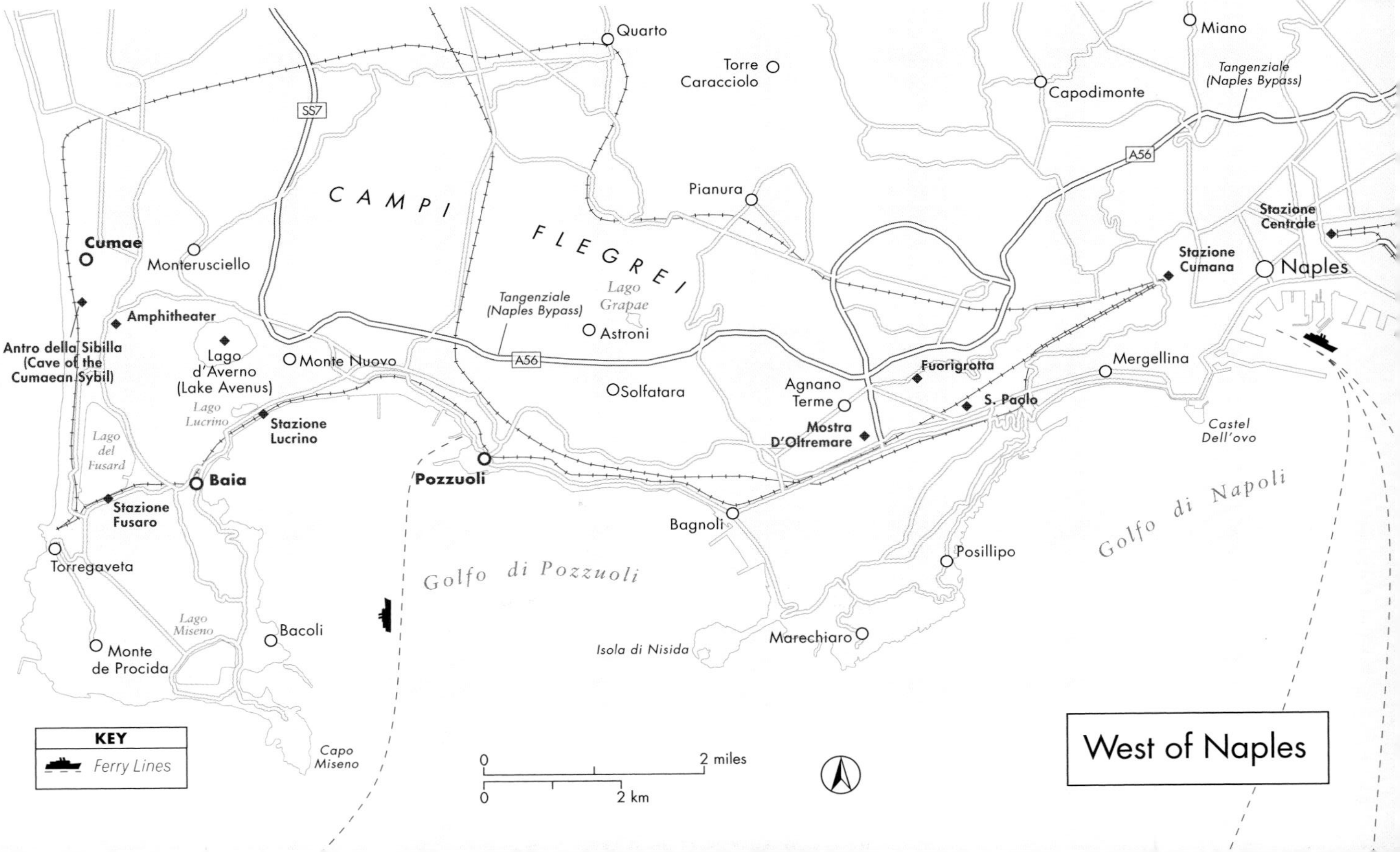
West of Naples
KEY
Ferry Lines
Quarto
Miano
Torre Caracciolo
Capodimonte
Tangenziale (Naples Bypass)
A56
SS7
Pianura
Stazione Centrale
Stazione Cumana
Naples
CAMPI FLEGREI
Cumae
Monterusciello
Lago Grapae
Amphitheater
Astroni
Antro della Sibilla (Cave of the Cumaean Sybil)
Lago d'Averno (Lake Avenus)
Monte Nuovo
Fuorigrotta
Mergellina
Agnano Terme
Solfatara
S. Paolo
Lago Lucrino
Stazione Lucrino
Mostra D'Oltremare
Castel Dell'ovo
Lago del Fusard
Pozzuoli
Baia
Stazione Fusaro
Golfo di Napoli
Bagnoli
Torregaveta
Posillipo
Golfo di Pozzuoli
Lago Miseno
Bacoli
Monte de Procida
Marechiaro
Isola di Nisida
Capo Miseno
0
2 miles
0
2 km

Today's Pozzuoli is a well-connected, busy town with about 80,000 inhabitants who are mainly employed by its fisheries, docks, and the tourism industry. Built on geologically unstable land, the area near the port was partially evacuated in the early 1980s due to a phenomenon known as *bradyseism,* or the rise and fall of the land surface. Since then it has been gradually recolonized and partially gentrified: many of the buildings in the Centro Storico have been given a face-lift, the main park (Villa Avellino) has become a mecca for open-air summer festivals, and the town's reputation as a center for gastronomy has been firmly established. Pozzuoli has also capitalized on its strategic position close to two of the islands in the Bay of Naples, Procida, and Ischia.

GETTING HERE AND AROUND

By car take the Tangenziale (bypass) from Naples toward Pozzuoli and get off at the Pozzuoli–Via Campana exit. At the roundabout, follow the signs for "Porto" to get to the port and the town center. There are subsequent signs for the "Anfiteatro" (amphitheater) and the "Volcano Solfatara." To get to Lake Avernus take the Pozzuoli–Arco Felice exit and follow the "Lago d'Averno" signs. The FS (state-run) Metropolitana Linea 2 from Naples (Piazza Garibaldi, Mergellina, Cavour, and Montesanto stations) stops at Pozzuoli–Solfatara near the Anfiteatro. For the town center get off at the main Pozzuoli station, which is nearer the sea. Bus No. 152 departs Naples Piazza Garibaldi and ends at the Port in Pozzuoli. The bus stops outside the main entrance to the Solfatara. It's a 1-km (½-mile) walk uphill from Pozzuoli's Metropolitana station to the Solfatara (or take Bus P9; no extra fare necessary).

FS Metropolitana Linea 2 ☎ *800/568866* 🌐 *www.trenitalia.com.*

EXPLORING

Anfiteatro Flavio (*Flavian Amphitheater*). Despite the wear and tear of the millennia and the loss of masonry during the Middle Ages, this site is one of the Campi Flegrei area's Roman architectural marvels. The amphitheater (seating capacity, 40,000) was probably built under Vespasian (AD 70–AD 79), although some historians maintain that work started under Nero (AD 54–AD 69) and was merely completed later. As you approach, note the exterior's combination of volcanic stone masonry, arranged in a net-shape pattern, and horizontal bands of brick. This technique, typical of the late 1st and early 2nd centuries, was designed to reduce stress and minimize damage during seismic events. Despite this precaution, much of the superstructure has been lost: the outside part consisted of three stories surmounted by a decorative attic, while the sitting area would have had a portico above the top row of seats, decorated with statues and supported by columns. A surviving passageway near the ticket office leads into a complex underground network of *carceres* (cells) that is well worth a visit.

In classical times, the entertainment here consisted mainly of animal hunts, public executions, and gladiator fights. The hunts often involved lions, tigers, and other exotic animals imported from far-flung corners of the Roman Empire. The *fossa,* or large ditch in the arena's middle, may have contained the permanent stage setting, which could be raised when necessary to provide a scenic backdrop. According to tradition, several Early Christians—including the Naples protector St. Januarius, or San Gennaro—were condemned to be savaged by wild beasts here under the Fourth Edict, passed in AD 304 by Diocletian, but the sentence was later commuted to a less spectacular decapitation, carried out farther up the hill in the Solfatara. **■ TIP→ The amphitheater is near the Pozzuoli Metropolitana railway station and a 15-minute walk from the Solfatara. The Pozzuoli tourist office has event and other information.** ✉ *Anfiteatro Grande, Via Terracciano 75, Pozzuoli* ☎ *081/5266007, 081/5262419 Pozzuoli tourist office* 🎫 *€4, including admission to Cumae and Museo Archeologico dei Campi Flegrei, and site of Baia* ⏲ *Wed.–Mon., 9–2:30, last admission 1 hr before closing.*

Lago d'Averno (*Lake Avernus*). Regarded by the ancients as the doorway to the Underworld, the fabled lake was well known by the time the great poet Virgil settled here to write the *Aeneid*. Forested hills rise on three sides of the lake, and the menacing cone of Monte Nuovo looms on the fourth. The water is indeed "black," the smell of sulfur sometimes hangs over the landscape, and blocked-off passages lead into long-abandoned caves into which Virgil might well have ventured. Not far away is the spring that was thought to flow directly from the River Styx. It was there that Aeneas descended into the Underworld with the guidance of the Cumaean Sibyl, as famously recounted in the *Aeneid*. In late 2013 an investigation began into an alleged 1997 incident involving the dumping of toxic materials into the lake. **■ TIP→ Bilingual information panels can be found at various stages along the pleasant skirting the lake.** ✉ *Via Lago Averno Lato Destro, off Via Italia.*

Fodor's Choice ★ **The Solfatara.** At this volcanic crater you can experience firsthand the otherworldly terrain of the Campi Flegrei. The only eruption of this semi-extinct volcano took place in 1198, though according to one legend every crater in the area is a mouth of a 100-headed dragon named Typhon, which Zeus hurled into the crater of Epomeo on the island of Ischia. According to another, the sulfurous springs all about are poisonous discharges from wounds the Titans received battling Zeus. The ancient Romans, who thought the god Vulcan resided here, named it *Forum Vulcani.*

After entering through the arch of the long-defunct baths complex—the ticket office is here—you approach the volcanically active area down an avenue of holm oak trees. Past the refreshment area you'll emerge from the vegetation into a light-clay expanse. Descriptive panels about the surrounding vegetation and the volcanic action at the crater's core will steer you past the century-old brick *stufe* (ovens) resembling a Roman *sudatorium* (sauna), where you can be parboiled in mere seconds. The sulfur fumes were thought to cure respiratory, skin, joint, and other ailments. From here, move on to the fenced-off area of the fumaroles, known as the *Bocca Grande,* where steam whooshes out at about 320°F (160°C). Continuing the circuit, note the *fangaia,* or mud baths, whose mineral-rich mud is highly prized for medicinal purposes.

The Anfiteatro Flavio is a marvel of ancient Roman architecture.

The Solfatara has lent its atmospheric splendor to several films, among them Roberto Rossellini's *Viaggio in Italia,* starring Ingrid Bergman; *Pink Floyd in Pompeii*; and John Turturro's *Passione,* whose song "Caravan Petrol," about striking oil in Naples," has its action set here. ✉ *Via Solfatara 161, Pozzuoli* ☎ *081/5262341* 🌐 *www.solfatara.it* 🎫 *€7* 🕒 *Daily 8:30–1 hr before sunset.*

WHERE TO EAT AND STAY

$$$$ NEAPOLITAN

✕ **Bobò.** A meal at this stylish but *simpatico* restaurant across from the ferry terminal is a fitting way to round out a day in the Campi Flegrei. The truly ravenous can partake of the *menu degustazione* (€55); the ample à la carte menu consists mainly of fish. The exquisite antipasti, delicately garnished pasta, and *pesce* straight off the boats make this a favorite with the locals, so book ahead on the weekends and at dinner. $ *Average main: €35* ✉ *Via C. Colombo 20, Pozzuoli* ☎ *081/5262034* 🌐 *www.ristorantebobo.com* 🕒 *Closed Tues. and 2 wks in Aug. No dinner Sun.*

$$$ NEAPOLITAN

✕ **La Cucina di Ruggiero.** In antiquity the site of celebrated oyster beds and fish farms, Lake Lucrino is now the setting for this rustic *trattoria*. Quirky Ruggiero runs the dining room with a whimsical charm—don't be shocked if he addresses you through his megaphone or warmly embraces you when you leave. Meanwhile his wife, Maria, lovingly prepares specialties from land, sea, and lake. ■ **TIP→ Locals cram into this place for its home cooking, reasonable prix-fixe menu, and convivial atmosphere; reservations are essential in the evening and on weekends.** $ *Average main: €30* ✉ *Via Intorno al Lago 3, Pozzuoli, loc. Lucrino* ☎ *081/8687473* ✍ *Reservations essential* ▭ *No credit cards* 🕒 *Closed Wed. No dinner Sun.*

$$ NEAPOLITAN **Ristorante Don Antonio.** Despite its unflattering location up a *vicolo* (alley) one block from the Pozzuoli waterfront, this restaurant is admired in Neapolitan circles for its fresh seafood, ample portions, and reasonable prices. Spaghetti with clams, octopus salad, grilled and fried fish, and seafood risotto are among the longtime favorites prepared here. *Average main: €24* *Vico Magazzini 20, off Piazza San Paolo, Pozzuoli* *081/5267941* *No credit cards* *Closed Mon.*

$$ NEAPOLITAN **Taverna Viola.** A three-minute walk down the road from the Solfatara, this rustic-style restaurant–pizzeria has a pleasing view over the Bay of Pozzuoli. This is the place to deviate from a pizza Margherita and have one *con prosciutto e rughetta* (with ham and arugula) or even branch out into a fish-based dish that draws on the day's catch from the famous Pozzuoli fish market. *Average main: €15* *Via Solfatara 76, Pozzuoli* *081/5269953.*

$ HOTEL **Hotel Solfatara.** A clean and functional property just outside the Solfatara entrance, the hotel is a 20-minute walk from the center of Pozzuoli. **Pros:** five-minute walk from train station; easy downhill walk to town; half and full board available; free parking. **Cons:** walk back from town is uphill; front rooms face main road; sulfur smell. *Rooms from: €85* *Via Solfatara 163, Pozzuoli* *081/5267017* *31 rooms* *Breakfast.*

5

BAIA

12 km (7 miles) west of Naples, 4 km (2½ miles) west of Pozzuoli.

Now largely under the sea, ancient Baia was once the most opulent and fashionable resort area of the Roman Empire, the place where Sulla, Pompey, Cicero, Julius Caesar, Tiberius, and Nero built their holiday villas. It was here that Cleopatra was staying when Julius Caesar was murdered on the Ides of March (March 15) in 44 BC; here that Emperor Claudius built a great villa for his third wife, Messalina (who is reputed to have spent her nights indulging herself at local brothels); and near here that Agrippina (Claudius's fourth wife and murderer) is believed to have been killed by henchmen sent by her son Nero in AD 59. Unfortunately, the Romans did not pursue the custom of writing official graffiti—"Here lived Crassus" would help—so it's difficult to assign these historical events to specific locations. Consequently, conjecture is the order of the day: Julius Caesar's villa is now thought to be at the top of the hill behind the archaeological site and not near the foot of the Aragonese castle, though we cannot be absolutely certain. We do know, however, that the Romans found this area staggeringly beautiful. A visit to the site can only confirm what Horace wrote in one of his epistles: *Nullus in orbe sinus Baiis praelucet amoenis* ("No bay on Earth outshines pleasing Baia").

GETTING HERE AND AROUND

To arrive by car take the Tangenziale from Naples and exit at Pozzuoli–Arco Felice and follow the indications for Baia. By train, take the Cumana railway (trains leave every 20 minutes from Montesanto in Naples, travel time 30 minutes, nearest stop Fusaro), followed by a SEPSA bus for the last 3 km (2 miles). On Friday, weekends, and public holidays, take the City Sightseeing Campi Flegrei bus from Piazza della Repubbblica in Pozzuoli (or from other sites in the area). Where the bus stops in the square outside the Baia station, cross the disused railway line on a footbridge. Continue upward for about five minutes until you reach the entrance to the site (limited parking is available). The same SEPSA bus also stops at the Museo Archeologico dei Campi Flegrei. To arrive from Naples by bus, take the SEPSA Linea 1 from Piazza Garibaldi and ask to get off at either the Parco Archeologico or the Museo.

EXPLORING

Baiasommersa. From the small modern-day port of Baia you can board a boat with glass panels on its lower deck and view part of the *città sommersa,* the underwater city of ancient Baia. The guided tour—usually in Italian, but given in English if arranged well in advance—lasts about 75 minutes and is best undertaken in calm conditions, when you can get good glimpses of Roman columns, roads, villa walls, and mosaics. Peer through fish-flecked Plexiglas at statues of Octavia Claudia (Claudius's sister) and of Ulysses, his outstretched arms and mollusk-eaten head once a part of the nymphaeum since sunk into the deeps after an outbreak of so-called bradyseism. (Actually these statues are replicas. The originals are up the hill in the Castle museum.) ☎ *3208350145* 🌐 *www.baiasommersa.it* 🎫 *€10* 🕑 *Sat. at noon and 3, Sun. at 10, noon, and 3.*

Museo Archeologico dei Campi Flegrei. The Castle of Baia, which commands a 360-degree view eastward across the Bay of Pozzuoli and westward across the open Tyrrhenian, provides a fittingly dramatic setting for the Archaeological Museum of Campi Flegrei. Though the castle's foundation dates to the late 15th century, when Naples was ruled by the House of Aragon and an invasion by Charles VIII of France looked imminent, the structure was radically transformed under the Spanish viceroy Don Pedro de Toledo after the nearby eruption of Monte Nuovo in 1538. Indeed, its bastions bear a striking resemblance to the imposing Castel Sant'Elmo in Naples, built in the same period.

Of the various exhibitions, the first on the suggested itinerary consists of plaster casts from the Roman period found at the Baia archaeological site. This gives valuable insights into the techniques used by the Romans to make copies from Greek originals in bronze from the classical and Hellenistic periods.

Pride of place goes to the *sacellum,* or small sanctuary, transported from nearby Misenum and tastefully displayed inside the Aragonese tower, the Torre Tenaglia. Standing about 20 feet high, the sacellum has been reconstructed, with two of its original six columns (the rest in steel) and a marble architrave with its dedicatory inscription to the husband-and-wife team who commissioned sanctuary's restoration in the 2nd century AD. The beneficent couple is depicted above this. Behind the facade are the naked marble figures of Vespasian (left) and Titus (right) in a flattering heroic pose, at least from the neck downward.

Unfortunately, what should be the museum's showpiece—Emperor Claudius's nymphaeum—has been closed for several years because of a dangerously unstable wall. Discovered in 1959 but only systematically excavated in the early 1980s, the original nymphaeum now lies under 20 feet of water in the Bay of Pozzuoli. Though you can't see the nymphaeum in person, Heculaneum's MAV museum contains a striking virtual reproduction.

■ TIP→ On weekdays except Friday, you can get to the museum on a regular bus from the old Baia railway station. Purchase a round-trip ticket at the kiosk outside and board the bus headed toward Bacoli. On Friday, weekends, and public holidays, take the Archeobus Flegreo from Piazza della Repubblica, Pozzuoli, or other sites. ✉ *Via Castello 39, Bacoli, Baia* ☎ *081/5233797* 🎫 *Free on weekdays, €4 on weekends, including Cumae, site at Baia, and Flavian amphitheater* ⏲ *Tues.–Sun. 9–2:30 (last admission at 1).*

Parco Archeologico e Monumentale di Baia (*Monumental and Archaeological Park of Baia*). In antiquity this whole area was the Palatium Baianum (the Palace of Baia), dedicated to *otium* (leisure) and the residence of emperors from Augustus to as late as Septimius Severus in the 3rd century AD. At the park's ticket office you should receive a small site map, and information panels in English are posted at strategic intervals. The first terrace, the Villa dell'Ambulatio, is one of the best levels from which to appreciate the site's topography: the whole hillside down to the level of the modern road near the waterfront has been modeled into flat terraces, each sporting different architectural features.

5

While up on the first terrace look for the depictions of dolphins, swans, and cupids in the *balneum* (thermal bathing, Room 13), and admire the elaborate theatrical motifs in the floor mosaic in Room 14. Below the balneum and inviting further exploration is a nymphaeum shrine, which can be reached from the western side. Make sure you get down to the so-called Temple of Mercury, on the lowest level, which has held much fascination for travelers from the 18th century onward. It has been variously interpreted as a frigidarium and as a *natatio* (swimming pool) and is the oldest example of a large dome (50 BC–27 BC), predating the cupola of the Pantheon in Rome. (Test the rich echo in the interior.) **■ TIP→ In summer the site provides an unusual backdrop for evening concerts and opera performances. The site office (☎ 84880288) or the tourist office website (🌐 www.infocampiflegrei.it) will have information about them.** ✉ *Parco Archeologico e Monumentale di Baia, Via Sella di Baia 22, Bacoli, loc. Baia* ☎ *081/8687592* 🎫 *€4 weekends and holidays, free Tues.–Fri.; admission good for visit to Cumae, Museo Archeologico dei Campi Flegrei in Baia, and Flavian amphitheater in Pozzuoli* ⏲ *Tues.–Sun. 9–2:30.*

WHERE TO EAT

$$$ NEAPOLITAN

✕ **Club il Casolare de Tobia.** Come here for the rare experience of dining within a 10,000-year-old volcanic crater (thankfully extinct). Though also a hotel, this place is known more for its restaurant, set on the volcano's inner slopes and offering a view of the crater floor's patchwork of farmed plots. Specializing in Neapolitan rustic cuisine, the owner Tobia Costagliola serves whatever is in season. Ordering from the prix-fixe menu you can expect a cornucopia of antipasti and some nouvelle vegetarian dishes such as pasta *e cicerchia* (with vetchling). The inn's four *mini-appartmenti* are small but tastefully furnished and provide a perfect base for exploring the surrounding area. *$ Average main: €30 ✉ Fondi di Baia 12, Bacoli ☎ 081/5235193 🌐 www.clubilcasolaredatobia.it 4 rooms ⏲ Closed Mon and Tues. No dinner Sun. No meals.*

$$ NEAPOLITAN **Il Tucano.** The Neapolitan chef here bakes delicious pizzas from half a meter (just under 20 inches) in diameter up to a full meter (39 inches)—as big as your table. The seafood options also stand out, among them grilled fish (the selection depends on the day's catch) and large prawns fresh from nearby Pozzuoli. The walls, some white and others powder blue, complement the blues of the bay, though cars parked in front of the building compromise the view. Il Tucano is popular with Americans from the nearby NATO base at Agnano. *$ Average main: €20 ✉ Via Molo di Baia 40, Bacoli ☎ 081/8545046 🌐 www.ristopizzailtucano.com.*

CUMAE

16 km (10 miles) west of Naples, 5 km (3 miles) north of Baia.

Fodor's Choice ★ Being perhaps the oldest Greek colony on mainland Italy, Cumae overshadowed the Phlegrean Fields and Neapolis in the 7th and 6th centuries BC, because it was home to the Antro della Sibilla, the fabled Cave of the Cumaean Sibyl—one of the three greatest oracles of antiquity—who is said to have presided over the destinies of men. In about the 6th century BC, the Greeks hollowed the cave (closed for restoration at time of writing) from the rock beneath the ridge leading up to the present ruins of Cumae's acropolis. Today you can walk—just as Virgil's Aeneas did—through a dark, massive 350-foot-long stone tunnel that opens into the vaulted Chamber of the Prophetic Voice, where the Sibyl delivered her oracles. Standing here in one of the most venerated sites of ancient times, the sense of the *numen*—of communication with invisible powers—is overwhelming. "This is the most romantic classical site in Italy," claimed the famed travelogue writer H. V. Morton. "I would rather come here than to Pompeii."

GETTING HERE AND AROUND

If driving, take the Cumae Exit 13 of the Naples Tangenziale and proceed along Montenuovo Licola Patria, following signs for Cumae. At the first major intersection, take a left onto Via Arco Felice Vecchio, pass under the arch, and make a right at the next intersection; after about 400 yards, turn left into the site. There is a free parking lot. There is no train station in Cumae, so to arrive from Naples, take the Cumana railway to Fusaro, then the SEPSA Miseno–Cumae bus to Cumae. SEPSA also runs buses to Cumae from Pozzuoli's station and Baia.

DID YOU KNOW?

In the Cave of the Cumaean Sibyl, ancient generals, aristocrats, and commoners alike would consult the oracle for guidance on everything from military campaigns to affairs of the heart.

EXPLORING

Cumae. Allow at least two hours to soak up the ambience of the ruins of Cumae, founded by Greek colonists late in the 8th century BC. The name has legendary origins: Myth has it that Euboean mariners found a woman who had miscarried a baby on the beach here, and the fetus was washed out to sea by great breakers. Thinking this an omen from the gods of fertility, the mariners built an altar here and called their new settlement *kuema* (or "fetus" in Greek). Centuries later Virgil wrote his epic of the *Aeneid,* the story of the Trojan prince Aeneas's wanderings, partly to give Rome the historical legitimacy that Homer had given the Greeks. On his journey, Aeneas had to descend to the underworld to speak to his father, and to find his way in, he needed the guidance of the Cumaean Sibyl. Virgil did not dream up the Sibyl's Cave or the entrance to Hades—he must have actually stood both in her chamber and along the rim of Lake Avernus, as you yourself will stand.

Although Cumae never achieved the status of Delphi, it was the most important oracular center in Magna Graecia (Great Greece), and the Sibyl would have been consulted on a whole range of matters. Governments consulted the Sibyl before mounting campaigns. Wealthy aristocrats came to channel their deceased relatives. Businessmen came to get their dreams interpreted or to seek favorable omens before entering into financial agreements or setting off on journeys. Love potions were a profitable source of revenue; women from Baia lined up for potions to slip into the wine of the handsome charioteers who drove up and down the street in their gold-plated four-horsepower chariots. Still, it was the Sibyl's prophecies that ensured the crowds here, prophecies written on palm leaves and later collected into the corpus of the Sibylline books.

■ TIP→ Unlike in Greek and Roman times, when access to Cumae was through a network of underground passages, an aboveground EAV bus service leaves outside Fusano station at regular intervals. (See website www.eavbus.it for times.) *Via Acropoli 1* *081/848800288* *€4, including Museo Archeologico dei Campi Flegrei and site at Baia, and Flavian amphitheater in Pozzuoli* *Wed.–Mon. 9–2:30.*

WHERE TO STAY

$$ B&B/INN **Villa Giulia.** Built with characteristic yellow tuff walls and restored in immaculate taste, this historic farmhouse provides an excellent base for the Cumae area provided you have a car. **Pros:** excellent food and service; charming grounds and garden; pool; family-friendly. **Cons:** car is essential; bugs an issue in summer. *Rooms from: €140* *Via Cuma–Licola 178* *081/8540163* *081/8044356* *www.villagiulia.info* *6 rooms* *Breakfast.*

6

NAPLES

WELCOME TO NAPLES

TOP REASONS TO GO

★ **A Spaccanapoli stroll:** For perfect people-watching, promenade through this historic district of Naples, whose packed streets, pungent aromas, and operatic hawking offer all the energy, chaos, and beauty that make this the most operatic of cities.

★ **A baroque extravaganza:** Gorge yourself on Naples's greatest moment in art history, the era of the baroque, by exploring the city's 17th-century churches, whose swirling gilt naves melt even the stoniest of hearts.

★ **Buried pleasures:** All the excavated treasures from Pompeii and Herculaneum ended up in Naples's Museo Archeologico Nazionale, the finest treasure trove of ancient art.

★ **Pizza:** There are hundreds of restaurants that specialize in pizza in Naples, and the best of these make nothing else. This is where the classic Margherita was invented, after all.

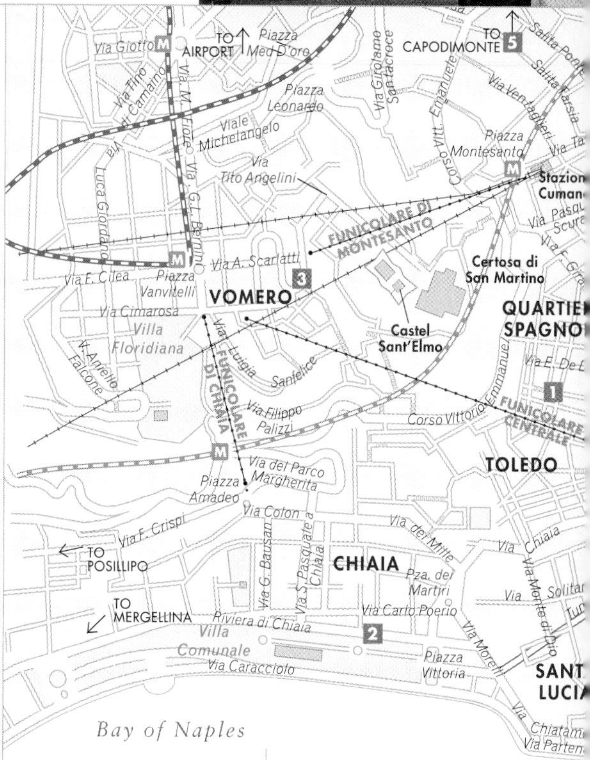

1 Toledo and Quartieri Spagnoli. The central Toledo district contains the sumptuous apartments of the Palazzo Reale and the broad open space of Piazza Plebiscito. Built by Viceroy Pedro di Toledo to bring some order to the city, the pedestrianized Via Toledo leads into the grid of Quartieri Spagnoli, a sort of NATO base of its time, where Spanish soldiers were deployed between campaigns to guard the palazzos of the ruling class. More accessible than ever, it now has a metro station.

2 The Lungomare. The area along the harbor south of Toledo consists of two quarters, Santa Lucia and Chiaia. Both are thin on culture and geared to *la dolce vita*: in Santa Lucia you can expect serenades from street musicians over dinner, while most locals head for their favorite trattoria up a side street in Chiaia.

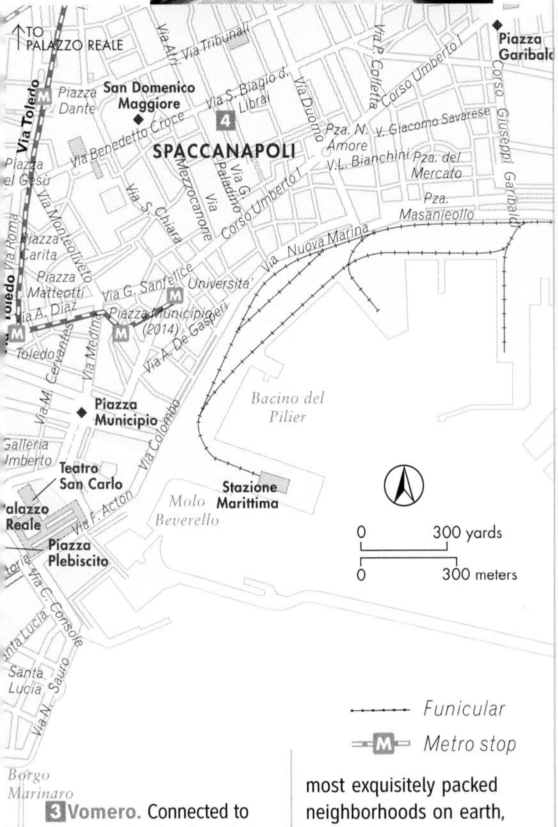

3 Vomero. Connected to the city below by three funiculars, the Vomero hill offers a peaceful contrast to the hustle downtown. The Certosa at San Martino, a monastery turned museum complex, is a highlight, with magnificent works of art, wraparound views of Naples, and gardens fit for contemplation.

4 Spaccanapoli. For art and archaeology, this must be one of the most exquisitely packed neighborhoods on earth, and at the same time it teems with vibrant street life. The United Nations has dubbed the district an open-air museum—which in this case feels like an understatement.

5 Capodimonte and Nearby. This upper neighborhood of ancient Naples is home to the most important museum of Greco-Roman antiquities in the world.

GETTING ORIENTED

In Naples "up and down" is often as accurate a form of direction as "to and fro." From the bay, the city rises up steep hillsides, which you can ascend with the help of three funiculars, as well as strategically placed *ascensori* (elevators). Via Toledo, one of the major thoroughfares, serves as a north–south axis, conveniently now with a metro station. Farther north, the long Corso Vittorio Emanuele, a panoramic strip of road, runs up along the Vomero, linking the sea-level southwest with the elevated northeast.

CAMPANIA'S SEAFOOD BOUNTY

Fish and other sea creatures are mainstays of the Campanian diet, especially along the region's stunning coastline, and on the islands ringing the Bay of Naples.

The waters along Campania's shore are regarded as some of the cleanest in Italy. Evidence of that claim comes from the ubiquity of anchovies (*alici* or *acciuga*), which are said to swim only in pristine waters. Fishermen in some villages still go out at night in lighted fishing boats to attract and net anchovies, which are cooked fresh or cured with salt.

The Mediterranean Sea's bounty extends far beyond alici. Some of the most popular fish varieties are listed on the following page, but there are scores more waiting to be tasted. Gustatory explorers eating their way down the coastline might also encounter these sea creatures: *agug-lie* (needle fish); *calamari* (squid); *cicale* (mantis shrimp); *mazzancolle* (a type of prawn); *orata* (sea bream or daurade); *pesce spada* (swordfish); *seppia* (cuttlefish); *scorfano di fondale* (ocean perch); *scorfano rosso* (scorpion fish); and *scampi* (langoustines).

MENU DECODER

Campanian chefs know how to treat fresh fish, using simple preparations that showcase the fresh flavors of the region. These are some of the typical preparations.

- baked (*al forno*)
- baked in a paper pouch (*al cartoccio*)
- cured (*salato*)
- fried (*fritto*)
- grilled (*alla griglia*)
- marinated (*marinato*)
- poached (*affogato*)
- raw (*crudo*)
- roasted (*arrostito*)
- roasted in salt (*al sale*)
- smoked (*affumicato*)

ALICI OR ACCIUGHE (ANCHOVY)
Highly flavored, small fish that may be served fresh or cured. Grilled or fried anchovies have a milder taste than the cured fish, which can be quite pungent. Fried anchovies are a popular snack along the coast.

BACCALÀ (SALT COD)
Cod that has been dried and cured in salt. Before use, the dried *baccalà* fillet is soaked repeatedly in water to reduce saltiness and reconstitute the flesh. Common dishes include sautéed baccalà with potatoes, and baccalà baked in spicy tomato sauce.

BRANZINO (EUROPEAN SEA BASS)
A medium-size fish with lean, flaky white meat and a slightly sweet, mild flavor. May also be called *spigola*. It is often grilled and served with potatoes, or baked *al cartoccio*.

COZZE (MUSSELS)
Extremely popular in the region since Roman times, these fat yellow delights are more likely than not to be farmed, as natural resources have been severely depleted. They are often served with a side plate for the shells.

GALLINELLA (GURNARD)
A meaty white fish that may also be called *mazzole* or tub fish. Gallinella *all'acqua pazza* is cooked in "crazy water" (oil mixed with water and flavored with tomatoes and herbs). A related fish is *cappone gallinella* (red gurnard).

POLPO (OCTOPUS)
The firmly textured, gently flavored octopus may be boiled in simple soups, stewed (*polpi in cassuola*), or simply sautéed with garlic and olive oil, among myriad preparations. *Polpetto* is the term used for little octopi.

SARDE (SARDINES)
Sardines are considered *pesce azzurro*—small blue fish that swim near the surface of the sea—along with the anchovy and *cecinelli* (smelt). These fish typically appear in seafood *fritto misto,* a mixture of small fried fish.

TOTANI (FLYING SQUID)
These squid closely resemble calamari, and likewise are a popular snack when cut into rings and deep-fried. May be stuffed with diced vegetables, fried as a snack, or boiled and served cold in salads.

TRIGLIA (RED MULLET)
Small bony fish with moderately fatty flesh and delicate flavor. Often featured in fish stews, and may also be served sautéed, baked, or roasted.

VONGOLE VERACI (STRIPED VENUS CLAMS)
These tiny, sweet clams are prized throughout Italy, where they play a starring role in *spaghetti con le vongole*.

6

Updated by Martin Bennett and Fiorella Squillante

"Built like a great amphitheater around her beautiful bay, Naples is an eternally unfolding play acted by a million of the best actors in the world," Herbert Kubly observed in his *American in Italy.* "The comedy is broad, the tragedy violent. The curtain never rings down." A huge zest for living and crowded conditions in the shadow of Vesuvius make Naples the most vibrant city in Italy—a steaming, bubbling, reverberating minestrone in which each block is a small village, every street the setting for a Punch-and-Judy show, and everything seems to be a backdrop for an opera not yet composed.

It's said that northern Italians vacation here to remind themselves of the time when Italy was *molto Italiana—really* Italian. In this respect, Naples—Napoli in Italian—doesn't disappoint: Neapolitan rainbows of laundry wave in the wind over alleyways open-windowed with friendliness, mothers caress children, men break out into impromptu arias at sidewalk cafés, and street scenes offer Fellini-esque slices of life. Everywhere contrasting elements of faded gilt and romance, rust and calamity, grandeur and squalor form a pageant of pure *Italianità*—Italy at its most Italian.

As the historic capital of Campania, Naples has been perpetually and tumultuously in a state of flux. Neapolitans are instinctively the most hospitable of people, and they've often paid a price for being so, having unwittingly extended a warm welcome to wave after wave of invaders. Lombards, Goths, Normans, Swabians, Spanish viceroys and kings, and Napoleonic generals arrived in turn; most of them proved to be greedy and self-serving. Still, if these foreign rulers bled the populace dry with taxes, they left the impoverished city with a rich architectural inheritance.

Much of that inheritance is on display in the Spaccanapoli district, where the Piazza Gesù Nuovo and the surrounding blocks are a showplace for the city's most beloved churches. Compared to most other great metropolises of the world, Naples has little tourist infrastructure, forcing you to become a native very quickly, as you'll find out if you spend some time wandering through the gridlike narrow streets of the old center.

NAPLES PLANNER

WHEN TO GO

High seasons in Naples are the so-called shoulder seasons elsewhere—from April to June and September to October. Book well in advance if visiting then. Christmas in Naples is also a good time to experience the city, Nativity scenes being a Neapolitan specialty. From July into September the entire area surrounding Naples—including the Amalfi Coast and Capri—fills up with local Italian holidaymakers, pushing up prices. Paradoxically, during August Naples empties, good for visitors except for the fact that police presence diminishes as well. With breezes coming in off the coast, summer temperatures are lower than one might think.

PLANNING YOUR TIME

From three to four days should be enough to give you a taste of the city and see you through the main monuments, as well as factor in a breather to one of the islands in the bay. Always make a contingency plan for each day. Naples can be fraying on the nerves and tiring in terms of legwork, so head for one of the city parks (Villa Comunale, Floridiana, or Capodimonte) for a well-earned break in between doses of culture. You may need a rest after touring the Spaccanapoli district, which, following the original Greek street plan is wonderfully compact, with more culture packed into a square mile or two than almost anywhere else in the world.

Sightseeing days should begin no later than 9, as most churches are usually open only from 7:30 until noon or 12:30, reopening only after the afternoon siesta, from 4 or 4:30 until about 7. Most museums have extended hours, with a few even open in evenings.

GETTING HERE AND AROUND

For standard public transportation, including the subways, buses, and funiculars, a Unico Napoli ticket costs €1.30 and is valid for 90 minutes as far as Pozzuoli to the west and Portici to the east; €3.70 buys a *biglietto giornaliero* (all-day ticket; €3.10 on weekends). The tickets are issued by Unico Campania, a consortium of transit companies.

Contact Unico Campania ☎ *081/5513109* 🌐 *www.unicocampania.it.*

BICYCLE TRAVEL

The Lungomare (also known as Via Partenope) is closed to car traffic, making bike travel along the waterfront safe and pleasant. Foxrent has bicycles for one, two, or even six, for adults and children, as well as skateboards and skates. The rental shop is adjacent to Castel dell'Ovo.

Contact Foxrent ✉ *Via Partenope 37, Santa Lucia* ☎ *081/7645060.*

BOAT TRAVEL

Ferries to Capri depart from the same port where cruise ships disembark; fast ferries leave from the Clata Porta di Massa, and hydrofoils leave from Molo Beverello. Hydrofoils (which are more frequent) make the trip in 40 minutes, other ferries 50 minutes. You can just walk on the ferry after buying a ticket. Fast-ferry prices are €17.80, and hydrofoils are €18.80–€20.20. Once on the island, the funicular railway from the port up to Capri Town is €1.40 round-trip.

BUS TRAVEL

Bus service has become viable over the last few years, especially with the introduction of larger buses on the regular R1, R2, R3, and R4 routes. Electronic signs display wait times at many stops.

CAR TRAVEL

Car travel within Naples is not recommended: it's difficult, parking is a nightmare, and theft of cars parked on the street is a persistent threat. If you come to Naples by car, find a garage, agree on the cost, and leave it there for the duration of your stay. Garage Cava, Grilli, and Turistico are three safe, centrally located garages. A car rental could be useful if you want to explore the Amalfi Coast, though you need to leave plenty of time to spare for your return because traffic along the coast can be heavy and slow moving. Expect to pay €55 per day for a compact manual vehicle.

Contacts **Garage Cava** ✉ *Via Mergellina 6* ☎ *081/660023* ⏲ *24 hrs.* **Grilli** ✉ *Hotel Ramada, Via Ferraris 40, near Stazione Centrale* ☎ *081/264344* ⏲ *6 am–midnight.* **Turistico** ✉ *Via de Gasperi 14, near port* ☎ *081/5525442* ⏲ *6:30 am–midnight.*

SUBWAY TRAVEL

Now with a couple of new art-decorated stations (Toledo and Università) recently voted among Europe's most attractive, Naples's rather old Metropolitana (subway system), provides fairly frequent service and can be the fastest way to get across the traffic-clogged city. The other urban subway system, Metropolitana Collinare, links the hill area of the Vomero and beyond with the National Archaeological Museum and Piazza Dante. Trains on both lines run from 5 am until 10:30 pm.

TAXI TRAVEL

Hailing a taxi is practically unheard of in Naples. Your best bet is to call Radio Taxi or ask someone at your hotel to book one. Taxi ranks can be found outside the central Piazza Garibaldi train station and the port (Molo Beverello), but there are few anywhere else. Watch out for overcharging at three locations: the airport, the railway station, and the hydrofoil marina. A taxi from the airport to the central station costs €37 euros, this covering three people, two large pieces of luggage, and two small pieces. City Airport Taxis has information about fees to other destinations within and near Naples.

Taxi trips around the city are unlikely to cost less than €10 or more than €20. You can pay a fixed price or ask for the meter to be switched on; the latter often results in your paying less. Other options besides Radio Taxi include Consorttaxi (☎ 081/5525252), Cotana (☎ 081/5707070), Free (☎ 081/5515151), and Napoli (081/5564444). In summer, most

CLOSE UP

Beyond First Impressions

If you're arriving in Naples by train, don't expect to be instantly charmed. Piazza Garibaldi, which is home to the Stazione Centrale, the main railroad terminal, is now a battered labyrinth—crowded, messy, and inhospitable, with the local bus station perched in the middle of a tangle of intersections. Longtime home to street sharks and souvenir hawkers, the piazza is now also a meeting point for Eastern European guest workers, who have become a growing presence in the city.

When you make your way beyond Piazza Garibaldi, first impressions begin to mellow: Delightfully and unforgettably, Naples reveals itself as a cornucopia of elegant boulevards, treasure-stocked palaces, the world's greatest museum of classical antiquities, the stage-set neighborhood of Spaccanapoli, and scores of historic churches. Naples becomes *Napoli la bella,* a city that centuries of romantics have deemed one of the most beautiful in the world.

cabs in Naples have no air-conditioning—which the city's buses and metro do have—and you can bake if caught in a traffic jam. Taxis charge approximately €3 initially (more on Sunday and holidays), then €0.05 per 65 meters or 10 seconds of idling.

Contacts City Airport Taxis *www.city-airport-taxis.com/airporttransfers/city/Naples-taxi.* **Radio Taxi Napoli** ☎ *081/5564444.*

TRAIN TRAVEL

The Naples area has four main-line train stations: Stazione Centrale, Piazza Garibaldi, Mergellina and Campi Flegrei. Stazione Centrale (ground level) and Piazza Garibaldi (lower level), which share the same building, receive many trains from Rome, and Mergellina also receives trains from the capital. ⇨ *For more information about traveling by train to Naples and for station and railroad contacts, see Train Travel in this book's Travel Smart chapter. For information about train travel to Mt. Vesuvius, Pompeii, and other areas just outside Naples, see the Planner section of the Bay of Naples chapter.*

RESTAURANTS

Naples has a wide choice of naturally elegant restaurants, but some Neapolitans will go out of town for a high-end restaurant meal, heading to gastronomic enclaves in the Pozzuoli area or on the Sorrentine Peninsula, or opting for a feast at one of the private dining clubs the Neapolitan aristocracy favors. If you stay in town, you're likely to be pleasantly surprised. Wherever you go, be prepared to deviate from the menu (locals rarely ask for one), and ask the waiter for the chef's special *piatto* (dish). At the lower end, service may be rough and ready, but then again, this is Naples, and you don't expect to be served by liveried waitstaff when your restaurant sits at the end of an alley. Note that many restaurants in Naples close for at least a week around August 15 to celebrate the Ferragosto holidays.

Prices in the reviews are the average cost of a main course at dinner, or, if dinner is not served, at lunch.

HOTELS

If you want seafront accommodation in Naples, remember that rooms with a view come at a sizable premium. With the coastal strip of Via Partenope recently having been decreed traffic-free, this area is all the more appealing a place to stay these days. Taking advantage of similar pedestrianization schemes, several competitively priced hotels close to Piazza Plebiscito and in the Chiaia occupy a more pleasing environment and offer public-transportation connections and many touring options within walking distance. Resist the temptation to stay near Piazza Garibaldi by the Stazione Centrale just because it's a transportation hub: the area is unsafe (and unpleasant) for evening strolls after 8:30 pm.

Prices in the reviews are the lowest cost of a standard double room in high season.

TOURS

Many companies run tours and excursions within Naples proper and to Vesuvius, Pompeii, the Amalfi Coast, and other places as well. Melody Travel has local tours to the top sights in Naples, for instance, or you can combine city tour with one to Pompeii. The company will also work with you to create a custom itinerary tailored to your interests.

The Centro di Accoglienza Turistica Museo Aperto Napoli, a welcome center based in the Museo Diocesano, in the old town, offers €6 audio tours. Close to the port, beside the main entrance to Castel Nuovo, is the terminal for the double-decker buses of City Sightseeing. For €22 (€11 for children, €66 per family) you can take four different excursions on weekends, three on weekdays. The weekday routes cover views of the gulf (72 minutes), art venues (61 minutes), and San Martino (90 minutes).

Contacts Centro di Accoglienza Turistica Museo Aperto Napoli ✉ *Museo Diocesano, Largo Donnaregina, Spaccanapoli* ☎ *081/5571365* 🌐 *www.museoapertonapoli.it.* **City Sightseeing** ✉ *Piazza Municipio* ☎ *081/5517279* 🌐 *www.napoli.city-sightseeing.it.* **Melody Travel** ☎ *081/0124931* 🌐 *www.melodytravel.it.*

VISITOR INFORMATION

The numerous tourist offices in Naples aren't always open when they claim to be, but most are generally open from Monday to Saturday between 8:30 and 8 (Sunday between 8:30 and 2) except where noted. The AACST specializes in information on old Naples but generally just supplies brochures. A second office, which is closed on Sunday, is handily inside the Palazzo Reale. There's an EPT (Ente Provinciale per il Turismo) office in Stazione Centrale staffed by a welcoming team of helpers. Pick up a free map and the latest "Art in Campania" brochure listing key venues and possible savings through the Campania Artecard (⇨ *see Campania Artecard box, below*). Other branches are in Piazza dei Martiri at Stazione Mergellina.

AACST ✉ *Piazza Gesù Nuovo, Spaccanapoli* ☎ *01/5523328.*

EPT ✉ *Stazione Centrale, Piazza Garibaldi* ☎ *081/268779* 🌐 *www.inaples.it* ⏲ *Daily 9–6* ✉ *Piazza dei Martiri 58, Chiaia* ☎ *081/4107211* ✉ *Stazione Mergellina* ☎ *081/7612102.*

EXPLORING NAPLES

Updated by Martin Bennett

Naples, a bustling city of a million people, can be a challenge for visitors because of its hilly terrain and its twisty, often congested streets. Though spread out, Naples invites walking; the bus system, funiculars, and subways are also options for dealing with weary legs.

The city stretches along the Bay of Naples from Piazza Garibaldi in the east to Mergellina in the west, with its back to the Vomero Hill. From Stazione Centrale, on Piazza Garibaldi, Corso Umberto I (known as the "Rettifilo") heads southwest to the monumental city center—commonly known as "Toledo"—around the piazzas Bovio, Municipio, and Trieste e Trento; here is the major urban set piece composed of the Palazzo Reale, Teatro San Carlo, and Galleria Umberto Primo.

To the north are the historic districts of old Naples, most notably Spaccanapoli, I Vergini, and La Sanità; to the south, the port. Farther west along the bay are the more fashionable neighborhoods of Santa Lucia and Chiaia, and finally the waterfront district of Mergellina. The residential area of Vomero sits on the steep hills rising above Chiaia and downtown.

At the center of it all is picturesque Spaccanapoli—the heart of the *centro storico* (historic center). The entire quarter takes its name from its main street, a partly pedestrianized promenade referred to as Spaccanapoli. Rather confusingly, this street changes its name—Via Benedetto Croce and Via San Biagio dei Librai, among others—as it runs its way through the heart of old Naples. Tying much of this geographic layout together is the "spine" of the city, Via Toledo—Naples's major north–south axis, which begins at Piazza Trieste e Trento and heads up all the way to Capodimonte. It's basically one straight road with four different names (five if you count the official name of Via Roma, which is how the locals refer to it).

Via Toledo links Piazza Trieste e Trento with Piazza Dante. Going farther north you get into Via Pessina for about 100 yards, which takes you up to the megajunction with the Museo Archeologico Nazionale. North of that, you head up to the peak of Capodimonte by traveling along Via Santa Teresa degli Scalzi and then Corso Amedeo di Savoia.

To make things a bit more confusing, parts of Via Toledo are pedestrianized—that means no buses or scooters, thankfully—from just south of Piazza Carità (where Via Toledo/Roma intersects with Via Diaz) all the way to Piazza Trieste e Trento.

TOLEDO

Naples's setting on what is possibly the most beautiful bay in the world has long been a boon for its inhabitants—the expansive harbor has always brought great mercantile wealth to the city—and, intermittently, a curse. Throughout history, a who's who of Greek, Roman, Norman, Spanish, and French despots has quarreled over this gateway to Campania. Each set of conquerors recognized that the area around the city harbor—today occupied by the Molo Beverello hydrofoil terminal and the 1928 Stazione Marittima—functioned as a veritable welcome mat to the metropolis and consequently should be a fitting showcase of regal and royal authority.

The monuments they created remain prominent features of the city center: one of the most magnificent opera houses in Europe, a palace that rivals Versailles, an impregnable *castello* (castle), a majestic church modeled on Rome's Pantheon, and a 19th-century shopping galleria are landmarks that characterized the shifts among the ruling powers, from the French Angevins to the Spanish Habsburgs and Bourbons and, later, the postunification rise of the bourgeoisie and the regime of Mussolini. In contrast to the intense intimacy of the Spaccanapoli district, the official center of Naples unrolls its majesty with great pomp along its spacious avenues and monumental piazzas.

TOP ATTRACTIONS

Castel Nuovo. Known to locals as Maschio Angioino, in reference to its Angevin builders, this imposing castle is now used more for marital than military purposes—a portion of it serves as a government registry office. A white four-tiered triumphal entrance arch, ordered by Alfonso of Aragon after he entered the city in 1443 to seize power from the increasingly beleaguered Angevin Giovanna II, upstages the building's looming Angevin stonework. At the arch's top, as if justifying Alfonso's claim to the throne, the Archangel Gabriel slays a demon.

Across the courtyard within the castle is the Sala Grande, also known as the Sala dei Baroni, which has a stunning vaulted ceiling 92 feet high. In 1486 local barons hatched a plot against Alfonso's son, King Ferrante, who reacted by inviting them to this hall for a wedding banquet, which promptly turned into a mass arrest. (Ferrante is also said to have kept a crocodile in the castle as his pet executioner.) You can also visit the Sala dell'Armeria, where a glass floor reveals recent excavations of Roman baths from the Augustan period. To one side are giant photographs of three Roman ships, wood amazingly intact, unearthed during recent digging of the nearby metro station and now in Pisa for restoration. In the next room on the left, the Cappella Palatina, look on the frescoed walls for Nicolo di Tomaso's painting of Robert Anjou, one of the first realistic portraits ever. Of the famous Giotto pictures described by Petrarch remain only a few tiny fragments.

The castle's first floor holds a small gallery that includes a beautiful early Renaissance Adoration of the Magi by Marco Cardisco, with the roles of the three Magi played by the three Aragonese kings: Ferrante I, Ferrante II, and Charles V. ✉ *Piazza Municipio, Toledo* ☎ *081/7955877* 🎟 *€5* ⏲ *Mon.–Sat. 9–7* Ⓜ *Toledo, Piazza Municipio (due 2014).*

Gallerie di Palazzo Zevallos Stigliano. Tucked inside this beautifully restored palazzo, which houses the Banca Intesa San Paolo, one of Italy's major banks, is a small museum that's worth seeking out. Enter the bank through Cosimo Fanzago's gargoyled doorway and take the handsome elevator to the upper floor. The first room to the left holds the star attraction, Caravaggio's last work, *The Martyrdom of Saint Ursula.* The saint here is, for dramatic effect, deprived of her usual retinue of a thousand followers. On the left, a face of pure spite, is

Castel Nuovo **7**

Galleria Umberto I **5**

Gallerie di Palazzo Zevallos Stigiano **9**

Palazzo Reale **3**

Piazza Plebiscito **1**

San Francesco di Paola **2**

Santa Brigida **6**

Sant' Anna dei Lombardi **8**

Teatro San Carlo **4**

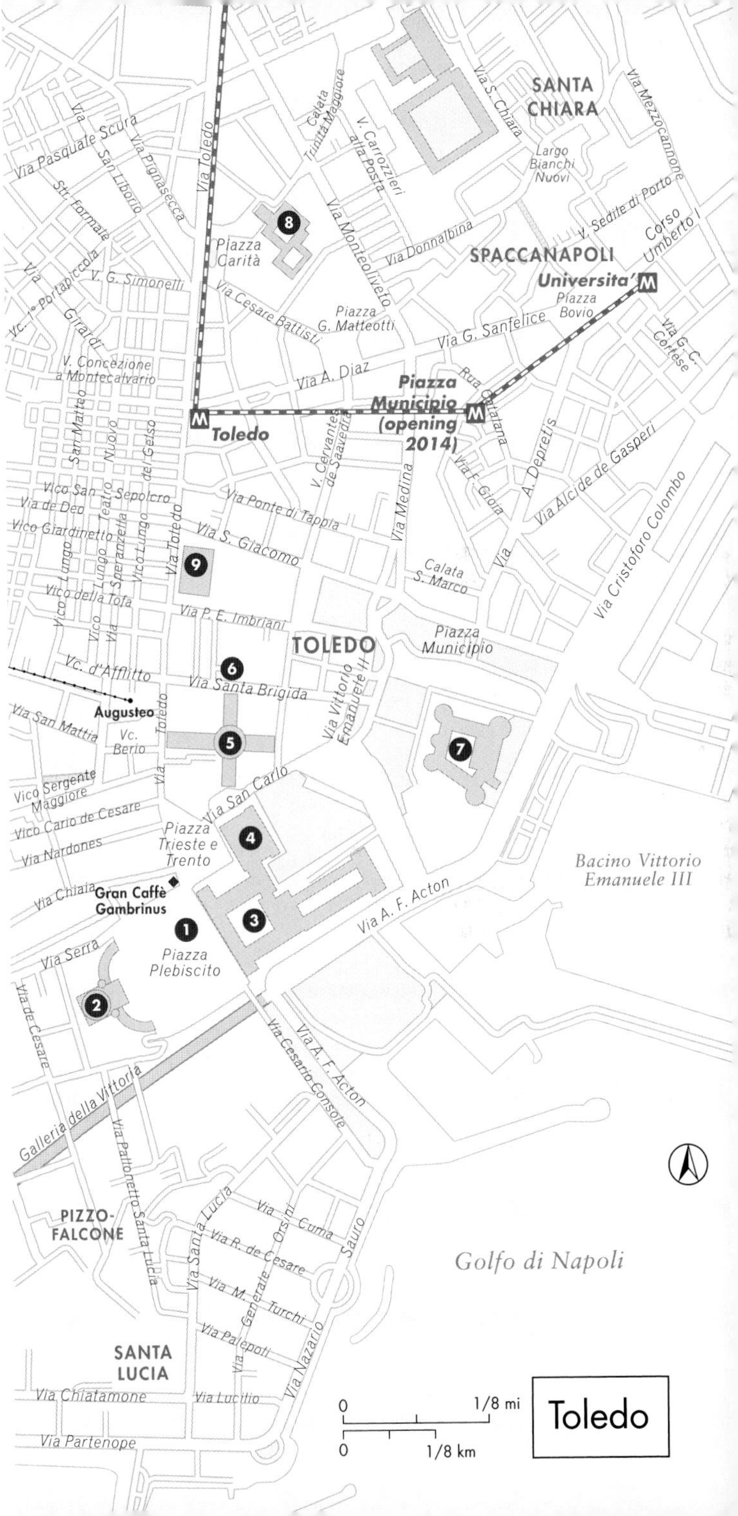

NAPOLI EVER AFTER: A GOOD WALK

In a day filled with monarchist grandeur, it's fitting to start out at **Gran Caffè Gambrinus,** in the very center of Naples on Piazza Trieste e Trento, between Piazza Plebiscito and Piazza Municipio. This ornate café was once the rendezvous for Italian dukes, prime ministers, and the literati, including Oscar Wilde. Treat yourself to a cappuccino and a pastry, then step outside into the grand **Piazza Plebiscito,** which makes an imposing setting for **San Francesco di Paola,** the domed 19th-century church built by Ferdinand I.

From here head directly across the piazza to take in the facade of the **Palazzo Reale,** then enter the palace from Piazza Trieste e Trento, walk up the grand staircase of its Scalone d'Onore, and tour the spectacular 18th- and 19th-century salons of the Museo dell'Appartmento Reale. To visit the adjacent **Teatro San Carlo,** head back down to the piazza and make a right turn in the Piazza Trieste e Trento. Guided English-language tours of the theater take place daily; you can book them in advance at the theater's website (🌐 *www.teatrosancarlo.it*). Across the way is the vast, elegant **Galleria Umberto I,** an ancestor of the shopping mall. Walk through it to Via Santa Brigida and tour the Church of **Santa Brigida.** Head back through the Galleria and then gently downhill on the Via San Carlo and the Via Vittorio Emanuele III; you'll come to the usually light-drenched Piazza Municipio, for years a sprawling building site for the Municipio metro station. To appreciate some of the technical difficulties faced by the subway engineers, peer down into the various layers of civilization from Roman times on. Above the piazza rises the imposing fortress of the **Castel Nuovo.** From the outside, study its sculpted triumphal arch of Alfonso of Aragon; inside, explore the museum and the spidery-roofed Hall of the Barons, plus giant photos of the Roman ships unearthed when the metro tube was being dug.

Head across Piazza Municipio to Via Medina until you reach the 20th-century complex at Piazza Matteotti. Then trip across the centuries by continuing up Via Monteoliveto to its pedestrianized piazza, where you can find both the quiet church of **Sant'Anna dei Lombardi** and the Tuscan-influenced rusticated facade of Palazzo Gravina.

Make a left leaving Sant'Anna dei Lombardi and head over to Piazza Carità for ice cream at La Scimmia, then take the 10 or so blocks down Via Toledo (the main thoroughfare of the area, often referred to as Via Roma) back to the Piazza Trieste e Trento; along the way, take in the 17th-century opulence of the **Gallerie di Palazzo Zevallos Stigliano,** do some window-shopping, and pick up a hot, flaky *sfogliatella* pastry at Mary's by the entrance to Galleria Umberto. You'll arrive back at Piazza Trieste e Trento in time to seek out a leisurely lunch. (*See the "Where to Eat" section for some good options.*)

TIMING

Not including stops at the Palazzo Reale and Castel Nuovo museums, this walk will take about three hours. There's no escaping the crowds, but if you start early you may catch the spectacular Piazza Plebiscito *senza gente* (without people).

Visited by Boccaccio and Giotto, massive Castel Nuovo sits near the shore of the Bay of Naples and once protected the heart of the medieval city.

the king of the Huns, who has just shot Ursula with an arrow after his proposal of marriage has been rejected. Opposite the painting is an elaborate map of the city of Caravaggio's day, not so different from now. ✉ *Via Toledo 185, Piazza Plebiscito* ☎ *800/16052007* 🌐 *www.palazzozevallos.com* 🎫 *€4* 🕐 *Tues.–Fri. and Sun. 10–6, Sat. 10–8* Ⓜ *Toledo.*

Galleria Umberto I. The galleria was erected during the "clean-up" of Naples following the devastating cholera epidemic of 1884, part of a massive urban-renewal plan that entailed the destruction of slum areas between Spaccanapoli and the Palazzo Reale. With facades on Via Toledo—the most animated street in Naples at the time—the structure, built between 1887 and 1890 according to a design by Emanuele Rocca, had a prestigious and important location. As with its larger predecessor, the Galleria Vittorio Emanuele II in Milan, the Galleria Umberto Primo exalts the taste of the postunification commercial elite in a virtuoso display of late 19th-century technology clothed in traditional style. Here are the iron-ribbed glass barrel vault and 188-feet-high dome by Paolo Boubée, which represented the latest advance in modern form yet is layered over with the reassuring architectural ornament of the 14th century (another era when the bourgeoisie triumphed in Italy). ✉ *Entrances on Via San Carlo, Via Toledo, Via Santa Brigida, Via Verdi, Toledo* Ⓜ *Toledo.*

Fodor's Choice ★ **Palazzo Reale.** A leading Naples showpiece created as an expression of Bourbon power and values, the Palazzo Reale dates to 1600. Renovated and redecorated by successive rulers, once lorded over by a dim-witted king who liked to shoot his hunting guns at the birds in

CLOSE UP

Artecard Discounts

The **Campania Artecard** entitles users to free or discounted admission to about four dozen museums and monuments in Naples and beyond. These are the main passes:

- Naples, three days (€21); three sights included and a fourth at up to 50% off, plus transportation discounts.
- Campania region, three days (€32), including Pompeii and other Bay of Naples sights and Ravello and Paestum; two sights included and a third at up to 50% off, plus transportation discounts.
- Campania region, three days, as above ($34); five sights included and a sixth for up to 50% off, no transportation discounts.

Other benefits (varies depending on the pass) include discounts on audio guides, theater and ferry tickets, city tours, and other activities, and visitors age 18 to 25 receive generous discounts. For more information visit the Campania Artecard website (🌐 *www.campaniaartecard.it*) or the tourist office in the Piazza Garibaldi station, which distributes a helpful booklet about the passes.

his tapestries, it is filled with salons designed in the most lavish 18th-century Neapolitan style. The Spanish viceroys originally commissioned the palace, ordering the Swiss architect Domenico Fontana to build a suitable new residence for King Philip III, should he chance to visit Naples. He died in 1621 before ever doing so. The palace saw its greatest moment of splendor in the 18th century, when Charles III of Bourbon became the first permanent resident; the flamboyant Naples-born architect Luigi Vanvitelli redesigned the facade, and Ferdinando Fuga, under Ferdinand IV, created the **Royal Apartments,** sumptuously furnished and full of precious paintings, tapestries, porcelains, and other objets d'art.

To access these 30 rooms, climb the monumental *Scalone d'Onore* (Staircase). On the right is the **Court Theater,** built by Fuga for Charles III and his private opera company. Damaged during World War II, it was restored in the 1950s; note the resplendent royal box. Antechambers lead to Room VI, the **Throne Room,** the ponderous titular object dating to sometime after 1850.

Decoration picks up in the **Ambassadors' Room,** choice Gobelin tapestries gracing the light-green walls. The ceiling painting honoring Spanish military victories is by local artist Belisario Corenzio (1610–20). Room IX was bedroom to Charles's queen, Maria Amalia. The brilliantly gold private oratory has beautiful paintings by Francesco Liani (1760).

The **Great Captain's Room** has ceiling frescoes by Battistello Caracciolo (1610–16). All velvet, fire, and smoke, they reveal the influence of Caravaggio's visit to the city; a jolly series by Federico Zuccari depicts 12 proverbs. More majestic is Titian's portrait (circa 1543) of Pier Luigi Farnese.

Room XIII was **Joachim Murat's writing room** when he was king of Naples; brought with him from France, some of the furniture is courtesy of Adam Weisweiler, cabinetmaker to Marie Antoinette. Room XVIII is notable for Guercino's depiction of Joseph's dream. The huge Room XXII, painted in green and gold with kitschy faux tapestries, is known as the **Hercules Hall,** because it once housed the *Farnese Hercules,* an epic sculpture of the mythological Greek hero. Pride of place now goes to the Sèvres porcelain.

The **Palatine Chapel,** redone by Gaetano Genovese in the 1830s, is gussied up with an excess of gold, although it has a stunning Technicolor marble intarsia altar from the previous chapel (Dionisio Lazzari, 1678). Also here is a Nativity scene with pieces sculpted by Giuseppe Sammartino and others. Pleasant 19th-century landscapes grace the next few rooms; then there is Queen Maria Carolina's Ferris wheel–like reading lectern (once enabling her to do a 19th-century reader's version of channel surfing). Speaking of reading, another wing holds the **Biblioteca Nazionale Vittorio Emanuele III.** Starting out from Farnese bits and pieces, it was enriched with the papyri from Herculaneum found in 1752 and opened to the public in 1804. The sumptuous rooms can still be viewed, and there's a tasteful garden that looks onto Castel Nuovo. ✉ *Piazza Plebiscito, Toledo* ☎ *081/5808111, 848/800288 schools and guided tours* 🌐 *www.palazzorealenapoli.it* 🎟 *€4, audio guide included* ⏲ *Thurs.–Tues. 9–8* Ⓜ *Toledo, Piazza Municipio (due 2014).*

6

NEED A BREAK?

Gran Caffè Gambrinus. The most famous coffeehouse in town, founded in 1850, sits across from the Palazzo Reale. Though its glory days as an intellectual salon are well in the past, the rooms inside, with mirrored walls and gilded ceilings, make this an essential stop. It was here that Oscar Wilde, down on his luck, would, for the price of a cup of tea, amaze Anglophone visitors with his still intact wit. ✉ ***Via Chiaia 1–2, near Piazza Plebiscito*** ☎ ***081/417582*** 🌐 ***www.grancaffegambrinus.com*** Ⓜ ***Toledo, Piazza Municipio (due 2014).***

Piazza Plebiscito (*People's Square*). After spending time as a parking lot, this square was restored in 1994 to one of Napoli Nobilissima's most majestic spaces, with a Doric semicircle of columns resembling Saint Peter's Square in Rome. On the left as you approach the church is a statue of Ferdinand and on the right one of his father, Charles III, both of them clad in Roman togas. Around dusk, floodlights come on, creating a magical effect. A delightful sea breeze airs the square, and on Sunday one corner becomes an improvised soccer stadium where local youths emulate their heroes. Ⓜ *Toledo, Piazza Municipio (due 2014).*

San Francesco di Paola. Modeled after Rome's Pantheon, this circular basilica is the centerpiece of the Piazza Plebiscito and remains one of the most frigidly voluptuous examples of the Stil Empire, or Neoclassical style, in Italy. Commissioned by Ferdinand I to fulfill a vow he had made in order to enlist divine aid in being reinstated to the throne of the Kingdom of the Two Sicilies, it rose at one end of the vast parade

DID YOU KNOW?

The French Enlightenment philosopher Montesquieu declared the Palazzo Reale's Scalone d'Onore the finest staircase in Europe.

ground built several years earlier by Joachim Murat. Completed in the late 1840s after 30 years of construction, it managed to transform Murat's inconveniently grandiose colonnade—whose architect was clearly inspired by the colonnades of St. Peter's in Rome—into a setting for restored Bourbon glory. Pietro Bianchi from Lugano in Switzerland won a competition and built a slightly smaller version of the Pantheon, with a beautiful coffered dome and a splendid set of 34 Corinthian columns in gray marble; but the overall lack of color (so different from the warm interior of the Pantheon), combined with the severe geometrical forms, produces an almost defiantly cold space. To some, this only proves the ancients did sometimes know their own architecture better. Art historians find the spectacle of the church to be the ultimate in Neoclassical *grandezza* (greatness); others think this Roman temple is only suitable to honor Jupiter, not Christ. In any event, the main altar, done in gold, lapis lazuli, and other precious stones by Anselmo Caggiano (1641), was taken from the destroyed Church of the Santi Apostoli and provides some relief from the oppressive perfection of the setting. **■ TIP→ On a hot summer day, the church's preponderance of marble guarantees sanctuary from the heat outside, with a temperature drop of ten or more degrees.** ✉ *Piazza Plebiscito, Toledo* ☎ *081/7645133* ⊙ *Mon.–Sat. 8:30–noon and 4–7, Sun. 8–noon* Ⓜ *Toledo, Piazza Municipio (due 2014).*

6

Sant'Anna dei Lombardi. Long favored by the Aragonese kings, this church, simple and rather anonymous from the outside, houses some of the most important ensembles of Renaissance sculpture in southern Italy. Begun with the adjacent convent of the Olivetani and its four cloisters in 1411, it was given a baroque makeover in the mid-17th century by Gennaro Sacco. This, however, is no longer so visible because the bombs of 1943 led to a restoration favoring the original *quattrocento* (15th-century) lines. The wonderful coffered wooden ceiling adds a bit of pomp. Inside the porch is the tomb of Domenico Fontana, one of the major architects of the late 16th century, who died in Naples after beginning the Palazzo Reale.

On either side of the original entrance door are two fine Renaissance tombs. The one on the left as you face the door belongs to the Ligorio family (whose descendant Pirro designed the Villa d'Este in Tivoli) and is a work by Giovanni da Nola (1524). The tomb on the right is a masterpiece by Giuseppe Santacroce (1532) done for the del Pozzo family. To the left of the Ligorio Altar (the corner chapel on the immediate right as you face the altar) is the Mastrogiudice Chapel, whose altar contains precious reliefs of the *Annunciation* and *Scenes from the Life of Jesus* (1489) by Benedetto da Maiano, a great name in Tuscan sculpture. On the other side of the entrance is the Piccolomini Chapel, with a *Crucifixion* by Giulio Mazzoni (circa 1550), a refined marble altar (circa 1475), a funerary monument to Maria d'Aragona by another prominent Florentine sculptor, Antonello Rossellino (circa 1475), and on the right, a rather sweet fresco of the Annunciation by an anonymous follower of Piero della Francesca.

Continued on page 244

GOING FOR *Baroque*

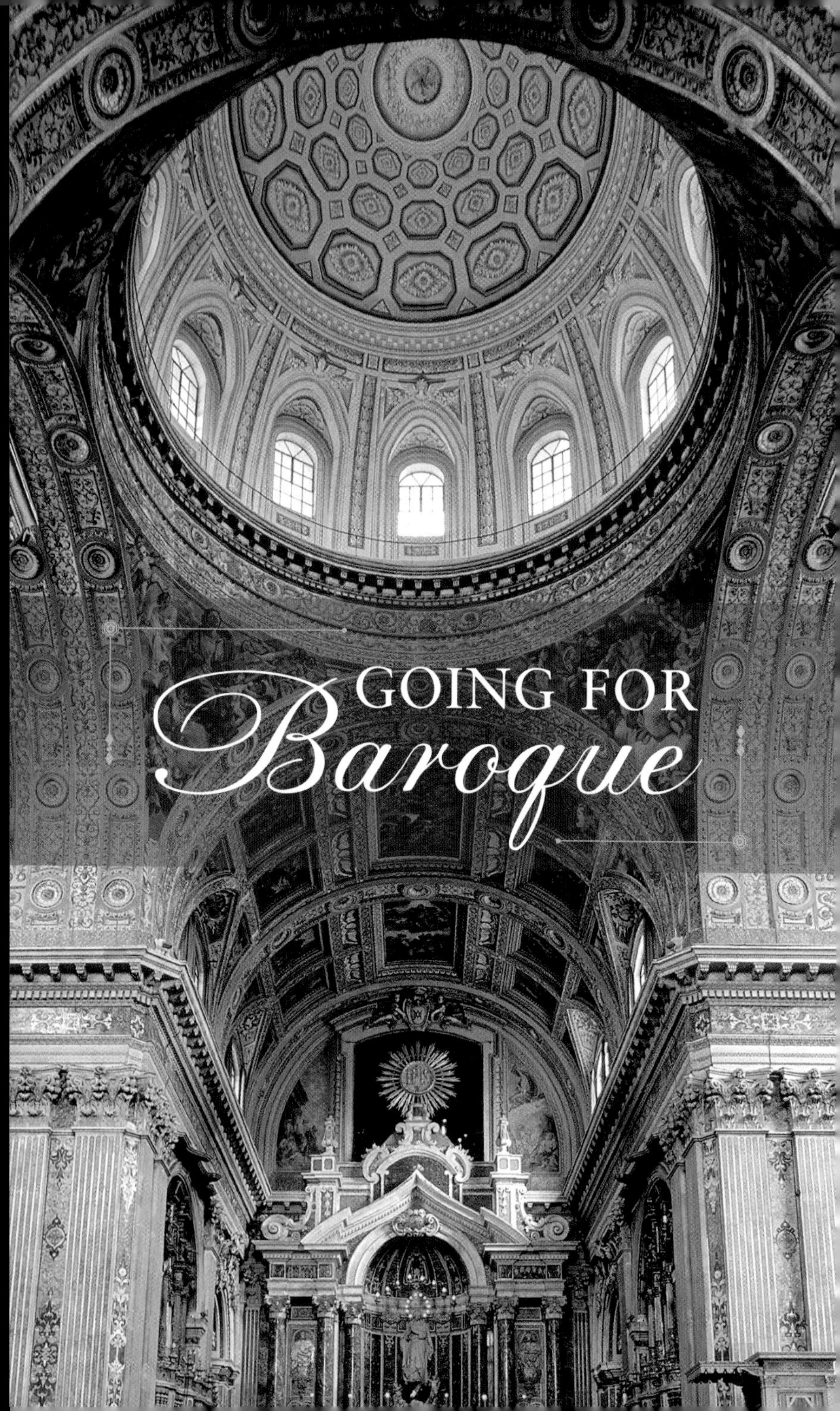

Even charitable observers would say that excess, fake opulence, and exaggeration are typical Neapolitan qualities. It's not surprising, then, that the baroque, an artistic style that revels in details added to swirls added to flourishes added to twists—a style that is playful, theatrical, dynamic, and seems permanently about to burst its bonds—should find one of its most spectacular showcases in Naples.

The very word "baroque" derives from a Portuguese word describing an impressive-looking but worthless type of pearl, and was originally used as an insult to describe the flagrantly emotional, floridly luxurious style that surfaced in Europe around 1600. Critics now use baroque to describe a style more than a period.

It's a style that found immediate favor in a city of volcanic passions. Like the city itself, the decorative scheme is diffuse and disjunctive, with little effort to organize everything into an easily understood scheme.

Contradictions still abound in Naples: plenty with want; grandeur with muddle; beauty with decay; the wide bay, lush countryside, and peaceful sky harboring the dense, chaotic city, sheltered by the ever-present threat of the slumbering Mount Vesuvius. In this context, the vivid, dramatic baroque style feels right at home.

NAPLES AND BAROQUE: A MATCH MADE FOR HEAVEN

At the beginning of the 17th century, thanks to the Counter-Reformation, the Catholic Church was busy making an overt appeal to its congregants, using emotion and motion to get its message across—and nowhere was this more blatant than in Naples, which, as the most populous city in Italy at the time, had more clerics (some 20,000) than even Rome. Baroque artists and architects, given an open invitation to indulge their illusionistic whims on church cupolas and the like, began arriving in Naples to strut their aesthetic stuff.

The most representative practitioner of Neapolitan baroque was **Cosimo Fanzago (1591–1678)**. A Lombard by birth, he traveled to Naples to study sculpture; even when decorating a church, he usually covered it head to toe with colored and inlaid marbles, as in his work at the Certosa di San Martino atop the Vomero hill.

Preceding Fanzago by two decades was **Caravaggio (1571–1610)**, who moved to Naples from Rome. This great painter took the city by storm, with an unflinching truthfulness and extroverted sensuality in his work. Experts will continue to argue to what degree Caravaggio was or wasn't a baroque painter, but certainly his use of chiaroscuro, a quality common in baroque art, can be seen dramatically in his Neapolitan paintings *The Flagellation of Christ* and *The Seven Acts of Mercy*.

(preceding page) The dome of Gesú Nuovo; (top) *St Bruno* by Cosimo Fanzago; (bottom) Caravaggio

BAROQUE TECHNIQUES: TRICKS OF THE TRADE

MEMENTO MORI. Lest all the sumptuous decoration should appeal too directly to the senses, the Church (as the major sponsor of the baroque) felt it was necessary to remind people of their ultimate message: *memento mori*—"remember that you will die." Don't be surprised if, in the midst of the most delicate and beautiful inlaid marble floor, you find leering skulls. In the tiny church of **Purgatorio ad Arco** ❶ in Spaccanapoli, a winged skull by Fanzago awaits salvation.

DOMES: LOOK UP! If there was one thing baroque architects loved, it was a dome—Exhibit One being the **Duomo di San Gennaro** ❷. Domes offered space and height and lots of opportunities to trompe your oeil. Even in the tightly packed old center of Naples, domes manage to make you feel as if you are in an enormous, heavenly space. This is in part due to their acoustic qualities, which reduce the city and its noisy inhabitants to swirling whispers and echoes.

MARVELOUS MARBLE. Making the most of the large quantities of marble quarries in Italy, baroque architects outdid their Renaissance predecessors. They used softer kinds of stone and developed intricate, interlaced patterns of different colored marble, such as seen in the **Certosa di San Martino** ❸.

KEEPING IT (HYPER)REAL. Getting solid marble or stone to "move" was one of the skills of any baroque sculptor worth his chisel. Giuseppe Sammartino, who sculpted the **Veiled Christ** ❹ in the Capella Sansevero, was so good at his craft that it was rumored (falsely) his boss had him blinded so he couldn't repeat his genius anywhere else. In Gesù Nuovo a dead Christ lies near the entrance in a glass case, often giving visitors cause

to stop momentarily as they think they've stumbled across a real person. It is common to find saints' marble effigies still dressed in real period clothes.

OUT OF THE SHADOWS. Chiaroscuro ("light-dark") is the word most often used to describe baroque painting, with its mixture of bright shafts of light and thick shadows. Figures loom out of the dark while the main action is highlighted by dazzling beams of light—as in Ribera's ***Apollo and Marsyas*** ❺ at the Museo di Capodimonte.

TROMPE L'OEIL. Literally "tricking the eye," trompe l'oeil is an illusionist method of painting that consists, quite simply, of making things look like something they're not. Angels lean over balconies and out of paintings, walls become windows, and skylights bestow views into heaven itself, as grandly displayed in Luca Giordano's ***Triumph of Judith*** ❻ at the Certosa di San Martino. There is something very baroque in trompe l'oeil's sense of trickery, of something being built upon nothing.

STAIRWAYS TO HEAVEN. The principles of movement and ascension naturally conveyed by a staircase made baroque architects drool with possibilities. Staircases can often be seen with winged banisters, as if those simply climbing the steps were on a journey into a higher realm. The staircase in the entrance of the Royal Palace in Naples splits and divides and splits again, its movement magnified and reflected dizzyingly by the windows and mirrors surrounding it. At the Palazzo della Spagnola in the Sanità neighborhood, the M.C. Escher–esque staircase boasts steps wide enough to ride a horse up them—which is precisely what they were used for in the 17th century.

ON STAGE. If some of the more extravagant interiors of Neapolitan churches remind you of theater sets, you're not far off. Many designers crossed over into ecclesiastical work, usually having first been noticed in the theater. Many arches over altars are made from a reinforced form of papier-mâché, originally used in theatrical productions.

One of the most frigidly voluptuous examples of the Neoclassical style, the church of San Francesco di Paola was designed to emulate Rome's Pantheon.

The true surprises of the church are to the right of the altar, in the presbytery and adjoining rooms. The chapel just to the right of the main altar, belonging to the Orefice family, is richly decorated in pre-baroque (1596–98) polychrome marbles and frescoes by Luis Rodriguez; from here you continue on through the Oratory of the Holy Sepulchre, with the tomb of Antonio D'Alessandro and his wife, to reach the church's showpiece: a potently realistic life-size group of eight terra-cotta figures by Guido Mazzoni (1492), which make up a Pietà; the faces are said to be modeled from people at the Aragonese court. Toward the rear of the church is Cappella dell'Assunta, with a fun painting in its corner of a monk by Michelangelo's student Giorgio Vasari, and the lovely Sacrestia Vecchia (Old Sacristy), adorned with one of the most successful decorative ensembles Vasari ever painted (1544) and breathtaking wood-inlay stalls by Fra' Giovanni da Verona and assistants (1506–10) with views of famous buildings. ✉ *Piazza Monteoliveto 15, Toledo* ☎ *081/5513333* 🕑 *Tues.–Sat. 9–noon* Ⓜ *Dante, Toledo.*

Teatro San Carlo. La Scala in Milan is the famous one, but San Carlo is more beautiful, and Naples is, after all, the most operatic of cities. The Neoclassical structure, designed by Antonio Niccolini, was built in a mere nine months after an 1816 fire destroyed the original. Many operas were composed for the house, including Donizetti's *Lucia di Lammermoor* and Rossini's *La Donna del Lago*. In the theater, nearly 200 boxes are arranged on six levels, and the 1,115-square-meter (12,000-square-foot) stage permits productions with horses, camels, and elephants, and even has a backdrop that can lift to reveal the Palazzo Reale Gardens. Above the rich red-and-gold auditorium is a

CLOSE UP

Attenzione! How to Cross Naples's Streets

Long considered a threatened species, the Naples pedestrian is gradually being provided with a friendlier environment. Once Piazza Garibaldi has been negotiated, traffic in much of Naples is no more off-putting than in other Italian cities. (Accident rates involving pedestrians are higher in Rome.) In fact, large tracts of Naples are open to pedestrians only. That's recently the case for the sea-hugging Via Partenope, and also for most of Via Toledo. Leading off it is the fashionable Via Chiaia, a destination for posh shopping and the birthplace of the pizza Margherita. Piazza Plebiscito, once reduced to a parking lot, is also now an ideal space to stroll through, touched by a pleasant sea breeze.

That being said, crossing major thoroughfares in Naples still takes some savvy. In a city where red traffic lights may be blithely ignored, especially by two-wheelers, walking across a busy avenue can be like a game of chess—if you hesitate, you capitulate. Some residents just forge out into the unceasing flow of traffic, knowing cars invariably slow down to let them cross. Look both ways even on one-way streets, as there may be motorcyclists riding against the flow. Areas where you have to be particularly vigilant—and cross at the lights—are around the Archaeological Museum and on Via Marina outside the port, as well as the ever-challenging Piazza Garibaldi.

ceiling fresco by Giuseppe Cammarano representing Apollo presenting poets to Athena. Performance standards are among Europe's highest—even the great Enrico Caruso was hissed here. If you're not attending an opera, you can still see the splendid theater on a 30-minute guided tour. Perhaps your experience will mirror that of the French author Stendhal, who wrote: "The first impression one gets is of being suddenly transported to the palace of an oriental emperor. There is nothing in Europe to compare with it, or even give the faintest idea of what it is like." **TIP→ English-language tours, which take place daily except on holidays, can be booked in advance on the theater's website.** ✉ *Via San Carlo 101–103, Toledo* ☎ *081/5534565 Mon.–Sat., 081/7972468 Sun.* 🌐 *www.teatrosancarlo.it* *Tour €6* ⏲ *Tour Mar.–Dec., Mon.–Thurs. 11:30 and 3:30, Fri. and Sat. on the half hr 10:30–12:30 and 2:30–4:30, Sun. on the half hr 10:30–12:30; Jan. and Feb. mornings only* Ⓜ *Toledo.*

WORTH NOTING

Santa Brigida. The Lucchesi fathers built this church around 1640 in honor of the Swedish queen and saint who visited her fellow queen, Naples's unsaintly Giovanna I, in 1372 and became one of the first people to publicly denounce the loose morals and overt sensuality of the Neapolitans. The height of the church's dome was limited to prevent its interfering with cannon fire from nearby Castel Nuovo, but Luca Giordano, the pioneer painter of the trompe l'oeil baroque dome, effectively opened it up with a spacious sky serving as the setting for an *Apotheosis of Saint Bridget* (1678), painted (and now in need of considerable restoration) in exchange for his tomb space, marked by a pavement inscription in the left transept. ✉ *Via Santa Brigida 72, Toledo* ☎ *081/5523793* ⏲ *Daily 6:45–12:45 and 4:30–7* Ⓜ *Dante, Piazza Municipio (due 2014).*

THE VOMERO, THE LUNGOMARE, AND NEARBY

Neapolitans often say their town's glories are vertical—the white *guglia* (religious obelisk) of the historic quarter, the eight-story tenements of Spaccanapoli, and Vomero, the towering hill that overlooks the city center. Even longtime residents love to head up here to gaze in wonder at the entire city from the balcony belvedere of the Museo di San Martino. Before them, a rich spread of southern Italian amplitude fills the eye: hillsides dripping with luxuriant greenery interspersed with villainously ugly apartment houses, streets short and narrow—leading to an unspeakable as well as unsolvable traffic problem—countless church spires and domes, and far below, the reason it all works, the intensely blue Bay of Naples. To tie together the lower parts and upper reaches of the city, everyone uses the *funicolare*—the funicular system that runs on three separate routes up and down the Vomero.

TIMING

As always in Naples, it's best to start out early in the morning to fit most of your sightseeing in before the lunch break—and summer's midday heat. Aim to get to the San Martino complex atop the Vomero hill at opening time and allow at least three hours to take it in along with the Castel Sant'Elmo and an additional half hour for the Villa Floridiana. If you prefer a leisurely wander or wish to visit an exhibition at Castel Sant'Elmo, go straight to the Borgo from the Riviera di Chiaia following the seafront, and then swing back to Villa Pignatelli and the Aquarium.

TOP ATTRACTIONS

Castel dell'Ovo (*Castle of the Egg*). The oldest castle in Naples, the 12th-century Castel dell'Ovo dangles over the Porto Santa Lucia on a thin promontory. Built atop the ruins of an ancient Roman villa, the castle these days shares its views with some of the city's top hotels. Its gigantic rooms, rock tunnels, and belvederes over the bay are among Naples's most striking sights.

You enter the castle through its main entrance, past its forbidding trio of cannons. On the right is a large picture of the castle in Renaissance times. Turn left and glimpse through the battlements the sleepy Borgo Marinaro below. An elevator on the left ascends to the castle top, or you can also continue along the walkway overlooking the ramparts. The roof's Sala della Terrazze offers a postcard-come-true view of Capri. This is a peaceful spot for strolling and enjoying the views, all the more so now that the Lungomare outside has recently been made a pedestrian-only area.

As for the castle's name, the poet Virgil is supposed have hidden inside it an egg that had protective powers as long as it remained intact. The belief was taken so seriously that to quell the people's panic after Naples suffered an earthquake, an invasion, and a plague in quick succession, its monarch felt compelled to produce an intact egg, solemnly declaring it to be the Virgilian original. ✉ *Santa Lucia waterfront, Via Eldorado 3, off Via Partenope* ☎ *081/7956180* 🎫 *Free* ⏲ *Mon.–Sat. 8–7:15, Sun. 8–1:45.*

Awash in gold and red velvet, the interior of the Teatro San Carlo, Naples's grand opera house, is almost more spectacular than its stage presentations.

Castel Sant'Elmo. Perched on the Vomero, this massive castle is almost the size of a small town. Built by the Angevins in the 14th century to dominate the port and the old city, it was remodeled by the Spanish in 1537. The parapets, configured in the form of a six-pointed star, provide fabulous views. The whole bay lies on one side; on another, the city spreads out like a map, its every dome and turret clearly visible; and to the east, is slumbering Vesuvius. Once a major military outpost, the castle these days hosts occasional cultural events. Its prison, the Carcere alto di Castel Sant'Elmo, is the site of the **Museo del Novecento Napoli,** which traces Naples's 20th-century artistic output, from the futurist period through the 1980s. ✉ *Largo San Martino, Vomero* ☎ *081/848800288* 🌐 *www.polomusealenapoli.beniculturali.it* 🎟 *€5* 🕑 *Wed.–Mon. 8:30–7:30* Ⓜ *Vanvitelli.*

Fodor's Choice ★ **Certosa di San Martino.** Atop a rocky promontory with a fabulous view of the entire city and majestic salons that would please any monarch, the Certosa di San Martino is a monastery that seems more like a palace. In fact, by the 18th century Ferdinand IV was threatening to halt the religious order's government subsidy, so sumptuous was this *certosa,* or charter house, which had been started in 1325. Although the Angevin heritage can be seen in the pointed arches and cross-vaulted ceiling of the **Certosa Church,** over the years dour Gothic was traded in for varicolored Neapolitan Baroque.

The sacristy leads into the **Cappella del Tesoro,** with Luca Giordano's ceiling fresco of Judith holding aloft Holofernes's head and the painting by Il Ribera (the *Pietà* over the altar is one of his masterpieces). The polychrome marble work of the architect and sculptor Cosimo Fanzago

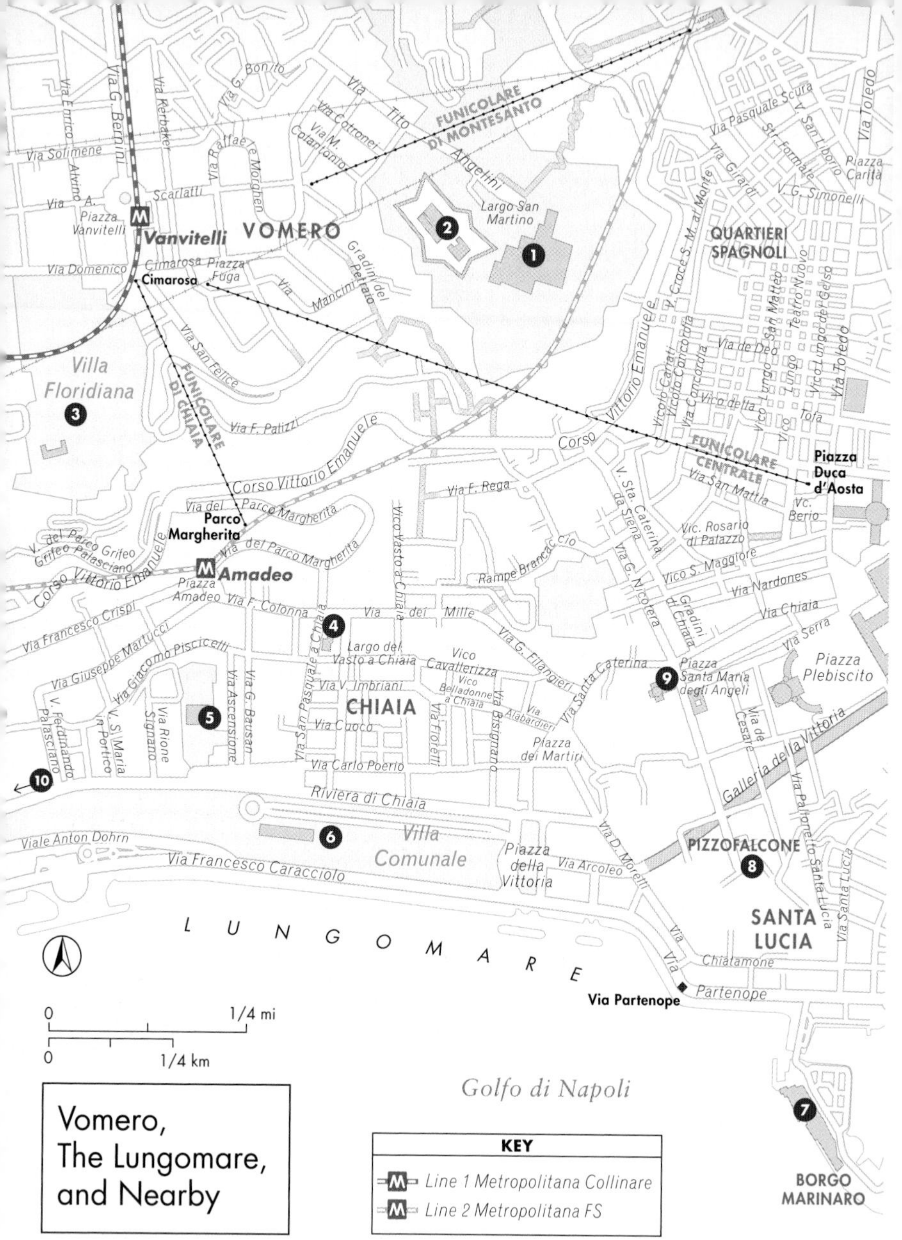

Vomero, The Lungomare, and Nearby

- Aquarium **6**
- Castel dell'Ovo **7**
- Castel Sant'Elmo **2**
- Certosa di San Martino **1**
- Museo Diego Aragona Pignatelli Cortes **5**
- Palazzo delle Arti di Napoli **4**
- Parco Vergiliano a Piedigrotta **10**
- Pizzofalcone **8**
- Santa Maria degli Angeli a Pizzofalcone **9**
- Villa Floridiana **3**

(1591–1678) is at its finest here, and he displays a gamut of sculptural skills in the **Chiostro Grande** (Great Cloister). Fanzago's ceremonial portals at each corner of the cloister are among the most spectacular of all Baroque creations, aswirl with Michelangelo-esque ornament.

The nearby **Museo dell'Opera,** not always open, contains sociological-themed rooms that add up to a chronological tour of the city. One room has 13 gouaches of Vesuvius, and another has paintings depicting the Plague.

The **Quarto del Priore** (Prior's Quarters), the residence of the only monk allowed contact with the outside world, is an extravaganza of salons filled with frescoes, majolica-tile floors, and paintings, plus extensive gardens where scenic *pergolati* (roofed balconies) overlook the bay.

Entering from the Quarto del Priore side, you come upon two splendid gilded coaches and then the **"Vessels of the King" museum,** beyond which lie two rooms with Early Renaissance masterpieces; subsequent rooms hold works by later artists, including the tireless Luca Giordano. Past the library, with its heavenly majolica-tile floor, comes the **Sezione Presepiale,** the world's greatest collection of Christmas cribs. Pride of place goes to the *Presepe* (Nativity scene) of Michele Cucineniello. Equally amazing in its own way is a crib inside an eggshell. ✉ *Piazzale San Martino 5, Vomero* ☎ *081/2294589* 🌐 *www.polomusealenapoli.beniculturali.it* 🎫 *€6* ⏱ *Thurs.–Tues. 9–7:30 (ticket office closes at 6:30); Christmas crèches Thurs.–Mon.; some rooms occasionally closed for lack of staffing* Ⓜ *Vanvitelli.*

6

WORTH NOTING

FAMILY **Aquarium.** The Greeks originally named their colony here for the mermaid Parthenope (who slew herself after being rejected by Odysseus, at least in the poet Virgil's version), so it's fitting that the city should have established one of Europe's first public aquariums in 1874. At the time Jules Verne's Captain Nemo and Hans Christian Andersen's Little Mermaid were stirring the public's imagination, and technological innovations came into place to funnel seawater directly from the bay into the aquarium tanks. Officially named the Stazione Zoologica and housed in a Stil Liberty building designed by Adolf von Hildebrandt, the aquarium's tanks showcase more than 200 species of fish. ✉ *Stazione Zoologica, Viale A. Dohrn, Villa Comunale 1, Chiaia* ☎ *081/5833263 for information and library visits* 🌐 *www.szn.it* 🎫 *€1.50* ⏱ *Mar.–Oct., Tues.–Sat. 9–6, Sun. 9:30–7:30; Nov.–Feb., Tues.–Sat. 9–5, Sun. 9–2* Ⓜ *Piazza Amedeo.*

Museo Diego Aragona Pignatelli Cortes. Set behind what, except for the palm trees, would be a very English expanse of lawn, this salmon-pink building with its Athenian-style porch was built in 1826 for Ferdinand Acton, the son of English aristocrat Sir John Acton. In 1841 it was bought up by the Rothschild banking family, who brought in Gaetano Genovese—he of the Palazzo Reale's sumptuous staircase—to design the Salotto Rosso and the ballroom. The villa then passed to a distant ancestor of Spanish conquistador Hernán Cortés, and eventually to the Italian State in 1955. The villa contains a sumptuous collection of porcelain and a *biblioteca-discoteca*—a collection of classical and operatic records. It exhibits part of Banco di Napoli's collection of paintings, including works by masters of Neapolitan Baroque, and has 18th- and 19th-century landscapes. ✉ *Riviera di Chiaia 200* ☎ *081/76112356* 🌐 *www.polomusealenapoli.beniculturali.it* 🎫 *€2* 🕐 *Wed.–Mon. 8:30–2* Ⓜ *Piazza Amedeo.*

Palazzo delle Arti di Napoli. Occupying the enormous Palazzo Rocella, PAN, as this arts organization calls itself, mounts temporary art exhibitions and operates a center for art research and documentation. Past exhibits have included the photographs of Joel-Peter Witkin, and internationally recognized contemporary artists working in other media have received shows, but the large space also showcases works by up-and-coming talents. Film and other events take place here, and the fine bookshop carries titles about Italian and international contemporary artists. ✉ *Via dei Mille 60, Chiaia* ☎ *081/7958605* 🎫 *€5 (some exhibitions; others free)* 🕐 *Mon. and Wed.–Sat. 9:30–7:30, Sun. 9:30–2:30; last admission 1 hr before closing* Ⓜ *Piazza Amedeo.*

Parco Vergiliano a Piedigrotta. An undervisited sight in western Naples, the park is named for the poet Virgil and is reputedly his burial site. Not to be confused with the Parco Virgiliano, at the western end of the Naples suburb of Posillipo, this patch of greenery is, however, more famous for its Bay of Naples vista, immortalized in countless postcards and pizza-parlor paintings—the ones showing a lone umbrella pine on a bluff overlooking bay and city, with Vesuvius in the background. The iconic pine no longer exists, but the view remains magnificent. A sign at the park's entrance indicates that not only (by legend) is Virgil's tomb here, but also the tomb-memorial of Giacomo Leopardi, the author of the evocative poem "L'infinito," who died during the 1837 cholera epidemic. As a safety precaution, victims of the disease were usually buried in mass graves, but the writer (and later politician) Antonio Ranieri, a close friend, arranged for this monument, which until 1939 was located elsewhere. ■ **TIP→ From the Mergellina metro station walk south to Salita della Grotta and turn right just before the church of Santa Maria di Piedigrotta; the park's entrance is just before the road tunnel.** ✉ *Salita della Grotta 20, off Piazza Piedigrotta, Mergellina* ☎ *081/669390* 🎫 *Free* 🕐 *9–1 hr before sunset* Ⓜ *Mergellina.*

Pizzofalcone (*Falcon's Beak*). In the 7th century BC, Pizzofalcone *was* Naples. The ancient Greeks had settled here because, legend says, the body of the siren Parthenope had washed ashore on the beach at the foot of the Pizzofalcone Hill, then known as Monte Echia. In the 18th century, the hill, mere feet from the bay and the Castel dell'Ovo, became a fashionable address as Naples's rich and titled sought to escape the congestion and heat of the city center. The rocky promontory soon became studded with baroque palaces and rococo churches. The leading sights these days are the palazzi along Via Monte di Dio—including Palazzo Serra di Cassano—and the churches of La Nunziatella and Santa Maria degli Angeli. ■ **TIP→ As with other parts of Naples, Pizzofalcone harbors both palaces and slums; unlike other parts, it's off the beaten path, so don't stop to answer questions from seemingly innocuous strollers.** ✉ *Piazza Santa Maria degli Angeli, accessed via elevator at Ponte di Chiaia on Via Chiaia (don't take dark stairway), Pizzofalcone.*

A GOOD WALK: VOMERO/LUNGOMARE

Begin at the main station of the Funicolare Centrale, on the tiny Piazza Duca d'Aosta, opposite the Via Toledo entrance to the Galleria Umberto I. After two hillside stops, get off at the end of the line, Stazione Fuga, near the top of the Vomero Hill. To get to the Castel Sant'Elmo/Certosa di San Martino complex, head out from the station, turning right across the pedestrianized Piazza Fuga toward the escalator, then left on Via Morghen. At the next junction, Via Scarlatti—the main thoroughfare of the neighborhood—turn right uphill and take the escalator (or steps), cutting twice across the snakelike Via Morghen, then follow the path around the left side of the Montesanto funicular until you run into the Via Tito Angelini. This street, lined with some of Naples's best Belle Epoque mansions, leads to the **Certosa di San Martino** past the adjoining **Castel Sant'Elmo,** which commands magnificent 360-degree vistas over city and sea to Vesuvius.

After viewing this enormous complex, backtrack to Via Scarlatti until you make a left on Via Bernini at Piazza Vanvitelli. This piazza, with no shortage of smart bars and trattorias, remains the center for the Vomero district, and is a gathering point for talented street performers.

Walk right onto Via Cimarosa for two blocks until you reach the entrance to the **Villa Floridiana,** today a museum filled with aristocratic knickknacks and surrounded by a once-regal park. After viewing the villa, make a right from the park entrance on Via Cimarosa for two blocks until you reach the Stazione Cimarosa of the Chiaia funicular, which will take you back down to the Lungomare area.

From the Amedeo funicular station walk down Via del Parco Margherita, past Piazza Amedeo, making a left onto Via Colonna. Stop at the rambling **Palazzo delle Arti Napoli** if there's an exhibition that catches your eye; otherwise take the first right turn down off Via Colonna onto the steps at the top of Via Bausan. The steps will take you down toward the Riviera di Chiaia (*chiaia* means "beach" in the Neapolitan dialect), where a final right turn brings you to the **Museo Diego Aragona Pignatelli Cortes.** From here cross the Riviera to the waterfront park of the Villa Comunale and its world-famous **Aquarium.**

Follow the Riviera past the Piazza della Vittoria for a stroll down Via Partenope to reach the spectacular **Castel dell'Ovo.** From here, a walk north on Via Chiatamone takes you to the Piazza dei Martiri, where you can join chic Neapolitans shopping the boutiques, bookstores, and antiques shops lining the streets that radiate off the piazza (particularly the designer-dense stretch between Via Carlo Poerio and Via dei Mille).

The area around Piazza dei Martiri is excellent for both snacking and more substantial meals. From here it's a relatively short walk back to one of the funiculars (the Centrale and Chiaia are roughly equidistant from the piazza), or you can catch any number of buses westward along the area's main artery, the Riviera di Chiaia.

Santa Maria degli Angeli a Pizzofalcone. In 1590 the princess of Sulmona, Costanza Doria del Carretto, commissioned this church not far from her palace on Pizzofalcone. In the 17th century the church was given to the Theatine order, which had it enlarged. The lively vault and dome frescoes are by Giovanni Beinaschi of Turin, better known as a painter of genre scenes, and there are some good paintings by Luca Giordano and Massimo Stanzione tucked away in the smaller side chapels and oratory. ✉ *Piazza Santa Maria degli Angeli, Pizzofalcone* ☎ *081/7644974* ⏲ *Daily 7:30–11:30 and 5:30–7.*

WORD OF MOUTH

"Although there is not much to see at the castle itself, the views of Naples from the walls make the Castel Sant'Elmo one of my favorite places."

—willit

Villa Floridiana. Now a chiefly residential neighborhood, the Vomero Hill was once the patrician address of many of Naples's most extravagant estates. La Floridiana is the sole surviving 19th-century example, built in 1817 on order of Ferdinand I for Lucia Migliaccio, duchess of Floridia—their portraits hang by the main entrance. Only nine shocking months after his first wife, the Habsburg Maria Carolina, died, when the court was still in mourning, Ferdinand secretly married Lucia, his longtime mistress. Scandal ensued, but the king and his new wife were too happy to worry, escaping high above the city to this elegant little estate. Designed by architect Antonio Niccolini in the Neoclassical style, the house is now occupied by the **Museo Nazionale della Ceramica Duca di Martina,** a museum devoted to the decorative arts of the 18th and 19th centuries. Countless cases on the upper floor display what Edith Wharton described as "all those fragile and elaborate trifles the irony of fate preserves when brick and marble crumble": Sèvres, Limoges, and Meissen porcelains, gold watches, ivory fans, glassware, enamels, majolica vases. Sadly, there are no period rooms left to see. Outside is a park done in the English style by Degenhardt, who also designed the park at Capodimonte. Too bad—graffiti defaces the Grecian Tempietto and the lawns are worn bare by aspiring soccer players. ✉ *Via Cimarosa 77, Vomero* ☎ *081/5788418* 🎫 *€2.50* ⏲ *Museum Wed.–Mon. 8:30–2, park daily 8:30–1 hr before sunset* Ⓜ *Vanvitelli.*

SPACCANAPOLI

If your plan for Naples is just to do the sights, you'll see the city, but you'll miss its essence. To get that, you need to discover Spaccanapoli, the unforgettable neighborhood that is the heart of old Naples. This is the Naples of peeling facades and enough waving laundry to suggest a parade; of small alleyways fragrant with freshly laid flowers at the many shrines to the Blessed Virgin. Here, where the cheapest pizzerias in town feed the locals like kings, the full raucous street carnival of Neapolitan popular culture is punctuated with improbable oases of spiritual calm. But the Spacca is not simply picturesque. It also contains some of Naples's most important sights, including a striking conglomeration of churches—Lombard, Gothic, Renaissance, Baroque, Rococo, and Neoclassical. Here are the majolica-adorned cloister of Santa Chiara;

Castel dell'Ovo provides impressive views of the bay, the city, and looming Vesuvius.

the sumptuous Church of the Gesù Nuovo; two opera-set piazzas; the city duomo (where the Festa di San Gennaro is celebrated every September); the Museo Cappella Sansevero; the greatest painting in Naples—Caravaggio's *Seven Acts of Mercy* altarpiece—on view at the museum complex of Pio Monte; and Via Gregorio Armeno, where shops devoted to *Presepe* Nativity scene (crèche) wares make every day a rehearsal for Christmas. And even though this was the medieval center of the city, night owls will find that many of Naples's most cutting-edge clubs and bars are hidden among its nooks and alleys. For soccer fanatics, there is even a shrine to Diego Maradona.

This area is best explored by starting out at its heart, the Piazza Gesù Nuovo (approachable from all directions but easily reachable from Via Toledo by heading eastward from Piazza Carità through the pedestrianized Piazza Monteoliveto and then up Calata Trinità Maggiore), then heading east along the Spacca street to the Duomo, then back along Via dei Tribunali. The Via dei Tribunali is often referred to as part of the city's Decumano Maggiore, but as it's only one block over from the Spacca, the entire region is also commonly grouped under the name Spaccanapoli.

TIMING

Because many churches open at 7:30 and close for the afternoon around 1, it's imperative to get an early start to fit in as many sights as possible before the midday break. Many shops close for three hours, from 1:30 to 4:30. By 4 many of the churches reopen. Plan on a good two hours to walk this route, plus a quarter to a half hour for each of the principal churches you decide to visit. But Spaccanapoli is the most memorable part of Naples so take a full day, if you can, to explore its varied pleasures.

TOP ATTRACTIONS

Complesso Museale Santa Maria delle Anime del Purgatorio ad Arco. This strange museum could exist only in Naples. Once a tavern, the Monte di Pietà charity in 1616 rebuilt it as a church, and its two stories are fascinatingly complementary. As bare as the upper church is lavish, the altar below-stairs is a stark black cross against a peeling gray wall. The nave covers what was a 1656 plague pit now set off by chains with four lamps to represent the flames of purgatory. As the pit filled up to accommodate more recent dead, the skulls of earlier plague victims were placed on the central floor. So was born the cult of *le anime pezzentelle* (wretched souls). By praying for them, the living could accelerate these souls' way to heaven, at which point the pezzentelle could intercede on behalf of the living.

During the 20th century, the Second World War left many Neapolitans with missing relatives. Some families found consolation by adopting a skull in their loved ones' stead. The skulls would be cleaned polished and then given a box-type *altarino.*

If all this verges on the pagan, the Catholic Church thought likewise, and in 1969 the practice was banned. The *altarini* were blocked off and eventually abandoned. In 1992 the church reopened. Most of the skulls were taken to Cimitero delle Fontanelle. Some, though, remain, like that of one Lucia, princess of skulls and patron of *amore infelice* (unhappy love). Then there's the skull of Giulio Mastrillo. In the church above you'll find his statue to the left of the 1653 altar he partly paid for. Winged to speed it heavenward, note the dentally challenged Fanzago skull. Yes, even skulls are subject to decay. ✉ *Via Tribunali 39, Spaccanapoli* 🌐 *www.purgatorioadarco.com* 🎫 *€4, upper church free* 🕙 *Mon.–Fri. 10–2, Sat. 10–5.*

Convento di San Domenico Maggiore. Saint Thomas Aquinas studied and taught at this Domenican monastery more recently noteworthy for its brilliant restoration and stint as a law court where crime bosses met their fates. Virtual photographs outside the **Chapter Hall** show how the monastery, parts of which date to the 13th century, would have looked before the suppression of monasteries under Napoleon. The hall itself contains a significant fresco of the Crucifixion by the late 17th-century Sicilian painter Michele Ragolia, and the ubiquitous Baroque master Fanzago is responsible for the stuccowork. Note the false windows, a work of optical illusion common to the period.

The standout work in the nearby **Grand Refectory** is Domenico Vaccaro's *Last Supper* mural, in which Christ comforts John while Judas, clutching a moneybag, glares at something else. Another mural in the refectory depicts a famous incident from Saint Thomas Aquinas's life here. Christ is shown directing at Thomas the words, *Bravo, Tommaso, che parlasti bene di me.* ("Well done, Thomas, for speaking well of me.") The refectory's many theatrical flourishes include pink columns as tall as trees; more down to earth are the remains of the stations where the monks would wash their hands before eating. More recently the refectory served as a law court. Two Camorra bosses—Raffaele Cutolo and Pupetta Maresca—were sentenced here as late as the 1990s.

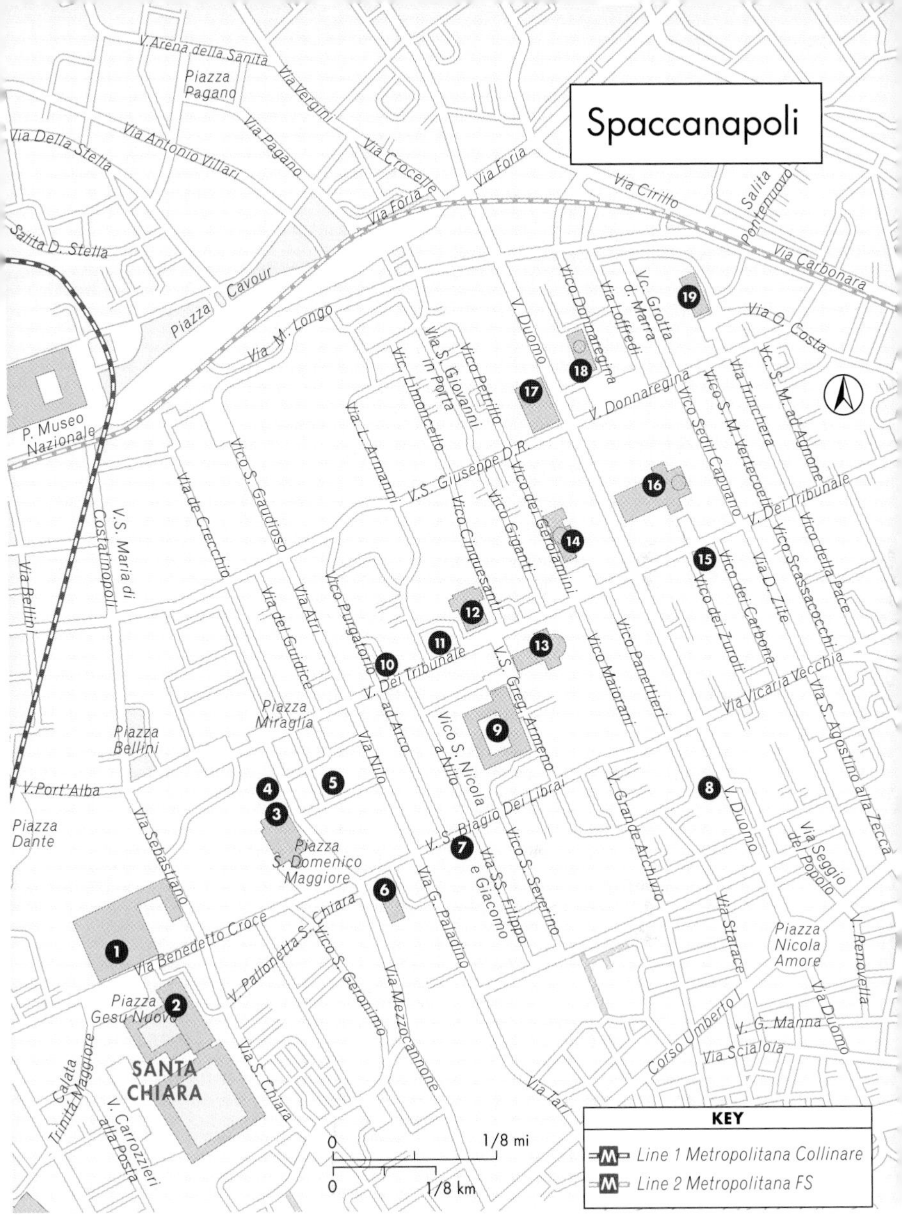

Complesso Museale Santa Maria delle Anime del Purgatorio ad Arco **10**

Convento di San Domenico Maggiore **4**

Duomo **16**

Gesù Nuovo **1**

Monumento Nazionale dei Girolamini **11**

Museo Cappella Sansevero **5**

Museo Diocesano Napoli **18**

Napoli Sotterranea **11**

Pio Monte della Misericordia **15**

Sacro Cappella di Diego Maradona **7**

San Domenico Maggiore ... **3**

San Giuseppe dei Ruffi **17**

San Gregorio Armeno **9**

San Lorenzo Maggiore **13**

San Paolo Maggiore **12**

San Severo al Pendino **8**

Sant'Angelo a Nilo **6**

Santa Chiara **2**

Santi Apostoli **19**

Also of note are the **cloisters,** originally for about a hundred monks, only nine of whom remain. It was here that Thomas Aquinas lived and studied and taught from 1272 to 1274. A magnificent doorway by Marco Bottiglieri marks his cell, now a chapel that is, alas, only rarely visitable. ✉ *Vico S. Domenico Maggiore 18, Spaccanapoli* ☎ *081/7956160* 🌐 *www.comune.napoli.it* 🎫 *Free* 🕒 *Mon.–Sat. 8–5.*

Duomo. Though the cathedral was established in the 1200s, the building you see was erected a century later and has since undergone radical changes—especially during the baroque period. Inside, 110 ancient columns salvaged from pagan buildings are set into the piers that support the 350-year-old wooden ceiling. Off the left aisle you step down into the 4th-century church of **Santa Restituta,** which was incorporated into the cathedral. Though Santa Restituta was redecorated in the late 1600s in the prevalent Baroque style, the mosaics in the **Battistero** (Baptistery) are claimed to be the oldest in the Western world.

On the right aisle of the cathedral, in the **Cappella del Tesoro di San Gennaro,** multicolor marbles and frescoes honor Saint Januarius, the miracle-working patron saint of Naples, whose altar and relics are encased in silver. Three times a year—on September 19 (his feast day); on the Saturday preceding the first Sunday in May, which commemorates the transfer of his relics to Naples; and on December 16—his dried blood, contained in two sealed vials, is believed to liquefy during rites in his honor; the rare occasions on which it does not liquefy portend ill, as in 1980, the year of the Irpinia earthquake. The most spectacular painting on display is Ribera's *San Gennaro in the Furnace* (1647), depicting the saint emerging unscathed from the furnace while his persecutors scatter in disarray. These days large numbers of devout Neapolitans offer up prayers in his memory. The **Museo del Tesoro di San Gennaro** houses a rich collection of treasures associated with the saint. Paintings by Solimena and Luca Giordano hang alongside statues, busts, candelabras, and tabernacles in gold, silver, and marble by Cosimo Fanzago and other 18th-century baroque masters. ✉ *Via Duomo 149, Spaccanapoli* ☎ *081/449097 Duomo, 081/294980 museum* 🎫 *Cathedral €7, baptistery €1.50* 🕒 *Cathedral daily 9–6; baptistery weekdays 8:30–12:30 and 3:30–6:30, holidays 8:30–1 and 3:30–6:30; Capella di San Gennaro weekdays 8:30–1 and 3:30–7:30, Sun. 8:30–1 and 4:30–6:30.*

Gesù Nuovo. A stunning architectural contrast to the plain Romanesque frontage of the nearby Santa Chiara, the oddly faceted stone facade of this elaborate baroque church dates to the late 16th century. Originally a palace, the building was seized by Pedro of Toledo in 1547 and donated to the Jesuits on the condition the facade remain intact. Recent research has revealed that the symbols on the stones on the front are Aramaic musical notes that produce a 45-minute concerto. Behind the entrance is Francesco Solimena's action-packed *Expulsion of Heliodorus from the Temple.* The bulk of the interior decoration took more than 40 years and was completed only in the 18th century. You can find the familiar baroque sculptors (Naccherino, Finelli) and painters. The gracious *Visitation* above the altar in the second chapel on the right is by Massimo Stanzione, who also contributed the fine frescoes in the main nave: they're in the presbytery (behind and around the main altar).

Continued on page 260

WALKING SPACCANAPOLI

Spaccanapoli is the informal designation given to the long, straight street running down the middle of Naples's *centro storico* (historic center). The name has also come to stand for the neighborhood surrounding the street, an area that's chaotic, vibrant, edgy, colorful, noisy, mysterious, and very beautiful. In other words, it's the essence of Naples. A walk along Spaccanapoli takes you past peeling palaces, artisans' workshops, many churches and street shrines, stores of all sorts, bars, and people young and old.

left, Via San Gregorio Armeno; top right, church of Gesú Nuovo; bottom right, a *presepe* shop window

A STROLL THROUGH THE HEART OF NAPLES

Santa Chiara

Frescoes, Santa Chiara

Morning is the best time to make this walk—many of the churches are closed in the afternoon. The route is a mile and a half long; done at a leisurely pace, with numerous stops along the way, it will take a full morning.

❶ **Start at Piazza Gesù Nuovo.** At this point Spaccanapoli goes by the name Via Benedetto Croce. The Guglia dell'Immacolata, an extravagant carved-stone spire honoring the Virgin Mary, stands in the middle of the district's largest square. The forbidding 15th-century facade of the church of **Gesù Nuovo** suits the building's original function as a fort; it was converted into the city's most extravagant baroque church by the Jesuits in the 18th century.

❷ **Cross the road and enter the church of Santa Chiara.** Originally built by Robert of Anjou in the early 1300s and reconstructed after a direct hit from a bomb in 1943, the church is light, airy, and spacious. Look for the traces of the Giotto frescoes behind the altar. A side entrance leads to a delightful vine-laden cloister decorated with hundreds of majolica tiles, an unexpected outbreak of peace in noisy Naples.

❸ **Head east on Spaccanapoli.** You'll cross Via San Sebastiano, a street filled with music shops frequented by students from the nearby conservatory; it can be a veritable symphony in the morning. **Palazzo Filomarino**, former home of philosopher Benedetto Croce and now the site of his library, is on the left as you continue. Next on your right is architect Cosimo Fanzago's **Palazzo Carafa della Spina**; coachmen once used the mouths of the gargoyles at the entrance to tamp out their torches.

Piazza Gesú Nuovo

❹ **Continue east to Piazza San Domenico Maggiore.** The rear of the church of San Domenico Maggiore, the Palazzo Corigliano (today part of the university), and another spire

Piazza San Domenico Maggiore

Chapel of San Gennaro

Capella Sansevero

Marionettes in a shop window.

contribute to one of Naples's most charming squares. Outdoor cafés (including Scaturchio, one of Naples's most celebrated pastry shops) give the piazza the feel of an open-air living room. Heading up the right-hand side of the piazza, swing right onto Via Francesco de Sanctis, where you find the fascinating **Cappella Sansevero**, the tomb-chapel of the Sangro di San Severo family.

❺ **Return to Spaccanapoli on Via Nilo.** Where the two streets intersect you pass a statue of the Egyptian river god Nile reclining on a pedestal. (A few steps beyond, Spaccanapoli's street name changes to Via San Biagio dei Librai.) Several blocks down is the storefront Ospedale delle Bambole (Doll Hospital).

❻ **Turn left (north) when you reach Via Duomo.** The next main intersection is Via Tribunali, the other great thoroughfare of the district. Take a right to reach the **Pio Monte della Misericordia**, which contains one of the greatest 17th-century altarpieces in Europe, Caravaggio's *Seven Acts of Mercy*. Return to the Via Duomo to visit the **Duomo di San Gennaro** and its spectacular chapel.

❼ **Head west on Via dei Tribunali.** After a short block you'll reach one of the street's many imposing churches, the gigantic **San Lorenzo Maggiore.** Its 18th-century facade hides a Gothic-era nave and—surprise—one of the most interesting archaeological sites in the city.

❽ **Turn left onto Via San Gregorio Armeno.** This may be the most charming street in Naples. The towering campanile of the Rococo church of **San Gregorio Armeno** arches over the street, which is lined with *presepe* (crèche) stores.

❾ **Continue west along Via Tribunali.** Stop to note the curious brass skulls outside the church of **Purgatorio ad Arco** on your right—touch them to bring good luck. At the end of Via Tribunali, turn right into Piazza Bellini and stop for a drink at one of the leafy square's many cafés.

Don't miss the votive chapel dedicated to the surgeon and university teacher Saint Giuseppe Moscato, along with a re-creation of his studio. Here hundreds of tiny silver images have been hung on the walls to give thanks to the saint, who was canonized in 1987, for his assistance in medical matters. On the opposite far left corner a smaller chapel similarly gives thanks to San Ciro (Saint Cyrus), also a doctor. Farther down are impressive statues of David and Jeremiah by Fanzago. Left of the altar the wooden heads of various saints are aligned like gods in an antique theater. ✉ *Piazza Gesù Nuovo, Spaccanapoli* ☎ *081/5578111* ⏲ *Daily 7–12:30 and 4–7:30* Ⓜ *Piazza Dante.*

WORD OF MOUTH

"Naples was really interesting. They say you'll love it or hate it. Put me on the side of love it."

—Flygirl

Fodor's Choice ★ **Museo Cappella Sansevero** (*Sansevero Chapel Museum*). The dazzling funerary chapel of the Sangro di Sansevero princes combines noble swagger, overwhelming color, and a touch of the macabre—which is to say, it expresses Naples perfectly. The chapel was begun in 1590 by Prince Giovan Francesco di Sangro to fulfill a vow to the Virgin if he were cured of a dire illness. The seventh Sangro di Sansevero prince, Raimondo, had the building modified in the mid-18th century and is generally credited for its current baroque styling, whose noteworthy elements include the splendid marble-inlay floor. A larger-than-life figure, Prince Raimondo was popularly believed to have signed a pact with the devil allowing him to plumb nature's secrets. He commissioned the young sculptor Giuseppe Sammartino to create numerous works, including the chapel's centerpiece: the remarkable *Veiled Christ,* which has a seemingly transparent marble veil some say was produced using a chemical formula provided by the prince. ■ **TIP→ If you have the stomach for it, take a look in the crypt, where some of the anatomical experiments conducted by the prince are gruesomely displayed.** ✉ *Via Francesco de Sanctis 19, off Vicolo Domenico Maggiore, Spaccanapoli* ☎ *081/5518470* 🌐 *www.museosansevero.it* 🎫 *€7/€5 with Artecard* ⏲ *Mon. and Wed.–Sat. 10–5:40, Sun. 10–1:10* Ⓜ *Dante.*

Museo Diocesano Napoli (*Diocesan Museum of Naples*). Instantly recognizable by the fresco of the Virgin above the entrance, this museum exhibits brilliantly restored works by late-Gothic, Renaissance, and Neapolitan baroque masters. The museum incorporates the baroque church of Santa Maria Donnaregina Nuova, started in 1617 and consecrated 50 years later for the Francescan nuns (*les Clarisses*) in the attached cloister. The church replaced the Gothic Donnaregina Vecchia, which was damaged by earthquake. In more modern times the building was used as legal offices before being closed completely, becoming prey to the occasional theft, not to mention bomb damage during World War II. In 2008 the space was reborn as a museum.

Ground-floor artworks center on the life of the Virgin Mary, beginning with the first chapel on the left and French painter Charles Mellin's beautiful *Immaculate Conception* (1646); on the other side of what was

Napoli Sotterranea (Naples Underground) is an extensive network of tunnels, caverns, and aqueducts.

the nave is an equally fine Madonna and Child by Massimo Stanzione. Also on the left is a space rich in Gothic and Renaissance statuary from the former church. You then take the elevator upstairs to where the nuns once attended Mass, concealed from the congregation by a special screen. The hundred works on display there follow the theme of life as an Imitation of Christ. There is also the rare chance to see the roof paintings close up, with state-of-the-art floodlights showing off their restoration to maximum effect.

The nave's vault contains frescoes by Francesco de Benedictis, including one depicting the Ascension of the Virgin (1654). In the former presbytery at the end are the last two works of Luca Giordano, *The Wedding at Cana* and a mystically lit *The Sermon on the Mount*, both from 1705. ✉ *Largo Donna Regina, opposite Archbishop's palace, Spaccanapoli* ☎ *081/5571365* 🌐 *www.museodiocesanonapoli.it* 🕒 *Mon. and Wed.–Sat. 9:30–4:30, Sun. 9:30–2* Ⓜ *Piazza Cavour (in construction: Duomo).*

FAMILY Fodor's Choice ★ **Napoli Sotterranea** (*Underground Naples*). Fascinating two-hour tours of a portion of Naples's fabled underground city provide an initiation into the complex layering of history in the city center. Efforts to dramatize the experience—amphoras lowered on ropes to draw water from cisterns, candles distributed to negotiate narrow passages as in pre-electric days, objects shifted to reveal secret passages—combined with excellent guiding in English make this particularly exciting for children.

After a descent into "Naples's stomach" (food storehouses), the first stop is an amphitheater where Nero famously performed three times. During one of his performances an earthquake struck and—so

Suetonius relates—the emperor forbade the 6,000 spectators to leave. The rumbling, he insisted, was only the gods applauding his performance. Across a small street above, another descent delivers you to a section of a 400-km (249-mile) system of quarries and aqueducts used from Greek times until the 1845 cholera epidemic. In 1942 a section was reopened to provide air-raid shelter big enough to sleep 3,000 people. A further descent takes you to a Greco-Roman quarry. Finally, prepare for a highly claustrophobic 1-km (½-mile) walk with only a candle to light your way.

At the end of the aqueduct you come to first a Greek and then a much larger Roman cistern. Near the entrance is the War Museum, which displays uniforms, armed transportation vehicles, and weapons from World War II. A room at the end of the tour contains examples of that most Neapolitan of art forms, *la presepe* (the crib). **■ TIP→ Be prepared on the underground tour to go up and down many steps and handle a few narrow corridors. Temperatures in summer will be much lower below than at street level, so bring a wrap.** ✉ *Piazza San Gaetano 68, along Via dei Tribunali, Spaccanapoli* ☎ *081/296944* 🌐 *www.napolisotterranea.org* 🎫 *€9.30* ⏲ *Tours every 2 hrs daily 10–6* Ⓜ *Piazza Cavour.*

Fodor's Choice ★ **Pio Monte della Misericordia.** One of Spaccanapoli's defining sites, this octagonal church was built around the corner from the Duomo for a charitable institution seven noblemen founded in 1601. The institution's aim was to carry out acts of Christian charity: feeding the hungry, clothing the poor, nursing the sick, sheltering pilgrims, visiting prisoners, ransoming Christian slaves, and burying the indigent dead—acts immortalized in the history of art by Caravaggio's famous altarpiece depicting the *Sette Opere della Misericordia* (*Seven Acts of Mercy*). In this haunting work the artist has brought the Virgin, borne atop the shoulders of two angels, down into the streets of Spaccanapoli (scholars have suggested a couple of plausible locations) populated by figures in whose spontaneous and passionate movements the people could see themselves. The original church was considered too small and was destroyed in 1655 to make way for a new church, designed by Antonio Picchiatti and built between 1658 and 1678. Pride of place is given to the great Caravaggio above the altar, but there are other important baroque-era paintings on view here. Some hang in the church—among them seven other works of mercy depicted individually by Caravaggio acolytes—while other works, including a wonderful self-portrait by Luca Giordano, are in the adjoining *pinacoteca* (picture gallery). ✉ *Via Tribunali 253, Spaccanapoli* ☎ *081/446973* 🌐 *www.piomontedellamisericordia.it* 🎫 *€6, includes audio guide* ⏲ *Daily 9–2* Ⓜ *Piazza Cavour (in construction: Duomo).*

San Domenico Maggiore. One of Spaccanapoli's largest churches, this Dominican house of worship was originally constructed by Charles I of Anjou in 1238. Legend has it that a painting of the Crucifixion spoke to St. Thomas Aquinas when he was at prayer here. Three centuries later a fire destroyed most of this early structure, and in 1850 a neo-Gothic edifice rose in its place, complete with a nave of awe-inspiring dimensions. In the second chapel on the right (if you

CLOSE UP

Murder in the Cathedral?

Most of the frescoes of the San Gennaro chapel are by the Bolognese artist Domenichino, but his compatriot Guido Reni was originally engaged to paint the cycle, and thereby hangs a tale.

When he arrived in Naples, Reni found himself so harassed and threatened by jealous local artists, who were indignant that the commission had been given to an outsider, that he gave up the job and fled town. Ultimately he was replaced by the great Domenichino, who came to Naples only after the viceroy himself guaranteed his protection.

Domenichino started painting under armed guard beginning in 1630 and had almost completed the work in 1641 when he died suddenly; poisoning was suspected. The committee charged with finding his replacement pointedly refused to consider a Neapolitan painter, instead selecting the Roman Giovanni Lanfranco, who bravely (and quickly) finished the dome. It was Lanfranco who painted the dome's frescoed vision of paradise. The most spectacular painting of all, however, is on the right—Ribera's depiction of the saint emerging from the furnace unscathed.

enter through the north door) are remnants of the earlier church—14th-century frescoes by Pietro Cavallini, a Roman predecessor of Giotto. Note the depiction of Mary Magdalene dressed in her own hair, and, in front, the crucifixion of Andrew as a devil strangles his judge, the Prefect Aegeas, just below. Along the side are some noted funerary monuments, including those of the Carafa family, whose chapel, to the left of Cosimo Fanzago's 17th-century altar, is a beautiful Renaissance-era set-piece. The San Carlo Borromeo chapel features an excellent *Baptism of Christ* (1564), by Marco Pino, a Michelangelo protégé. Other interesting works are the unusual *Madonna di Latte*, in the Cappella di S. Maria Maddalena, and a beautiful Madonna by Agostino Tesauro in the Cappella San Giovanni. A Ribera painting in the San Bartolomeo chapel depicts the saint's martyrdom. Near the back of the church, looking like a giant gold peacock's tail, is the so-called Machine of 40 Hours, a devotional device for displaying the sacrament for the 40 hours between Christ's burial and resurrection. ✉ *Piazza San Domenico Maggiore 8, Spaccanapoli* ☎ *081/459188* ⏲ *Mon.–Sat. 8:30–noon and 4–7, Sun. 9–1 and 4:30–7 Sala di Tesoro: 8:30–1, 4–7, €3. Guided visit: Sat. 9:30–noon, 4:43–7, Sun. 9:30–noon* Ⓜ *Dante.*

San Gregorio Armeno. This convent is one of the oldest and most important in Naples. Set on Via San Gregorio Armeno, the street lined with Naples's most adorable *Presepe*—or Nativity crèche scene–emporiums—the convent is landmarked by a picturesque campanile. The nuns who lived here, often the daughters of Naples's richest families, must have been disappointed with heaven when they arrived—banquets here outrivaled those of the royal court, hallways were lined with paintings, and the church was filled with gilt stucco and semiprecious stones. Described as "a room of Paradise on Earth" by Carlo Celano

CLOSE UP

Caravaggio's Seven Acts of Mercy

The most unforgettable painting in Naples, Michelangelo Merisi da Caravaggio's *Seven Acts of Mercy*—in Italian, the *Sette Opere della Misericordia*—takes pride of place in the Church of Pio Monte della Misericordia, as well as in nearly all of southern Italy, for emotional spectacle and unflinching truthfulness.

Painted in 1607, it combines the traditional seven acts of Christian charity in sometimes-abbreviated form in a tight, dynamic composition under the close, compassionate gaze of the Virgin (the original title was *Our Lady of Mercy*).

Borne by two of the most memorable angels ever painted, she flutters down with the Christ child into a torch-lighted street scene.

Illuminated in the artist's landmark chiaroscuro style (featuring pronounced contrasts of light, *chiaro*, and deep shadow, *scuro*), a man is being buried, a nude beggar is being clothed, and—this artist never pulled any punches—a starving prisoner suckles a woman.

Caravaggio, as with most geniuses, was a difficult artist and personality. His romantic bad-boy reputation as the original bohemian, complete with angry, nihilistic, rebel-with-a-cause sneer and roistering lifestyle, has dominated interpretations of his revolutionary oeuvre, undermining its intense religiosity, in which the act of painting almost becomes an act of penance.

This is perhaps understandable—most of the documents pertaining to his life relate to his problems with the law and make for a good story indeed (he came to Naples after killing a man in a bar brawl in Rome, where his cardinal patrons could no longer protect him).

But in spite of (or perhaps because of) his personal life, Caravaggio painted some of the most moving religious art ever produced in the West, whittling away all the rhetoric to reveal the emotional core of the subject.

His genuine love of the popular classes and for the "real" life of the street found expression in his use of ordinary street folk as models.

If his art seems to surge directly from the gut, his famous "objectivity" of observation and reduced palette have clear antecedents in paintings from his home region in northern Italy.

The simplicity and warts-and-all depictions of his characters show a deeply original response to the Counter-Reformation writings on religious art by Carlo Borromeo, a future saint, also from Lombardy.

The *Seven Acts of Mercy,* the first altarpiece commissioned for the new church of the charitable institution, has been called "the most important religious painting of the 17th century" by the great 20th-century Italian art critics Roberto Longhi and Giuliano Argan. This astonishing painting immediately inspired the seven imitative Acts of Mercy individually depicted by other Neapolitan artists on the remaining seven walls of the same chapel, and the painting could lay claim to having kick-started the Neapolitan Baroque, with visual relations being expressed purely in terms of dramatic light and shadow, further exalting the contrasts of human experience.

and designed by Niccolò Taglicozzi Canle, the church has a highly detailed wooden ceiling, unique papier-mâché choir lofts, a shimmering organ, candlelit shrines, and important Luca Giordano frescoes of scenes of the life of St. Gregory, whose relics were brought to Naples in the 8th century from Byzantium. From the convent's cloister (entrance off the small square up the road—buzz on the entry phone) you can gain access to the nuns' gallery shielded by 18th-century jalousies and see the church from a different perspective. Other areas off the cloister, such as the Salottino della Badessa—generally not on view, as this is still a working convent—are preserved as magnificent 18th-century interiors. ✉ *Piazzetta San Gregorio Armeno 1, Spaccanapoli* ☎ *081/5520186* ⏲ *Mon.–Sat. 9–noon, Sun. 9–1* Ⓜ *Dante.*

San Lorenzo Maggiore. One of the grandest medieval churches of the Decumano Maggiore, San Lorenzo features a very unmedieval facade of 18th-century splendor. Due to the effects and threats of earthquakes, the church was reinforced and reshaped along baroque lines in the 17th and 18th centuries. Begun by Robert d'Anjou in 1265 on the site of a previous 6th-century church, the church has a single, barnlike nave that reflects the Franciscans' desire for simple spaces with enough room to preach to large crowds. A grandiose triumphal arch announces the transept, and the main altar (1530) is the sculptor Giovanni da Nola's masterpiece; notice the fascinating historical views of Naples in the reliefs.

The apse, designed by an unknown French architect of great caliber, is pure French Angevin in style, complete with an ambulatory of nine side chapels that is covered by a magnificent web of cross arches. The church's most important monument is found here: the tomb of Catherine of Austria (circa 1323), by Tino da Camaino, among the first sculptors to introduce the Gothic style into Italy. The left transept contains the 14th-century funerary monument of Carlo di Durazzo and yet another Cosimo Fanzago masterpiece, the **Cappellone di Sant'Antonio.** Outside the 17th-century cloister is the entrance to the **Greek and Roman *scavi*,** or excavations, under San Lorenzo. Near the area of the forum, these digs have revealed streets, markets, and workshops of another age.

Next door to the church is the **Museo dell'Opera di San Lorenzo,** installed in the 16th-century palazzo around the *torre campanaria* (bell tower). In Room 1 ancient remains from the Greek agora beneath combine with modern maps to provide a fascinating impression of import and export trends in the 4th century BC. The museum also contains ceramics dug up from the Svevian period, many pieces from the early Middle Ages, large tracts of mosaics from the 6th-century basilica, and helpful models of how the ancient Roman forum and nearby buildings must have looked. A multimedia facility has recently been added to do justice to a place that exists in several historical dimensions. ✉ *Via dei Tribunali 316, Spaccanapoli* ☎ *081/2110860* 🌐 *www.sanlorenzomaggiore.na.it* 🎫 *Excavations and museum €9/€7 for students and pensioners/€6 for under 18s* ⏲ *Museum, Mon.–Sat. 9:30–5:30, Sun. 9:30–1:30; Church daily 8–1 and 5:30–7; closed to sightseers during services* Ⓜ *Dante.*

San Severo al Pendino. Erected in the 16th century atop a previous church, this building has metamorphosed many times—from church of San Severo into a private palace, a monastery later suppressed by Napoleon, a state archive, a World War II bomb shelter, and an earthquake-damaged relic—before a long and painstaking renovation restored its luster. To the right of the nave rests the tomb of Charles V's general—and original church benefactor—Giovanni Bisvallo. In addition to its aesthetic highlights, the complex also provides a telling disquisition on mortality. Aboveground one can view the grandeur of monuments to the dead. Less grandly, a brief excursion downstairs reveals the *scolatoi*. These are draining holes where the recently deceased, seated upright and left to dry of bodily fluids, were not abandoned but visited daily by Domenican monks seeking to reinforce their sense of the fragility of human existence. **■TIP→ This is a rather amazing place, and the admission is free.** ✉ *Via Duomo 286, Spaccanapoli* 🎫 *Free* 🕑 *Mon.–Sat. 9–7.*

Santa Chiara. Offering a stark and telling contrast to the opulence of the nearby Gesù Nuovo, Santa Chiara is the leading Angevin Gothic monument in Naples. The fashionable house of worship for the 14th-century nobility and a favorite Angevin church from the start, the church of St. Clare was intended to be a great dynastic monument by Robert d'Anjou. His second wife, Sancia di Majorca, added the adjoining convent for the Poor Clares to a monastery of the Franciscan Minors so she could vicariously satisfy a lifelong desire for the cloistered seclusion of a convent. This was the first time the two sexes were combined in a single complex. Built in a Provençal Gothic style between 1310 and 1328 (probably by Guglielmo Primario) and dedicated in 1340, the church had its aspect radically altered, as did so many others, in the baroque period. A six-day fire started by Allied bombs on August 4, 1943, put an end to all that, as well as to what might have been left of the important cycle of frescoes by Giotto and his Neapolitan workshop. The church's most important tomb towers behind the altar. Sculpted by Giovanni and Pacio Bertini of Florence (1343–45), it is, fittingly, the tomb of the founding king: the great Robert d'Anjou, known as the Wise. Nearby are the tombs of Carlo, duke of Calabria, and his wife, Marie de Valois, both by Tino da Camaino.

Around the left side of the church is the **Chiostro delle Clarisse,** the most famous cloister in Naples. Complemented by citrus trees, the benches and octagonal columns comprise a light-handed masterpiece of painted majolica designed by Domenico Antonio Vaccaro, with a delightful profusion of landscapes and light yellow and green floral motifs realized by Donato and Giuseppe Massa and their studio (1742). ✉ *Piazza Gesù Nuovo, Spaccanapoli* ☎ *081/5516673* 🌐 *www.monasterodisantachiara.eu* 🎫 *Museum and cloister €6* 🕑 *Church daily 7:30–1 and 4:30–8, museum and cloister Mon.–Sat. 9:30–5:30, Sun. 10–2:30* Ⓜ *Dante, Università.*

WORTH NOTING

Monumento Nazionale dei Girolamini. *Il Girolamini* is another name for the Oratorians, followers of St. Philip Neri, to whom the splendid church I Girolamini is dedicated. The church is part of a larger complex managed as the Monumento Nazionale dei Girolamini. The Florentine architect Giovanni Antonio Dosio designed I Girolamini, which was erected between 1592 and 1619; the dome and facade were rebuilt (circa 1780) in the most elegant Neoclassical style after a design by Ferdinando Fuga. Inside the entrance wall is Luca Giordano's grandiose fresco (1684) of Christ chasing the money-changers from the temple. The intricate carved-wood ceiling, damaged by Allied bombs in 1943, has now been restorted to its original magnificence.

The Oratorians also built the **Casa dei Padri dell'Oratorio** (House of the Oratorio Fathers). Step through its gate to see the two cloisters designed by Dosio and other Florentine architects around 1600. The gallery in this section contains 16th- and 17th-century paintings by Ribera and other baroque masters. One of Europe's most gloriously decorated 18th-century libraries, the **Biblioteca dei Girolamini** (Girolamini Library), still used by scholars, helped make this an intellectual nexus during the Renaissance and Baroque periods. ■ **TIP→ The ticket office is on Via Duomo, behind the church.** ✉ *Via Duomo 142, Spaccanapoli* ☎ *142/08129444* 💵 *Free* ⏲ *Mon.–Sat. 9–12:50* Ⓜ *Piazza Cavour.*

Sacro Cappella di Diego Maradona. By Pop Art standards this homemade shrine to Napoli's all-time favorite soccer player, Diego Maradona, is a masterpiece. "The hand of god, the head of Maradona," quoth the famous Argentine-born superstar after scoring a much-disputed World cup goal against England. The sentiment, in its ability to mix the earthly and fallible with the divine, is also peculiarly Neapolitan. The shrine, appropriately bearing the colors of Argentina's flag, has the footballer flanked by San Gennaro and Nuestra Senora de Lujan, here a clipping from *La Gazzetta dello Sport* (*Sports Gazette*), there an ampoule containing tears from the fateful year (1991) when the champion left Naples and his team's winning streak promptly ended. Have a coffee in Bar Nilo, whose hospitable owner will be happy to let you take a photo. ■ **TIP→ At night and on holidays, the shrine is dismantled and taken inside, perhaps to safeguard it from not-so-adoring English or rival Italian fans of long ago.** ✉ *Bar Nilo, Via S. Biagio dei Librai 129, Spaccanapoli.*

San Giuseppe dei Ruffi. On most mornings around 7:30, Sacramentine nuns, or the *Perpetue Adoratrici,* beautifully sing early Mass beneath Francesco de Mura's *The Paradise,* this late-17th-century church's dome painting. Dressed in immaculate red, black, and white habits, the nuns, after singing, prostrate themselves before the altar, which stretches upward, with layer after baroque layer of Dionisio Lazzari's sumptuous gold and marble (1686), topped by the putti and the figures of Hope and Charity by Matteo Bottigliero (1733). Upon entering or exiting, take note of San Giuseppe dei Ruffi's dramatically baroque facade, designed, as was the interior, by Lazzari, a renowned architect and sculptor. ■ **TIP→ Hearing the nuns sing is a unique, if little known, Naples experience, and well worth rising early for.** ✉ *Piazza San*

The unique majolica-decorated cloister at Santa Chiara serves as a tranquil oasis amid hectic Spaccanapoli.

Giuseppe dei Ruffi 2, half block from Duomo, Spaccanapoli ⏲ *Mon.–Sat. 7:30–9:30, Sun. 7:30–10:30* Ⓜ *Piazza Cavour.*

San Paolo Maggiore. Like the nearby Santi Apostoli, this church was erected for the Theatin fathers in the late 16th century (1583–1603), the period of their order's rapid expansion. This was another instance where Francesco Grimaldi, the (ordained) house architect, erected a church on the ruins of an ancient Roman temple, then transformed it into a Christian basilica. Spoils from the temple survive in the present incarnation, especially the two monumental Corinthian columns on the facade. An earthquake knocked down the original facade in 1688, and damage during World War II, coupled with decades of neglect, led to further deterioration that has since been reversed. Two large murals by Francesco Solimena in the sacristy have been restored. In the first Simon Magus is depicted flying headlong down to Earth as biblical or Neapolitan figures either look on or continue their activities. Similarly spectacular is the fresco depicting the imminent conversion of Saul: illuminated by a light-projecting cloud, the future Saint Paul tumbles off a horse in the picture's center. ✉ *Piazza San Gaetano, Spaccanapoli* ☎ *081/454048* ⏲ *Weekdays 9–1 and 3–6, Sat. 9–1* Ⓜ *Dante.*

Sant'Angelo a Nilo. Amid this church's graceful interior can be found the earliest evidence of the Renaissance in Naples: the funerary monument (1426–27) of Sant'Angelo's builder, Cardinal Brancaccio, sculpted by the famous Donatello and the almost-as-famous Michelozzo. The front of the sarcophagus bears Donatello's contribution, a bas-relief *Assumption of the Virgin,* upheld by angels, the Virgin seeming to float in air. Built in the late 1300s the church was redesigned in the 16th century by Arcangelo Guglielminelli. ✉ *Piazzetta Nilo, along Via San Biagio dei Librai, Spaccanapoli* ☎ *081/5516227* ⏲ *Mon.–Sat. 9–1 and 4–6, Sun. 8:30–noon* Ⓜ *Dante.*

WORD OF MOUTH

"Stay in the old town where you can walk around, visit the archaeology museum (where the treasures from Pompeii are located), and eat pizza!"

—yorkshire

Santi Apostoli. This baroque church in a basic Latin-cross style with a single nave shares the piazza with a contemporary art school in a typically anarchic Neapolitan mix. The church, designed by the architect Francesco Grimaldi for the Theatin fathers and erected between 1610 and 1649, replaced a previous church, itself constructed on the remains of a temple probably dedicated to Mercury. Santi Apostoli is worth a quick peek for its coherent, intact baroque decorative scheme. Excellent (circa 1644) by Giovanni Lanfranco each narrate a different martyrdom, and there are works by his successors, Francesco Solimena and Luca Giordano. **■ TIP→ An altar in the left transept by the architect Francesco Borromini is the only work in Naples by this noted architect whose freedom from formality so inspired the exuberance of the baroque.** ✉ *Largo Santi Apostoli 9, Spaccanapoli* ☎ *081/299375* ⏲ *Mon.–Sat. 9–noon, Sun. 9–1* Ⓜ *Piazza Cavour.*

MUSEO ARCHEOLOGICO NAZIONALE AND NEARBY

It's only fitting that the Museo Archeologico Nazionale—the single most important and remarkable museum of Greco-Roman antiquities in the world (in spite of itself, some observers say)—sits in the upper *decumanus,* or neighborhood, of ancient Neapolis, the district colonized by the ancient Greeks and Romans. Happily, it's open all day (its core collection, that is). But if two hours are your limit for gazing at ancient art, nearby you can discover some of the lesser-known delights of medieval and Renaissance Naples, along with the city's lush botanical gardens. Along the way are churches that are repositories for magnificent 15th- and 16th-century art and sculpture; the Museo Madre, the city's flagship museum of modern art; and the famed Porta Capuana, one of the historic gates to the city walls.

TOP ATTRACTIONS

Madre (*Museum of Contemporary Art Donnaregina*). With 8,000 square meters (86,111 square feet) of exhibition space and a host of young and helpful attendants, the Madre, as this facility is commonly known, is one of the most visited museums in Naples. Most of the artworks on the first floor were installed in situ by their creators, and the second-floor "historic" gallery exhibits works by international and Italian contemporary artists. The museum also hosts temporary shows by major international artists. ✉ *Via Settembrini 79, San Lorenzo* ☎ *081/19313016* 🌐 *www.madrenapoli.it/en* 🎫 *€7, free on Mon.* ⏲ *Mon., Wed.–Sat. 10–7:30, Sun. 10–8* Ⓜ *Piazza Cavour.*

Fodor's Choice ★ **Museo Archeologico Nazionale** (*National Museum of Archaeology*). Those who know and love this legendary museum—now restyled as MANN (Museo Archeologico Nazionale Napoli), though the name has yet to catch on—have the tendency upon hearing it mentioned to heave a sigh: it's famous not only for its unrivaled collections but also for its cordoned-off rooms, missing identification labels, poor lighting, billows of dust, suffocating heat in summer, and indifferent personnel, a state of affairs seen by some critics as an encapsulation of everything that's wrong with southern Italy in general.

Precisely because of this emblematic value, the National Ministry of Culture has decided to lavish attention and funds on the museum in a complete reorganization. This process has been ongoing for some time and looks as if it will continue for a while longer, although improvements are gradually becoming visible: ticketing has been privatized and opening hours extended—for the core "masterpiece" collection, that is; other rooms are subject to staffing shortages and sometimes close on a rotating basis. Some of the "newer" rooms, covering archaeological discoveries in the Greco-Roman settlements and necropolises in and around Naples, have helpful informational panels in English. A fascinating free display of the finds unearthed during digs for the Naples metro has been set up in the Museo station, close to the museum's entrance.

Though some rooms may be closed when you visit, world-renowned archaeological finds that put most other museums to shame are always on view. These include the legendary Farnese collection of ancient sculpture, some of the best mosaics and paintings from Pompeii and Herculaneum, and *Iliou Persis* (*The Taking of Troy*), one of several dozen objects returned to Italy by the J. Paul Getty Museum in Los Angeles. ✉ *Piazza Museo 19, Spaccanapoli* ☎ *081/440166* 🌐 *cir.campania.beniculturali.it/museoarcheologiconazionale* 🎫 *€8* ⏲ *Wed.–Mon. 9–7:30* Ⓜ *Museo.*

Orto Botanico. Founded in 1807 by Joseph Bonaparte and Prince Joachim Murat as an oasis from hectic Naples, this is one of the largest of all Italian botanical gardens, comprising some 30 acres. Nineteenth-century greenhouses and picturesque paths hold an important collection of tree, shrub, cactus, and floral specimens from all over the world. Next to the Orto Botanico, with a 1,200-foot facade dwarfing Piazza Carlo III, is one of the largest public buildings in Europe, the Albergo dei Poveri, built in the 18th and 19th centuries to house the city's destitute and homeless; it's now a UNESCO World Heritage site awaiting an ambitious restoration scheme. ✉ *Via Foria 223, Carlo III* ☎ *081/449759* 🌐 *www.ortobotanico.unina.it* 🎫 *Free* ⏲ *By appointment weekdays 9–2.*

San Giovanni a Carbonara. An engaging complex of Renaissance architecture and sculpture, this church is named for its location during medieval times near the city trash dump, where refuse was burned (carbonized). The church's history starts in 1339, when the Neapolitan nobleman Gualtiero Galeota donated a few houses and a vegetable garden to Augustinian monks who ministered to the poor neighborhood nearby.

San Giovanni's dramatic piperno-stone staircase, with its double run of elliptical stairs, was modeled after a 1707 design by Ferdinando

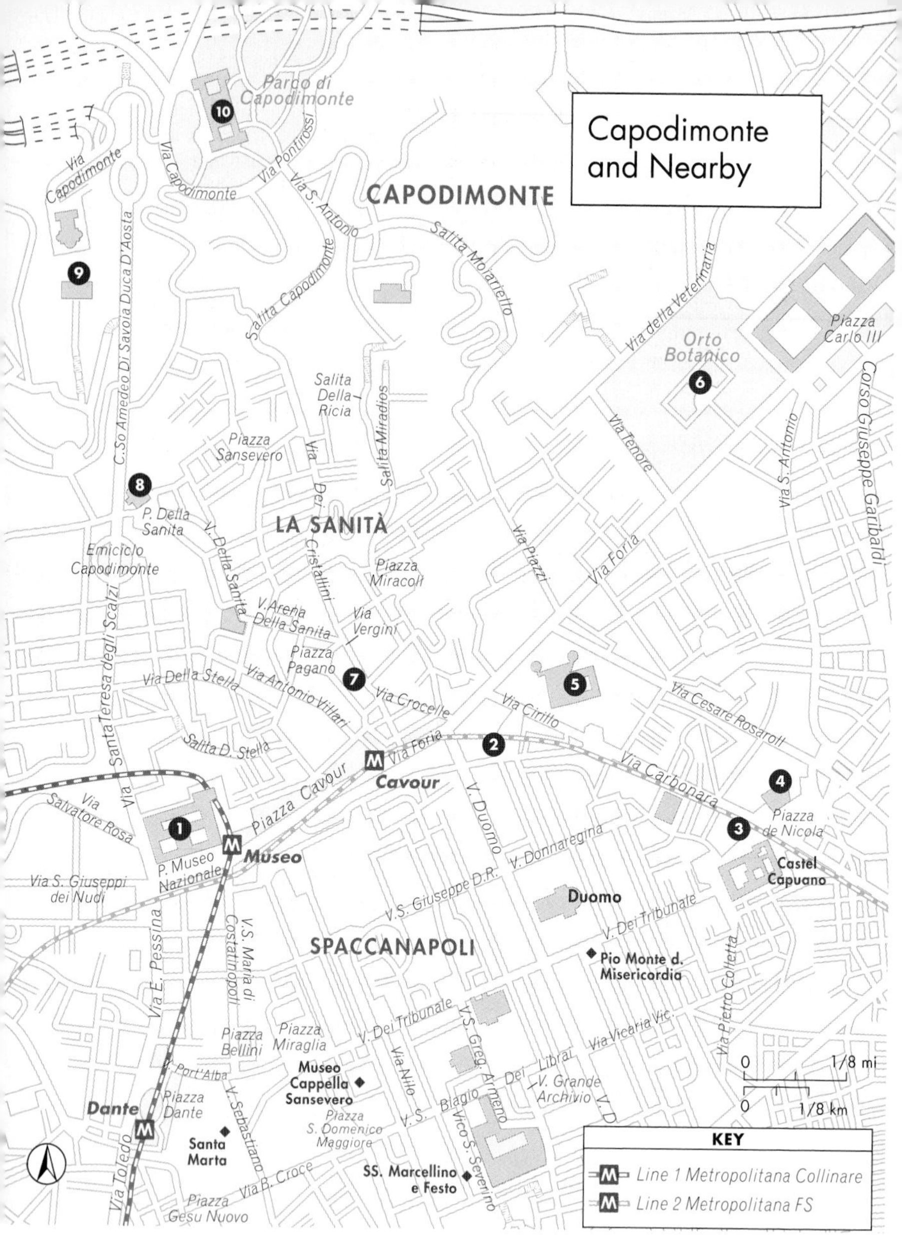

Basilica Santa Maria della Sanità **8**
Catacomba di San Gennaro **9**
Madre **2**
Museo Archeologico Nazionale **1**
Museo di Capodimonte **10**
Orto Botanico **6**
Palazzo della Spagnola **7**
Porta Capuana **3**
San Giovanni a Carbonara **5**
Santa Caterina a Formiello **4**

Sanfelice similar to other organ-curved stairways in Rome, such as the Spanish Steps. Upon entering the rectangular nave, the first thing you see is the monument of the Miroballo family, which is actually a chapel on the opposite wall, finished by Tommaso Malvito and his workshop in 1519 for the Marchese Bracigliano; the magnificent statues in the semicircular arch immediately set the tone for this surprising repository of first-class Renaissance sculpture.

Beyond the skeletal main altar, which has been stripped of its 18th-century baroque additions, is the 59-foot-tall funerary monument of King Ladislas and Joan II, finished by Marco and Andrea da Firenze in 1428. A door underneath this monument leads to the **Ser Caracciolo del Sole Chapel,** with its rare and beautiful original majolica pavement. The oldest (1427) produced in Italy, from a workshop in Campania, it shows the influence of Arab motifs and glazing technique.

The dating of the circular **Caracciolo di Vico Chapel** is the subject of debate. Usually given as 1517, with the sculptural decor complete by 1557, the design (often attributed to Tommaso Malvito) may go back to 1499 and thus precede the much more famous Tempietto in Rome, by Bramante, which it so resembles. Other artworks of note in the church are an impressively restored *Crucifixion* by Giorgio Vasari, some brightly colored frescoes by an anonymous 16th-century master, and an intriguing sculpture of a knight taking a nap in his armor. **■TIP→ Because this great church is off the path of tour groups, you can absorb the ordered beauty of the decoration in peace.** ✉ *Via San Giovanni a Carbonara 5, Decumano Maggiore* ☎ *081/295873* ⏲ *Mon.–Sat. 9:30–1* Ⓜ *Piazza Cavour.*

6

WORTH NOTING

Porta Capuana. Its elegance heightened by the spruced-up pedestrianized piazza on which it stands, this great ceremonial gateway is one of Naples's finest landmarks of the Renaissance era. Ferdinand II of Aragon commissioned the Florentine sculptor and architect Giuliano da Maiano to build this white triumphal arch—perhaps in competition with the Arco di Trionfo found on the facade of the city's Castel Nuovo—in the late 15th century. As at Castel Nuovo, this arch is framed by two peperino stone towers, here nicknamed Honor and Virtue, while the statue of Saint Gennaro keeps watch against Mount Vesuvius in the distance. Across Via Carbonara stands the medieval bulk of the **Castel Capuano,** once home to Angevin and Aragonese rulers until it was transformed in 1540 by the Spanish viceroy into law courts, a function it still fulfills today. **■TIP→ On Sunday this is a meeting place for Naples's extracommunitari (immigrants), who chat in their native tongues—from Ukrainian and Polish to Twi and Igbo.** ✉ *Piazza San Francesco, Carlo III.*

Santa Caterina a Formiello. After a complete makeover in 2008, this church is eminently visitable, the full explanations of its paintings and sculptures on display worthy of a good museum. The Formiello in the name refers to the *formali,* the nearby underground aqueduct, which, history relates, the Aragonese also used to capture the town from beneath. The church facade in dark piperno stone was designed for the Dominicans by the Tuscan architect Romolo Balsimelli, a student of Brunelleschi.

The side chapels are as interesting for their relics as for their art. In the **Orsini Chapel,** on the left, are the elaborately framed remains of St. Helodorus and other Dominican saints, while the fourth chapel displays some 20 skulls of the martyrs of Otranto, brought to Naples by King Alfonso in 1490. The event referred to is the Ottoman sack of Otranto in 1480, when 813 Christians were executed for refusing to renounce their faith. (More martyrs' skulls occupy a much larger cabinet in Otranto's cathedral.) Depicted in the rather surrealistic altar painting is the headless Antonio Primaldo, whose body, through the strength of faith, stands upright to confound his Ottoman executioner.

In the fifth chapel a cycle of paintings by Giacomo del Po depicts the life and afterlife of St. Catherine, while in the vault Luigi Garzi depicts the same saint in glory. Up in the faded dome painted by Paolo di Mattei, Catherine, together with the Madonna, implores the Trinity to watch over the city. Below are the tombs of the Spinelli family, feudal loyalty to the Aragonese cause being rewarded by something of a family Pantheon. The sumptuous altar is by Lorenzo Fontana. ✉ *Via Carbonara, Decumano Maggiore* ☎ *081292316* 🌐 *www.portacapuana.info* ⏲ *Mon.–Sat. 8.30–1, Sun. Mass at 11* Ⓜ *Piazza Garibaldi.*

LA SANITÀ, CAPODIMONTE, AND NEARBY

The Parco di Capodimonte is the crowning point of the vast mountainous plain that slopes down through the city to the waterfront area. Nearly 5 km (3 miles) removed from the madding crowds in the *centro storico,* it is enjoyed by locals and visitors alike as a favored escape from the overheated city center. With picture-perfect views over the entire city and bay, the park was first founded in the 18th century as a hunting preserve by Charles of Bourbon. Before long, partly to house the famous Farnese collection that he had inherited from his mother, he commissioned a spectacular Palazzo Reale for the park. Today this palace is the Museo di Capodimonte, which contains among its treasures the city's greatest collection of old-master paintings. If you're feeling intrepid—and not carrying anything of value—you might like to deviate into La Sanità, one of Naples's most densely populated and uncomfortably lawless neighborhoods, still studded with legendary palaces and gilded churches. Alternatively, avoid the hassle at street level by taking a fascinating tour with Napoli Sotterranea (🌐 *www.napolisotterranea.org*) to the Cimitero delle Fontanelle.

TOP ATTRACTIONS

Museo di Capodimonte. The grandiose 18th-century Neoclassical Bourbon royal palace houses fine and decorative art. Capodimonte's greatest treasure is the excellent collection of paintings well displayed in the **Galleria Nazionale,** on the palace's first and second floors. Aside from the artworks, part of the royal apartments still has a complement of beautiful antique furniture (most of it on the splashy scale so dear to the Bourbons), and a staggering range of porcelain and majolica from the various royal residences. Most rooms have fairly comprehensive information cards in English, whereas the audio guide is overly selective and somewhat quirky. The main galleries on the first floor are devoted to

The Salone della Meridiana, on the top floor of the Museo Archeologico, is one of the largest rooms in Europe.

work from the 13th to the 18th century, including many pieces by Dutch and Spanish masters. On the second floor look for stunning paintings by Simone Martini (circa 1284–1344), Titian (1488/90–1576), and Caravaggio (1573–1610). The palace is in the vast Bosco di Capodimonte (Capodimonte Park), which served as the royal hunting preserve and later as the site of the Capodimonte porcelain works. ✉ *Via Miano 2, Porta Piccola, Via Capodimonte, Capodimonte* ☎ *199/199100 for information and tickets for special exhibitions, 081/7499111* 🌐 *www.polomusealenapoli.beniculturali.it* 🎫 *€7.50* ⏲ *Thurs.–Tues. 8:30–7:30; ticket office closes at 6:30.*

WORTH NOTING

Basilica Santa Maria della Sanità. Dominican friars commissioned this baroque, Greek cross–shape basilica, replete with majolica-tile dome, in the early 17th century. The church contains a small museum of the era's Counter-Reformation art—the most flagrantly devotional school of Catholic art—and includes no less than five Luca Giordano altarpieces. Elsewhere, the richly decorated elevated presbytery, complete with double staircase, provides the only note of color in the gray-and-white decoration. **■ TIP→ This provides access to the noted Catacomba di San Gaudioso.** ✉ *Via della Sanità 124, Sanità* ☎ *081/5441305* 🌐 *www.catacombedinapoli.it* ⏲ *Weekdays 9:30–1, Sat. 9:30–1 and 5–7, Sun. 9:30–1:30.*

Catacomba di San Gennaro. These catacombs—designed for Christian burial rather than as refuges—date back at least as far as the 2nd century AD. This was where St. Gennaro's body was brought from Pozzuoli in the 4th century, after which the catacombs became a key pilgrimage center. The 45-minute guided tour of the two-level site takes you down a series of vestibules with frescoed niche tombs. Looming over the site is the imposing bulk of the early-20th-century Madre del Buon Consiglio Church, whose form was apparently inspired by St. Peter's in Rome. **■TIP→ Under the general site name of Catacombe di Napoli these catacombs are now linked ticket wise with the Catacombs of St. Gaudioso, in the Sanità district.** ✉ *Via Capodimonte 13, next to Madonna del Buon Consiglio church, Capodimonte* ☎ *0817443714* 🌐 *www.catacombedinapoli.it* 🎫 *€8, includes visit to Catacomba di San Gaudioso* ⏲ *Guided tours Mon.–Sat. 10–5, Sun. 10–1.*

Palazzo dello Spagnolo. Built in 1738 for the Neapolitan aristocrat Marchese Moscati, this palazzo is famed for its external "hawk-winged staircase," believed to follow the design of star architect Ferdinando Sanfelice and decorated with sumptuous stucco and a bust and panel at the top of each flight. The palace was at one point owned by a Spanish nobleman, Don Tommas Atienza, thus the name "dello Spagnolo." In the left corner of the courtyard in the back, a nondescript metal door leads to a tunnel running all the way to Piazza Carlo III—another example of the Neapolitan underground. The palace was recently immortalized in *Passione,* John Turturro's excellent film about Naples and music, each distinctive green archway filled with a nubile Neapolitan beauty gyrating to *"Come facette mammeta"* (loosely translated as "How my mother made me"). ✉ *Via Vergini 19, Sanità* ⏲ *Daily 7–7.*

NEED A BREAK?

Pasticceria dei Vergini. On teeming Via dei Vergini, give in to temptation and try one of this pastry shop's bursting-with-calories Neapolitan specialties. ✉ ***Via dei Vergini 66, Vergini*** ☎ ***081/455989.***

WHERE TO EAT

Updated by Fiorella Squillante

Let's be honest: You really want a traditional Neapolitan dinner against the backdrop of Vesuvius with a great show of Neapolitan love songs to get you crying into your limoncello liqueur. There's no reason to feel guilty, because even the natives love to get into the spirit. But listening to someone warble "Santa Lucia" while feasting on a pizza *Margherita* from a table overlooking the bay is just one example of the pleasures awaiting diners in Naples.

As the birthplace of pizza, Naples prides itself on its vast selection of pizzerias, the most famous of which—Da Michele (where Julia Roberts filmed her pizza scene in *Eat Pray Love*) or Sorbillo—deserve the encomium "incomparable." Many Neapolitans make lunch their big meal of the day, and then have a pizza for supper.

DINING NEIGHBORHOODS

Appropriately, the monumental city center—the area around **Piazza Municipio and Toledo**—contains Naples's most iconic restaurants. Nearby **Spaccanapoli** is now one of *the* evening locations where *buona cucina* (good food) meets low- and high-brow culture after 9 pm. The upscale area of **Chiaia** is a favorite with locals and discerning expatriates and will likely offer better value. If you are looking for an international cuisine,

CLOSE UP

Neapolitan Classic Cuisine

The city expresses its gastronomic self in many ways. Those in search of nouvelle flights of fantasy served on designer plates should look elsewhere. Although these can be found, the cuisine in Naples is by and large earthy, pungent, and *buonissima*, as attested to by those signature dishes: *mozzarella in carrozza* (mozzarella cheese fried in a "carriage" of two slices of bread); *polpo alla luciana* (octopus stewed with garlic, chili peppers, and tomatoes); *risotto ai frutti di mare* (seafood risotto); and *spaghetti alla puttanesca* (streetwalker's spaghetti with black olives and capers in sea salt). In Naples it is still the old reliables that apply—the recipes time-tested by centuries of mammas who still manage to put meat on your bones and smiles on your faces. When it comes to *i secondi* (main dishes), you won't be disappointed by the *salsicce* (pork sausages), but the reason visitors to Naples want to eat seafood is a good one: geography. As for seafood Neapolitan style, the best—*spigola* (sea bass), *pesce spada* (swordfish), and, if you can find it, *San Pietro* (sort of a sole for grown-ups)—is grilled simply and ennobled with a splash of olive oil and a squeeze of lemon. When it's not on the menu—and many top delicacies are only available if you ask the waiter—go for the *pezzogna* (blue-spotted bream), as you can be almost sure it hasn't been fish-farmed. Fresh calamari, kissed lightly by a grill, can be exquisitely delicate, but the fried version, which can be uniquely satisfying, is, alas, too often done these days with frozen squid.

Should you stumble across such breaks with tradition, you can always console yourself with a creamy, wonderful pastry. On the whole, Neapolitan pastry tends to suffer from the excesses that mark most southern Italian desserts, but the Neapolitan tradition is an old and venerable one, and the most classic local invention in matters of *pasticceria* (pastry making), the *sfogliatella*, is a true baroque masterpiece, with puff pastry cut on a bias and wrapped around a nugget of sugar ricotta to form a simple but intricate shell. These are best eaten hot.

there are many choices along tiny Via Bausan, off the Riviera di Chiaia. **Santa Lucia** is a classic choice for its chic and touristy fish restaurants with that just-how-you-imagined-Naples sea view. The ritzy bay-side suburbs of **Mergellina** and **Posillipo** host some of the Naples area's most popular restaurants. Several occupy space on secluded waterfront culs-de-sac, so unless you have your own wheels, taking a taxi will be the most convenient option. Atop a hill, the wealthy and residential **Vomero** doesn't seem like a place to dine, but if you've been shopping on Via Scarlatti or taking in the Castel Sant'Elmo, this isn't a bad place to grab a nontouristy bite. The **Piazza Garibaldi** area is known for fine no-nonsense eating, mostly from traditional restaurants offering excellent value for the money. If returning to your base after dark, stick to well-lighted main roads or ask a restaurant staffer to order a taxi.

Use the coordinate (⊕ B2) at the end of each review to locate a property on the Where to Eat and Stay in Naples map.

CLOSE UP

Neapolitan Folk Songs at Your Table

If you want to hear *canzoni napoletane*—the fabled Neapolitan folk songs—performed live, you can try to catch the city's top troupes, such as the Cantori di Posillipo and I Virtuosi di San Martino, in performances at venues like the Teatro Trianon or the Teatro Sannazzaro. But an easier alternative is to head for one of the city's traditional restaurants, such as La Bersagliera or Mimì alla Ferrovia, where most every night you can expect your meal to be interrupted by a *posteggiatore*. These singers aren't employed by the restaurants, but they're encouraged to come in, swan around the tables with a battered old guitar, and belt out classics such as "Santa Lucia," "O' Surdato Innamurato," "Torna a Surriento," and, inevitably, "Funiculì Funiculà."

These songs are the most famous of a vast repertoire that found international fame with the mass exodus of southern Italians to the United States in the early 20th century. "Funiculì Funiculà" was written by Peppino Turco and Luigi Denza in 1880 to herald the new funicular railway up Vesuvius. "O Sole Mio," by Giovanni Capurro and Eduardo di Capua, has often been mistakenly taken for the Italian national anthem. "Torna a Surriento" was composed by Ernesto de Curtis in 1903 to help remind the Italian prime minister how wonderful he thought Sorrento was (and how many government subsidies he had promised the township).

The singers are more than happy to do requests, even inserting the name of your *innamorato* or *innamorata* into the song. When they've finished they'll stand discreetly by your table. Give them a few euros and you'll have friends for life (or at least for the night).

PIAZZA MUNICIPIO/TOLEDO

$ SOUTHERN ITALIAN — **7 Soldi.** Just off Via Toledo, this simple restaurant with outside tables in summer serves good pizza and other southern Italian favorites. Try the *gamberoni alla Posillipo* (prawns in a seafood sauce made with cherry tomatoes) or the *Pignatiello di mare* (octopus, calamari, prawns, and other seafood on fried bread), and you'll be happy for the rest of the day. $ *Average main: €11 ✉ Vico Tre Re a Toledo 6, Toledo ☎ 081/418727 ⊕ D4.*

$ PIZZA — **Brandi.** Forget that this historic place gave the world *pizza Margherita*—the classic combo of tomato sauce, mozzarella, and basil, named after King Umberto's queen. This is, hands down, one of the most picturesque restaurants in Italy. Set on a cobblestone alleyway just off chic Via Chiaia, it welcomes you with an enchanting wood-beam salon festooned with 19th-century memorabilia, saint shrines, gilded mirrors, and bouquets of flowers, beyond which you can see the kitchen and the *pizzaioli* (pizza makers) at work. That's the good news. Unfortunately, most of Naples stays away, considering the pizzas are far, far better elsewhere. But there's no denying the decor is *delizioso* and if tourists like Chelsea Clinton, Bill Murray, and Gerard Depardieu have dined here, why not you? $ *Average main: €13 ✉ Salita Sant'Anna di Palazzo 1, Toledo ☎ 081/416928 ⊙ Closed Mon. ⊕ D4.*

$$ NEAPOLITAN **Ciro a Santa Brigida.** Just off Via Toledo, Ciro has been an obligatory entry on any list of Neapolitan cooking (as opposed to cuisine) since 1932, when Toscanini and Pirandello used to eat here. Popular with business travelers, artists, and journalists, Ciro is famous for a variety of favorites, with an emphasis on rustic food, from very fine pizzas and justly famed versions of pasta *e fagioli* to the classic *sartù*—rice loaf first concocted by baroque-era nuns—and the splendid *pignatiello e vavella,* shellfish soup. The menu, which includes gluten-free items, looks too large for all its items to be good, but the owners must be doing something right, as the place is often packed with Neapolitan regulars. **TIP→ The old waiters are darling wherever you sit, but try to get a table upstairs, which has a more pleasant atmosphere.** *Average main: €17 Via Santa Brigida 71, Toledo 081/5524072 www.ciroasantabrigida.it Closed Sun. Oct.–Jan. D4.*

$ NEAPOLITAN **Gay-Odin.** Chocolate lovers will be relieved to know that Gay-Odin, Naples's most famous *cioccolateria,* has seven stores around town, all recognizable by their inviting dark-wood Art Nouveau decor; try the signature chocolate forest cake (*foresta*) or the unusual "naked" chocolates (*nudi*), a suave mixture of chestnuts and walnuts, some with a whole coffee bean wrapped in the center. *Average main: €3 Via Toledo 214, Toledo 081/400063 www.gay-odin.it D4.*

$ SOUTHERN ITALIAN **Il Cuoco Galante.** This multimenu restaurant serves a good choice of traditional Neapolitan dishes, including vegetarian and dietetic options (although starting a diet in Naples is beyond foolhardy!). The small room is nicely designed, perfect for a light lunch or a relaxing supper. Don't be in a hurry, though, because this is not a fast-food place. Take your time and watch the cook at work in the kitchen. Among the specialties he whips up are *millefoglie di vitello con verdurine croccanti* (thin layers of veal meat with crispy vegetables) and sea bass with zucchini. *Average main: €12 Via Broggia 12, Toledo 081/0664058 www.cuocogalante.it Closed Sun. and 2 wks in Aug. No dinner Mon., Tues., Sat. E1.*

$ NEAPOLITAN **La Sfogliatella Mary.** This excellent bakery at the Via Toledo entrance to the Galleria Umberto crafts a broader array of delicacies than the name (for puff pastries) suggests. *Average main: €1 Galleria Umberto 66, Toledo 081/402218 No credit cards D4.*

$ NEAPOLITAN **L.U.I.S.E.** At this perfect place for a lunchtime snack, you point to what you want in the tempting glass counter, and pay for it at the cash desk. Among the specialties are the usual *frittura* (fried dough balls and potato croquets stuffed with mozzarella), tangy cheese pies (*sfoglino al formaggio*), pizza *scarola* (an escarole pie with black olives), and slices of omelets stuffed with spinach, peppers, or onions. **TIP→ If you can't find a seat, you can stand against the wall, as some customers do, or just get your order to go and have your meal outside.** *Average main: €3 Via Toledo 266–269, Toledo 081/415367 No credit cards D4.*

$ NEAPOLITAN **Pintauro.** The classic address for *sfogliatelle* (puff pastries) is Pintauro, which rarely disappoints. *Average main: €1 Via Toledo 275, Toledo 081/417339 No credit cards D4.*

6

$ NEAPOLITAN **Tandem.** Come here to taste traditional Neapolitan *ragù*, a meat-based sauce generally served with pasta and prepared from cuts of beef and pork. At Tandem, opened in 2013 by a young actress—which explains the hilarious ragù videos that sometimes play on the screens here—local cervellatine sausages are included in the sauce. The young and enthusiastic staff keeps the mood lighthearted and fun. If you're game, the waiter will bring you a little bowl of ragù and start a stopwatch—you pay just €1 for every minute spent eating. **TIP→ Enjoy your ragù with ziti spezzati (broken ziti pasta) and Parmesan cheese, mop the sauce up with the celestial Neapolitan rustic bread, and forget about time!** *Average main: €8 Via Paladino 51, Toledo 081/19002468 No credit cards F2.*

$ NEAPOLITAN Fodor's Choice ★ **Trattoria San Ferdinando.** This cheerful trattoria seems to be run for the sheer pleasure of it. Try the excellent fish or the traditional (but cooked with a lighter modern touch) pasta dishes, especially those with *verdura* (fresh leaf vegetables) or with potatoes and smoked mozzarella (*pasta e patate con la provola*). Close to Teatro San Carlo and aptly decorated with playbills and theatrical memorabilia, both ancient and modern, this is an excellent place to stop after a visit to the opera. **TIP→ Look for the entrance almost immediately on the right as you go up Via Nardones from Piazza Trieste e Trento—ring the bell outside to be let in.** *Average main: €12 Via Nardones 117, Toledo 081/421964 Closed Sun., Mon., and last 3 wks of Aug. No dinner Sat., Tues. D4.*

SPACCANAPOLI

$ NEAPOLITAN **Cioccolateria Perzechella.** Cioccolateria Perzechella looks set to challenge Gay-Odin's supremacy in the chocolate world. How can it not, because owners Pina and Giulia have rather shamelessly devised the *Tre Re* ("three kings")—three hazelnuts stuck together with chocolate in honor of King Ferdinand II, revolutionary Masaniello, and Naples's unofficial saint, the soccer player Diego Maradona. They just may tip the scales in their favor with the *Torna a Surriento*—Sorrento orange peel dipped in dark chocolate. *Average main: €3 Vico Pallonetto a S. Chiara 36, Spaccanapoli 081/5510025 F2.*

$ PIZZA **Friggitoria Pizzeria Giuliano.** A favorite haunt of students from the adjacent school of architecture, Giuliano has an old-style glass cabinet in which are kept *arancini* (balls of fried rice) the size of tennis balls, and deep-fried pizzas filled with mozzarella, tomato, prosciutto, or ricotta, that can fill that yawning void in your stomach—even if you have to sit down on the steps in the square afterward to recover. *Average main: €3 Calata Trinità Maggiore 31–33, Spaccanapoli 081/5510906 No credit cards E3.*

$ NEAPOLITAN **Gallucci.** A small alleyway leading off the side of the Gesù Nuovo toward Via Toledo hides a little-known jewel that is worth the detour: Gallucci, founded in 1890, specializes in fruit-filled chocolates (the cherry and grape are memorable) and also produces a delightfully original local cult item, chestnuts filled with marsala. It also produces the most fantastically packaged Easter eggs, all with huge silver or gold bows, that you are ever likely to see. *Average main: €5 Via Cisterna dell'Olio 6, Spaccanapoli 081/5513148 E3.*

Sfogliatelle are a classic Neapolitan pastry, a multilayered wonder best enjoyed while hot.

$ PIZZA **Gino Sorbillo.** There are three restaurants called Sorbillo along Via dei Tribunali; this is the one with the crowds waiting outside. Order the same thing the locals come for: a basic Neapolitan pizza (try the unique pizza al pesto or the stunningly simple marinara—just tomatoes and oregano). They're cooked to perfection by the third generation of pie makers who run the place. The pizzas are enormous, flopping over the edge of the plate onto the white marble tabletops. *Average main: €6 Via dei Tribunali 32, Spaccanapoli 081/446643 Closed Sun. (except Dec.) and 3 wks in Aug. E2.*

$ CAFÉ **Gran Caffè Neapolis.** For a fine coffee in the heart of historic Spaccanapoli, visit Gran Caffè Neapolis and sit out on the Piazza San Domenico or inside in the modern tearoom. *Average main: €3 Piazza San Domenico Maggiore 14/15, Spaccanapoli 081/6584536 Reservations not accepted E2.*

$ PIZZA **I Decumani.** Every pizzeria along Via dei Tribunali is worth the long wait (all the good ones are jam-packed) but none more so than the Decumani, thanks to the superlative *pizzaioli* (pizza makers)—say hello to Gianni and Enzo for us—at work here. They turn out a wide array of pizzas and do them all to perfection. If you aren't on a diet, try the *frittura* and you'll be pleasantly surprised with this mix of Neapolitan-style tempura: zucchini, eggplants, rice-balls, and many other delicacies. *Average main: €6 Via dei Tribunali 58, Spaccanapoli 081/5571309 Closed Mon. (except Dec.) E2.*

$$ SOUTHERN ITALIAN **La Stanza del Gusto.** This restaurant's name translates roughly to "room of taste," but the tastes here are many and extend from the traditional to the gourmet to the ultramodern. Start with the *antipasto di pesce* (seafood appetizer), experience the glory that is Naples in

the *gattò delle due Sicilie* (cake of the two Sicilies; Sicilian eggplant with a cheese fondue and a pesto mustard), or bow to contemporary sensibilities with the *menu vegetariano km zero* (all local vegetables of the season). With its recycled chairs and tables and vintage-style ads outside, this place exhibits a strong but pleasing personality. The cheese-and-wine parlor downstairs has an easygoing ambience, while the room upstairs is more of a slow-food den. *Average main: €17 ✉ Via S. Maria di Costantinopoli 100, Spaccanapoli ☎ 081/401578 🌐 www.lastanzadelgusto.com ⏲ Closed Sun, no lunch Mon. ✥ E2.*

$ NEAPOLITAN **La Campagnola.** This well-known trattoria–wineshop sees everyone from foodies to students and professors from the nearby university. The menu changes daily and there is always a good selection of pastas, meat, fish, and vegetable side dishes. Go for a plate of *pasta e fagioli* or octopus salad and fried anchovies with a carafe of a good local wine. *Average main: €9 ✉ Via Tribunali 47, Spaccanapoli ☎ 081/459034 ⏲ Closed Tues. ✥ E2.*

$ NEAPOLITAN **La Cantina di Via Sapienza.** With a balanced array of mainly land-based cuisine, owner-manager Gaetano attracts students and young professionals to this unpretentious eatery—mainly regulars from the school of medicine around the corner. It's busy and not big enough (expect to share a table—and if your fellow diners are not shy, why should you be?), but the prices can't be beat, and the daily selection of a good dozen vegetable side plates merits a detour of its own, even if you're not a vegetarian. *Average main: €9 ✉ Via Sapienza 40, Spaccanapoli ☎ 081/459078 ▭ No credit cards ⏲ Closed Sun. and Aug. No dinner ✥ E2.*

$ NEAPOLITAN **La Vecchia Cantina.** On a rather dark side street in the scruffier section of Spaccanapoli, this place is well worth seeking out for its combination of old-style Neapolitan hospitality and attention to the quality of its food and wine. The place is run as a family affair, much like a typical Neapolitan household. An accumulation of kitsch decorations completes the feeling, and everyone who comes here seems to know each other. The pasta with chickpeas is a must, and *baccalà fritto* (fried salt cod) is a specialty. Backed up with a selection of wines from all over Italy, this place is a great value. *Average main: €11 ✉ Via S. Nicola alla Carità 13–14, Spaccanapoli ☎ 081/5520226 ⏲ No dinner Sun. ✥ E3.*

$ NEAPOLITAN **Le Sorelle Bandiera.** For a mere €8 you can eat in the presence, if not of the original Pizza Queen, then at least that of her bust: Margherita no less, also honored in this restaurant by a wood-fired oven set in the tufa stone below. This is how pizza was supposed to be, though the restaurant has renamed it "geo-thermal." To bolster the sense of authenticity, the tables are set with the majolica tiling unearthed during the excavation of the historic San Paolo convent below. In short, this is a restaurant that doubles as a museum, or vice versa. ■ **TIP→ Le Sorelle is in the running for the best-tasting Margherita around, and at a price considerably lower than that of many imitations.** *Average main: €8 ✉ Vico Cinquesanti 33, Spaccanapoli ✥ F2.*

Continued on page 288

AN APPETITE FOR NAPLES

"But there's nothing to it!" cry food snobs when Neapolitan cuisine is mentioned among the higher rungs of the world's culinary ladder. And they might be right—after all, there are no secret spices or special skills needed in its preparation.

The best fresh ingredients are all you need when the local produce is this good

But indeed, simplicity is the key, and the best fresh ingredients are what Napoli has in spades. Long, fleshy, deep-red San Marzano tomatoes grow on the fertile slopes of Vesuvius. The olive groves of the Cilento provide fragrant oil. Buffalo chew the grass on the plains toward Caserta, north of Naples, producing milk that makes the best mozzarella cheese in the world. And Neapolitans have long used the fish-filled waters of the bay to their gastronomic advantage. Tiny fish are marinated, fried, and eaten whole, or used to flavor sauces. Swordfish are sliced up to make steaks. Clams, mussels, and octopus are ubiquitous, and usually enhanced with oil, lemon juice, garlic, and parsley, rather than masked with sauces.

With it all being so simple, you'd think you could replicate it at home. But it's never quite the same: perhaps it's that the water is different, or that you can never quite get the right variety of tomato. Or maybe it doesn't taste the same simply because you're not in Napoli anymore.

Classic Neapolitan dishes featuring the best of the sea and the field.

PIZZA: THE CLASSIC MARGHERITA

Locally grown San Marzano tomatoes are a must.

The best pizza should come out with cheese bubbling and be ever-so-slightly charred around its edges.

Only buffalo-milk mozzarella or fior di latte cheese should be used.

The dough must be made from the right kind of durum wheat flour and be left to rise for at least six hours.

Be prepared: ranging from the size of a plate to that of a Hummer wheel, Neapolitan pizza is different from anything you might find elsewhere in Italy—not to mention what's served up at American pizza chains. The "purest" form is the marinara, topped with only tomatoes, garlic, oregano, and olive oil.

OTHER FAVORITES ARE . . .

- **CAPRICCIOSA** (the "capricious"), made with whatever the chef has on hand.
- **SICILIANA** with mozzarella and eggplant.
- **DIAVOLA** with spicy salami.
- **QUATTRO STAGIONI** ("four seasons"), made with produce from each one.
- **SALSICCIA E FRIARIELLI** with sausage and a broccoli-like vegetable.

A PIZZA FIT FOR A QUEEN

During the patriotic fervor following Italian unification in the late 19th century, a Neapolitan chef decided to celebrate the arrival in the city of the new Italian queen Margherita by designing a pizza in her—and the country's—honor. He took red tomatoes, white mozzarella cheese, and a few leaves of fresh green basil—reflecting the three colors of the Italian flag—and gave birth to the modern pizza industry.

ONLY THE BEST

An association of Neapolitan pizza chefs has standardized the ingredients and methods that have to be used to make pizza certified DOC (*denominazione d'origine controllata*) or STG (*specialità tradizionale garantita*). See the illustration on the opposite page for the basic requirements.

FIRED UP!

The Neapolitan pizza must be made in a traditional wood-burning oven. Chunks of beech or maple are stacked up against the sides of the huge, tiled ovens, then shoved onto the slate base of the oven, where they burn quickly at high temperatures. If you visit Pompeii, you will see how similar the old Roman bread-baking ovens are to the modern pizza oven. The *pizzaiolo* (pizza chef) then uses a long wooden paddle to put the pizza into the oven, where it cooks quickly.

PIZZERIE

Hundreds of restaurants specialize in pizza in Naples, and the best of these make pizza and nothing else. As befits the original fast food, *pizzerie* tend to be simple, fairly basic places, with limited menu choices, and quick, occasionally brusque service.

THE REAL THING

Naples takes its contribution to world cuisine seriously. The Associazione Verace Pizza Napoletana (www.pizzanapoletana.org) was founded in 1984 in order to share expertise, maintain quality levels, and provide courses for aspiring pizza chefs and pizza lovers. The group also organizes the annual Pizzafest—three days in September dedicated to the consumption of pizza, when *maestri* from all over the region get together and cook off.

Margherita of Savoy

Buffalo-milk mozzarella

A pizzaiolo at work

Typical pizzeria in Naples

Simple, fresh toppings

REMEMBRANCE OF THINGS PASTA . . .

Studded with clams, spaghetti con vongole is a top menu favorite.

The most famous of Neapolitan foods can be eaten standing up, but there's more to local cuisine than pizza. Don't leave Naples without sitting down to a few of these Napoli classics.

HOW SIMPLE IS NEAPOLITAN CUISINE?

Take a handful of tomatoes and squeeze them into a pan along with a drizzle of olive oil, a pinch of salt, and some fresh basil leaves. Leave them in just long enough to warm through. Boil some pasta for just as long as it needs. Put it all together, and you have pasta al pomodoro fresco, one of the most delicious dishes Italy has to offer. There really is nothing to it!

- **SPAGHETTI CON LE VONGOLE:** spaghetti topped with different kinds of clams, from the tiny lupini to the big red fasullari, still in their shells.
- **IMPEPATA DI COZZE:** mussels, thrown in a pot, heated up, and served with lots of fresh black pepper.
- **BACCALÀ:** dried salt cod, fried and served with some fresh herbs. Once you try it, you'll understand why many Neapolitans regard it as the authentic taste of home.
- **POLPETTINE AL RAGÙ:** meatballs in tomato sauce. Italian food's biggest export has never tasted as good as in Napoli.
- **PESCE ALL'ACQUA PAZZA:** fish in "crazy water," with garlic, a few small tomatoes, then some of the water from the fish added to the hot oil. The bubbles are what make it "crazy."
- **PARMIGIANA DI MELANZANE:** layers of eggplant, mozzarella, and tomato sauce baked in the oven.
- **PASTA ALLA GENOVESE:** not from Genoa, as its name might suggest, but, some claim, invented by a Neapolitan chef named Genovese. Beef and onions are slow-cooked for hours and then folded into the pasta.

"POOR FOOD"

During the winter when the best fresh produce isn't so abundant, Neapolitans head for the store cupboard and soak large quantities of dried cannellini beans, chickpeas, and lentils. These are then made into hearty soups, to which any kind of pasta can be added. They're great as filling and warm dishes, but because *pasta e fagioli*, *pasta e ceci*, and *pasta e lenticchie* are regarded as "poor food" (the kind of thing you make at home), they aren't often found on restaurant menus.

LA FRITTURA

Forget all that stuff about the Mediterranean diet being so healthy. Lots of pizzerie and roadside stalls will offer you a selection of *frittura*—deep-fried balls of dough and seaweed, fried sliced eggplant, fried potato croquettes, fried zucchini flowers. Eat them with your fingers, and don't feel guilty.

CAKE SEASON

Like everything else, cakes are seasonal. If you're visiting over Christmas, check out the teeth-challenging *rococò*, made of hazelnuts, or the softer *struffoli*, tiny balls of fried pastry doused in honey. Carnival time (mid-February to mid-March) is for *chiacchiere*—large, flat slices of light pastry sprinkled with icing sugar—while Easter sees rivalries for the best *pastiera*, a rich cake filled with ricotta, sifted grain, and orange or rose water. Around All Souls' Day (late October), cake shops fill up with *torrone* (soft or hard nougat). Two Napoli classics are, thankfully, available year-round: the large soft sponge *babà*, soaked in rum, and the *sfogliatella*, sweet and spicy ricotta cheese wrapped in short crust or puff pastry.

LIMONCELLO

No serious meal is complete without a final *liquore*, and the local limoncello is the best of the lot. Made from the zest of lemons, lots of sugar, and pure alcohol, limoncello is very sweet, very strong, and must be served very cold.

O' CAFÈ

Whether to help you digest a big meal, give you a morning pickup, or accompany a cake, *o' cafè* (to give coffee its name in the local dialect) is a Neapolitan rite. You can have it in its pure state, small and black with a teaspoonful of sugar, or order *nocciola* (with hazelnut syrup), *macchiato* (with a dash of frothy milk), or *corretto* (with a shot of liqueur) varieties. If you want to keep to local customs, never ask for a cappuccino after a meal. It's considered bad for digestion.

Baccalà alla vicentina, a traditional Italian codfish stew

Fried zucchini flowers

Divine pies and pasteria

Many brands of limoncello

O' Cafè

$ PIZZA ✕ **Lombardi a Santa Chiara.** Opposite the Palazzo Croce, home to the philosopher and historian Benedetto Croce, this is one of the city's most famous pizzerias, packed night after night. The young crowd heads down into the more boisterous basement, while the atmosphere upstairs is calmer and more congenial to conversation at standard decibel levels. On the ground floor you can watch the *pizzaioli* working the pizza dough, manipulating each pie as if it were a live creation. ■ **TIP→ In summer there are tables outside on the pedestrian zone.** $ *Average main: €7* ✉ *Via Benedetto Croce 59, Spaccanapoli* ☎ *081/5520780* ✣ *E2.*

WORD OF MOUTH

"Sorbillo has the best pizza ever as far as I am concerned. I went to Naples just to eat here again. Da Michele is also a classic, only two choices, pizza marinara or Margherita. But I give the edge to Sorbillo. I loved the mushroom pizza!"
—kellyee21

$ ITALIAN ✕ **Osteria da Carmela.** Conveniently close to the archaeological museum, yet surprisingly off the tourist beat, this small eatery is patronized by *professori* from the nearby Academy of Fine Arts and theatergoers from the Teatro Bellini next door. A specialty here is the blend of seafood with vegetables—try the *tubettoni con cozze e zucchini* (tube-shaped pasta with mussels and zucchini) or *paccheri al baccalà* (large pasta with codfish). If you prefer meat, try the *brasato alla Genovese* (onion and meat sauce). The service at Osteria is both swift and obliging. $ *Average main: €11* ✉ *Via Conte di Ruvo 11–12, Spaccanapoli* ☎ *081/5499738* ⊙ *Closed Sun.* ✣ *E2.*

$$$ NEAPOLITAN ✕ **Palazzo Petrucci.** In a 17th-century mansion facing the grand Piazza San Domenico Maggiore, Palazzo Petrucci doesn't lack for dramatic dining options—under the vaulted ceiling of the former stables, in the gallery where a glass partition reveals the kitchen, or in the cozy room overlooking the piazza. Fortify yourself with a complimentary glass of Prosecco before agonizing between the à la carte offerings and the menu *degustazione* (€55). A popular starter is mille-feuille of local mozzarella with raw prawns and vegetable sauce. The *paccheri all'impiedi* (large tube pasta served standing on end) in a rich ricotta-and-meat sauce is an interesting twist on an old regional favorite. The interior is elegantly minimal; the culinary delights are anything but. $ *Average main: €25* ✉ *Piazza San Domenico Maggiore 4, Spaccanapoli* ☎ *081/5524068* 🌐 *www.palazzopetrucci.it* ✍ *Reservations essential* ⊙ *Closed 2 wks in Aug. No dinner Sun., no lunch Mon.* ✣ *E2.*

$ NEAPOLITAN ✕ **Ristorante Bellini.** Worth visiting just to observe the waiters, who all seem to have just stepped off the stage of a Neapolitan comedy at the nearby Teatro Bellini, this spot claims a proud perch on the corner of the chicly bohemian Piazza Bellini. But if the neighborhood remains suave, this staple Neapolitan restaurant proudly retains its old-world feel. Good bets here include a fine (if rather small) pizza, and classic fish dishes such as linguine *al cartoccio* (baked in paper) or *all'astice* (a type of small lobster). Go up the narrow stairs to get to the spacious upper rooms, or squeeze in at one of the pavement tables in summer. $ *Average main: €13* ✉ *Via Santa Maria di Costantinopoli 79, Spaccanapoli* ☎ *081/459774* ⊙ *Closed Sun. June–Sept. and 1 wk in Aug.* ✣ *E2.*

CLOSE UP

Naples is for Coffee Lovers

Espresso was invented here and is still considered by the Neapolitans to be an essential and priceless part of their cultural patrimony (the word *espresso,* by the way, should probably be understood here in its meaning "pressed out," rather than the more common interpretation of "quick"). Even Italian bars (meaning coffee bars) are generally tied to a coffee roaster–distributor, as English pubs once were with brewers. The sponsoring brand is indicated with a sign on the outside, so you can choose your bar by looking for the sign of your favorite brand. Brands tend to be highly regional; the most widely advertised Neapolitan brand is Kimbo, but Moreno, Salimbene, and Tico are considered superior by those in the know. Some small, family-run cafés still roast their own.

You won't find any double low-fat mochas with extra vanilla, though there are certain permitted variations: *corretto,* with a shot of grappa or the local moonshine thrown in; *al vetro,* in a glass; *macchiato,* "stained" with a burst of steamed milk; and, of course, cappuccino. On the whole, coffee is a Neapolitan sacred ritual with precise rules. Cappuccino, for instance, is essentially a breakfast beverage, accepted in the afternoon with a pastry but looked strangely at after a meal (some claim it's bad for the liver). Many Italians like to order a glass of water (*bicchiere d'acqua*) with their coffee as a chaser. Coffee is perhaps the one feature of life in which Neapolitans don't gild the lily. As with so much about the traditional cuisine here, why fix what works?

6

$ CAFÉ **Scaturchio.** This is the quintessential Neapolitan pastry shop. Although the coffee is top-of-the-line and the ice cream and pastries are quite good—including the specialty, the *ministeriale,* a pert chocolate cake with a rum-cream filling—it's the atmosphere that counts here. Nuns, punks, businesspeople, and housewives all commune in this unprepossessing yet remarkable space. *Average main: €2 Piazza San Domenico Maggiore 19, Spaccanapoli 081/5516944 E2.*

$ NEAPOLITAN **Timpani e Tempura.** A tiny shrine to local culinary culture with three small tables and a bar-style counter, this place is worth the squeeze for its *timballi di maccheroni* (baked pasta cakes) and its unique *mangiamaccheroni,* spaghetti in broth with caciocavallo cheese, butter, basil, and pepper. High-quality wines by the glass make this a spot for a swift but excellent lunch. You can also buy cheese and salami to take home with you. *Average main: €7 Vico della Quercia 17, Spaccanapoli 081/5512280 www.timpanietempura.it No credit cards Closed Aug. No dinner E2.*

$ NEAPOLITAN **Vaco 'e Press.** Stoke up here before or after your visit to the Museo Archeologico, a five-minute walk away. This busy eatery close to the metro station in Piazza Dante has a bewildering variety of hot meals, pizzas, vegetable pies, and rolls. As usual in this type of establishment, pay at the *cassa* before you eat. There's seating in the back. *Average main: €5 Piazza Dante 87, Spaccanapoli 081/5499424 No credit cards D2.*

CHIAIA

$$ SOUTHERN ITALIAN ✕ **Amici Miei.** Favored by meat eaters who can't abide another bite of sea bass, this small, dark, and cozy den is known for dishes such as tender carpaccio with fresh artichoke hearts. There are also excellent pasta selections, including orecchiette with chickpeas or *alla barese* (with chewy green turnips), or that extravaganza, the *carnevale lasagne,* an especially rich concoction that sustains revelers in the build-up before Lent. Everyone finishes with a slice of chocolate and hazelnut *torta caprese.* *Average main: €16 ✉ Via Monte di Dio 78, Chiaia ☎ 081/7646063 🌐 www.ristoranteamicimiei.com Reservations essential Closed Mon. and June–Aug. No dinner Sun ✣ D5.*

$$$ NEAPOLITAN Fodor's Choice ★ ✕ **Da Dora.** Despite its location up an unpromising-looking *vicolo* (alley) off the Riviera di Chiaia, this small restaurant has achieved cult status for its seafood platters. It's remarkable what owner-chef Giovanni can produce in his tiny kitchen. Start with linguine *alla Dora,* laden with local seafood and fresh tomatoes, and perhaps follow up with grilled *pezzogna* (blue-spotted bream). Like many restaurants on the seafront, Dora has its own guitarist, who is often robustly accompanied by the kitchen staff. *Average main: €25 ✉ Via Fernando Palasciano 30, Chiaia ☎ 081/680519 Reservations essential Closed Oct.–May. No dinner Sun. ✣ A5.*

$ NEAPOLITAN ✕ **Gran Caffè Cimmino.** Connoisseurs often say the most refined pastries in town can be found at Gran Caffè Cimmino. Many of the city's lawyers congregate here, to celebrate or commiserate with crisp, light cannoli; airy lemon eclairs; *choux* paste in the form of a mushroom laced with chocolate whipped cream; and delightful wild-strawberry tartlets. *Average main: €2 ✉ Via G. Filangieri 12/13, Chiaia ☎ 081/418303 ✣ C5.*

$ NEAPOLITAN ✕ **Gran Caffè Gambrinus.** The most famous coffeehouse in town is the Caffè Gambrinus, catty-corner to the Palazzo Reale across the Piazza Trieste e Trento. Founded in 1850, this 19th-century jewel functioned as a brilliant intellectual salon in its heyday but has unfortunately fallen into a Sunset Boulevard–type existence, relying on past glamour, at the mercy of tourists and their pitiless cameras, and with at times indifferent service. Nevertheless, the renovation and reopening of some of its long-closed inside rooms, replete with amazing mirrored walls and gilded ceilings, makes it an essential stop for any visitor to the city. Have a coffee and a chocolate or a pastry, and soak up the grandeur and the history. *Average main: €2 ✉ Via Chiaia 1/2, Chiaia ☎ 081/417582 ✣ D4.*

$ NEAPOLITAN ✕ **Gran Caffè La Caffettieria.** A classic address in the chic Chiaia district, La Caffetteria has a second space in Vomero. Both locations sell the famous coffee-flavored chocolates in the shape of tiny coffeepots. *Average main: €3 ✉ Piazza dei Martiri 30, Chiaia ☎ 081/7644243 ✣ C5.*

$ ITALIAN ✕ **La Focaccia.** While the flat, pan-cooked focaccia is enough to make pizza fundamentalists wince (coming as it does from Rome), this place makes mouthwatering slices of crunchy-bottomed snacks with a variety of toppings. Skip the predictable tomato variations and go for the delicious potato-and-rosemary focaccia with melted *provola* (smoked mozzarella). Washed down with a beer, this makes for a great speedy lunch or late-night snack. *Average main: €3 ✉ Vico Belledonne a Chaia 31, Chiaia ☎ 081/412277 No credit cards ✣ C5.*

$$ NEAPOLITAN ✕ **L'Altro Loco.** This stylish place took the Naples dining scene by storm a few years back, and it remains popular thanks to the innovative cuisine of master chef Diego Nuzzo. A bar runs the length of the restaurant, where salami and other glorious tidbits are served. But for the real deal, take a table and be pampered with subtle dishes such as *insalata di aragosta e gamberi alla catalana* (lobster and prawn salad garnished with citrus). Large groups can book a private room. *$ Average main: €18 ✉ Vicoletto Cappella Vecchia 4/5, east of Piazza dei Martiri, Chiaia ☎ 081/7641722 🌐 www.ristorantelaltroloco.com ⏲ Closed 3 wks in Aug. No lunch July–Sept. ✥ D5.*

$ NEAPOLITAN ✕ **La Torteria.** This café is beloved not only for its excellent coffee but also for its beautiful cakes—concoctions of cream, chocolate, and fruit whose swirls of color make them look like Abstract Expressionist paintings. *$ Average main: €3 ✉ Via Filangieri 75, Chiaia ☎ 081/405221 ✥ C5.*

$ ITALIAN ✕ **L'Ebbrezza di Noè.** A simple enoteca by day and in a way more of a place to sip drinks and snack than to have a full meal, L'Ebbrezza has a dining area in the back that fills up in the evening. Owner Luca's enthusiasm for what he does is quite moving—as you sample a recommended wine you can sense that he hopes you like it as much as he does. The attention paid to the quality of the wine carries over to the food. Here you can taste *paccheri* (large pasta) stuffed with eggplant *parmigiana*—or try one of the fantastic soups. Other highlights include the rare cheeses, among them the Sicilian *ragusano di razza modicana* and the local *caciocavallo podolico*, and the daily selection of hot dishes. *$ Average main: €12 ✉ Vico Vetriera a Chiaia 8b/9, Chiaia ☎ 081/400104 🌐 www.lebbrezzadinoe.com ⏲ Closed Mon. No lunch. Closed Aug. ✥ C4.*

$ NEAPOLITAN ✕ **Moccia.** Another candidate for the finest pasticceria in the city, Moccia has great babas—decorated, should you wish, with whipped cream and wild strawberries—and an out-of-this-world pound cake injected with just the right dose of intense lemon curd. *$ Average main: €3 ✉ Via San Pasquale a Chiaia 21, Chiaia ☎ 081/411348 ✥ C5.*

$ SOUTHERN ITALIAN Fodor's Choice ★ ✕ **Pescheria Mattiucci.** Four nights a week this fourth-generation fish shop becomes a trendy spot to enjoy an aperitif and a light meal. If you want to experience superb Neapolitan sushi and cold wine while sitting on a buoy stool, get here early. On the nights the place is open, service is from 7:30 to 10:30; a full fish lunch is served daily except Monday. *$ Average main: €12 ✉ Vico Belledonne a Chiaia 27, Chiaia ☎ 081/2512215 🌐 www.pescheriamattiucci.com/naples 💳 No credit cards ⏲ Closed Mon. No dinner Wed. and Sun. ✥ C5.*

$$ NEAPOLITAN ✕ **Trattoria dell'Oca.** The bright, clean, simple decor reflects this place's lighter take on occasionally heavy Neapolitan food, also echoed in the youngish crowd that packs in here on weekends. The soupy pasta *e piselli* (with peas) is a wonderful surprise for anyone who has bad memories of pea soup, and the penne *alla scarpariello* (pasta quills with fresh tomato, basil, and pecorino cheese) is a specialty to set the taste buds quivering. *$ Average main: €16 ✉ Via S. Teresa a Chiaia 11, Chiaia ☎ 081/414865 ⏲ Closed 3 wks in Aug. and Sun. June–Sept. No dinner Sun. Oct.–May ✥ B5.*

Where to Eat and Stay in Naples

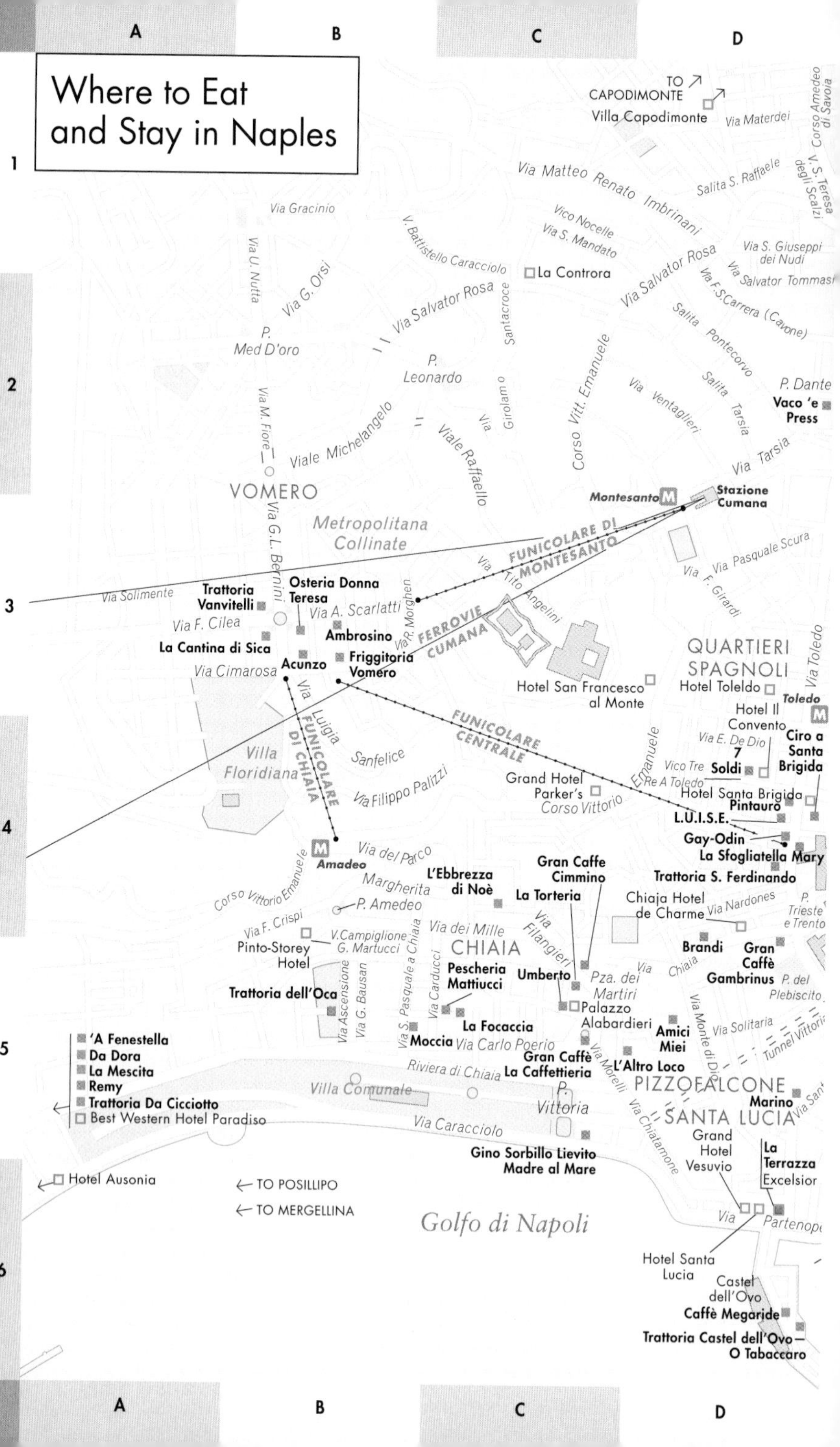

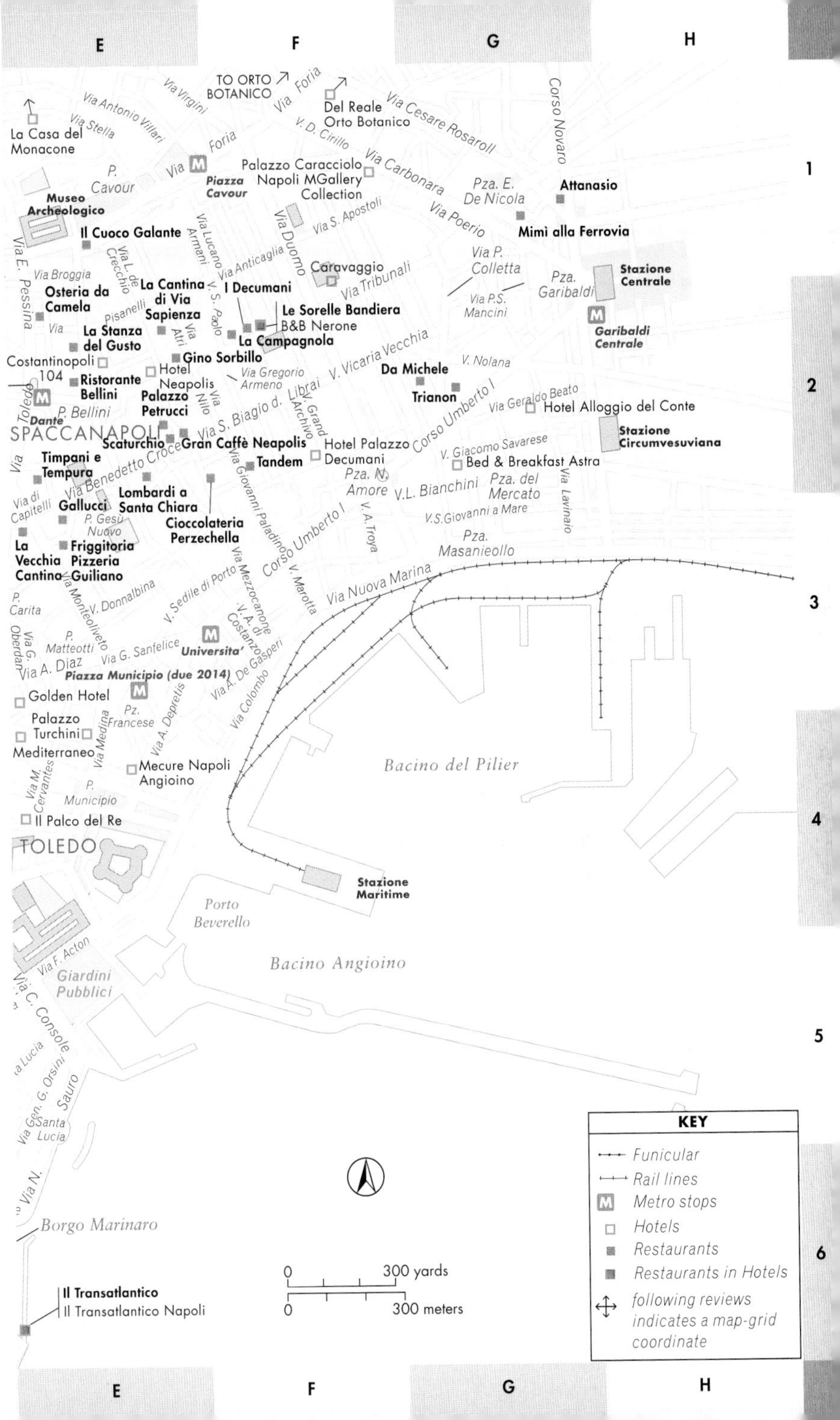
E
F
G
H
1
2
3
4
5
6
TO ORTO BOTANICO
La Casa del Monacone
Del Reale Orto Botanico
Via Antonio Villari
Via Stella
Via Virgini
Via Foria
Via Cesare Rosaroll
V. D. Cirillo
Corso Novaro
P. Cavour
Via Foria
Piazza Cavour
Palazzo Caracciolo Napoli MGallery Collection
Via Carbonara
Pza. E. De Nicola
Attanasio
Museo Archeologico
Via S. Apostoli
Via Poerio
Mimì alla Ferrovia
Il Cuoco Galante
Via Lucano Armanì
Via Duomo
Via E. Pessina
Via L. de Crecchio
Via Anticaglia
Caravaggio
Via Tribunali
Via P. Colletta
Stazione Centrale
Via Broggia
La Cantina di Via Sapienza
I Decumani
Pza. Garibaldi
Osteria da Camela
Pisanelli
V. S. Paolo
Le Sorelle Bandiera
B&B Nerone
Via P.S. Mancini
Garibaldi Centrale
La Stanza del Gusto
Via Atri
La Campagnola
V. Vicaria Vecchia
Costantinopoli 104
Gino Sorbillo
V. Nolana
Ristorante Bellini
Hotel Neapolis
Via Gregorio Armeno
Da Michele
Via Toledo
Dante
Palazzo Petrucci
Via Nilo
Via S. Biagio d. Librai
Trianon
Via Geraldo Beato
Hotel Alloggio del Conte
P. Bellini
V. Grand Archivio
Corso Umberto I
SPACCANAPOLI
Scaturchio
Gran Caffè Neapolis
Hotel Palazzo Decumani
Stazione Circumvesuviana
V. Giacomo Savarese
Timpani e Tempura
Via Benedetto Croce
Tandem
Pza. N. Amore
Bed & Breakfast Astra
Via Lavinaio
Via di Capitelli
Lombardi a Santa Chiara
Via Giovanni Paladino
V.L. Bianchini
Pza. del Mercato
Gallucci
P. Gesù Nuovo
Cioccolateria Perzechella
V. A. Troya
V.S. Giovanni a Mare
La Vecchia Cantina
Friggitoria Pizzeria Guiliano
Corso Umberto I
Pza. Masanieollo
Via Mezzocannone
V. Sedile di Porto
Via Nuova Marina
V. Marotta
P. Carita
Via Monteoliveto
V. Donnalbina
Via G. Oberdan
P. Matteotti
Via G. Sanfelice
Universita'
V.A. di Costanzo
Via A. Diaz
Piazza Municipio (due 2014)
Via A. De Gasperi
Golden Hotel
Via Colombo
Palazzo Turchini
Pz. Francese
Via A. Depretis
Mediterraneo
Via Medina
Bacino del Pilier
Mecure Napoli Angioino
Via M. Cervantes
P. Municipio
Il Palco del Re
TOLEDO
Stazione Maritime
Porto Beverello
Via F. Acton
Giardini Pubblici
Bacino Angioino
Via C. Console
Via Lucia
Via Gen. G. Orsini
Sauro
Santa Lucia
Via N.
Borgo Marinaro
Il Transatlantico
Il Transatlantico Napoli
0
300 yards
0
300 meters
KEY
Funicular
Rail lines
Metro stops
Hotels
Restaurants
Restaurants in Hotels
following reviews indicates a map-grid coordinate

$$ NEAPOLITAN **Umberto.** Run by the Di Porzio family since 1916, Umberto is one of the city's classic restaurants. It combines the classiness of its neighborhood, Chiaia, and the friendliness one finds in other parts of Naples. Try the *tubettoni 'do tre dita* ("three-finger" pasta with octopus, tomato, olives, and capers); it bears the nickname of the original Umberto, who happened to be short a few digits. Owner Massimo and sisters Lorella and Roberta (Umberto's grandchildren) are all wine experts and oversee a fantastic cellar. Note that Umberto is also one of the city's few restaurants catering to diners with a gluten allergy, as well as to vegetarians. *Average main: €15 Via Alabardieri 30–31, Chiaia 081/418555 www.umberto.it No lunch Mon. C5.*

SANTA LUCIA

$ CAFÉ **Caffè Megaride.** After a visit to Castel dell'Ovo this café under its shadow provides a romantic outdoor setting for a snack and a coffee or aperitif. *Average main: €2 Via Borgo Marinaro 1, Santa Lucia 081/7645300 D6.*

$ PIZZA **Gino Sorbillo Lievito Madre al Mare.** For excellent pizza and a spectacular view head to this hip little pie palace on the seaside promenade. Locally grown and made peppers, olives, basil, prosciutto, ricotta, mozzarella, and other ingredients top a masterful wood-fired crust made with the *lievito madre* yeast starter. Nearly as tasty and just as tempting are such sinfully delicious snacks as the *frittatina di maccheroni* (macaroni frittata) and the potato croquets. Enjoy them all, then walk along the *lungomare* (harborfront) to digest. **TIP→ In fine weather there are few nicer places for people-watching and pizza eating than the outdoor patio at Gino Sorbillo.** *Average main: €7 Via Partenope 1, Santa Lucia 081/19331280 C5.*

$$ NEAPOLITAN **Il Transatlantico.** Within the picturesque Borgo Marinaro harbor, in the shadow of Castel dell'Ovo, it's as if you're eating aboard a transatlantic cruise ship. With the Bay of Naples setting and Vesuvius the backdrop, you can understand the nautical decor, blue tablecloths, and the menu abrim with fish delicacies. (Foodies will also wish to note that this was the site of the Roman villa of Lucullus, the moneyed aristocrat famous for his passion for luxurious dining.) A best bet is the *schiaffoni* with *astice* and *pescatrice* (large flat tube pasta with lobster and angler fish), or one of the tasty pizzas, but leave room for the dolce of the day (great homemade tiramisu or pear cake with ricotta). If after one too many limoncellos you feel like crashing, just head upstairs in this make-believe ocean liner and book one of the bright and airy guest rooms in this newly opened hotel. *Average main: €18 Via Luculliana 15, Borgo Marinaro, Santa Lucia 081/7648842 Closed Tues. D6.*

$$$ ITALIAN **La Terrazza.** The Hotel Excelsior's Terrazza restaurant attracts visiting A-list stars with its marble floorings and brown-leather furnishings (all aimed at highlighting the silver cutlery). The à la carte menu fuses Italian regional culinary styles—try the rhombus fish fillet with potatoes and black olives from Gaeta *al cartoccio* (baked and served in a transparent paper). Dress up, and expect to be impressed. *Average main: €28 Hotel Excelsior, Via Partenope 48, Santa Lucia 081/7640111 www.laterrazzaexcelsior.com Closed Sun. D6.*

$ PIZZA **Marino.** Just around the corner from the Borgo Marinaro and the Hotel Vesuvio, this famous pizzeria offers up its delights in a cool white-and-blue room. Try the house specialty, the Anastasia, with cherry tomatoes and lots of premium mozzarella. A wide sidewalk and the partial pedestrianization of Via Santa Lucia make this a pleasant venue for alfresco dining in summer. *Average main: €7 Via Santa Lucia 118/120, Santa Lucia 081/7640280 Closed Mon. and Aug. D5.*

$ NEAPOLITAN **Trattoria Castel dell'Ovo—O Tabaccaro.** If you're trying to keep to a budget but want to enjoy the splash-out of a seafood feast side by side with the yachts of the Borgo Marinaro harbor, head to this former tobacco store. While your eyes feast on all the pretty boats, the Lungomare hotels, the Castel dell'Ovo, and Vesuvius, your tongue can savor classic Neapolitan seafood spaghetti or an *impepata di cozze* (mussels with pepper and garlic). Or just opt for the special made with the fish of the day. *Average main: €12 Borgo Marinaro, Santa Lucia 081/7646352 No credit cards Closed Thurs., and Oct.–Mar. No dinner Sun. D6.*

MERGELLINA AND POSILLIPO

$$ NEAPOLITAN **'A Fenestella.** This restaurant perches over a beach in Posillipo near the end of a long winding side road, and has long capitalized on its location. The landmark comes with its own legend: the story goes that in the 19th century any Juliet would promise herself simply by appearing at the window ("fenestella" in the local dialect) to the Romeo sailing in the boat below, thus inspiring the Neapolitan folk song "*Marechiare.*" Today, the restaurant is blatantly traditional, with a comfortable decor and the usual suspects on the menu. **TIP→ For more stylish food and people, and better value for money, head across the road to Da Cicciotto.** *Average main: €18 Calata del Ponticello a Marechiaro 23, Posillipo 081/7690020 www.afenestella.it Closed Tues. Sept.–May A5.*

$$ NEAPOLITAN **La Mescita.** Close to Cape Posillipo and a short walk from the Parco Virgiliano, this trattoria and pizzeria is a good place for a plate of fresh seafood like *spaghetti ai ricci* (spaghetti with sea urchins) or a land-based *paccheri alla Genovese* (pasta garnished with an onion and meat sauce). There's a good wine list, and the service is cordial. *Average main: €15 Discesa Coroglio 88, Posillipo 081/5983375 Closed Mon. and 2 wks in Aug. A5.*

$ NEAPOLITAN **Remy.** Just off Via Gramsci, a five-minute walk west of the Villa Comunale and the American Consulate, is the highly rated gelateria Remy. If you're going to abandon your low-cholesterol diet, this is definitely the place to do it, preferably with a selection of the *semi-freddi* (a cross between ice cream and mousse). *Average main: €3 Via F. Galiani 29/A, Mergellina 081/667304 A5.*

$$$ NEAPOLITAN Fodor's Choice ★ **Trattoria da Cicciotto.** Chic and charming Da Cicciotto corrals more than a few members of the city's fashionable set—if you dine here, there's a fair chance you'll find a Neapolitan count or off-duty film star enjoying this jewel. A tiny stone terrace overlooks a pleasant anchorage, centered on an antique column, with seats and canopy exquisitely upholstered in blue-and-white matching-but-mixing fabrics. You can

appreciate the outdoor setting at either lunch or dinner, and don't even bother with a menu—just start digging into the sublime antipasti and go with the waiter's suggestions. ■TIP→ Cicciotto sits at the end of the same long winding road that leads to the famed 'A Fenestella restaurant and shoreline, so phone for the restaurant's free shuttle service if starting out from the city center. ⑤ *Average main: €25* ⊠ *Calata del Ponticello a Marechiaro 32, Posillipo* ☎ *081/5751165* ⚠ *Reservations essential* ✛ *A5.*

VOMERO

$

PIZZA

✕ **Acunzo.** If you see a line of hungry-looking patrons near the top station of the Chiaia Funicular, you'll know you are close to Pizzeria Acunzo. To avoid anxious waits, many like to get here as soon as it opens for the busier evening session at 7:30. When ordering, note that few variations on the pizzas are permitted; but then owner Michele and his wife, Caterina, have been running the establishment since 1964 and have a tried-and-tested product. The house specialty, pizza Acunzo, comes replete with a daunting list of ingredients, but ends up being *fenomenale.* ⑤ *Average main: €8* ⊠ *Via Cimarosa 60–62, Vomero* ☎ *081/5785362* ⊘ *Closed Sun.* ✛ *B3.*

$

NEAPOLITAN

✕ **Ambrosino.** At Ambrosino, ideal for a quick snack, you can take your pick of the pizzas and pasta dishes, or ask the owners to whip up a *panino* (sandwich) made from the excellent cheeses, vegetables, and meats on display. The uniformly high-quality ingredients make up for this place's spartan surroundings. ⑤ *Average main: €7* ⊠ *Via Scarlatti 49, Vomero* ☎ *081/3721170* ⊘ *Closed Sun. in July and Aug., and 3 wks in Aug.* ✛ *B3.*

$

NEAPOLITAN

✕ **Friggitoria Vomero.** Popular with kids heading home from school, this spot also often draws guilty-looking adults attracted by its greasy brown-paper bags filled with deep-fried eggplant, zucchini, zucchini flowers, *zeppole* dough balls, or potato croquets—the Neapolitan versions of Proust's madeleines. Forget all that stuff about the Mediterranean diet being so healthy and indulge in some oil-drenched bliss. ⑤ *Average main: €3* ⊠ *Via Cimarosa 44, Vomero* ☎ *081/5783130* ▬ *No credit cards* ⊘ *Closed Sun. and Aug.* ✛ *B3.*

$$

NEAPOLITAN

✕ **La Cantina di Sica.** This rustically elegant trattoria serves variations on traditional faves: the *tubettoni al pesce spada* (small pasta tubes with succulent pieces of swordfish), *peperoni imbottiti* (peppers stuffed with bread crumbs, olives, and capers), and *parmigiana di melanzane* (layers of tomato, eggplant, and mozzarella baked in the oven) are all excellent. The kitchen's take on the traditional Neapolitan *pastiera* (a pie) is as good as, if not better than, anybody's mamma ever made it. ⑤ *Average main: €15* ⊠ *Via Bernini 17, Vomero* ☎ *081/5567520* ⊘ *Closed Mon. and Aug., no dinner Sun.* ✛ *B3.*

$

NEAPOLITAN

✕ **Osteria Donna Teresa.** A tiny place, this restaurant is always full of clients who are treated like children (and that means being encouraged, if not actually forced, to eat everything on their plates). Patrons flock here at lunchtime, in particular for a fill of classic *pasta e fagioli* (with beans), *pasta e ceci* (with chickpeas), or solid helpings of fried anchovies or baccalà (salt cod). ⑤ *Average main: €8* ⊠ *Via Kerbaker 58, Vomero* ☎ *081/5567070* ▬ *No credit cards* ⊘ *Closed Sun. and Aug.* ✛ *B3.*

$ ✕ **Trattoria Vanvitelli.** A small low-key entrance on Piazza Vanvitelli opens
ITALIAN into a labyrinth of underground cellars and a large covered courtyard surrounded by palazzos. This bustling eatery suits a range of palates and budgets: pizzas and several variants of *filletto* (beef tenderloin) are highly recommended. **■ TIP→ Portions are large, so be conservative when ordering.** *Average main: €14 ✉ Piazza Vanvitelli 9c, Vomero ☎ 081/5563015 ⊕ B3.*

PIAZZA GARIBALDI

$ ✕ **Attanasio.** For a hot-out-of-the-oven morsel as soon as you get off the
NEAPOLITAN train, Attanasio, hidden away off Piazza Garibaldi, is justifiably famous. *Average main: €4 ✉ Vico Ferrovia 2, Piazza Garibaldi ☎ 081/285675 No credit cards ⊕ G1.*

$ ✕ **Da Michele.** You may recognize Da Michele from the movie *Eat, Pray,*
PIZZA *Love,* but for more than 140 years before Julia Roberts arrived this place was a culinary reference point. Despite offering only two types of pizza—marinara (with tomato, garlic, and oregano) and *Margherita* (with tomato, mozzarella, and basil)—plus a small selection of drinks, it still manages to attract long lines. The prices have something to do with it. But the pizza itself suffers no rivals, so even customers waiting in line are good-humored: the boisterous, joyous atmosphere wafts out with the smell of yeast and wood smoke onto the street. **■ TIP→ Get a number at the door, and then hang outside until it's called.** *Average main: €5 ✉ Via Sersale 1/3, off Corso Umberto, between Piazza Garibaldi and Piazza Nicola Amore, Piazza Garibaldi ☎ 081/5539204 ⊕ www.damichele.net No credit cards ⊙ Closed 2 wks in Aug. and Sun June–Nov. ⊕ G2.*

$ ✕ **Mimì alla Ferrovia.** Patrons of this Neapolitan institution have included
NEAPOLITAN the filmmaker Federico Fellini and that true-Neapolitan comic genius and aristocrat, Totò. Mimì cheerfully lives up to its history, serving fine versions of everything from pasta *e fagioli* (with beans) to the sea bass *al presidente,* baked in a pastry crust and enjoyed by any number of visiting Italian presidents. The owner's son Salvatore is the new chef, working wonders in the kitchen. This is not so much a see-and-be-seen place as common ground for the famous and the unknown to mingle, feast, and be of good cheer. **■ TIP→ Given the fairly seedy neighborhood, travel here and back by taxi, especially at night.** *Average main: €13 ✉ Via A. D'Aragona 19/21, Piazza Garibaldi ☎ 081/5538525 ⊕ www.mimiallaferrovia.com ⊙ Closed Sun. (except Dec.) and last wk in Aug. ⊕ G1.*

$ ✕ **Trianon.** Across the street from its archrival Da Michele—and without
PIZZA the lines outside—this is a classic pizzeria with a simple yet upscale Art Nouveau ambience expressed in soothing tile and marble. More relaxed and upmarket than its rival, Trianon does the classics (Margherita, marinara) in an exemplary manner, but you can also feast on pizza with sausage and broccoli greens. The signature pizza Trianon comes with eight different toppings. *Average main: €5 ✉ Via P. Coletta 46, Piazza Garibaldi ☎ 081/5539426 No credit cards ⊕ G2.*

6

WHERE TO STAY

Updated by Martin Bennett

Naples is not known for peace and quiet, but many hotels here deliver exactly that, from top-end hideaways to simple, family-run B&Bs and *pensioni*. Usually small and intimate, and often set in historic palazzi, their staffs raise traditional Neapolitan hospitality to an art form. But whether you're in a five-star hotel or a more modest establishment, you may enjoy one of the greatest pleasures of all: a view. Some of the best can be found in the Santa Lucia hotels along the waterside Lungomare. Be sure to ask for a bay-side room if your hotel can provide one, though be warned that *"camere panoramiche"* (panoramic rooms) often cost more than regular rooms.

Another amenity that might cost you more is air-conditioning—Naples hotels offer some of the strongest air-conditioning around—so when making reservations, be sure to inquire if there's an additional charge. The peak visiting times are from April to June and September to October; book well in advance if visiting then.

LODGING NEIGHBORHOODS

Santa Lucia and the Lungomare offer visitors an unsurpassed view of the Bay of Naples, all the more so for now being traffic-free. This area has the city's greatest concentration of luxury hotels, although more reasonable lodging is available on the side streets. **Spaccanapoli** is Naples's most picturesque quarter, so if you're looking for classic Neapolitan atmosphere, this is the place to roost. The flip side of the coin is the nearby **Piazza Municipio/Toledo** area; it's the bustling heart of the modern city, and it has a collection of upscale, large-capacity business hotels, along with some quirky finds in historic buildings. **Chiaia** is the ritziest residential neighborhood in town, studded with 19th-century mansions and containing an elegant shopping district. Above Chiaia rises the **Vomero** hill, offering great bay vistas. The bay-side atmosphere continues at **Mergellina,** a transportation hub set at the far western end of the Riviera di Chiaia, and beyond at the suburban coastal district of **Posillipo.** North of the city center in gritty **La Sanità** is a B&B that's part of a 17th-century church complex. Also noisy and edgy is the **Piazza Garibaldi** area. It's handy if you have to catch an early-morning train, but otherwise you're better off putting some distance between you and the central station.

Use the coordinate (✥ B2) at the end of each review to locate a property on the Where to Eat and Stay in Naples map.

For expanded hotel reviews, visit Fodors.com.

SANTA LUCIA

$$$ HOTEL Fodor's Choice ★

Grand Hotel Vesuvio. You'd never guess from the modern exterior that this is the oldest of Naples's great seafront hotels—the place where Enrico Caruso died, Oscar Wilde dallied with lover Lord Alfred Douglas, and Bill Clinton charmed the waitresses. **Pros:** luxurious atmosphere; historic setting; directly opposite Borgo Marinaro; traffic-free Lungomare is just outside. **Cons:** spa, pool, and Internet cost extra; reception staff can be snooty; not all rooms have great views. *Rooms from: €230 ✉ Via Partenope 45, Santa Lucia ☎ 081/7640044 ⊕ www.vesuvio.it 149 rooms, 21 suites Breakfast ✥ D6.*

$$$ HOTEL **Hotel Excelsior.** Maharajahs, emperors, and Hollywood legends have stayed at this grand-tradition outpost that opened in 1909. **Pros:** delicious breakfasts; great views from breakfast room and rooftop terrace; spacious rooms. **Cons:** the busy road outside is a challenge to cross; traffic noise may keep you up; decor seems dated. *Rooms from: €205* ✉ *Via Partenope 48, Santa Lucia* ☎ *081/7640111* *www.excelsior.it* *109 rooms, 12 suites* *Breakfast* ✣ *D6.*

$$$ HOTEL **Hotel Santa Lucia.** Neapolitan enchantment can be yours if you stay at this luxurious, quietly understated hotel that overlooks the port immortalized in the song "Santa Lucia." **Pros:** great views from most rooms; proximity to the port is convenient for trips to the islands; bikes for hire at €5 an hour. **Cons:** rooms disappointingly boxy. *Rooms from: €220* ✉ *Via Partenope 46, Santa Lucia* ☎ *081/7640666* *www.santalucia.it* *95 rooms* *Breakfast* ✣ *D6.*

$ B&B/INN Fodor's Choice ★ **Il Transatlantico Napoli.** Enjoying perhaps the most enchanting setting in all of Naples, this modestly priced hotel tops many travelers' dream list of places to stay. **Pros:** fabulous location; gentle prices. **Cons:** cheap and ugly furniture. *Rooms from: €120* ✉ *Via Lucculliana 15, Santa Lucia* ☎ *081/768842* *www.transatlanticonapoli.com* *8 rooms* *No meals* ✣ *E6.*

CHIAIA

$ HOTEL **Chiaja Hotel de Charme.** No views here, but this 18th-century palazzo has a great location and its apartments, all on the first floor, have plenty of atmosphere. **Pros:** near Piazza del Plebiscito, the Royal Palace, and nightlife; on bustling pedestrians-only street. **Cons:** no views in a town with some great ones; even with air-conditioning, some rooms get hot in summer; difficult to reach by car. *Rooms from: €100* ✉ *Via Chiaia 216, Chiaia* ☎ *081/415555* *www.hotelchiaia.it* *33 rooms* *Breakfast* ✣ *D4.*

$$ HOTEL Fodor's Choice ★ **Hotel Palazzo Alabardieri.** Just off the chic Piazza dei Martiri, this is the most fashionable choice among the city's smaller luxury hotels—for some, there is simply no other hotel in Naples. **Pros:** impressive public salons; central yet quiet location; polite, pleasant staff. **Cons:** no sea view; difficult to reach by car. *Rooms from: €145* ✉ *Via Alabardieri 38, Chiaia* ☎ *081/415278* *www.palazzoalabardieri.it* *39 rooms* *Breakfast* ✣ *C3.*

$$ B&B/INN **Il Palco del Re.** Here's a lodging with just one room—but what a room: with its frescoed ceiling and an overall luxurious feel, you'll feel like you're living inside a dream. **Pros:** convenient to Palazzo Reale and city center; lodging fit for royalty; excellent breakfast; friendly, accommodating host. **Cons:** books up far in advance. *Rooms from: €155* ✉ *Piazza Plebiscito, Via San Carlo, Chiaia* ☎ *3356871272 (cell phone)* *www.ilpalcodelre.com* *1 room* *Breakfast* ✣ *E4.*

$$ HOTEL **Pinto-Storey Hotel.** The name juxtaposes a 19th-century Englishman who fell in love with Naples with a certain Signora Pinto; together they went on to establish this hotel that overflows with warmth and charm. **Pros:** safe neighborhood; near public transit; option of not using air-conditioning for an €8-a-day reduction; courteous reception; traditional Anglophile atmosphere. **Cons:** not close to major sights; only a few rooms have views; can be hard to find (look for the large

diagonal wooden door and press for the fourth floor). *Rooms from: €88* ✉ *Via G. Martucci 72, Chiaia* ☎ *081/681260* 🌐 *www.pintostorey.it* *16 rooms* 🍴 *No meals* ✥ *B4.*

PIAZZA MUNICIPIO/TOLEDO

$ HOTEL **Hotel Il Convento.** A 17th-century palazzo in the Quartieri Spagnoli contains this hotel whose small but elegant guest rooms have original architectural features such as arched or beamed ceilings. **Pros:** close to cafés and shops; free Internet access; warm Neapolitan reception; personal touch. **Cons:** locale sometimes dicey; church bells may wake you in the morning; just off the busy Via dei Tribunali; tiny lobby. *Rooms from: €120* ✉ *Via Speranzella 137/A, Toledo* ☎ *081/403977* 🌐 *www.hotelilconvento.com* *12 rooms, 2 suites* 🍴 *Breakfast* ✥ *D4.*

$$$ HOTEL **Hotel Santa Brigida.** Masterfully designed by local architect Antonio Scala, formerly of New York City, this concept lodging combines the ultramodern with a playful, at times arcane, take on Neapolitan tradition. **Pros:** a stay here is an experience; painstaking yet playful design; ultramodern decor; artistically presented breakfast. **Cons:** tucked away on Via Santa Brigida; views not what they would be on Via Partenope. *Rooms from: €210* ✉ *Via S. Brigida 6, near Piazza Plebiscito, Toledo* 🌐 *www.hotelsantabrigida.it* *12 rooms, 2 suites* 🍴 *Breakfast* ✥ *D4.*

$$ HOTEL **Hotel Toledo.** A centuries-old palazzo has been tastefully transformed into this boutique hotel, a two-minute walk up from Via Toledo, near Spaccanapoli and the Royal Palace. **Pros:** convenient to Via Toledo shopping; great views from roof garden; helpful reception staff; two suites have a private roof garden. **Cons:** rooms are small; hotel is a steep walk up Via Montecalvario. *Rooms from: €120* ✉ *Via Montecalvario 15, Toledo* ☎ *081/406800* 🌐 *www.hoteltoledo.com* *14 rooms* 🍴 *Breakfast* ✥ *D3.*

$$ HOTEL **Mercure Napoli Angioino.** Right off Piazza Municipio, in the shadows of Castel Nuovo, and close to the Teatro San Carlo, this popular hotel is a good choice if you're taking a boat from Molo Beverello. **Pros:** good location near the port and sights; meals other than breakfast are available for groups by special arrangement. **Cons:** on a busy road; lacks character compared to many Naples hotels. *Rooms from: €170* ✉ *Via De Pretis 123, Toledo* ☎ *081/5529500* 🌐 *www.mercure.com* *85 rooms* 🍴 *Breakfast* ✥ *E4.*

$$ HOTEL **Palazzo Turchini.** Adjacent to the impressive *fontana di Nettuno* (Fountain of Neptune), just a few-minutes' walk from the Castel Nuovo, Palazzo Turchini is one of the city center's more attractive smaller hotels. **Pros:** good location for the port; more intimate than neighboring business hotels; breakfast is included. **Cons:** close to a metro-related construction site. *Rooms from: €160* ✉ *Via Medina 21, Toledo* ☎ *081/5510606* 🌐 *www.palazzoturchini.it* *27 rooms* 🍴 *Breakfast* ✥ *E4.*

$$ HOTEL **Renaissance Naples Hotel Mediterraneo.** A modern, efficient business hotel, the Mediterraneo is within walking distance of both the Teatro San Carlo and Spaccanapoli. **Pros:** convenient to the port; attractive rooftop breakfast terrace. **Cons:** restaurant's food is mediocre. *Rooms from: €170* ✉ *Via Nuova Ponte di Tappia 25, Toledo* ☎ *081/7970001* 🌐 *www.mediterraneonapoli.com* *256 rooms* 🍴 *Breakfast* ✥ *E4.*

SPACCANAPOLI

$ B&B/INN **B&B Nerone.** One of the most original and historic lodgings you're likely to find anywhere, this inn has rooms overlooking part of the Napoli Sotterranea (Naples Underground). **Pros:** welcoming management; in the heart of Spaccanapoli; it's an "experience" to stay here. **Cons:** accessible only through Napoli Sotterranea, which manages the property; rooms aren't particularly airy or light. *Rooms from: €60 ✉ Vico Quattro Santi, Piazza San Gaetano 68, Spaccanapoli ☎ 081/296944 www.napolisotterranea.org 4 rooms No meals ✣ F2.*

$ HOTEL **Caravaggio Hotel.** In a 17th-century palazzo on a tiny square behind the Duomo, this place takes its name from the painter of the amazing *Sette Opere della Misericordia* altarpiece, which can be seen in the chapel opposite. **Pros:** great base for sightseeing. **Cons:** old building; small rooms; unreliable climate control; neighborhood might be too rough around the edges for some travelers. *Rooms from: €120 ✉ Piazza Riario Sforza 157, Spaccanapoli ☎ 081/2110066 www.caravaggiohotel.it 16 rooms Breakfast ✣ F2.*

$$ HOTEL Fodor's Choice ★ **Costantinopoli 104.** An oasis of what Italians call *stile liberty* (Art Nouveau style), with impressive stained-glass fittings and striking artwork, this serene, elegant hotel is well placed for touring the Museo Archeologico Nazionale and Spaccanapoli. **Pros:** pool (a rarity in Neapolitan hotels) and garden; pleasant service. **Cons:** buildings surround the pool; hotel can be difficult to find (look for the sign that reads Villa Spinelli, the place's former name). *Rooms from: €176 ✉ Via Costantinopoli 104, Spaccanapoli ☎ 081/5571035 www.costantinopoli104.com 19 rooms Breakfast ✣ E2.*

$ HOTEL **Golden Hotel.** A "techno-style" hotel that opened in 2010, this is one of the most plugged-in lodgings in Naples. **Pros:** Wi-Fi connection in every room; good tech facilities; polite and obliging multilingual staff; safe large enough to store a laptop; in the middle of things yet out of the whirlwind. **Cons:** rooms lack views. *Rooms from: €120 ✉ Via dei Fiorentini 51, Spaccanapoli ☎ 081/2514192 www.goldenhotel.it 15 rooms Breakfast ✣ E4.*

$ HOTEL **Hotel Neapolis.** On a narrow alley off the humming Via Tribunali, close to Piazza Bellini, this hotel looks out over the 13th-century Pietrasanta bell tower. **Pros:** great location in the historic center; breakfast included; data ports in every room; two quadruple rooms and three triples available. **Cons:** difficult to find; a closed window won't always keep out the roar of passing scooters. *Rooms from: €90 ✉ Via Francesco Del Giudice 13, Spaccanapoli ☎ 081/4420815 081/4420819 www.hotelneapolis.com 18 rooms Breakfast ✣ E2.*

$$ HOTEL Fodor's Choice ★ **Hotel Palazzo Decumani.** This contemporary upscale hotel near transportation links and Spaccanapoli's major sights occupies an early-20th-century palazzo. **Pros:** convenient to major sights; large rooms and bathrooms; soundproofed windows. **Cons:** can be hard to find—follow signs from Corso Umberto. *Rooms from: €140 ✉ Piazzetta Giustino Fortunato 8, Spaccanapoli ☎ 081/4201379 www.palazzodecumani.com 28 rooms Breakfast ✣ F2.*

6

VOMERO

$$$ HOTEL **Grand Hotel Parker's.** Midway up the Vomero hill, with fine views of the bay and distant Capri, this landmark hotel, first opened in 1870, continues to serve up a supremely elegant dose of old-style atmosphere to visiting VIPs, ranging from rock stars to Russian leaders. **Pros:** excellent restaurant; fabulous views. **Cons:** a long walk from the funicular; a very long walk or taxi ride from city center and seafront; not quite as grand as it once was. *Rooms from: €300* *Corso Vittorio Emanuele 135, Vomero* *081/7612474* *www.grandhotelparkers.it* *73 rooms, 9 suites* *Breakfast* *C4.*

$$ HOTEL **Hotel San Francesco al Monte.** This high-end hotel retains hints of its former life as a Franciscan monastery: the small lobby leads to narrow corridors lined with doors that look dauntingly cell-like, until you enter and find surprisingly spacious, simply decorated rooms, many with their own hot tubs and furnishings no monk would dream of. **Pros:** rooftop pool; several dining options. **Cons:** isolated location; taxi needed to go out at night. *Rooms from: €150* *Corso Vittorio Emanuele 328, Vomero* *081/4239111* *www.hotelsanfrancesco.it* *45 rooms* *Breakfast* *D3.*

$ B&B/INN **La Controra.** You get a unique experience here, at what is probably the cheapest place to stay in the city. **Pros:** energetic, artsy vibe; international clientele; a few private rooms; one "suite" available for a mere €33. **Cons:** hostel-style dorm rooms (for 2 to 10 people); shared baths; minimal facilities; odd location, higher up than the old town but lower than the Vomero; hidden behind a crumbling church. *Rooms from: €33* *Piazzetta Trinità alla Cesarea 231, Vomero* *081/5494014* *www.lacontrora.com* *3 rooms with shared bath, 4 dorms* *Breakfast* *C2.*

MERGELLINA AND POSILLIPO

$ HOTEL **Best Western Hotel Paradiso.** This impressive hotel on the hillside of Posillipo is famous for its Bay of Naples view, its roof-garden restaurant, and its garden terrace. **Pros:** sweeping bay view; posh Posillipo neighborhood is quieter and safer than city center. **Cons:** some rooms face inland (ask instead for a *camera con vista*); funicular service is infrequent, and the alternative is a long walk up a steep hill or a taxi ride into the city center; removed from Naples, so guests miss out on city life. *Rooms from: €70* *Via Catullo 11, Posillipo* *081/2475111* *www.bestwestern.it* *74 rooms* *Breakfast* *A5.*

$ HOTEL **Hotel Ausonia.** In the courtyard of a building on the Mergellina waterfront, this hotel is handy if you're coming or going from the Mergellina pier. **Pros:** one of the few Mergellina-area hotels; away from the city-center hubbub; convenient to the port; hotel has won hospitality awards. **Cons:** inside a larger palazzo, so it's hard to find (be sure to write down the address). *Rooms from: €90* *Via Caracciolo 11, Mergellina* *081/682278* *www.hotelausonianapoli.com* *6 rooms* *Breakfast* *A5.*

LA SANITÀ

$ **La Casa del Monacone.** It's not every day you can be a "guest" of a
B&B/INN famed 17th-century church, but this distinctive B&B was once part of the giant complex of Santa Maria della Sanità, the main landmark of the Rione Sanità quarter. **Pros:** dynamic and friendly staff; beautiful terrace. **Cons:** La Sanità quarter; small bathrooms; hard to locate. *Rooms from: €60 Via Sanità 124, Sanità 081/7441305 www.catacombedinapoli.it 6 rooms No credit cards Breakfast D1.*

PIAZZA GARIBALDI

$ **Bed & Breakfast Astra.** Though it occupies an unattractive neighbor-
B&B/INN hood whose only bright spots—literally and figuratively—are the neon shrines illuminating nearly every corner each night, this B&B between Corso Umberto and the port wins points for its distinctly homespun appeal. **Pros:** charming, hospitable owner; breakfast included (British or American if requested); cooking facilities available. **Cons:** neighborhood, southwest of Piazza Garibaldi, isn't that great; ambience is homey rather than luxurious. *Rooms from: €47 Vico Campagnari 21, Piazza Garibaldi 081/200167 bb-astra.com 9 rooms Breakfast G2.*

$ **Del Real Orto Botanico.** Near Naples's noted botanical gardens, this
HOTEL 18th-century building has been turned into a spacious hotel whose owner's attention to detail makes the place stand out. **Pros:** near the Archaeological Museum; eight-minute taxi ride from the airport; short bus ride from city center; some rooms overlook the botanical gardens. **Cons:** far from other attractions; noisy location. *Rooms from: €64 Via Foria 192, Carlo III 081/4421528 www.hotelrealortobotanico.it 36 rooms Breakfast F1.*

$ **Hotel Alloggio del Conte.** Southwest from Piazza Garibaldi with a few
B&B/INN twists and turns, this B&B can be difficult to find: once here, however, a warm Neapolitan welcome is assured. **Pros:** quiet; computer connection in hallway; pleasant manager (Michele); breakfast included; *una cena* (a dinner) cooked free for every five days stayed; communal terrace. **Cons:** dodgy TV reception; difficult to find; area not well policed. *Rooms from: €45 Via Salaiolo 27, Piazza Garibaldi 081/200322 www.alloggiodelconte.it 12 rooms Breakfast G2.*

$$$$ **Palazzo Caracciolo Napoli MGallery Collection.** Sleek, soigné, and swank,
HOTEL this hotel is definitely a diamond in the rough—the rough being its immediate neighborhood, a bit far from the tourist or historic quarters. **Pros:** absolute soundproofing; multilingual receptionists; well placed for visiting Spaccanapoli; good breakfast; supermodern design. **Cons:** rough neighborhood. *Rooms from: €480 Via Carbonara 111, Piazza Garibaldi 081/0160111 www.hotel-palazzo-caracciolo-naples.com 139 rooms, 3 suites Breakfast G1.*

NIGHTLIFE AND THE ARTS

THE ARTS

Lively and energetic yet also chaotic and often difficult to follow, the cultural scene in Naples reflects the city's charming yet frustrating character. Event schedules are published in daily newspapers, particularly *Il Mattino, La Repubblica,* and *Corriere della Sera,* or advertised on websites such as ⊕ *www.napolidavivere.it.* Bear in mind, though, that they can't be relied on to reveal everything that is happening or the frequent last-minute changes of program or venue. Word of mouth (hotel staffers are often good sources) is your best source of information, and keep your eyes peeled for the theater and concert posters that wallpaper much of the city center. Neapolitans take their cinema seriously: Several cinemas run "cineforums" one day a week to cater to discerning cinemagoers, and from the end of June to mid-September, open-air cinemas provide aficionados with a chance to catch up on movies missed during the year.

Ticket Agencies Box Office ✉ *Galleria Umberto I 17, Piazza Municipio* ☎ *081/5519188* ⊕ *www.boxofficenapoli.it.* **Concerteria** ✉ *Via Schipa 23, Chiaia* ☎ *081/7611221* ⊕ *www.concerteria.it.* **FNAC** ✉ *Via Luca Giordano 59, Vomero* ☎ *081/2201000* ⊕ *www.fnac.it.*

CLASSICAL MUSIC AND OPERA

CHIAIA

Associazione Alessandro Scarlatti. The association organizes chamber-music concerts at various venues, including the auditorium of the Castel Sant'Elmo, the Villa Pignatelli, and Palazzo Zevallos. ✉ *Piazza dei Martiri 58, Chiaia* ☎ *081/406011* ⊕ *www.associazionescarlatti.it.*

Villa Pignatelli. The 19th-century residence of the Rothschild banking family makes a fitting venue for the concerts that are often held in the summer here. ✉ *Riviera di Chiaia 200, Chiaia* ☎ *081/76123561.*

PIAZZA MUNICIPIO/TOLEDO

Teatro San Carlo. Opera is a serious business in Naples. Not the music, that is, but the costumes, the stage design, the players, and the politics. At the season's major openings, what's happening on the stage and in the pit is secondary to the news of who is there, with whom, and what they're wearing. All this takes place in the historic Teatro San Carlo, the luxury liner of opera houses in southern Italy. The company, which favors the classics over contemporary works but performs both, is usually of high quality. Should the players falter, though, the audience lets them know—rotten vegetables may be passé, but catcalls and hisses are perfectly acceptable.

Teatro San Carlo also hosts ballet performances and musical concerts. For the opera and ballet season (generally from December through June), many seats are presold by subscription, but unless a superstar is performing, some seats will usually be available if you go to the box office several days before the performance you wish to attend. You can also book ahead on the theater's website. If you are under 30, you can buy an unsold ticket one hour before the curtain rises for a steep discount.

Each opera or ballet is usually scheduled for a run of 10 days or so. Prices vary according to seat location and date. The front rows of the stalls, known as *poltronissime,* might cost as much as €200 for a performance on the first night of an opera, while up in the sixth tier, the *Balconata VI,* you would pay a fifth of that price, or much less if you go on a later night. Prices are always highest on first nights with the best opera divas, then fall off as top performers are sometimes substituted after a few nights. Ballet and concert performances are up to 50% less expensive than operas. ✉ *Via San Carlo 101–103, Piazza Municipio* ☎ *081/7972412 box office, 081/7972331* 🌐 *www.teatrosancarlo.it.*

SPACCANAPOLI

Centro di Musica Antica Pietà de' Turchini. Based in the early-baroque church of Santa Caterina da Siena, the center presents an excellent season of early music that runs from October to early May. Even if madrigals aren't your thing, it's worth visiting just for the location. ✉ *Via Santa Caterina da Siena 38, Toledo* ☎ *081/402395* 🌐 *www.turchini.it.*

CONCERT HALLS AND THEATERS

CHIAIA

Teatro Politeama. This venue presents a challenging bill of fare that includes a healthy dose of contemporary dance. The Teatro San Carlo company uses the space to present contemporary works it wouldn't dare unveil in its hallowed headquarters. ✉ *Via Monte di Dio 80, Chiaia* ☎ *081/7645001* 🌐 *www.teatropoliteama.it.*

Teatro Sannazzaro. For a satisfying Neapolitan "soul" experience, catch a local singer like Lina Sastri or Lara Sansone at Teatro Sannazzaro; traditional Neapolitan plays by Edoardo di Filippo are also often presented here, and the venue also books shows by younger Italian bands and singers. ✉ *Via Chiaia 157, Chiaia* ☎ *081/418824* 🌐 *www.teatrosannazaro.it.*

TAM Tunnel. For those with a knowledge of Italian, the TAM Tunnel has a solid program of cabaret and stand-up. ✉ *Gradini Nobili 1, Chiaia* ☎ *081/682814* 🌐 *www.tamteatro.it.*

TOLEDO

Galleria Toledo. The hip set comes here to watch high-quality fringe and avant-garde theater presentations. ✉ *Via Montecalvario 36, Spaccanapoli* ☎ *081/425824* 🌐 *www.galleriatoledo.org.*

Teatro Augusteo. A large, centrally located theater off Via Toledo, the Augusteo usually presents commercial Italian theater and concerts. ✉ *Piazza Augusteo, Piazza Municipio* ☎ *081/414243* 🌐 *www.teatroaugusteo.it.*

Teatro Mercadante. A Belle Epoque theater with an ultramodern foyer, Teatro Mercadante hosts high-quality touring productions. ✉ *Piazza Municipio, Piazza Municipio* ☎ *081/5513396* 🌐 *www.teatrostabilenapoli.it.*

Teatro Nuovo. Another exciting venue for avant-garde performances, Teatro Nuovo occupies a historic theater building. ✉ *Via Montecalvario 16, Spaccanapoli* ☎ *081/425958* 🌐 *www.teatronuovonapoli.it.*

SPACCANAPOLI

Teatro Bellini. Teatro Bellini is a gilded Belle Epoque theater that presents plays and concerts of a more traditional flavor. ✉ *Via Conte di Ruvo 14, Spaccanapoli* ☎ *081/5491266* 🌐 *www.teatrobellini.it.*

Teatro Instabile. You can sample the expressive Neapolitan avant-garde, experimental, and innovative arts at this basement venue in an old building. ✉ *Vico Fico Purgatorio ad Arco 38, Spaccanapoli* ☎ *338/4731271* 🌐 *www.teatroinstabile.ning.com.*

Teatro Trianon. An old cinema refurbished to provide a "home for Neapolitan song," this theater mixes showings of classic Neapolitan movies with local comedies and comedy acts, and frequent concerts by traditional Neapolitan musicians. ✉ *Piazza Calenda 9, Spaccanapoli* ☎ *081/2258285* 🌐 *www.teatrotrianon.org.*

FILM

CHIAIA

Warner Village Metropolitan. Mainstream movies are the primary fare at this American-style city-center multiplex. ✉ *Via Chiaia 149, Chiaia* ☎ *081/5511247* 🌐 *www.cinemametropolitan.it.*

VOMERO

America Hall. The city's love affair with the movies reaches its high point every year with the Napoli Film Festival, which takes place in autumn at several locations across the city. ✉ *Via Tito Angelini 21, Vomero* ☎ *081/5788982* 🌐 *www.napolifilmfestival.com.*

SPACCANAPOLI

Modernissimo. This Italian-style multiplex is in the historical center. ✉ *Via Cisterna dell'Olio 59, Spaccanapoli* ☎ *081/5800254* 🌐 *www.modernissimo.it.*

NIGHTLIFE

Nightlife in Naples begins well after the sun has gone down. If you're going to a club, don't even think about turning up before 11, and don't plan on going to bed much before 3. Yet if you're willing to stay up late enough, and prepared to hang around outside places—with the rest of the *perdi-tempo* ("time wasters")—where there's sometimes more going on in the street than in the clubs themselves, Naples offers distractions for night owls of all persuasions. The designer-clad young and not so young hang out in the area around Chiaia and Mergellina; a more artsy poststudent crowd congregates around Piazza Bellini; the rawer, punkier edge prefers to hang around on Piazza Dante or Piazza San Domenico. Clubs tend to open and close or change name, style, or ownership with bewildering rapidity, so be sure to check locally before planning a night out. The best way to find out what's going on is to keep your eyes on the flyers that cover Spaccanapoli or check the monthly publication *Zero 81*.

Many dance clubs issue a drink card (prices vary, €15 is average) at the door that must be returned when you leave, stamped to show you've consumed at least one drink. After the first or second drink, other drinks usually run less (about €5).

If chaotic nightlife is more than you can take after a day experiencing the all-too-chaotic daylife of Naples, there's the civilized option of the *enoteca,* not exactly a wine bar, but a place where you can stop for a drink or meet up with friends without having to shout over the music or hang around on the street outside for hours, and have something more substantial to eat than peanuts and pretzels.

BARS

CHIAIA

66. The bar entitled simply 66 describes itself as a "fusion bar." Some prefer it as a chic place to have an aperitif (help yourself to the snacks beautifully laid out on the bar). Other patrons, who look like they've just popped out of one of the area's designer-clothing shops, come here to dine and listen to the chilled-out DJ in one of the ethnic-theme rooms upstairs. ✉ *Via Bisignano 58, Chiaia* ☎ *081/415024.*

Enoteca Belledonne. Between 8 and 9 in the evening it seems as though the whole upscale Chiaia neighborhood has descended into the tiny space for an *aperitivo* (cocktail). The small tables and low stools are notably uncomfortable, but the cozy atmosphere and the pleasure of being surrounded by glass-front cabinets full of wine bottles with beautiful labels more than makes up for it. Excellent local wines are available by the glass at great prices. ✉ *Vico Belledonne a Chiaia 18, Chiaia* ☎ *081/403162* 🌐 *www.enotecabelledonne.com.*

L'ebbrezza di Noè. A particularly quiet and refined option in Chiaia is L'ebbrezza di Noè, which is both a stand-up bar and a sit-down eatery. ✉ *Vico Vetriera a Chaia 9, Chiaia* ☎ *081/400104* 🌐 *www.lebbrezzadinoe.com.*

S'move. With its high-tech bar leading into an Oriental-style room complete with scatter cushions on the floor, S'move is something between a bar and a club. It fills around midnight with a young crowd that wears its clothes with the designer labels showing. ✉ *Vico dei Sospiri 10, Chiaia* ☎ *081/7645813.*

SPACCANAPOLI

Caffè Intramoenia. The granddaddy of all the bars in Piazza Bellini was set up as a bookstore in the late 1980s and still has its own small publishing house with a variety of attractive titles. Seats in the heated veranda are at a premium in winter, though many customers sit outside all year round. ✉ *Piazza Bellini 70, Spaccanapoli* ☎ *081/290988* 🌐 *www.intramoenia.it.*

Kestè Art Bar. The cool chrome furnishings at Kestè contrast with the old arched ceiling inside, but try to get a table out in the beautiful square in front of the Orientale University. A DJ spins tunes, and there's live jazz on the tiny stage on weekends. ✉ *Largo S. Giovanni Maggiore 26, Spaccanapoli* ☎ *081/5513984* 🌐 *www.keste.it.*

Nea. A beautiful café and contemporary art gallery, Nea is a highly atmospheric spot to just hang out, especially in fine weather at the tables outside. ✉ *Via Costantinopoli 53, Spaccanapoli* ☎ *081/451358* 🌐 *www.spazionea.it.*

Perditempo. If Piazza Bellini is too packed, head around the corner to Perditempo, which advertises *libri, vini e vinili* ("books, wine, and vinyl"). Set up as a used book and record store, it is now a relaxed place to enjoy a glass or two and peruse the merchandise. ✉ *Via San Pietro a Maiella 8, Spaccanapoli* ☎ *081/444958* 🌐 *www.perditempo.org.*

Portico 340. Drink in a little culture along with a coffee or a cocktail at this literary café known for its friendly staff and a lively slate of arts events. ✉ *Via Tribunali 340, Spaccanapoli* ☎ *081/0127030* 🌐 *www.portico340.it.*

Superfly. Via Cisterna dell'Olio hosts the tiny but agreeably funky Superfly, where a DJ spins classic jazz and changing photography exhibitions line the walls. ✉ *Via Cisterna Dell'Olio 12, Spaccanapoli* ☎ *347/1272178.*

MUSIC CLUBS

CHIAIA

Trip. A large space that hosts artistic and musical events, many of them surprising or unique, Trip holds many themed evenings. It's worth it to find out what's on tap when you're in town. ✉ *Via Martucci 64, Chiaia* ☎ *081/19568994* 🌐 *www.tripnapoli.com.*

SPACCANAPOLI

Bourbon Street. This small club in the historic district books jazz musicians and hosts jam sessions and live DJ sets. The cocktails are as good as the music is. ✉ *Via Bellini 52, Spaccanapoli* ☎ *338/8253756* 🌐 *www.bourbonstreetjazzclub.com.*

Volver. You can play board games while having a drink at Volver, a lounge that hosts live music, tango (classes are given, too), and other events. ✉ *Via Bellini 56, Spaccanapoli* ☎ *081/0606630.*

SHOPPING

Updated by Fiorella Squillante

Naples is a fascinating city for shopping. Shops are generally open from around 9:30 in the morning to 1:30, when they close for lunch, reopening around 4:30 and staying open until 7:30 or 8. Most stores are closed on Sunday, but certain higher-volume addresses are open on Sunday morning. Sales run twice a year, from mid-January to mid-March for the fall–winter collections and from mid-July to early September for the spring–summer collections, with half-price discounts common.

The classic handicraft of Naples is the Presepe—or Nativity crèche scene—with elaborate sets and terra-cotta figurines and elements of still life. The tradition goes back to the medieval period, but its acknowledged golden age arrived in the 18th century. The tradition is alive and flourishing; although the sets and figurines retain their 18th-century aspect, the craftsmen keep their creativity up-to-date with famous renditions of current political figures and other celebrities. The scenes contain a profusion of domestic animals and food of all sorts, meticulously rendered. Some of the smaller articles make great Christmas tree ornaments.

SHOPPING NEIGHBORHOODS

Most of the luxury shops in Naples lie along a crescent that descends the Via Toledo to Piazza Trieste e Trento and then continues along Via Chiaia to Via Filangieri and on to Piazza Amedeo, as well as continuing south toward Piazza dei Martiri and the Riviera di Chiaia. Within this area, the Via Chiaia probably has the greatest concentration and variety of shops—the café–pastry shop Gran Caffé Cimmino (⇨ *see Where to Eat, above*), on the corner of Via Filangieri and Via Chiaia, makes for an excellent rest stop along this route. In Vomero the area around Piazza Vanvitelli, and Via Scarlatti in particular, has some good shops. Funiculars from Piazza Amedeo, Via Toledo, and Montesanto serve this portion of Vomero. Secondhand book dealers tend to collect between Piazza Dante, Via Port'Alba, and Via Santa Maria di Costantinopoli. The charming shops specializing in Nativity scenes are in Spaccanapoli, on the Via San Gregorio Armeno. Via San Sebastiano, close to the Conservatory, is the kingdom of musical instruments.

CHIAIA

ART GALLERIES

Galleria Lia Rumma. Cindy Sherman, Anselm Kiefer, and Vanessa Beecroft are among international artists represented by this gallery, whose lineup also includes the Neapolitan photographer Mimmo Jodice. ✉ *Via Vannella Gaetani 14, Chiaia* ☎ *081/7643619* 🌐 *www.gallerialiarumma.it.*

Galleria Trisorio. The gallery exhibits the works of international artists of the caliber of Rebecca Horn and William Eggleston. ✉ *Riviera di Chiaia 215, Chiaia* ☎ *081/414306* 🌐 *www.studiotrisorio.com.*

Umberto Di Marino. Young and promising Italian and international artists are shown here, along with their established counterparts. ✉ *Via Alabardieri 1, Chiaia* ☎ *081/0609318* 🌐 *www.galleriaumbertodimarino.com.*

BOOKS AND PRINTS

Arethusa. Collectible posters are the specialty of this gallery that has an excellent selection of rare and inexpensive editions. ✉ *Riviera di Chiaia 202/b, Chiaia* ☎ *081/411551.*

Bowinkel. For antique prints, postcards, watercolors, photographs, engravings, and some books, the most famous shop in town is Bowinkel, where the lucky collector can often pick up pricey treasures, including delectable views of 19th-century Naples. ✉ *Piazza dei Martiri 24, Chiaia* ☎ *081/7644344* 🌐 *www.bowinkel.it.*

La Feltrinelli. The largest bookstore in town carries books, CDs, and DVDs, and has an inviting coffee bar on the lower ground floor. The Toledo branch, at Via Tommaso D'Aquino 70, also has a large selection of English books. ✉ *Piazza dei Martiri, Chiaia* ☎ *081/2405411* 🌐 *www.lafeltrinelli.it.*

CLOTHING AND ACCESSORIES

Argenio. An exclusive address for men's accessories, Argenio is the former supplier of scarves, cuff links, buttons, tiepins, and so forth to the royal Bourbons of the House of the Two Sicilies. ✉ *Via Filangieri 15, Chiaia* ☎ *081/418035.*

Eddy Monetti. The original Eduardo Monetti opened his doors in 1887 as a hat designer, soon bringing in customers such as the tenor Enrico Caruso. The shop remains a landmark Neapolitan name in sartorial splendor for men. Women can now find Monetti fashions on Via Santa Caterina. ✉ *Via dei Mille 45, Chiaia* ☎ *081/427716* 🌐 *www.eddymonetti.com.*

Emporio Armani. Designer Giorgio Armani's mass-market brand does business in chic Piazza dei Martiri. ✉ *Piazza dei Martiri 64, Chiaia* ☎ *081/425816* 🌐 *www.armani.com/it.*

Furla. The shop carries accessories—scarves, bags, shoes, and more—at surprisingly accessible prices. ✉ *Via Filangieri 58, Chiaia* ☎ *081/414218* 🌐 *www.furla.com/it.*

Hermès. The French brand Hermès has a shop on the increasingly chic Via Filangieri. ✉ *Via Filangieri 53/57, Chiaia* ☎ *081/4207054* 🌐 *www.hermes.com.*

Jossa. Menswear by Italian and international designers at reasonable prices can be found here. ✉ *Via Carlo Poerio 43, Chiaia* ☎ *081/7649835.*

Livio de Simone. The wife and daughter of the late Neapolotian designer Livio de Simone, famous for his bright, printed-textile designs worn by 1950s and 1960s celebrity femmes, run the still-sexy line now. ✉ *Via Domenico Morelli 15, Chiaia* ☎ *081/7643827* 🌐 *www.lds-fabrics.com.*

Lo Stock. Come to this large basement store prepared to rummage for designer-label remainders at hugely reduced prices. ✉ *Via Fiorelli 7, Piazza dei Martiri* ☎ *081/7648763.*

Mariano Rubinacci. If you feel like indulging in a custom-made suit or shirt, try this world-famous haberdashery that's been in business since the 19th century. ✉ *Palazzo Cellammare via Chiaia 149, Chiaia* ☎ *081/415793.*

Marinella. Count the British royal family among the customers of this shop that sells old-fashioned made-to-measure ties. ✉ *Via Riviera di Chiaia 287/a, Chiaia* ☎ *081/2451182.*

Salvatore Ferragamo. Although based in Florence, Ferragamo is also beloved by Neapolitans who appreciate fine Italian taste and craftsmanship. ✉ *Piazza dei Martiri 56/60, Chiaia* ☎ *081/412123 men's, 081/415454 women's* 🌐 *www.ferragamo.com.*

Tramontano. Since 1865 this place has been crafting fine leather luggage, bags, shoes, belts, and wallets. ✉ *Via Chiaia 142, Chiaia* ☎ *081/414837* 🌐 *www.tramontano.it.*

DECORATION AND ANTIQUES

Domenico Russo e Figli. This shop continues the centuries-old Neapolitan tradition of marble-inlay work, creating precious tables and console tops. ✉ *Via Bisignano 51, Chiaia* ☎ *081/7648387.*

Galleria Navarra. One of the largest expositions of antique and vintage furniture, paintings, rugs, tapestries, objets d'art, clothing, and urban architecture is at the Galleria Navarra. ✉ *Piazza dei Martiri 23, Chiaia* ☎ *081/7643595.*

JEWELRY

Bulgari. The posh brand showcases its internationally famous jewelry on posh Via Filangieri. ✉ *Via Filangieri 40, Chiaia* ☎ *081/409551.*

Damiani. Award-winning Damiani sells high-end watches and jewelry to the likes of Sophia Loren, Brad Pitt, and Gwyneth Paltrow. ✉ *Via Filangieri 15, Chiaia* ☎ *081/405043* 🌐 *www.damiani.com/it.*

DoDo. The unusual jewelry at DoDo comes in the form of gold, silver, and other charms. ✉ *Via Filangieri 58, Chiaia* ☎ *081/418245* 🌐 *www.dodo.it.*

Ventrella. The chic salon of this most exclusive contemporary jewelry workshop sells the original designs of its gifted artisans. ✉ *Via Carlo Poerio 11, Chiaia* ☎ *081/7643173.*

MARKETS

Bancarelle di San Pasquale. High-quality shoes, bags, and clothing can be found every morning at this market in Chiaia that also has a large section of foods, spices, fruits, and vegetables. ✉ *Via San Pasquale, Chiaia.*

SPACCANAPOLI

ART GALLERIES

Fondazione Morra Greco. The influential collector Maurizio Morra Greco has put all his private holdings on display at this gallery that also mounts shows by emerging artists. ✉ *Largo Avellino 17, Spaccanapoli* ☎ *081/210690* 🌐 *www.fondazionemorragreco.com.*

Palazzo Bagnara. The palazzo is the headquarters of the Fondazione Morra, whose founder Giuseppe Morra has been one of the leading patrons promoting visual poetry, Actionism, and conceptual art in Naples since the 1960s. ✉ *Piazza Dante 89, Spaccanapoli* ☎ *081/5641655* 🌐 *www.fondazionemorra.org.*

Raucci Santamaria. This gallery specializes in international artists, including Mat Colishaw, Ugo Rondinone, and Tim Rollins. ✉ *Corso Amedeo di Savoia 190, Spaccanapoli* ☎ *081/7443645* 🌐 *www.raucciesantamaria.com.*

BOOKS AND PRINTS

Alpha. If you're an art-history student and pictures are what matter, browse the booksellers near Piazza Bellini and take Via Port'Alba to Piazza Dante, where Alpha has a great selection of cut-rate art books. ✉ *Via Sant'Anna dei Lombardi 10, Spaccanapoli* ☎ *081/5525013* 🌐 *www.alphalibri.com.*

Colonnese. The antique wooden cabinets and tables at this old-fashioned bookstore are laden with volumes about art, local history, and esoterica. ✉ *Via San Pietro a Maiella 32/33, Spaccanapoli* ☎ *081/459858.*

Libreria Guida. Expert staff members preside over this shop that carries local-interest books in English and Italian. ✉ *Via Port'Alba 20/23, Spaccanapoli* ☎ *081/446377* 🌐 *www.guida.it.*

Libreria Neapolis. A small store with many books about Neapolitan art and history, this place stocks a few English titles and has a wide selection of DVDs and music CDs. ✉ *Via San Gregorio Armeno 4, Spaccanapoli* ☎ *081/5514337* 🌐 *www.librerianeapolis.it.*

CLOTHING AND ACCESSORIES

Melinoi. Its originality separates Melinoi from the many small boutiques in Naples; it stocks clothes and accessories by Romeo Gigli as well as a number of French designers. ✉ *Via Benedetto Croce 34, Spaccanapoli* ☎ *081/5521204.*

Oblomova. The club set heads to perky Oblomova for vintage and handmade clothing and accessories but also books, vinyl, CDs, and even cassettes. ✉ *Via San Sebastiano 20, Spaccanapoli* ☎ *081/4420855* 🌐 *www.oblomova.com.*

CRAFTS AND GIFTS

Egraphe. A tiny hole in the wall, Egraphe is crammed with notebooks of every style and size, different kinds of handmade papers, and unusual pens and pencils. ✉ *Piazza L. Miraglia 391, Spaccanapoli* ☎ *081/446266* 🌐 *www.egraphe.it.*

Ferrigno. Shops selling Nativity scenes cluster along the Via San Gregorio Armeno in Spaccanapoli, and they're all worth a glance. The most famous is Ferrigno: Maestro Giuseppe Ferrigno died in 2008, but the family business continues, still faithfully using 18th-century techniques. ✉ *Via San Gregorio Armeno 10, Spaccanapoli* ☎ *081/5523148* 🌐 *www.arteferrigno.it.*

La Scarabattola. The store's Scuotto family creates *Presepi* (Nativity scenes) in both classic Neapolitan and contemporary styles. Past customers include the Spanish royal family. ✉ *Via Tribunali 50, Spaccanapoli* ☎ *081/291735.*

Liuteria Calace. Several generations of the Calace family have contributed to this prestigious shop's reputation for exquisitely made mandolins. ✉ *Vico San Domenico Maggiore 9, Spaccanapoli* ☎ *081/5515983* 🌐 *www.calace.it.*

Marisa Catello. You can find rare antique Nativity figures at Marisa Catello. ✉ *Via Santa Maria Costantinopoli 124, Spaccanapoli* ☎ *081/444169.*

Nel Regno di Pulcinella. This is the workshop of Lello Esposito, a Neapolitan artist renowned for his renderings of a popular puppet named Pulcinella. A statue of his creation was recently unveiled in Vico dei Fico al Purgatorio, just off Via dei Tribunali. ✉ *Vico San Domenico Maggiore 9, Spaccanapoli* ☎ *081/5514171* 🌐 *www.lelloesposito.com.*

FAMILY **Ospedale delle Bambole.** This tiny storefront operation with a laboratory across the street is a world-famous "hospital" for dolls. In business since 1850, it's a wonderful place to take kids. ✉ *Via San Biagio dei Librai 81, Spaccanapoli* ☎ *339/5872274* 🌐 *www.ospedaledellebambole.it* 🕒 *Weekdays 10–3.*

JEWELRY

Gioielleria Lo Scrigno. Near the center of the Spacca along pedestrian-friendly Via Benedetto Croce, this shop sells jewelry and accessories. ✉ *Via Benedetto Croce 26/27, Spaccanapoli* ☎ *081/5520464.*

MARKETS

Mercatino della Pignasecca. The best place in the city for fruit and vegetables, this market can be found several blocks west of Piazza Carità off Via Toledo. ✉ *Spaccanapoli* 🕒 *Mon.–Sat. 8–2.*

Bringing smiles to even the stoniest hearts, the Doll Hospital in Spaccanapoli is a Neapolitan institution.

VOMERO

BOOKS AND PRINTS

FNAC. The Neapolitan branch of the French chain has a huge basement brimming with books and CDs; there's also a coffee bar and meeting space. ✉ *Via Luca Giordano 59, Vomero* ☎ *081/2201000* 🌐 *www.fnac.it.*

MARKETS

Mercatino di Antignano. For low-price and surprisingly high-quality clothing and linen, head to the Mercatino di Antignano. ✉ *Piazza degli Artisti, Vomero* 🕓 *Daily 8–1.*

PIAZZA MUNICIPIO/TOLEDO

CLOTHING AND ACCESSORIES

Barbaro. "Made in Italy" is the trademark of this popular shop that showcases the fashions of top-name designers. ✉ *Galleria Umberto I 1/7, Piazza Municipio* ☎ *081/414940* 🌐 *www.barbaro.eu.*

Benetton. A good selection of affordable clothes can be found at Benetton, which continues to represent easy Italian chic to most of the world. ✉ *Via Chiaia 203/204, Chiaia* ☎ *081/405385.*

Zara. Trendy Zara, part of a Spanish chain known for its cheap-and-hip fashions, delivers the goods at a reasonable price. ✉ *Via Toledo 210, Toledo* ☎ *081/4238060.*

JEWELRY

Ascione. A family firm established in 1855 and known for its traditionally made coral jewelry and artworks, Ascione, has a showroom-gallery in a wing of the Galleria Umberto. ✉ *Piazzetta Matilde Serao 19, Piazza Municipio* ☎ *081/4211111* 🌐 *www.ascione.it.*

Brinkmann. Watches that incorporate rare coins are the trademark of this Piazza Municipio shop. ✉ *Piazza Municipio 21, Piazza Municipio* ☎ *081/5520555.*

Leonardo Gaito. For antique wonders or eclectic creations in gold, precious stones, and silver, make yourself at home on one of the velvet chairs inside Leonardo Gaito and get ready to be regaled with some fabulous Neapolitan-style jewels. ✉ *Via Toledo 278, Toledo* ☎ *081/421104.*

PIAZZA GARIBALDI

MARKETS

Borgo di Sant'Antonio. Groceries and household items are sold at the cheapest prices at this market (nicknamed *O'Buver'* in the Neapolitan dialect) near Piazza Garibaldi. ✉ *Via S. Antonio Abate, Piazza Garibaldi* ⏲ *Daily 8–2.*

Mercatino di Poggioreale. This market is only open three days a week and is a little farther out than most, but it has a vast selection of shoes in all styles and sizes, and at uniformly low prices. Clothes, antiques, and other items are also for sale. ■ **TIP→ Some locals insist that the best bargains can be found on Friday.** ✉ *Via Nuova Poggioreale, Piazza Garibaldi* ⏲ *Fri.–Sun. 7–2.*

Mercato di Porta Capuana. Jeans, shoes, and a surprising number of untagged name-brand items at half price or better can be found at this popular market. ✉ *Porta Capuana/Piazza Leone, Piazza Garibaldi* ⏲ *Mon.–Sat. 8–1:30.*

ITALIAN VOCABULARY

ENGLISH	ITALIAN	PRONOUNCIATION

BASICS

Yes/no	Sí/no	see/no
Please	Per favore	pear fa-**vo**-ray
Yes, please	Sí, grazie	see **grah**-tsee-ay
Thank you	Grazie	**grah**-tsee-ay
You're welcome	Prego	**pray**-go
Excuse me, sorry	Scusi	**skoo**-zee
Sorry!	Mi dispiace!	mee dis-spee-**ah**-chay
Good morning/ afternoon	Buongiorno	bwohn-**jor**-no
Good evening	Buona sera	**bwoh**-na **say**-ra
Good-bye	Arrivederci	a-ree-vah-**dare**-chee
Mr. (Sir)	Signore	see-**nyo**-ray
Mrs. (Ma'am)	Signora	see-**nyo**-ra
Miss	Signorina	see-nyo-**ree**-na
Pleased to meet you	Piacere	pee-ah-**chair**-ray
How are you?	Come sta?	**ko**-may **stah**
Very well, thanks	Bene, grazie	**ben**-ay **grah**-tsee-ay
Hello (phone)	Pronto?	**proan**-to

NUMBERS

one	uno	**oo**-no
two	due	**doo**-ay
three	tre	tray
four	quattro	**kwah**-tro
five	cinque	**cheen**-kway
six	sei	say
seven	sette	**set**-ay
eight	otto	**oh**-to
nine	nove	**no**-vay
ten	dieci	dee-**eh**-chee
eleven	undici	**oon**-dee-chee
twelve	dodici	**doe**-dee-cee

thirteen	tredici	**tray**-dee-chee
fourteen	quattordici	kwa-**tore**-dee-chee
fifteen	quindici	**kwin**-dee-chee
sixteen	sedici	**say**-dee-chee
seventeen	diciassete	dee-cha-**set**-ay
eighteen	diciotto	dee-**cho**-to
nineteen	diciannove	dee-cha-**no**-vay
twenty	venti	**vain**-tee
twenty-one	ventuno	vain-**too**-no
twenty-two	ventidue	vain-tee-**doo**-ay
thirty	trenta	**train**-ta
forty	quaranta	kwa-**rahn**-ta
fifty	cinquanta	cheen-**kwahn**-ta
sixty	sessanta	seh-**sahn**-ta
seventy	settanta	seh-**tahn**-ta
eighty	ottanta	o-**tahn**-ta
ninety	novanta	no-**vahn**-ta
one hundred	cento	**chen**-to
one thousand	mille	**mee**-lay
ten thousand	diecimila	dee-eh-chee-**mee**-la

USEFUL PHRASES

Do you speak English?	Parla inglese?	**par**-la een-**glay**-zay
I don't speak Italian	Non parlo italiano	non **par**-lo ee-tal-**yah**-no
I don't understand	Non capisco	non ka-**peess**-ko
Can you please repeat?	Può ripetere?	pwo ree-**pet**-ay-ray
Slowly!	Lentamente!	**len**-ta-men-tay
I don't know	Non lo so	non lo **so**
I'm American	Sono americano(a)	**so**-no a-may-ree-**kah**-no(a)
I'm British	Sono inglese	so-no een-**glay**-zay
What's your name?	Come si chiama?	**ko**-may see kee-**ah**-ma
My name is . . .	Mi chiamo . . .	mee kee-**ah**-mo

What time is it?	Che ore sono?	kay **o**-ray **so**-no
How?	Come?	**ko**-may
When?	Quando?	**kwan**-doe
Yesterday/today/ tomorrow	Ieri/oggi/domani	**yer**-ee/**o**-jee/do-**mah**-nee
This morning/	Stamattina/Oggi	sta-ma-**tee**-na/**o**-jee
afternoon	pomeriggio	po-mer-**ee**-jo
Tonight	Stasera	sta-**ser**-a
What?	Che cosa?	kay **ko**-za
What is it?	Chee cos'é?	kay ko-**zay**
Why?	Perché?	pear-**kay**
Who?	Chi?	kee
Where is . . .	Dov'è . . .	doe-**veh**
the bus stop?	la fermata dell'autobus?	la fer-**mah**-tadel ow-toe-**booss**
the train station?	la stazione?	la sta-tsee-**oh**-nay
the subway?	la metropolitana?	la may-tro-po-lee-**tah**-na
the terminal?	il terminale?	eel ter-mee-**nah**-lay
the post office?	l'ufficio postale?	loo-**fee**-cho po-**stah**-lay
the bank?	la banca?	la **bahn**-ka
the . . .hotel?	l'hotel . . .?	lo-**tel**
the store?	il negozio?	eel nay-**go**-tsee-o
the cashier?	la cassa?	la **kah**-sa
the . . .museum?	il museo . . .?	eel moo-**zay**-o
the hospital?	l'ospedale?	lo-spay-**dah**-lay
the first-aid station?	il pronto soccorso?	eel **pron**-to so-**kor**-so
the elevator?	l'ascensore?	la-shen-**so**-ray
a telephone?	un telefono?	oon tay-**lay**-fo-no
the restrooms?	Dov'è il bagno?	do-**vay** eel **bahn**-yo
Here/there	Qui/là	kwee/la
Left/right	A sinistra/a destra	a see-**neess**-tra/ a **des**-tra
Straight ahead	Avanti dritto	a-**vahn**-tee **dree**-to
Is it near/far?	È vicino/lontano?	ay vee-**chee**-no/ lon-**tah**-no
I'd like . . .	Vorrei . . .	vo-**ray**
a room	una camera	**oo**-na **kah**-may-ra
the key	la chiave	la kee-**ah**-vay
a newspaper	un giornale	oon jor-**nah**-lay
a stamp	un francobollo	oon frahn-ko-**bo**-lo

I'd like to buy . . .	Vorrei comprare . . .	vo-**ray** kom-**prah**-ray
How much is it?	Quanto costa?	**kwahn**-toe **coast**-a
It's expensive/cheap	È caro/economico	ay **car**-o/ ay-ko-**no**-mee-ko
A little/a lot	Poco/tanto	**po**-ko/**tahn**-to
More/less	Più/meno	pee-**oo**/**may**-no
Enough/too (much)	Abbastanza/troppo	a-bas-**tahn**-sa/**tro**-po
I am sick	Sto male	sto **mah**-lay
Call a doctor	Chiama un dottore	kee-**ah**-mah oon doe-**toe**-ray
Help!	Aiuto!	a-**yoo**-toe
Stop!	Alt!	ahlt
Fire!	Al fuoco!	ahl **fwo**-ko
Caution/Look out!	Attenzione!	a-ten-**syon**-ay

DINING OUT

A bottle of . . .	Una bottiglia di . . .	**oo**-na bo-**tee**-lee-ahdee
A cup of . . .	Una tazza di . . .	**oo**-na **tah**-tsa dee
A glass of . . .	Un bicchiere di . . .	oon bee-key-**air**-ay dee
Bill/check	Il conto	eel **cone**-toe
Bread	Il pane	eel **pah**-nay
Breakfast	La prima colazione	la **pree**-ma ko-la-**tsee**-oh-nay
Cocktail/aperitif	L'aperitivo	la-pay-ree-**tee**-vo
Dinner	La cena	la **chen**-a
Fixed-price menu	Menù a prezzo fisso	may-**noo** a **pret**-so **fee**-so
Fork	La forchetta	la for-**ket**-a
I am diabetic	Ho il diabete	o eel dee-a-**bay**-tay
I am vegetarian	Sono vegetariano/a	**so**-no vay-jay-ta-ree-**ah**-no/a
I'd like . . .	Vorrei . . .	vo-**ray**
I'd like to order	Vorrei ordinare	vo-**ray** or-dee-**nah**-ray
Is service included?	Il servizio è incluso?	eel ser-**vee**-tzee-o ay een-**kloo**-zo

It's good/bad	È buono/cattivo	ay **bwo**-no/ka-**tee**-vo
It's hot/cold	È caldo/freddo	ay **kahl**-doe/**fred**-o
Knife	Il coltello	eel kol-**tel**-o
Lunch	Il pranzo	eel **prahnt**-so
Menu	Il menù	eel may-**noo**
Napkin	Il tovagliolo	eel toe-va-lee-**oh**-lo
Please give me . . .	Mi dia . . .	mee **dee**-a
Salt	Il sale	eel **sah**-lay
Spoon	Il cucchiaio	eel koo-kee-**ah**-yo
Sugar	Lo zucchero	lo **tsoo**-ker-o
Waiter/Waitress	Cameriere/cameriera	ka-mare-**yer**-ay/ ka-mare-**yer**-a
Wine list	La lista dei vini	la **lee**-sta **day**-ee **vee**-nee

TRAVEL SMART AMALFI COAST, CAPRI & NAPLES

GETTING HERE AND AROUND

AIR TRAVEL

Air travel to Italy is frequent and virtually problem-free, except for airport- or airline-related union strikes that may cause delays. Alitalia, Italy's national flag carrier, has the most nonstop flights to Rome and Milan, from which you can fly on to Naples.

Flying time to Milan or Rome is approximately 8–8½ hours from New York, 10–11 hours from Chicago, 11½ hours from Dallas (via New York), and 11½ hours from Los Angeles. Flights from Rome to Naples are around 30 minutes and from Milan to Naples, about 1 hour.

You are advised to confirm flights within Italy the day before travel. Labor strikes are frequent and can affect not only air travel, but also the local trains that serve the airport. Your airline will have information about strikes directly affecting its flight schedule. If you are taking a train to get to the airport, check with the local tourist agency or rail station about upcoming strikes.

Airline Security Transportation Security Administration (*TSA*). The agency has answers for almost every security question that might come up. 🌐 *www.tsa.gov*. A helpful website for information (location, phone numbers, local transportation, etc.) about all the airports in Italy is 🌐 *www.airport-authority.com/browse-IT*.

AIRPORTS

The major gateways to Italy include Rome's Aeroporto Leonardo da Vinci (FCO), better known as Fiumicino, and Milan's Aeroporto Malpensa (MXP). Most flights to Naples from North America and Australia make connections at Fiumicino and Malpensa or another European airport, though a number of budget airlines offer direct flights to Naples from European destinations. You can also take the FS airport train to Termini, Rome's main station, to connect with a train to Naples. It will take about 35 minutes to get from Fiumicino to Termini.

Just outside Naples, Aeroporto Capodichino (NAP) serves the Campania region. It handles domestic and international flights, including several flights daily between Naples and Rome (flight time 30 minutes). The airport is run by GESAC, part of BAA (British Airports Authority), the majority stakeholder.

Although it was completely renovated in 2009, being so close to Naples's city center—a 10-minute drive at nonpeak travel times—Capodichino Airport has little room for expansion. There are skeletal facilities at the airport, so no Internet center, no fitness center, and no airport hotels: On short stopovers—especially if you have to leave early the next morning before road traffic builds up—you're better off staying in the city center. The nearest thing to an airport hotel is the Holiday Inn (shuttle service every hour to the airport): in the *Centro Direzionale* (Business District) close to the industrial eastern suburbs, this is not the sort of place for evening strolls by the Mediterranean.

Airport Information Aeroporto Capodichino ✉ *Viale Umberto Maddalena, 5 km (3 miles) north of Naples, Italy* ☎ *081/7896111* 🌐 *www.gesac.it*. **Aeroporto Fiumicino** (*FCO, also called Leonardo da Vinci*). ✉ *35 km [20 miles] southwest of Rome, Italy* ☎ *06/65951* 🌐 *www.adr.it*. **Aeroporto Malpensa** (*MPX*). ✉ *45 km [28 miles] north of Milan, Italy* ☎ *02/232323* 🌐 *www.airportmalpensa.com*.

FLIGHTS

You may choose to fly Alitalia to Italy—as the national flag carrier, it has the greatest number of nonstops. However, domestic and international carriers, such as Meridiana, Air Italy, EasyJet, and Air Berlin may have direct connections between Naples and destinations in other European countries and slightly cheaper flights within Italy.

Meridiana connects New York's JFK Airport to Naples's Aeroporto Capodichino once a week from late June to early September (it also flies to Palermo). Alitalia (operating with Air One) offers an extensive schedule of daily flights connecting Naples with the major international hubs of Rome and Milan, as well as Bologna, Catania, Genoa, Palermo, Trieste, Turin, and Venice. It also offers nonstop flights to Italy from the United States as part of a transatlantic joint venture with Air France-KLM and Delta. Alitalia has direct flights to Boston, Chicago, Miami, New York City, and seasonal flights to Los Angeles. Domestic connections to Naples are also handled by other carriers, such as EasyJet (Milan Malpensa and Venice), Meridiana (Catania, Cagliari, Alghero, Olbia, Milan Linate, Turin, and Verona) and Lufthansa (Milan Linate). For connections from abroad, Alitalia also offers direct flights from Athens, Vueling offers a daily flight from Barcelona, and Air Berlin competes with Lufthansa on direct flights from German airports. Several other carriers link major European cities with Naples—for instance, British Airways offers a direct route from London-Gatwick, and Transavia serves connections from Amsterdam and Paris. Other connections are offered between Naples and Dublin (Aer Lingus), and Budapest and Prague (WizzAir).

Airline Contacts **Aer Lingus** ☎ *02/43458326 from Italy, 516/622 4022 from U.S.* 🌐 *www.aerlingus.com.* **Air Berlin** ☎ *199/400737 within Italy* 🌐 *www.airberlin.com.* **Alitalia** ☎ *800/223–5730 in U.S., 892/010 in Italy, 06/65640 Rome office* 🌐 *www.alitalia.it.* **British Airways** ☎ *800/247–9297 in U.S., 02/69633602 in Italy* 🌐 *www.britishairways.com.* **EasyJet** ☎ *+44843/104 5454 from outside U.K., 199/201 840 in Italy, 0843/104 5000 from inside U.K.* 🌐 *www.easyjet.com.* **Meridiana** ☎ *892/928 call center, 866/751–4499 from U.S., 0871/222 9319 from U.K.* 🌐 *www.meridiana.it.* **Transavia** ☎ *899/009901* 🌐 *www.transavia.com.* **Vueling** ☎ *899/399 888 within Italy* 🌐 *www.vueling.com.* **Wizz Air** ☎ *899/018874 within Italy* 🌐 *www.wizzair.com.*

BOAT TRAVEL

As one of the great harbors of the world, Naples offers a wide array of boat, ferry (*traghetti*), and hydrofoil (*aliscafo*) services between the city, the islands of the bay, the Sorrentine Peninsula, and other Mediterranean destinations. Hydrofoils leave from the main station of Molo Beverello—the port harbor of Naples opposite the Castel Nuovo (and not too far from the Toledometro stop)—along the waterfront of Piazza Municipio. Less frequent ferries leave from Calata Porta di Massa, a short distance to the east. Companies such as Caremar, SNAV, and Alilauro run services connecting Naples with Sorrento, Capri, Ischia, and Procida. The trip to Ischia and Procida is shorter and cheaper if you use the ferry that departs from Pozzuoli harbor (the nearest metro station is on the Cumana line at Pozzuoli). Next to the Molo Beverello is the Stazione Marittima (Molo Angioino), where larger ferries make trips to Ponza, the Aeolian Islands, Sicily, and Sardinia.

Hydrofoil service is generally twice as fast as ferries and almost double the price. The service is considerably more frequent in summer. *For specific information about boat, ferry, and hydrofoil travel between Naples and other destinations on the Bay of Naples and the Amalfi Coast, see the "Getting Here and Around" sections near the beginning of each regional chapter.* Car ferries operate to the islands of the Bay of Naples, but advance reservations are best.

FARES AND SCHEDULES

The most comprehensive coverage of ferry, hydrofoil, and boat services and schedules is found in the local paper *Il Mattino*, which features a *Per chi Parte* ("For Those Departing") section every day. *Qui Napoli*, the helpful monthly English-language periodical for visitors to Naples also lists ferry and hydrofoil schedules. As there are substantial seasonal variations, double-check departure times and days, especially when traveling further afield on low-frequency services.

Boat Information Alilauro ☎ *081/4972222* 🌐 *www.alilauro.it.* **Caremar** ☎ *081/5513882* 🌐 *www.caremar.it.* **Navigazione Libera del Golfo** *(NLG).* ☎ *081/5520763* 🌐 *www.navlib.it.* **SNAV** ✉ *Italy* ☎ *081/4285555* 🌐 *www.snav.it.* **Tirrenia** ✉ *Italy* ☎ *892/123* 🌐 *www.tirrenia.it.*

BUS TRAVEL

Campania's bus network is extensive and in some areas buses can be more direct (and, therefore, faster) than local trains, so it's a good idea to compare bus and train schedules. Bus services outside cities are organized on a regional level, and often by private companies. Campania has three main bus companies, *listed below.* ANM handles buses within Naples, while SITA services longer trips, including the Amalfi Coast. Taking buses from Naples requires both research and patience, because there's no central bus station as such: different bus lines leave from different city squares, with the situation being compounded by regular traffic reorganization in Piazza Garibaldi to accommodate the ongoing metro construction. Once you've tracked down the schedule and departure point, you'll find the service fairly reliable and uniform. All buses—as indeed all public transport—are no-smoking.

CUTTING COSTS

For bus services within the region of Campania you should buy a **Unicocampania** ticket. For bus trips to Benevento, for example, where bus connections are better than train, you should buy a Fascia 6 ticket (€5.30, valid 190 minutes). This will cover combined use of other buses, funiculars, trains, trams, and trolley buses on an outward journey. Note that if you purchase a three-day **Artecard,** you get free transport within the region, regardless of the Fascia. Children up to 1 meter (just over 3 feet) tall travel free.

Artecard ☎ *800/600601 toll-free in Italy* 🌐 *www.campaniartecard.it.* **Unicocampania** ☎ *081/5513109* 🌐 *www.unicocampania.it.*

WORD OF MOUTH

"You can get by without speaking Italian, but if you do have some language, it will make your trip much more satisfying, even if it is only to order coffees and drinks. Italians respond well to people attempting to speak their language—even if your Italian is as bad as mine."

—Peter_S_Aus

PAYING

Tickets are not sold onboard buses so you must purchase them in advance (cash only) by machine (often no change given), at newsstands, at tobacconists, or at metro stations. Remember to time-stamp your ticket after you board as conductors sometimes do spot checks. Keep in mind that many ticket sellers close for several hours at midday, so it's always wise to stock up on bus tickets when you have the chance.

Bus Information ANM ✉ *Via G. Marino 1, Naples, Italy* ☎ *800/639525 toll-free in Italy* 🌐 *www.anm.it.* **SITA** ✉ *Varco Immacolata, inside Molo Beverello port, Naples, Italy* ☎ *089/405145* 🌐 *www.sitasudtrasporti.it.*

CAR TRAVEL

Combine the cost of gasoline (as much as €1.80 per liter, or $6.50 per gallon, at this writing), the weak and ever changeable dollar, the gridlock traffic in and around Naples, parking fees, and driving standards in southern Italy, and you get some good reasons for not traveling by car in Campania. There's an extensive network of *autostrade* (toll highways), complemented by equally well-maintained but free *superstrade* (expressways). The ticket you're issued on entering an autostrada must be returned when you exit and pay the toll; on some shorter highways, like the *tangenziale* around Naples, the flat-rate toll €0.90 is paid on exiting; the Naples–Salerno toll €2 is paid on entry. Viacard cards, on sale for €25, €50, or €75 at many autostrada locations, allow you to pay for tolls in advance, although if you're just using the car on local autostrade within Campania you may find yourself with substantial surplus credit on your card at the end of your trip. It is easier to simply use your credit card. At special lanes, identifiable by the blue sign, you simply slip the card into a designated slot at many autostrada locations, make paying tolls easier and faster. Here are some important signage words to know. A *raccordo* is a ring road surrounding a city, while a *tangenziale* bypasses a city entirely. An *uscita* is an exit. *Strade regionale* and *strade provinciale* (regional and provincial highways, denoted by *S*, *SS*, *SR*, or *SP* and numbers) may be single-lane roads, as are all secondary roads; directions and turnoffs aren't always clearly marked.

Your driver's license may not be recognized outside your home country. An International Driver's Permit is a good idea; it's available from the American or Canadian automobile association, and, in the United Kingdom, from the AA or RAC. These international permits are universally recognized, and having one in your wallet may save you a problem with the local authorities.

If you want to hire a driver, this service can usually be arranged through hotels or travel agents. Agree on a flat daily rate beforehand, which will include the driver, car, and gasoline. In most cases you would be expected to pay extra for the driver's meals, as well as any parking fees incurred.

AUTO CLUBS

There are two major automobile clubs operative in Italy: ACI (Automobile Club d'Italia), which also provides breakdown assistance coverage; subscription to the TCI (Touring Club Italiano) provides motorists with maps and logistical assistance when planning journeys and holidays, besides taking an active interest in Italian heritage preservation. For an annual surcharge of €22, the TCI will also provide breakdown assistance.

Automobile Club D'Italia ☎ *081/7253811* 🌐 *www.aci.it.* **Touring Club Italiano** ☎ *840/888802* 🌐 *www.touringclub.it.*

GASOLINE

Gas stations are along the main highways. Those on *autostrade* are open 24 hours. Otherwise, gas stations are generally open Monday through Saturday from 7 am to 7 pm with a break at lunchtime. Many stations also have self-service pumps, which usually accept bills of €5, €10, or €20. Gas stations on autostrade offer motorists the choice of self-service or full-service gasoline (more expensive per liter, no tip required). Credit cards are widely accepted, especially at major stations along main roads. Gas, so-called *benzina verde* (unleaded fuel known as "green gasoline"), costs about €1.70–€1.80 per liter. Confusingly, the Italian word *gasolio* means diesel fuel. It costs about €1.60 per liter (if you are renting a car, ask about the fuel type before you leave the agency).

PARKING

Parking space is at a premium in Naples and most towns, but especially in the *centri storici* (historic centers), which are filled with narrow streets and restricted circulation zones. It's often a good idea (if not the only option) to park your car in a designated (preferably attended) lot. The *parcometro*, the Italian version of metered parking in which you purchase prepaid tickets (from a newsstand or tobacconist's) that you scratch to indicate time and date of arrival and leave on the dashboard, is common both in Naples and in many of the surrounding towns. You will also find coin-only parking ticket machines at regular intervals. Watch the display panel at the front of the machine, which gives you the expiration time as you insert the coins. If driving to the more popular venues in Naples at night, you may be encouraged to park by a *parcheggiatore abusivo* (unlicensed parking attendant) who will expect a tip (about €1). Bear in mind that this will not stop your car from being clamped or towed away, and such practices are really just fueling the submerged economy.

A red sign with a horizontal white stripe through it means do not enter; a blue circular sign with a red slash or an X means no parking, as do the signs "Vietato Sostare, Divieto di Sosta" and "Non Parcheggiare." Wheel clamping is increasingly common in Naples, making parking offenses potentially costly and time-consuming. **TIP→ If you have baggage in the car, always park your car in an attended car park or garage.**

RENTALS

Most American chains have affiliates in Italy, but the rates are usually lower if you book a car before you leave home. To rent a car in Italy, generally you must be at least 23 years old. Additional drivers must be identified in the contract and must qualify with the age limits. There may be an additional daily fee for more than one driver. Upon rental, all companies require credit cards as a warranty; to rent bigger cars (2,000 cc or more), you must often show two credit cards. There are no special restrictions on senior-citizen drivers. Book car seats, required for children under age three, in advance (the cost is generally about €50 for the duration of the rental). Most rentals are standard transmissions. You must request an automatic and often pay a higher rate. A satellite navigation system will cost around €10 per day, and is an extremely useful investment.

All rental agencies operating in Italy require that you buy a collision-damage waiver and a theft-protection policy, but those costs will already be included in the rates you are quoted. Be aware that coverage may be denied if the named driver on the rental contract is not the driver at the time of the incident. Also ask your rental company about other included coverage when you reserve the car and/or pick it up.

LOCAL AGENCIES

Car and Driver Your Driver In Italy ☎ *328/830–7748* 🌐 *www.yourdriverinitaly.com.*

Major Agencies Alamo ☎ *888/222–9075* 🌐 *www.alamo.com.* **Auto Europe** ☎ *800/223–5555 toll free* 🌐 *www.autoeuropa.it.* **Avis** ☎ *800/331–1212* 🌐 *www.avis.com.* **Budget** ☎ *800/527–0700* 🌐 *www.budget.com.* **Hertz** ☎ *800/654–3131* 🌐 *www.hertz.com.* **National** ☎ *877/222–9058* 🌐 *www.nationalcar.com.* **Nova** ☎ *866/668–2227* 🌐 *www.novacarhire.com.*

ROAD CONDITIONS

Autostrade are well maintained, as are most interregional highways. The condition of provincial (county) roads varies, but road maintenance at this level is generally decent in Campania. Street and road signs are often challenging—a satellite navigator or good map and patience are essential. When stopping to ask locals for directions, it's usually pointless to refer to maps as there is no widespread map-reading culture in southern Italy. Just say the name of your destination and listen carefully or watch for hand gestures. In general, driving standards are poor: some drive fast and are impatient with those who don't, while others dawdle along oblivious to those behind them. Widespread nonuse of direction indicators means you have to do a lot of guesswork while motoring.

ROADSIDE EMERGENCIES

In the event of a breakdown, if you're on a major highway or autostrada, you should stay in your car and wait for assistance. It can be extremely dangerous to walk by the roadside. If you have to abandon your vehicle, make sure you use the reflective triangle and wear the orange jacket that every vehicle in Italy should contain.

In the event of an accident that goes beyond a mild bump or scratch, make sure the emergency services are notified as soon as possible—there should be an emergency number on the rental contract or on the key ring.

Emergency Services ACI Emergency Service offers 24-hour road service. Dial ☎ 803116 from any phone to reach the ACI dispatch operator.

RULES OF THE ROAD

Driving is on the right. Regulations are similar to those in the United States, except that a right turn is not permitted on a red light. Daytime use of headlights is now obligatory on all roads outside urban areas, and seat belts must be worn at all times—despite high noncompliance rates in Campania. In most Italian towns the use of the horn is forbidden; a large sign, "Zona di Silenzio," indicates where. Elsewhere, according to the Italian Highway Code, horns can only be used in situations where there is "immediate and real danger." Some drivers interpret this as covering every sharp bend on the Amalfi Coast, although an alternative noise-free technique is to slow down and keep a foot hovering over the brake pedal. In winter you'll often be required to have snow chains, especially when traveling south on the main autostrada from Salerno to Reggio Calabria, and in upland areas within the region. Speed limits are 130 kph (80 mph) on autostrade, 110 kph (70 mph) on *superstrade,* and 90 kph (55 mph) on state and provincial roads, unless otherwise marked. If your mobile phone rings while driving, you should either ignore it or pull over and stop when it's safe to do so—stiff sanctions have been introduced to reduce the use of handheld mobile phones while driving. Fines for driving after drinking are heavy, including the suspension of license and the additional possibility of six months' imprisonment.

TRAIN TRAVEL

The fastest trains in Italy are the state-run Freccia Rossa (red arrow), Alta Velocità, and the competing Nuovo Trasporto Viaggiatori (NTV) Italo, launched by Ferrari mogul Montezemolo in 2012. These operate between Rome and Naples (70 minutes), and also run the length of the peninsula, including Naples–Milan via Rome, Florence, and Bologna. A close second come the Freccia Bianca (white arrow) trains (1 hour 45 minutes); Some Eurostars (the ETR 460 trains) have little aisle and luggage space (although there's a space near the door where you can put large bags). Car numbers are displayed on their exterior. Next-fastest trains are the Intercity (IC) trains; seat reservations are included in the fare. *Interregionale* trains usually make more stops and are a little slower. *Regionale* and *locale* trains are the slowest; many serve commuters.

Almost all trains leave from the Stazione Centrale although you may be directed to Piazza Garibaldi on the lower level of the complex—take the escalator down to the level below Napoli Centrale (follow signs to the *Metropolitana*). Some trains to Rome leave from the classy station of Mergellina, four stops away from Piazza Garibaldi on the Metropolitana. As many as four trains—of varying speed and cost—connect Roma Termini and Napoli Centrale every hour (Alta Velocità and Italo: 1 hour 10 minutes, €43, second class; Freccia Bianca Eurostar: 1 hour 45 minutes, €37.50, second class; Intercity: about 2 hours 10 minutes, €24.50, second class. Substantial discounts are available when booking in advance); fewer departures on Sunday and after 5 pm.

CUTTING COSTS

If Italy is your only destination in Europe, consider purchasing a Eurail Italy pass, which allows unlimited travel on the Italian Rail network (but not Italo) for a set number of travel days within two months: $328 for 4 days of travel in first class ($267 second class); 8 days of travel ($471 first class, $383 second class); and 10 days of travel ($542 first class, $441 second class). Prices are further reduced for groups of two to five people traveling together. More information can be found at 🌐 *www.raileurope.com.*

Those under 26 should inquire about discount travel fares under the Carta Verde (Green Card) and Euro Domino Junior schemes. If you are over 60, enquire about the Carta Argento (Silver Card) (€30 for one year, free for over 75s), which allows a 15% discount on all first- and second-class rail travel. Toddlers under four travel free on trains, though they have no right to a seat, while children under 14 travel for half the fare, but must be accompanied by an adult.

Many travelers assume that rail passes guarantee them seats on the trains they wish to ride. Not so. You need to book seats ahead even if you're using a rail pass.

If you're on a tight schedule or just want to avoid unpleasant surprises, double-check beforehand whether there's a strike (*sciopero*) planned for the day you're traveling—these can happen three or four times a year. On average, industrial action is usually planned for 24-hour periods on Friday or Monday, and only limited service may be provided while the strike lasts.

FARES AND SCHEDULES

To avoid long lines at station windows, you can buy tickets with seat reservations up to two months in advance at travel agencies displaying the Trenitalia or Italo emblem. The self-service machines in major stations will also save you time. Tickets can be purchased at the last minute; if you board without a ticket, you will have to pay a surcharge of €50 on application to train staff.

On trains without reservations tickets must be date-stamped in the small yellow or green machines near the tracks before you board. Once stamped, your ticket is valid for six hours if your destination is within 200 km (124 miles), for 24 hours for destinations beyond that. You can get on and off at will at stops in between for the duration of the ticket's validity. If you forget to stamp your ticket in the machine, or you didn't buy a ticket, you are liable to a hefty €50 fine, over and above the fare to your destination. Don't wait for the conductor to find out that you're without a valid ticket (unless the train is overcrowded and walking becomes impossible), as he might charge you a much heavier fine. You can buy train tickets for nearby destinations (within a 200-km [124-mile] range) at tobacconists and at ticket machines in stations.

USEFUL STATIONS

The main train station in Campania is Naples's **Stazione Centrale**. The Ferrovia Circumvesuviana leaves for points east from the **Stazione Circumvesuviana**; all trains also stop on the lower level of Stazione Centrale. Destinations include Ercolano (Herculaneum), Pompei Scavi–Villa dei Misteri (Pompeii), and Sorrento. Note that there are two Circumvesuviana stations in the town of Pompeii, served by different lines. For the archaeological site, take the Sorrento line. SEPSA manages two railway lines that leave from the **Stazione Cumana**. Both end at Torregaveta, at the west end of the Bay of Naples; the Cumana line goes along the coast and stops at Pozzuoli and Lucrino (near Baia), among other places. **Salerno's train station** is a stop on the Milan–Reggio Calabria line.

Information **Circumvesuviana** ✉ *Italy* 🌐 *www.eavcampania.it.* **Stazione Cumana** ✉ *Piazzetta Montesanto, near Montesanto Metro station, Italy* ☎ *800/211388 toll free* 🌐 *www.eavcampania.it.* **Salerno's train station.** Salerno's train station is a stop on the Milan–Reggio Calabria line. ✉ *Piazza V. Veneto, Italy* ☎ *199/892021 within Italy* 🌐 *www.trenitalia.com.* **Stazione Centrale** ✉ *Piazza Garibaldi, Naples, Italy* ☎ *892021* 🌐 *www.trenitalia.com, www.italotreno.it.*

Other Resources **NTV Italo** ✉ *Naples, Italy* ☎ *06/0708* 🌐 *www.italotreno.it.* **Trenitalia** ☎ *892021 in Italy (fee charged)* 🌐 *www.trenitalia.com.* **Trenitalia** ✉ *Naples, Italy* ☎ *199/892021 within Italy* 🌐 *www.trenitalia.com.*

ESSENTIALS

ACCOMMODATIONS

Campania has a varied and abundant number of hotels, bed-and-breakfasts, *agriturismi* (farm stays), and rental properties. Throughout the cities and the countryside you can find very sophisticated, luxurious palaces and villas as well as rustic farmhouses and small hotels. Six-hundred-year-old *palazzi* and converted monasteries have been restored as luxurious hotels, while retaining the original atmosphere. At the other end of the spectrum, boutique hotels inhabit historic buildings using chic Italian design for the interiors. Increasingly, the famed Italian wineries are creating rooms and apartments for three-day to week-long stays.

The lodgings we list are the cream of the crop in each price category. When pricing accommodations, always ask what's included and what costs extra (air-conditioning often incurs an extra charge). Properties are assigned price categories based on the range between their least- and most-expensive standard double room at high season (excluding holidays).

Note that this region of Italy has many resort hotels and in peak-season months (usually June to September), some of them require either half- or full-board arrangements, whereby your (increased) room tab includes one or two meals provided by the hotel restaurant. Board plans, which are usually an option offered in addition to the basic room plan, are generally only available with a minimum two- or three-night stay and are, of course, more expensive than the basic room rate, running from €10 to €50 per meal. Note that the hotel prices in this book reflect basic room rates only. Inquire about board plans when making your reservations; details and prices are often stated on hotel websites.

Useful terms to know when booking a room are *aria condizionata* (air-conditioning), *bagno in stanza* (private bath), *letto matrimoniale* (double bed), *letti singoli* (twin beds), *letti singoli uniti* (twin beds pushed together). Italy does not really have queen- or king-size beds, although some beds, particularly in four- and five-star accommodations, can be larger than standard.

APARTMENT AND HOUSE RENTALS

Renting an apartment, a farmhouse, or a villa can be economical depending on the number of people in your group and your budget. Issues to keep in mind when renting an apartment in a city or town are the neighborhood (street noise and ambience), the availability of an elevator or number of stairs, the furnishings (including pots and pans and linens), and the cost of utilities (ask if they are included in the rental rate). Inquiries about countryside properties should also include how isolated the property is. (Ask about accessibility to the nearest town.)

Contacts **At Home Abroad** ☎ *212/421–9165* 🌐 *www.athomeabroadinc.com.* **Barclay International Group** ☎ *800/845–6636, 516/364–0064* 🌐 *www.barclayweb.com.* **Drawbridge to Europe** ☎ *541/482–7778* 🌐 *www.drawbridgetoeurope.com.* **Home Away** ✉ *Italy* ☎ *512/493–0382* 🌐 *www.homeaway.com.* **Interhome** ✉ *Italy* ☎ *800/882–6864* 🌐 *www.interhomeusa.com.* **Rent A Villa** ☎ *877/250–4366, 206/417–3444* 🌐 *www.rentavilla.com.* **Villas & Apartments Abroad** ☎ *212/213–6435* 🌐 *www.vaanyc.com.* **Villas of Distinction** ☎ *800/289–0900* 🌐 *www.villasofdistinction.com.* **Villas International** ☎ *800/221–2260, 415/499–9490* 🌐 *www.villasintl.com.*

BED-AND-BREAKFASTS

Although these may represent substantial cost savings, be aware that quality varies. When booking, try to find out exactly what's on offer. For further information, contact the local tourist information office or one of the agencies below.

Reservation Services Bed & Breakfast.com ☎ *512/322-2710* 🌐 *www.bedandbreakfast.com.* **Bed & Breakfast Inns Online** ✉ *Italy* ☎ *800/215-7365* 🌐 *www.bbonline.com.* **BnB Finder.com** ☎ *888/469-6663* 🌐 *www.bnbfinder.com.* **Rent a Bed** ✉ *Italy* ☎ *081/417721* 🌐 *www.rentabed.it.*

HOME EXCHANGES

With a direct home exchange you stay in someone else's home while they stay in yours. Some outfits also deal with vacation homes, so you're not actually staying in someone's full-time residence, just their vacant weekend place.

Exchange Clubs Home Exchange.com. Membership is $7.95 monthly. ☎ *800/877-8723, 310/798-3864* 🌐 *www.homeexchange.com.* **HomeLink International.** Membership is $89 for one year, $142 for two; additional listings are $25. ☎ *800/638-3841, 954/566-2687, 0422/815575 in Italy* 🌐 *www.homelink.org.* **Intervac Home Exchange.** One-year membership is $99. ☎ *800/756-4663* 🌐 *www.intervac-homeexchange.com.*

COMMUNICATIONS

INTERNET

Getting online in and around Naples isn't difficult: free Wi-Fi is available in many places, and there are also public Internet stations and Internet cafés. Prices differ from place to place, so spend some time to find the best deal. Bear in mind that you are required by law to show a photo ID before logging on. Some hotels in Campania have in-room modem lines and have implemented Wi-Fi systems but, as with phones, using the hotel's line is relatively expensive. Always check rates before logging on. You might need an adapter for your computer for the European-style plugs. As always, if you're traveling with a laptop, carry a spare battery and an adapter. Never connect your computer to any socket before asking about surge protection. IBM sells a pea-size modem tester that plugs into a telephone jack to check whether the line is safe to use.

Contact Cybercafes. This website lists more than 4,000 Internet cafés worldwide. 🌐 *www.cybercafes.com.*

PHONES

Calling from a hotel is almost always the most expensive option; cell phone calls are still usually a much cheaper option than calling from your hotel.

In Naples, you can phone from call centers, many of which are found around Stazione Centrale. Public pay phones are becoming increasingly scarce. Pay phones require a *sceda telefonica* (prepaid phone card). You buy the card (values vary) at Telecom centers, post offices, and tobacconists. Break off the corner of the card, and insert it in the slot on the phone. When you dial, the card's value appears in the window. After you hang up, the card is returned so you can use it until its value runs out.

When calling Italy from the United States, begin by entering 011 (begin with 00 in other countries), followed by Italy's country code, 39. Note that Italian telephone numbers do not have a standard number of digits (they can range anywhere from four to eight). The area code for Naples is 081. Essentially, the region from Naples to the islands (Capri, Ischia, Procida) and around the Bay of Naples to Sorrento uses the area code 081; the region along the Amalfi Coast from Positano to Salerno uses the area code 089. When dialing an Italian number from abroad, you do not drop the initial 0 from the local area code. The same goes for when you're in Italy. When dialing numbers within Italy, you must always use the area code (e.g., 081 for Naples) even if the number you're calling is just down the road. Mobile phone numbers can be easily recognized; they begin with the digit 3, and run up to about 10 numbers.

LOCAL DO'S AND TABOOS

GREETINGS

Upon meeting and leave-taking, both friends and strangers wish each other good day or good evening (*buongiorno, buonasera*); *ciao* isn't used between strangers. Italians who are friends greet each other with a kiss, usually first on the left cheek, then on the right. When you meet a new person, shake hands.

SIGHTSEEING

Italy is full of churches, and many of them contain significant works of art. They are also places of worship, however, so be sure to dress appropriately. Shorts, tank tops, and sleeveless garments are taboo in most churches throughout the country. Some churches provide scarves at the entrance, but to be safe carry a sweater or other item of clothing to wrap around your bare shoulders before entering.

You should never bring food into a church, and do not sip from your water bottle while inside. If you have a cell phone, switch it to silent mode. And avoid entering a church when a service is in progress, especially if it is a private affair such as a wedding or baptism.

OUT ON THE TOWN

Table manners in Italy are formal; rarely do Italians share food from their plates. In a restaurant, be formal and polite with your waiter—don't call across the room for attention.

When you've finished your meal and are ready to go, ask for the check (*il conto*); unless it's well past closing time, or there is a waiting list, it is unlikely a waiter will put a bill on your table until you've requested it.

Wine, beer, and other alcoholic drinks are almost always consumed along with food. Public drunkenness is very much looked down on.

Smoking has been banned in all public establishments, much as it has in much of the United States, although you may spot some people flouting the law.

Flowers, chocolates, or a bottle of wine are appropriate hostess gifts when invited to dinner at the home of an Italian.

DOING BUSINESS

Showing up on time for business appointments is the norm and expected in Italy, although there is some flexibility with this in Naples. There are more business lunches than business dinners, and even business lunches aren't common, as Italians view mealtimes as periods of pleasure and relaxation.

Business cards are used throughout Italy, and business suits are the norm for both men and women. To be on the safe side, it is best not to use first names or a familiar form of address until invited to do so.

Business gifts are not the norm, but if one is given it is usually small and symbolic of your home location or type of business.

LANGUAGE

One of the best ways to make connections with the locals is to learn a little of the language. You need not strive for fluency; even just mastering a few basic words and terms is bound to make chatting with the locals more rewarding. "Please" is *per favore*, "thank you" is *grazie*, and "you're welcome" is *prego*.

In most of the places listed in this guide, language is not a big problem. Most hotels have English speakers at their reception desks, and if not, they can always find someone who speaks at least a little English.

You may have trouble communicating in the countryside, but a phrase book and expressive gestures will go a long way. A phrase book and language-tape set can help get you started before you go.

MOBILE PHONES

If you have a triband phone and your service provider uses the world-standard GSM network, you can probably use your phone abroad. Roaming fees can be steep, however: 99¢ a minute is considered reasonable. And overseas you normally pay the toll charges for incoming calls. It's almost always cheaper to send a text message than to make a call.

TIP→ If you're carrying a laptop, tablet, or smartphone, investigate apps and services such as Skype, Viber, and Whatsapp, which offer free or low-cost calling or texting services.

If you just want to make local calls, consider buying a new SIM card (note that your provider may have to unlock your phone for you to use a different SIM card) and a prepaid service plan in the destination. You'll then have a local number and can make local calls at local rates. If your trip is extensive, you could also simply buy a new cell phone in your destination, as the initial cost will be offset over time.

TIP→ If you travel internationally frequently, save one of your old mobile phones or buy a cheap one on the Internet; ask your cell phone company to unlock it for you, and take it with you as a travel phone, buying a new SIM card with pay-as-you-go service in each destination.

The cost of cell phones is dropping; you can purchase a cell phone with a prepaid calling card (no monthly service plan) in Italy for less than €50. Inexpensive cell phones are dual band and will not allow you to call the United States, but using an international calling card and the cell phone solves that problem in an inexpensive manner. You will need to present your passport to purchase the SIM card that goes with the phone.

Rental cell phones are available from some tour operators in Naples and the Amalfi Coast. Most rental contracts require a refundable deposit that covers the cost of the cell phone (€75–€150) and then set up a monthly service plan that is automatically charged to your credit card. Frequently, rental cell phones will be triple band and allow you to call the United States. Be sure to check the rate schedule before you rent a cell phone and commence calling to prevent a nasty surprise when you receive your credit-card bill two or three months later.

TIP→ Beware of cell phone (and PDA) thieves. Keep your phone or PDA in a secure pocket or purse. Do not lay it on the bar when you stop for an espresso. Do not zip it into the outside pocket of your backpack in the city or public transport. Do not leave it in your hotel room. If you are using a phone with a monthly service plan, notify your provider immediately if it is lost or stolen.

Contacts Cellular Abroad. This is a good source for SIM cards that work in many countries; travel-friendly phones can also be purchased or rented. ☎ *800/287-5072* 🌐 *www.cellularabroad.com*. **Mobal.** GSM phones that will operate in 190 countries are available for purchase (starting at $29) and rent. Per-call rates in Italy are $1.25 per minute; sending a text costs $.80. ☎ *888/888-9162, 212/785-5800 Support* 🌐 *www.mobal.com.*

CUSTOMS AND DUTIES

You're always allowed to bring goods of a certain value back home without having to pay any duty or import tax. But there's a limit on the amount of tobacco and liquor you can bring back duty-free, and some countries have separate limits for perfumes; for exact figures, check with your customs department. The values of so-called duty-free goods are included in these amounts. When you shop abroad, save all your receipts, as customs inspectors may ask to see them as well as the items you purchased. If the total value of your goods is more than the duty-free limit, you'll have to pay a tax (most often a flat percentage) on the value of everything beyond that limit.

U.S. residents are normally entitled to a duty-free exemption of $800 on items accompanying them. As a general rule, mature cheeses like Parmesan—especially if they're vacuum-packed—are fine, but soft cheeses are not. Condiments such as oil, vinegar, honey, jelly, and jam, are generally admissible. You cannot bring back any of that delicious prosciutto or salami or any other meat product. Fresh mushrooms, truffles, or fresh fruits and vegetables are also forbidden. There are also restrictions on the amount of alcohol allowed in duty-free. Export of antiques and antiquities is best avoided unless you have access to specialist advice; you must have documents such as export permits and receipts when importing such items into the United States. In any case, to avoid unpleasant surprises—and such regulations change with the arrival of every health scare—check with the relevant authorities listed below.

Of goods obtained anywhere outside the EU or goods purchased in a duty-free shop within an EU country, the allowances are: (1) 200 cigarettes or 100 cigarillos or 50 cigars or 250 grams of tobacco; (2) 4 liters of still table wine or 1 liter of spirits over 22% volume or 2 liters of spirits under 22% volume or 2 liters of fortified and sparkling wines; and (3) 60 milliliters of perfume and 250 milliliters of toilet water.

To bring pets into Italy, the animal has to have a certificate of health and origin from a recognized public authority in your country, and may also need a certificate that it's free of infectious diseases. For cats and dogs the health certificate must include a declaration of an anti-rabies vaccination at least 20 days and no more than 11 months after issuing the certificate. Similar rules apply to exporting pets from Italy to the United States.

Information in Italy Italian Customs *(Dipartimento delle Dogane e Imposte Indirette).* ✉ *Via A. de Gasperi 20, Naples, Italy* ☎ *081/7803036, 081/5521759* 🌐 *www.agenziadogane.it.*

U.S. Information U.S. Customs and Border Protection ☎ *877/227-5511* 🌐 *www.cbp.gov.*

EATING OUT

Though pizza, mozzarella, and pasta with seafood are the flagship dishes in the Naples region, regional cuisine in Campania is both varied and distinctive. This is reflected by the choice of eateries, especially in Naples and Sorrento: meals range from on-the-hoof one-euro pizzas at kiosks, to earthy *osterie* serving *cucina povera* (land-based cuisine with a good dose of vegetables), and upscale restaurants where service, location, and *piatti* (dishes) should be worth the higher price tag. Italian restaurateurs have become sensitive to those with special dietary requirements, though vegetarians may still have a rough ride, especially as bacon or kindred pork products may be used to flavor many land dishes but never appear as an item on the menu.

MEALS AND MEALTIMES

Breakfast (*la colazione*) is usually served from 7 to 10:30, lunch (*il pranzo*) from 12:30 to 2:30, dinner (*la cena*) from 7:30 pm until midnight. Although it's not usually necessary to reserve a table, remember that you'll find restaurants deserted before 8 in the evening and packed by 9:30, while lunch can extend until as late as 5 pm on Sunday. Menus can sometimes seem to be an optional extra in many restaurants, and often those that do exist bear little relation to what is actually on offer that day. Tune in carefully as the waiter reels off a list of what's good today—following their advice often pays off. A full-scale meal consists of a selection of *antipasti* followed by a *primo* (pasta or rice), then a *secondo* (meat or fish), rounded off with *frutta o dolci* (fruit or dessert). In general, Neapolitans have moved away from the classic *abbuffata* (Satyricon-style blowout) toward healthier two-course, or even one-course, meals. You should not feel guilty about skipping the main course, especially if you've already had a rich antipasto and primo.

Enoteche (wine bars) are open also in the morning and late afternoon for a snack at the counter. An enoteca menu is often limited to a selection of cheese, cured meats, salads, and desserts, but if there's a kitchen you'll also find soups, pastas, and main courses, too. Most pizzerias are open all day, closing around midnight, or later in summer and on weekends. Most bars and cafés are open nonstop from 7 am until 8 pm; a few stay open until midnight or so. They can usually fix you up with *un toast* (a toasted sandwich) if every other option is closed.

Bars are primarily places to get a coffee and a bite to eat, rather than drinking establishments. Most bars have a selection of *panini* (sandwiches) warmed up on the griddle (*piastra*) and *tramezzini* (sandwiches made of untoasted white bread triangles). Most bars offer beer and a variety of alcohol as well as wines by the glass (sometimes good but more often mediocre). A café (*caffè* in Italian) is like a bar but usually with more tables. Pizza at a café should be avoided—it's usually heated in a microwave.

If you place your order at the counter, ask if you can sit down: some places charge for table service, others do not. In self-service bars and cafés it's good manners to clean your table before you leave. Note that in some places you have to pay a cashier, then place your order and show your *scontrino* (receipt) at the counter. Menus are posted outside most restaurants (in English in tourist areas). Although mineral water makes its way to almost every table, you can order a carafe of tap water (*acqua dal rubinetto*).

Wiping your bowl clean with a piece of bread (*fare la scarpetta*) is usually considered a sign of appreciation, not bad manners. Spaghetti should be eaten with a fork, although a little help from a spoon won't horrify locals the way cutting spaghetti into little pieces might. Don't ask for a doggy bag.

Unless otherwise noted, the restaurants listed in this guide are open daily for lunch and dinner.

PAYING

As indicated on *il conto*—the restaurant check—prices for goods and services in Italy include tax. Most restaurants have a cover charge per person, usually listed at the top of the check as *coperto* or *pane*. It should be a modest charge (around €2 per person), except at the most expensive restaurants. Some restaurants add an additional service charge (*servizio*), a percentage of the total bill, but this must be clearly stated on the menu. Although the vast majority of eateries now accept major credit cards, tips are still left in cash. The price of fish dishes is often given by weight (before cooking), so the price you see on the menu is for 100 grams or a kilo of fish, not for the whole dish. An average fish portion is about 350 grams. When it comes to smaller cafés and pizzerias, you sometimes place your order and then show your *scontrino* (receipt) when you move to the counter. Like the rest of Italy, there's a two-tier pricing system in many cafés, one for drinks consumed at the counter, and another if you sit down. If there's waiter service in a café, you should sit down and patiently wait for service, and resist the temptation to pay first (counter prices), pick up your drink, and walk to the table.

When you leave a dining establishment, take your meal bill or receipt with you; although not a common experience, the Italian finance (tax) police can approach you within 100 yards of the establishment at which you've eaten and ask for a receipt. If you don't have one, they can fine you and will fine the business owner for not providing the receipt.

RESERVATIONS AND DRESS

Regardless of where you are, it's a good idea to make a reservation if you can. We only mention them specifically when reservations are essential (there's no other way you'll ever get a table) or when they are not accepted. For popular restaurants, book as far ahead as you can (a week or two in advance), and reconfirm as soon as you arrive. (Large parties should always call ahead to check the reservations policy.)

We mention dress only when men are required to wear a jacket or a jacket and tie. But unless they're dining outside or at an oceanfront resort, Italian men rarely wear shorts or running shoes in a restaurant. The same applies to women: no casual shorts, running shoes, or plastic sandals when going out to dinner. Shorts are acceptable in pizzerias and cafés.

WINES, BEER, AND SPIRITS

Refreshingly, there's a fairly low markup on bottled wines, and a liter of house wine rarely costs more than €8–€10. At the end of your meal you may well be offered some of the house liqueur, probably *limoncello* (a lemon-based liqueur with varying proportions of sugar) or *nocillo* (from green walnuts).

In general, the southern Italians have a relaxed attitude to alcohol consumption. In many homes, a bottle of wine on the dining table is a necessary accompaniment to any meal, like salt and olive oil. All bars and cafés are licensed to serve alcohol, and even takeaway pizzas can be enjoyed with a beer in a city park.

ELECTRICITY

The electrical current in Italy is 220 volts, 50 cycles alternating current (AC); wall outlets take Continental-type plugs, with two or three round prongs.

Consider making a small investment in a universal adapter, which has several types of plugs in one lightweight, compact unit. Most laptops and mobile-phone chargers are dual voltage (i.e., they operate equally well on 110 and 220 volts), so require only an adapter. These days the same is true of small appliances such as hair dryers. Always check labels and manufacturer instructions to be sure. Don't use 110-volt outlets marked "For Shavers Only" for high-wattage appliances such as hair dryers. Adaptors can be found at some *ferramente* (hardware stores) in Naples and the Amalfi Coast. Ask for *"un adatattore per una presa americana."*

Contacts Steve Kropla's Help for World Travelers. Steve Kropla's Help for World Travelers has information on electrical and telephone plugs around the world. *www.kropla.com.*

EMERGENCIES

No matter where you are in Italy, dial 113 for all emergencies, or find somebody (your concierge, a passerby) who will call for you, as not all 113 operators speak English; the Italian word to use to draw people's attention in an emergency is *"Aiuto!"* (Help!, pronounced "ah-YOU-toh"). *"Pronto soccorso"* means "first aid" and when said to an operator will get you an *ambulanza* (ambulance). If you just need a doctor, you should ask for *un medico*; most hotels will be able to refer you to a local doctor. Don't forget to ask the doctor for *una ricevuta* (an invoice) to show to your insurance company in order to get a reimbursement. Other useful Italian words to use in an emergency are *"Fuoco!"* (Fire!, pronounced "fuh-WOE-co"), and *"Ladro!"* (Thief!, pronounced "LAH-droh").

Italy has a national police force (*carabinieri*) as well as local police (*polizia*). Both are armed and have the power to arrest and investigate crimes. Always report the loss of your passport to either the carabinieri or the police, as well as to your embassy. When reporting a crime, you'll be asked to fill out *una denuncia* (official report); keep a copy for your insurance company. Local traffic officers are known as *vigili* (though their official name is *polizia municipale*)—they are responsible for, among other things, giving out parking tickets and clamping cars (note that there are also private firms licensed to do this). Should you find yourself involved in a minor car accident in town, you should contact the vigili.

Car Breakdowns and Emergencies (☎ *803, 116*).

Foreign Embassies U.S. Consulate Naples ✉ *Piazza della Repubblica, Naples, Italy* ☎ *081/5838111* 🌐 *naples.usconsulate.gov.* **U.S. Embassy** ✉ *Via Vittorio Veneto 121, Rome, Italy* ☎ *06/46741* 🌐 *italy.usembassy.gov.*

General Emergency Contacts Ambulance ✉ *Naples, Italy* ☎ *118.* **Emergencies** ☎ *115 Fire, 118 Ambulance.* **Medical emergency.** Ask for an English-speaking nurse. ✉ *Naples, Italy* ☎ *081/7613466, 081/2547082 after 8 pm.* **National and State Police** ☎ *112 Polizia (National Police), 113 Carabinieri (State Police).* **Police Station.** Naples' Main Police Station has an *ufficio stranieri* (foreigners' office) that usually has an English speaker on staff and can help with passport problems. ✉ *Via Medina 75, Naples, Italy* ☎ *081/7941111.*

HOURS OF OPERATION

Before you travel, check ahead for public holidays, especially April 25, May 1, and June 2, when public offices and most shops are closed. When holidays fall on a Sunday, it is business as usual on Monday.

Banks are open weekdays 8:30 to 1:15 and 2:45 to 3:45.

Post offices are open weekdays 8:30 to 2 and Saturday from 9 to 1; central and main district post offices stay open until 6 weekdays, 9 to 1 on Saturday.

Gas stations open about 7 am and close at about 8 pm. In sleepy country areas away from major roads they close for lunch between 1 and 4, and on Sunday, so make sure you fill up beforehand. Services open around the clock can be found on *autostrade* and the *tangenziale* around Naples, and there are about 20 *benzinai notturni* (night-shift gas-stations) operating in various parts of Naples. Details can be found in local newspapers.

The major museums in Naples, such as Museo Archeologico Nazionale, Museo di Capodimonte, Palazzo Reale, and San Martino, are often open through to the evening, although you may find some rooms closed due to lack of staff. Many smaller private museums are only open from 9 am to 1 or 2 pm. The opening times of archaeological sites are subject to seasonal variations, with most sites closing an hour before sunset, and preventing access as much as two hours before. When this book refers to summer hours, it means approximately Easter to October; winter hours run from November to Easter. Most museums are closed one day a week, often Monday or Wednesday. Always check locally.

Most churches are open from early morning until noon or 12:30, when they close for three hours or more; they open again in the afternoon, closing about 7 pm or later. Be as discreet as possible when services are in progress.

Pharmacies are generally open weekdays from 8:30 to 1 and from 4 to 8, and Saturday morning 9 to 1. Local pharmacies cover the off-hours in shifts: On the door of every pharmacy is a list of pharmacies that will be open in the vicinity on Saturday afternoon, Sunday, or 24 hours. If the *farmacia* (pharmacy) in Naples's Stazione Centrale is closed, it will post the address of one that's open; the newspaper *Il Mattino* also prints a list of pharmacies that are open nights and weekends.

Most shops are open Monday–Saturday 10–1 and 3:30 or 4–7:30 or 8. Most shops in downtown Naples will close for two to four weeks in August. They observe extended hours for the three weeks leading up to Christmas and many close from December 25 to January 6.

HOLIDAYS

National holidays include January 1 (New Year's Day); January 6 (Epiphany); Easter Sunday and Monday; April 25 (Liberation Day); May 1 (Labor Day or May Day); June 2 (Founding of the

Italian Republic); August 15 (Assumption of Mary, also known as *Ferragosto*); November 1 (All Saints' Day); December 8 (Immaculate Conception); and December 25 and 26 (Christmas Day and St. Stephen's Day). During these holidays many shops and restaurants are closed, while decisions about whether to open major museums and archaeological sites like Pompeii and Herculaneum are usually made at the 11th hour.

The feast days of patron saints are observed locally in various towns and villages; some of the more famous *feste* are: San Costanzo, Capri, May 14; San Antonio, Anacapri, June 13; Sant'Andrea, Amalfi, June 25–30; San Pietro, Positano, June 29; Sant'Anna, Ischia, July 26; and San Pantaleone, Ravello, July 27. In Naples, two annual celebrations are held at the Duomo on the first Sunday in May and on September 19 to celebrate the Festa di San Gennaro, or the Liquefaction of the Blood of San Gennaro.

MAIL

The Italian mail system has made great progress in speed and reliability, although it can still be slow, so allow up to 10 days for mail to and from the United States and Canada, about a week to and from the United Kingdom. You should be able to buy postage stamps at tobacconists without having to line up in post offices.

To send urgent letters and papers to the United States and elsewhere, consider the *Paccocelere Internazionale* system, which is similar to a courier system, but not necessarily cheaper. This service is offered at several major post offices in Naples and in town post offices throughout the area.

Correspondence can be addressed to you in care of the Italian post office. Letters should be addressed to your name, "c/o Ufficio Postale Centrale," followed by "Fermo Posta" on the next line, and the name of the city (preceded by its postal code) on the next. You can collect it at the central post office by showing your passport or photo-bearing ID and paying a small fee. American Express also has a general-delivery service. There's no charge for cardholders, holders of American Express traveler's checks, or anyone who booked a vacation with American Express. When shipping a package out of Italy, it is virtually impossible to find an overnight delivery option—the fastest delivery time is 48 to 72 hours.

MONEY

Italy's prices are in line with those in the rest of Europe, with costs in its main cities comparable to those in other major capitals, such as Paris and Madrid. As in most countries, prices vary from region to region and are a bit lower in the countryside than in the cities. Good value for money can still be had in many places in Naples and on the Amalfi Coast.

Prices throughout this guide are given for adults. Substantially reduced fees are almost always available for children, students, and senior citizens from the European Union.

TIP→ Banks never have every foreign currency on hand, and it may take as long as a week to order. If you're planning to exchange funds before leaving home, don't wait until the last minute.

ATMS AND BANKS

Your own bank will probably charge a fee for using ATMs abroad; the foreign bank you use may also charge a fee. Nevertheless, you'll usually get a better rate of exchange at an ATM than you will at a currency-exchange office or even when changing money in a bank. Check with your bank to confirm that you have an international PIN (*codice segreto*) that will be recognized in Italy, to find out your maximum daily withdrawal allowance, and to learn what the bank fee is for withdrawing money. **TIP→ Be aware that PINs beginning with a 0 (zero) tend to be rejected in Italy.**

Don't count on finding ATMs in tinier towns and rural areas. Italian ATMs are reliable, and are commonly attached to a bank—you won't find one, for example, in a supermarket. The word for ATM in Italian is *bancomat,* for PIN, *codice segreto.*

CREDIT CARDS

It's a good idea to inform your credit-card company before you travel. Record all your credit-card numbers—as well as the phone numbers to call if your cards are lost or stolen—in a safe place. Both MasterCard and Visa have general numbers you can call (collect if you're abroad) if your card is lost, but you're better off calling the number of your issuing bank, since MasterCard and Visa generally just transfer you to your bank.

If you plan to use your credit card for cash advances, you'll need to apply for a PIN at least two weeks before your trip. Although it's usually cheaper (and safer) to use a credit card abroad for large purchases (so you can cancel payments or be reimbursed if there's a problem), note that some credit-card companies *and* the banks that issue them add substantial percentages to all foreign transactions, whether they're in a foreign currency or not. Check on these fees before leaving home.

■ TIP→ Before you charge something, ask the merchant whether he or she plans to do a dynamic currency conversion (DCC). In such a transaction the credit-card processor (shop, restaurant, or hotel, not Visa or MasterCard) converts the currency and charges you in dollars. In most cases you'll pay the merchant a 3% fee for this service in addition to any credit-card company and issuing-bank foreign-transaction surcharges.

Dynamic currency conversion programs are becoming increasingly widespread. Merchants who participate in them are supposed to ask whether you want to be charged in dollars or the local currency, but they don't always do so. And even if they do offer you a choice, they may well avoid mentioning the additional surcharges. The good news is that you *do* have a choice. And if this practice really gets your goat, you can avoid it entirely thanks to American Express; with its cards, DCC simply isn't an option.

MasterCard and Visa are preferred by Italian merchants, so don't expect American Express to be accepted everywhere, even in tourist spots; Travelers Checks are also seldom accepted. If you want to pay with a credit card in a small shop, hotel, or restaurant, it's a good idea to make your intentions known early on. In general, use cash, not credit cards, for purchases below €20. Southern Italy is still very much a cash-based society.

Reporting Lost Cards American Express ☎ *800/528–4800 in U.S., 905/474–0870 collect from abroad* 🌐 *www.americanexpress.com.* **Diners Club** ☎ *800/234–6377 in U.S., 514/881–3735 collect from abroad, 800/393939 in Italy* 🌐 *www.dinersclub.com.* **MasterCard** ☎ *800/627–8372 in U.S., 636/722–7111 collect from abroad, 800/151616 in Italy* 🌐 *www.mastercard.us.* **Visa** ☎ *800/847–2911 in U.S., 303/967–1096 from abroad, 800/819014 in Italy* 🌐 *usa.visa.com.*

CURRENCY AND EXCHANGE

The unit of currency in Italy is the euro, currently adopted in 17 countries of the European Union. This is printed in bills of 500 (practically impossible to change outside of banks), 200, 100, 50, 20, 10, and 5. Coins are €2, €1, 50 cents, 20 cents, 10 cents, 5 cents, 2 cents, and 1 cent (although Neapolitans tend to ignore these last two). **■ TIP→ When changing money, make sure you ask for small-denomination notes, preferably of 50 euros and below, as retailers in Naples and the surrounding area are notoriously bereft of small change.**

The euro continues to fluctuate considerably against other currencies. At the time of this writing the exchange rate was about €0.76 to the U.S. dollar.

■ TIP→ Even if a currency-exchange booth has a sign promising no commission, rest assured that there's some kind of huge, hidden fee. As for rates, you're almost always better off getting foreign currency at an ATM or exchanging money at a bank.

PACKING

In summer, stick with clothing that is as light as possible, although a sweater may be necessary for cool evenings, especially in the Lattari Mountains along the Amalfi Coast (even during the hot months). Sunglasses, a hat, and sunblock are essential, now more than ever due to global warming, which often sends the temperature soaring to 95°F or more in the middle of summer. But, contrary to myth, the sun does not shine all day, every day on Campania: brief summer thunderstorms are common in Naples, while typhoon-like storms occasionally arrive along the Amalfi Coast, so an umbrella will definitely come in handy. In winter bring a medium-weight coat and a raincoat; winters in Naples can be both humid *and* cold. Even in Naples, central heating may not be up to your standards, and interiors can be chilly and damp; take wools or flannel rather than sheer fabrics. Bring sturdy shoes for winter, and comfortable walking shoes in any season.

For sightseeing, pack a pair of binoculars; they will help you get a good look at Naples' wondrous painted ceilings and domes. If you stay in budget hotels, take your own shampoo and soap.

PASSPORTS AND VISAS

U.S. citizens need only a valid passport to enter Italy for stays of up to 90 days. Ensure that the passport is valid for six months after the date of arrival. Children are required to have their own passport or be included in the passport of the parent with whom they are traveling.

PASSPORTS

■ TIP→ Before your trip, make two copies of your passport's data page (one for someone at home and another for you to carry separately). Or scan the page and e-mail it to someone at home and/or yourself.

VISAS

When staying for 90 days or less, U.S. citizens are not required to obtain a visa prior to traveling to Italy. A recent law requires you fill in a declaration of presence within eight days of your arrival. The stamp on your passport at Airport Arrivals substitutes this.

U.S. Passport Expediters

A. Briggs Passport & Visa Expeditors ☎ *800/806–0581 toll-free, 202/338–0111* 🌐 *www.abriggs.com.* **American Passport Express** ☎ *800/455–5166* 🌐 *www.americanpassport.com.* **Passport Express** ☎ *800/362–8196* 🌐 *www.passportexpress.com.* **Travel Document Systems** ☎ *800/874–5100* 🌐 *www.traveldocs.com.* **Travel the World Visas** ☎ *866/886–8472, 202/223–8822* 🌐 *www.world-visa.com.*

U.S. Passport Information

U.S. Department of State ☎ *877/487–2778* 🌐 *www.travel.state.gov/passport.*

RESTROOMS

Public restrooms are rather rare in Naples; the locals seem to make do with well-timed pit stops and rely on the local bar. Although private businesses can refuse to make their toilets available to the passing public, some bars will allow you to use the restroom if you ask politely. Alternatively, it's not uncommon to pay for a little something—a euro for a mineral water or coffee—to get access to the facilities. Standards of cleanliness and comfort vary greatly. In downtown Naples, restaurants, hotel lobbies, department stores such as Coin, and McDonald's restaurants tend to have the cleanest restrooms. Pubs and bars rank among the worst and, for these, it may help to have your own small supply of tissues. There are bathrooms in most museums and in all airports and train stations. In major train stations you'll also find well-kept pay toilets for around €0.50. There are also bathrooms at highway rest stops and gas stations: a small tip to the cleaning person is always appreciated. There are no bathrooms in churches, post offices, public beaches, although some stops on the Naples metro have one.

SAFETY

Naples, like any modern metropolis, has had certain problems with crime. Although great inroads have been made since the 1990s and the city today is as safe as many other big urban centers in Europe, you should continue to be vigilant, especially around the main rail station of Piazza Garibaldi where petty theft is common. In Italy, in general, violent crimes are rare.

TIP→ Distribute your cash, credit cards, IDs, and other valuables between a deep front pocket, an inside jacket or vest pocket, and a hidden money pouch. Don't reach for the money pouch once you're in public.

LOCAL SCAMS

The areas round Piazza Garibaldi and near the port in Naples are infamous for a variety of scams. Avoid getting involved in the three-card monte around the station, and never buy any goods from an unlicensed street vendor—you may discover on returning to your hotel or cruise ship that the package with the digital camera you bought at an unbeatable price near the port actually contains little more than wooden chocks. Besides, under current Italian law, any purchase—except at a newsstand or tobacconist's—has to be accompanied by a proper receipt. Without one, both purchaser and vendor are liable to a fine, so you're putting yourself at risk by buying bootleg goods.

Be especially vigilant if traveling on public transport, especially crowded buses, as pickpockets can materialize from seemingly nowhere in large numbers. Dress down rather than up to attract less attention, and never wear gold jewelry.

Both in town and out on the highway, one scam is the *cavallo di ritorno*. Car owners lose their cars by some ruse—usually they're told they have a problem at the back or under the chassis; once they get out, the car is driven off. The owner is then traced and contacted by an intermediary, who will stipulate the ransom for the car (as much as €1,500–€2,500). You do need to stop if you're flagged down by the police; otherwise act with due caution.

The difficulties encountered by women traveling alone in Italy are often overstated. Younger women have to put up with much male attention, but it's rarely dangerous. Ignoring whistling and questions is the best way to get rid of unwanted attention. Fortunately, the vast majority of locals are extremely protective both of foreign visitors and women. As a general rule, in urban areas you're fine walking at street level when the shops are open (until about 8:30 pm). At other times, especially around the seedier parts of Naples, taking a taxi is a sound investment.

TAXES

Value-added tax (IVA or V.A.T.) is 22% on clothing and luxury goods. On most consumer goods, it's already included in the amount shown on the price tag, whereas on services it may not be.

At hotels, the service charge and the 10% IVA, or value-added tax, are included in the rate except in five-star deluxe establishments, where the IVA (10%) may be a separate item added to the bill at departure. If your purchases in a single store total more than €155 you may be entitled to a refund of the V.A.T.

When making a purchase, ask for a V.A.T. refund form and find out whether the merchant gives refunds—not all stores do, nor are they required to. Have the form stamped like any customs form by customs officials when you leave the country or, if you're visiting several European Union countries, when you leave the EU. After you're through passport control, take the form to a refund-service counter for an on-the-spot refund (which is usually the quickest and easiest option), or mail it to the address on the form (or on the envelope with it) after you arrive home. You receive the total refund stated on the form, but the processing time can be long, especially if you request a credit-card adjustment.

Global Refund is a Europe-wide service with 225,000 affiliated stores and more than 700 refund counters at major airports and border crossings. Its refund form, called a Tax Free Check, is the most common across the European continent. The service issues refunds in the form of cash, check, or credit-card adjustment.

V.A.T. Refunds Global Blue ☎ *866/706–6090 in North America, 421 232/111111 from abroad, 00800/32 111 111 from Italy* 🌐 *www.global-blue.com.*

TIPPING

In tourist areas like Capri and the Amalfi Coast, a 10% to 15% service charge may appear on your check; this must be clearly written on the menu in order to be applied. If service is added to the bill, it's not necessary to leave an additional tip, although this charge does not actually go to the waiters, so a few euros will not go amiss. If service is not included, leave a cash tip of a couple of euros per person. Usually there will not be a line item on your credit-card slip for a tip—but even if there is, tip in cash. Tip checkroom attendants €1 per person and restroom attendants €0.50 (more in expensive hotels and restaurants). A service charge is added at cafés for table service, so it is not necessary to leave additionally gratuity. At a hotel bar tip €1 for a round or two of drinks. At a café, tip €0.10 per coffee.

Italians rarely tip taxi drivers, and at most round up to the nearest euro. That said, a euro or two is appreciated, particularly if the driver helps with luggage. Service-station attendants are tipped only for special services; give them €1 for checking your tires. Railway and airport porters charge a fixed rate per bag. Tip an additional €0.50 per person, more if the porter is helpful. On large group sightseeing tours, tip guides about €5 per person for a half-day group tour, more if they are especially knowledgeable. In monasteries and other sights where admission is free, a contribution (€1–€2) is expected.

In hotels leave the chambermaid about €1 per day, or about €5 a week in a moderately priced hotel; tip a minimum of €1 for valet or room service. Double these amounts in an expensive hotel. In expensive hotels tip doormen €0.50 for calling a cab and €1.50 for carrying bags to the check-in desk and bellhops €1.50–€2.50 for carrying your bags to the room.

TOURS

Guided tours are a good option when you don't want to do it all yourself. A knowledgeable guide can take you places that you might never discover on your own, and you may be pushed to see more than you would have otherwise. Whenever you book a guided tour, find out what's included and what isn't. Also keep in mind that the province of Naples has tour guides licensed by the government. Some are eminently qualified in relevant fields such as architecture and art history, but most, especially those that linger outside Pompeii have simply managed to pass the test (or purchase the license!). Few local guides have their own websites, though all reputable agencies do. Check online before you leave home.

Tourist offices and hotel concierges also can provide the names of knowledgeable local guides and the rates for certain services. Before you hire a local guide, ask about their background and qualifications and make sure you agree on a price, content, and scheduling. Tipping is appreciated, but not obligatory, for local guides.

Recommended Generalists
Abercrombie & Kent *800/554-7016* *www.abercrombiekent.com.* **Andante** *888/331-3476* *www.andantetravels.com.* **Context Travel** *888/467-1986* *www.contexttravel.com.* **Tauck** *800/788-7885* *www.tauck.com.* **Travcoa** *800/992-2003, 310/649-7104* *www.travcoa.com.*

Biking and Hiking Tour Contacts
Backroads *800/462-2848, 510/527-1555* *www.backroads.com.* **Butterfield & Robinson** *866/551-9090, 416/864-1354* *www.butterfield.com.* **Ciclismo Classico** *800/866-7314, 781/646-3377* *www.ciclismoclassico.com.*

Culinary Tour Contact **Epiculinary** *707/815-1415* *www.epiculinary.com.* **Italian Connection** *0932/462-7911 Italy, 335/438-5712 Italy mobile* *www.italian-connection.com.* **Vesuvius vs Pompeii.** For guided tours of the Sorrentine Peninsula (but also departing from Sorrento to Capri, Pompeii, and the Naples area) check out the knowledgeable and passionate team of Vesuvius vs. Pompeii. They can also arrange private transfers and vehicles for people with disabilities. *Italy* *333/6409000* *www.vesuviusvspompeii.com.*

Volunteer Programs **Road Scholar** *800/454-5768, 978/323-4141* *www.roadscholar.org.*

Wine Tour Contacts **Cellar Tours** *310/496-8061* *www.cellartours.com.*

VISITOR INFORMATION

EPT *Stazione Centrale, Piazza Garibaldi, Naples, Italy* *081/268779* *www.inaples.it* *Daily 9-6* *Piazza dei Martiri 58, Chiaia, Naples, Italy* *081/4107211* *Stazione Mergellina, Naples, Italy* *081/7612102.*

Italian Government Tourist Board (*ENIT*). *Amalfi, Italy* *212/245-5618 in New York, 310/820-1898 in Los Angeles, 312/644-0996 in Chicago, 416/925-4882 in Toronto* *www.italiantourism.com.*

Ufficio Informazioni Turistiche *Piazza del Gesù, 7, Naples, Italy* *081/551-2701* *www.inaples.it* *Via San Carlo 9, Naples, Italy* *081/402-394* *www.inaples.it.*

The official site of the local region (*www.regione.campania.it*) also provides some coverage (in Italian).

TRAVEL TOOLS

The site for Trenitalia (the national rail), *www.trenitalia.com* is a good source for train information and journey planning, although you can only purchase tickets online with an Italian credit card—PayPal is, however, accepted. The website for the local bus service is *www.anm.it* while the website *www.eavcampania.it* has public transport information for getting around the bay on the Circumvesuviana and Ferrovia Cumana/Circumflegrea lines. The site for the metro in Naples is *www.metro.na.it.* The SITA site (Italian only) has schedules for bus travel in Campania, *www.sitasudtrasporti.it.* The website for the municipality of Naples is *www.commune.napoli.it.* A handy site for Capri is *www.capri.net*; Ischia has its official website at *www.ischia.com* while *www.ravellotime.it* is the best-maintained site of the Amalfi Coast.

Circumvesuviana *Corso Garibaldi 387, Naples, Italy* *800 toll free* *www.eavcampania.it.*

INDEX

PHOTO CREDITS

Front cover: Günter Gräfenhain/fototeca 9x12. 1, Robert I. C. Fisher. 2–3, Demetrio Carrasco/age fotostock. 5, capripalace.com. Chapter 1: Experience the Amalfi Coast, Capri & Naples: 8–9, Chris Sargent/Shutterstock. 10, Allerina & Glen/Flickr. 11 (left), Alfi o Ferlito/Shutterstock. 11 (right), iStockphoto. 14, Campania Tourism. 15 (left), ollirg/Shutterstock. 15 (right) and 16 (left), iStockphoto. 16 (top center), Public Domain. 16 (top right), Khirman Vladimir/Shutterstock. 16 (bottom right), Vacclav/Shutterstock. 17 (top left), Capri Tourism. 17 (bottom left), Campania Tourism. 17 (top center), Robert I. C. Fisher. 17 (bottom center), Floriano Rescigno/ iStockphoto. 17 (right), Tina Lorien/iStockphoto. 19, Public Domain. 21 (left and right), Campania Tourism. 22, Jan Greune/age fotostock. 23, Maurizio Grimaldi/age fotostock. 24, Gina Sanders/Shutterstock. Chapter 2: The Amalfi Coast: 25, Robert I. C. Fisher. 26, Floriano Rescigno/iStockphoto. 27, ary6/Shutterstock. 28, Robert I. C. Fisher. 37,Bruce Bi/age fotostock. 41, José Fuste Raga/age fotostock. 42 (top), Khirman Vladimir/Shutterstock. 42 (bottom), george green/Shutterstock. 43. (left), Robert I. C. Fisher. 43 (center), ollirg/Shutterstock. 43 (right), Robert I. C. Fisher. 44 (top), Alfi o Ferlito/Shutterstock. 44 (bottom), Khirman Vladimir/Shutterstock. 45 (left), Robert I. C. Fisher. 45 (center), Allerina & Glen/Flickr. 45 (right), ollirg/Shutterstock. 50–53, Robert I. C. Fisher. 57, Atlantide S.N.C./age fotostock. 60, Danilo Donadoni/age fotostock. 65, Demetrio Carrasco/age fotostock. 67, Atlantide S.N.C./age fotostock. 72, Bruno Morandi/ age fotostock. 80, Richard T. Nowitz/age fotostock. 84, Jensens/wikipedia.org. 87, Wojtek Buss/ age fotostock. Chapter 3: Capri, Ischia, and Procida: 89, Matz Sjöberg / age fotostock. 90 (top and bottom), Capri Tourism. 91, Vladimir Khirman/iStockphoto. 92, Malgorzata Kistryn/Shutterstock. 93 (top), Elena Uspenskaya/Shutterstock. 93 (bottom), Vacclav/Shutterstock. 94, Matz Sjöberg/age fotostock. 98, Massimo Rivenci/Alamy. 104, FAN/age fotostock. 107, Danita Delimont/Alamy. 109, Juneisy Hawkins/iStockphoto. 113, Ken Gillham/age fotostock. 114 (top), Danilo Donadoni/age fotostock. 114 (bottom), Kiedrowski, R/age fotostock. 115 (top), deepblue–photographer/Shutterstock. 115 (bottom left), De Agostini Picture Library/ Fototeca ENIT. 115 (bottom right), caprirelaxboats.com/salsa/it. 116 (top), capripalace.com. 116 (bottom left), Capri Tourism. 116 (bottom right), Colin Sinclair/ age fotostock. 117 (top), SCPhotos/Alamy. 117 (bottom), caprirelaxboats.com/salsa/it. 121, Capri Tourism. 123, scanpress/Alamy. 129, Demetrio Carrasco/age fotostock. 137, Paola Ghirotti/Fototeca ENIT. 143, Adam Eastland/Alamy. 146, Maurizio Grimaldi/age fotostock. 149, CuboImages srl/Alamy. Chapter 4: Sorrento and the Sorrentine Peninsula: 151, Robert I. C. Fisher. 152, Danilo Ascione/iStockphoto. 153 (top), Khirman Vladimir/Shutterstock. 153 (bottom), iStockphoto. 154, Atlantide S.N.C./age fotostock. 155 (top), Campania Tourism. 155 (bottom), iStockphoto. 156, keepwaddling1/Flickr. 161, Adam Eastland/Alamy. 165, John Mole Photography/Alamy. 169, Robert I. C. Fisher. Chapter 5: The Bay of Naples: 179, Danilo Donadoni/age fotostock. 180 (top), Pierdelune/Shutterstock. 180 (bottom), iStockphoto. 181, Paola Ghirotti/Fototeca ENIT. 182, Castello aragonese by Ferdinando Marfella www.fl ickr.com/photos/fotofm/1268328710/ Attribution– ShareAlike License. 183 (top), Angela Sorrentino/iStockphoto. 183 (bottom), Angela Sorrentino/iStockphoto. 184, DEA PICTURE LIBRARY/ age fotostock. 192, Demetrio Carrasco/age fotostock. 196, DEA/ S AMANTINI/age fotostock. 199, GARDEL Bertrand/age fotostock. 201 (top), The Print Collector / age fotostock. 201 (bottom), SuperStock/age fotostock. 202, kated/Shutterstock. 203 (top), skyfi sh/ Shutterstock. 203 (bottom), Walter Rawlings / age fotostock. 204 (top), Vito Arcomano/Fototeca ENIT. 204 (bottom left), Boris Stroujko/ Shutterstock. 204 (right), Alastair Johnson/iStockphoto. 205, Doug Scott/age fotostock. 206, Katie Hamlin. 207, Demetrio Carrasco/Agency Jon Arnold Images/age fotostock. 214, Danilo Donadoni/age fotostock. 219, DEA/S VANNINI/age fotostock. Chapter 6: Naples: 221, Atlantide S.N.C./age fotostock. 222, wikipedia.org. 223 (top), Fabiuccio/wikipedia.org. 223 (bottom), Khirman Vladimir/Shutterstock. 224, Robert I. C. Fisher. 225 (top), gallimaufry/Shutterstock. 225 (bottom), Dave Gordon/ Shutterstock. 226, Tony French/Alamy. 235, Demetrio Carrasco/age fotostock. 238, Kiedrowski, R/age fotostock. 240, Doug Scott/age fotostock. 241 (top), Public Domain. 241 (bottom), wikipedia.org. 242 (top left), CuboImages srl/Alamy. 242 (bottom left), Neil Setchfi eld/Alamy. 242 (right), Sylvain Grandadam/ age fotostock. 243 (top), Doug Scott/age fotostock. 243 (bottom left and right), Public Domain. 244, Khirman Vladimir/Shutterstock. 247, Sylvain Grandadam/age fotostock. 253, De Agostini Picture Library/Fototeca ENIT. 257 (left), AEP/Alamy. 257 (top and bottom right), Robert I. C. Fisher. 258 (top left), Lalupa/wikipedia.org. 258 (top right), Marisa Allegra Williams/iStockphoto. 258 (bottom), Tibor Bognar/Alamy. 259 (top left), Peter Horree/Alamy. 259 (top center), Vittorio Sciosia/Alamy. 259(top right), Doug Scott/age fotostock. 259 (bottom), Robert I. C. Fisher. 261, Ethel Davies/age fotostock. 265, CuboImages srl/Alamy. 269, vittorio sciosia/age fotostock. 275, Paolo Gallo/Alamy. 281, iStockphoto. 283, Robert I. C. Fisher. 284, Campania Tourism. 285 (top), Mary Evans Picture Library/Alamy. 285 (second from top), Elena Elisseeva/Shutterstock. 285 (third from top), Concettina D'Agnese/iStockphoto. 285 (fourth from top), Kiedrowski R / age fotostock. 285 (bottom), iStockphoto. 286, Sami